Defectors

DEFECTORS

How the Illicit Flight of Soviet Citizens Built the Borders of the Cold War World

Erik R. Scott

OXFORD
UNIVERSITY PRESS

Oxford University Press is a department of the University of Oxford. It furthers
the University's objective of excellence in research, scholarship, and education
by publishing worldwide. Oxford is a registered trade mark of Oxford University
Press in the UK and certain other countries.

Published in the United States of America by Oxford University Press
198 Madison Avenue, New York, NY 10016, United States of America.

CIP data is on file at the Library of Congress

ISBN 978–0–19–754687–1

DOI: 10.1093/oso/9780197546871.001.0001

Printed by Sheridan Books, Inc., United States of America

To K & S

CONTENTS

ACKNOWLEDGMENTS

This book began in Tbilisi, where I stumbled upon a multivolume KGB investigation of two Soviet citizens who sought to defect from the socialist superpower and transcend Cold War borders by hijacking an airplane. My effort to understand what had led them to undertake such a desperate act, what befell them afterwards and what defection meant more broadly in the context of the Cold War brought me back to Georgia, and then to Ukraine and Russia. It also pushed me to places I was unused to traveling as a historian of the Soviet Union: to the United Kingdom, to public and private emigre collections in far-flung locations, and even to archives within driving distance of my home in Kansas. As my project expanded thematically and geographically, the debts I accumulated also grew. I am eager to acknowledge them.

I am grateful for the support I received to research and write this book. Grants and fellowships from the American Council of Learned Societies, the American Philosophical Society, the National Endowment for the Humanities, and the University of Kansas gave me the resources I needed to undertake archival research as well as the time required to sift through what I found. The history department of the University of Kansas was endlessly supportive, and I would like to acknowledge my past and present chairs, Eve Levin and Luis Corteguera, for their understanding and encouragement. At KU, Kathy Porsch of the Hall Center for the Humanities helped me to hone my grant applications; later, the Hall Center graciously provided me with a quiet space to complete an initial draft of the manuscript.

The archival traces left by defectors were often scattered among the records of multiple organizations in different countries. I am grateful for the help offered by the staff of the Archive of the Ministry of Internal Affairs of Georgia, the Sectoral State Archive of the Security Services of Ukraine, the Foreign Policy Archive of the Russian Federation, the State Archive of the Russian Federation, the Russian State Archive for Literature and the Arts, the Russian State Archive of Contemporary History, the Russian State Archive of Socio-Political History, the Russian State Military Archive, and the National Archives of the UK. Although I completed my overseas research in 2019, my thoughts remain with my colleagues in Ukraine who are bravely resisting Russia's invasion of their country even as I finish this book. In the United States, I was assisted by the capable staff of the US National Archives in College Park, the Hoover Institution Archives in Stanford, the Eisenhower Presidential Library in Abilene, the Kennedy Presidential Library in Boston, the Truman Presidential Library in Independence, the National Security Archive in Washington, and the New York Public Library. I am especially grateful to Victoria Wohlsen and the staff of the Tolstoy Foundation for allowing me to peruse their records in Valley Cottage even as they were busy running the foundation's nursing center. Edward Kasinec guided me to the published and unpublished records of Soviet emigres, and Jon Giullian of KU Libraries helped me gain access to many of them.

My understanding of migration, borders, and the Cold War was informed by many conversations I had with colleagues and friends as I pursued my research and writing. I am indebted to the insights of Rachel Applebaum, Gregory Afinogenov, Emily Baran, Stephen Bittner, Oleg Budnitskii, Vitaly Chernetsky, Ed Cohn, Michael David-Fox, Alex Diener, Bob Edelman, David Engerman, Christine Evans, Dina Fainberg, David Farber, Gosia Fidelis, Victoria Frede, Juliane Fürst, Przemysław Gasztold, Megan Greene, Steve Harris, Kristy Ironside, Marike Janzen, Denis Kozlov, Andy Janco, Oleg Khlevniuk, Diane Koenker, Victor Krupyna, Jo Laycock, Laurie Manchester, Bruce Menning, Kevin Riehle, Josh Sanborn, Yuri Slezkine, Victoria Smolkin, Alexander Titov, Ben Tromly, Svetlana Vassileva-Karagyozova, and Tara Zahra. Ken Yalowitz and the late Tony Olcott kindly helped me to secure interviews. Burton Gerber and Jeff Smith shared their experiences working with defectors, and Albert White described his difficult journey to the United States. Presentations at the Berkeley Kruzhok, Columbia University, Georgetown University, Stetson University, the University of Chicago, the University of London, and the University of Sheffield helped me develop the book's chapters. I would like to thank Seth Bernstein, Sheyda Jahanbani, Alexis Peri, and Nathan Wood for reading portions of the manuscript. Special thanks are owed to Andy Denning and Lewis Siegelbaum for reading the entire thing. An earlier version of Chapter 6 appeared as an article in *Past & Present*, and I am grateful to the journal for allowing me to include it here in updated form.

At Oxford University Press, Susan Ferber shepherded the project from proposal to finished book. Her detailed comments on my draft chapters, and the constructive suggestions offered by the two anonymous readers, helped me clarify my arguments and tighten my prose. Patterson Lamb further refined the text, and Jeremy Toynbee supervised production. Jayne Rising contributed the index. The maps were designed by Di Shi of KU's cartographic lab.

Family and friends helped me on the long and circuitous path that led to this book. Georgios Athanasakopoulos, Patrick Davis, Berdia Natsvlishvili, John Popadic, Marat Umerov, and Alfonso Vega were familiar faces when I was far from home. Helen Bernstein shared her house in East Palo Alto. My parents, grandmother, sister, and brother-in-law were a steady source of encouragement and wonderful family meals. My daughter, Sabina, grew up with this book in the background, and sometimes in the foreground as she accompanied me on research trips to Moscow and Washington. Watching her progress from a curious toddler to an inquisitive middle schooler has been a privilege. My greatest debt is to my wife, Keeli. She was the first to hear about my findings in the archives and the first to read my early drafts. She shared her intelligence, humor, and fine-tuned sense of what makes for a compelling story with generosity, through the pandemic and on countless walks together. Without her love and support, this book would not have been written.

Defectors

Introduction

Defectors and the Spaces in Between

In the early twilight of a summer day in 1958, the shores of the Bosporus were still, even as large ships streamed through the straits that connected the Black Sea to the Mediterranean, separated Europe from Asia, and divided Istanbul in two. No one saw the young man jump from the deck of a hulking Soviet cargo ship returning from a voyage abroad. The identity of the man who swam to shore with nothing but the soaked clothes on his back remained mysterious even after the Turkish police took him into custody. An American CIA officer posted to Turkey put the young sailor through a lie detector test to determine whether he was a Soviet agent. The Turkish press, whether by mistake or to conceal him from Soviet officials seeking his return, initially misreported his name as Grigory Dimitriev. Soviet authorities subsequently identified him as Viktor Oreshkov, a low-ranking sailor on his way home to the USSR.

Oreshkov's leap into the Bosporus was quickly invested with political meaning. Turkish reporters described him as a valiant defector who swam to freedom. A Soviet court charged him with the crime of "betrayal of the Motherland in the form of flight abroad" and sentenced him to death for treason. Expeditiously granted a Turkish passport, he was placed on a plane to New York to keep him out of the reach of Soviet prosecutors. Upon arrival, he was greeted by a representative of the Tolstoy Foundation, a Russian emigre group that received funding from the US government to help defectors resettle in the West. He found work in New York, saved his earnings, and gained American citizenship in 1965.

Up to that point, Oreshkov's story read like a classic case of Cold War flight. It would soon unravel in ways that confounded expectations on both sides of the Iron Curtain. Just two years after receiving his US citizenship papers, he embarked on a two-month journey to socialist Bulgaria. While America's CIA officers had relied on the cooperation of their Turkish allies, Soviet authorities could count on Bulgarian intelligence to provide a careful account of Oreshkov's visit. A report dispatched from the Bulgarian capital of Sofia recounted his stay in minute detail, from the conversations he struck up with locals to his relationship with a waitress at a restaurant near where he was staying. After his return to the United States, he appeared restless. He subsequently showed up unannounced at the gates of the Soviet Embassy in Washington in 1973, requesting that he be allowed to go back to the land of his birth.

Officials in both Moscow and Washington struggled to understand his motivations. The KGB scrutinized his biography and behavior for clues as to why he had left, the reasons for his return, and whether he was acting at the behest of American intelligence. Questioned after he went back to the USSR at the end of 1973, he explained to Soviet investigators that he had jumped into the Bosporus on an impulse, frustrated by an argument with the ship's captain over a dog that the sailor kept on board against regulations. His KGB interlocutors were perplexed but ultimately decided to let the matter rest. Following a psychiatric screening, he was released to live near his parents in central Russia, his death sentence commuted.[1] Yet the following summer, Oreshkov showed up at the US Embassy in Moscow, asking the Americans to take him back. Secretary of State Henry Kissinger questioned whether Oreshkov was still an American citizen and even suggested that the man at the embassy might be an imposter. Until US officials spent time "scrutinizing [the] identity question based on available photographs," Kissinger wrote, they could not be sure he was who he claimed to be.[2] In the end, the American side relented. Oreshkov was flown back to New York in April 1975 and quietly resettled out of public view.[3]

This account of Oreshkov's story, traced through archives on both sides of the Cold War conflict, diverges from the tales of defection told in spy novels, dramatized in films, and celebrated in Western news coverage. Popular portrayals heralded those who fled, jumped, or flew across the border separating socialist "captivity" from the "free" West. Rather than a one-way journey, Oreshkov's defection was the beginning of a decade and a half spent crossing the political and ideological fault lines of the Cold War. In some instances, cases of defection provoked fierce competition between the Soviet Union and the United States. But when Oreshkov sought to return to the USSR, American officials seemed eager to be rid of him and

Soviet authorities were unsure whether to regard him as a covert agent or a schizophrenic. His movements lacked clear meaning; his journey's arc was a recurrent loop.

Oreshkov's story, though more obscure than the defection of a high-ranking Soviet official or a world-class ballet dancer, was far more representative of the experiences of migrants who sought to transcend the borders of the Cold War world and manipulate the migration policies of the superpowers for their own ends. While the capitalist and socialist camps vied for defectors and were quick to view their migration through an ideological lens, governments on both sides were wary of spontaneous movement. Over time, the Cold War superpowers used their global reach to restrict the pathways open to defectors even as they facilitated migration flows through checkpoints that they could manage and control. In a mutually reinforcing way, both sides shored up borders to regulate movement in previously ungoverned spaces across the globe, targeting the liminal areas favored by those fleeing the socialist bloc. Meanwhile, new embassies and consulates were opened, official delegations were cleared for travel, air networks connected the world like never before, and cargo ships like the one from which Oreshkov had jumped continued to sail through the Bosporus.

DEFECTION AND BORDER-MAKING IN A GLOBALIZED WORLD

Oreshkov's journey illustrates how the histories of migration and globalization were intertwined. Both accelerated amid the Cold War but are typically treated as separate subjects. The Cold War began in part as a "battle for refugees," as the dramatic movement of people from East to West reified the distinction between the two opposing camps.[4] The Cold War also saw the expansion of globalization, though the limits placed on migration during this period have been dismissed as simply "an exception to the general trend toward global integration."[5] Migration experts have pointed to the naturalization of the right to leave one's country at the Cold War's end. Specialists on globalization have emphasized the role of the United States in promoting the spread of capital and culture across borders and tended to portray the Soviet Union as a secondary actor in this process, or even a victim of it.[6]

Defectors, by contrast, argues that restraints on human mobility were an integral part of globalization and were imposed by both superpowers. During the Cold War, border technologies grew more advanced, screening measures more extensive, and spaces previously beyond the reach of state control more thoroughly regulated by law. The way that borders continue to limit the movement of people in the contemporary world is not an exception to globalization's advance nor a sign of its demise. Rather, it is a key feature of globalization's architecture, shaped by the interaction between two rival systems for governing international migration in the Cold War. Defectors were both the catalysts for the delimiting of previously open spaces and the most visible representatives of the consequences of enclosure. While other migrants were rendered as anonymous statistics, defectors were tracked by state intelligence agencies, interviewed by nongovernmental organizations that advocated on their behalf, and subjected to extensive media coverage in the capitalist and socialist camps, whether in celebration or condemnation of their actions.

Defection occurred in the spaces that lay between two global mobility regimes. One, supported by the United States and upheld by its allies, was devoted to managing entry and selectively attracting certain classes of migrants. The other, maintained by the Soviet Union and most other socialist states, was intent on retaining and returning wayward citizens.[7] Both systems aimed to assert control over international migration in the wake of the Second World War, which uprooted populations on a massive scale. The American regime was justified by a strategically defined humanitarian universalism; its Soviet counterpart claimed to protect migrants from capitalist exploitation. US policymakers worked through international institutions to construct an asylum system that emphasized the freedom to leave one's country but did not guarantee the right to enter the United States; the Soviet Union and its allies cast the effort as a cynical attempt to lead socialist citizens astray. Defection was jointly produced by the criminalization of emigration by socialist states, the strategic encouragement of departure by capitalist states, and the tactics of migrants who sought to navigate the era's turbulent politics.

Unlike most migrants before and after the Cold War, defectors were pursued by the states they left even as they were sought by the states that received them. Wherever they moved, they carried competing claims of sovereignty with them. Their global journeys helped map out the contested spaces of the Cold War. Some, like Vladimir Pronin, a private in the Red Army, abandoned their posts in Soviet-controlled Germany and crossed through the shadowlands of Berlin before the Wall went up in 1961. Others plotted an escape from the periphery of the Soviet Union. A year after the Berlin Wall's construction, two young men, Revaz Mkheidze and Yuri Orekhov, stole a classified map detailing the Soviet Union's border with Turkey and journeyed to the Black Sea city of Batumi, where they hoped swim with the aid of a hand-held propeller to the Turkish coast, or to a foreign ship willing to pick them up. Eight years later, in the same city, a father and son, Pranas and Algirdas Brazinskas, undertook the first hijacking of a Soviet civilian airplane; they also hoped to reach nearby Turkey, a member of the NATO alliance opposed to the Soviet Union.

Others sought to flee from the Soviet Union's extraterritorial outposts in the West. While Soviet official Victor Kravchenko, who abandoned his post in Washington as the Second World War drew to a close, may have been among the first to "choose freedom" in this manner, the most dramatic escape belonged to Oksana Kasenkina, a schoolteacher to the children of Soviet diplomats in New York. Kasenkina made a stunning "leap to freedom" from the window of the Soviet consulate as a crowd of onlookers gathered on the Manhattan sidewalk. On the high seas, defectors traveled beyond the reach of the Soviet state, as happened with the crew of the Soviet tanker *Tuapse*, detained in the South China Sea in 1954 and subsequently scattered across the globe. Some found points of departure in neutral countries that hoped to avoid taking sides in the Cold War, even if it was difficult to do so. The most famous case was that of Svetlana Allilueva, Stalin's daughter, who sought refuge at the US Embassy in New Delhi. She was shuttled to Rome and questioned by American officials in Geneva before arriving in the United States.

While flight from all socialist states galvanized public attention, none of the defectors were pursued so relentlessly, or sought so eagerly, as those from the Soviet Union. The struggle for fugitive Soviet citizens was an imperial contest waged far beyond the domestic borders of the United States and the Soviet Union and against the backdrop of waning European influence across the globe.[8] It played out in a crowded courtroom in postwar Paris, among rival intelligence agencies operating in the shadows of occupied Europe, in the western reaches of the socialist superpower, around the walls of Soviet embassies, in the disputed straits of the South China Sea, and thousands of feet in the air above the Soviet Union's neighbors. A closer look at the movement of defectors through these contested spaces confirms that the Cold War world's borders were more tentative than the monolithic "Iron Curtain" paradigm suggests.[9] They were not simply imposed by one state, but instead formed through the interaction between East and West and as the result of a broader dialectic between migrants and state boundaries.[10] However, their fluid and evolving nature did not hamper their effectiveness in limiting human migration. German author Peter Schneider, writing about the Berlin Wall, observed that "every improvement in the border system . . . spurred the creative drive to find a new loophole."[11] Yet each illegal crossing in turn tightened the governance

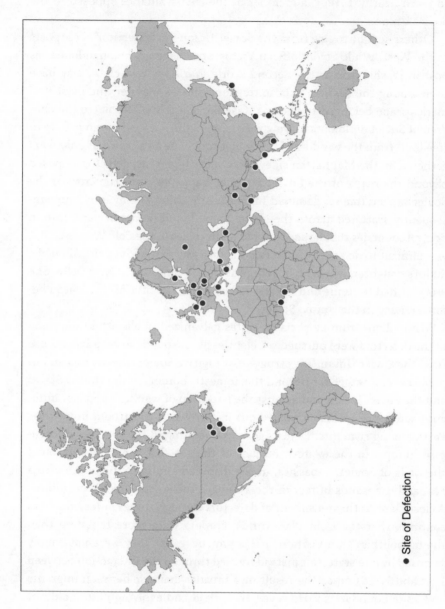

Figure I.1 Soviet Defections across the Globe: Cases of Illicit Flight in *Defectors*, 1944–1991

● Site of Defection

of the border regime. Policies deployed by both superpowers to manage defectors followed in the wake of their movements.

Surprisingly, the competition for runaway Soviet citizens paved the way for collusion between the superpowers, who shared an interest in regulating the spaces crossed by defectors. As part of an effort to maintain their authority in the face of the decolonization that followed the demise of Europe's empires, the Soviet Union and the United States sought to lock newly independent countries into a set of rules governing diplomatic missions, the high seas, and airspaces.[12] While they pursued different models of economic development, both superpowers sought to harness the power of international trade, which required protecting foreign delegations, shipping lines, and air routes.[13] This effort at global rule-making, begun in the late 1950s as the Cold War order was being institutionalized, carved out exceptions for the superpowers but left less powerful countries and unauthorized migrants at a disadvantage.[14] Although defection would all but disappear after the Cold War, it helped shape the governance of global borders in enduring ways. Disputes over these liminal wanderers brought what French philosopher Michel Foucault called "governmentality" into uncharted spaces, turning people into populations managed by state power.[15] At the same time, defection's ideological framework hardened international borders for migrants by reinforcing the view, still widely held, that asylum should only apply to those with clearly delineated political claims.

During the Cold War, the physical crossing of international borders by defectors seemed to speak for itself as a political act. Defectors' bestselling memoirs, often ghostwritten, reinforced the impression that flight was an ideologically motivated decision. Victor Kravchenko, the Soviet official who fled while on assignment in Washington, published *I Chose Freedom* in 1946, just as the battle lines between the Cold War's superpowers were being drawn. The book's title neatly signposted his journey from tyranny to liberty. Yet upon closer inspection, even some of the more famous cases of defection resembled the experience of Oreshkov, the wandering sailor. Although defection promised the possibility of international mobility and personal reinvention, it flattened the complexity of migrant motivations and shoehorned their stories into Cold War narratives. The silencing of certain experiences, and the full-throated promotion of others, makes it difficult for historians to recover the full complexity of defectors' lives. Defection often left people trapped physically and symbolically between the two camps. Some reached the United States but died in obscurity; others remained stranded beyond the borders of the Western countries they longed to reach; a prominent few returned to the Soviet Union but had difficulty finding a place for themselves in their old homeland. Although the two superpowers competed to claim defectors, they were more interested in interpreting and channeling movement, and they were prepared to prevent it when it was not in their national interests.

DEFECTORS AND OTHER MIGRANTS

The term "defector" rose and fell with the Cold War. It first became a common way of describing unauthorized flight around 1948. Nearly four decades later, the frequency of its usage had increased by more than 8,000 percent. The sudden disappearance of the term after 1991 was nearly as dramatic.[16] Although originally used to describe those who fled from the Soviet Union and its Warsaw Pact allies, it came to encompass migrants from China, Vietnam, Cuba, and elsewhere in the socialist world. Defectors were treated as a special class of migrants. Following their dramatic arrival in the West, some were able to traverse previously insurmountable boundaries, including the racialized immigration restrictions maintained by the United States.[17] Defection emphasized migrants' individual identities, allowing them to claim asylum on the basis of their "political opinion."[18] At the same time, it narrowed the scope of political choice to capitalism versus communism.

Curiously, the word that defined Cold War migration for English speakers had no single equivalent inside the Soviet Union. The most direct translation was *perebezhchik*, a person who flees to the other side. The Russian term dated to the early nineteenth century and, appropriately for the Cold War, had military connotations, as it originally referred to soldiers who went to fight for the opposing army. Other terms, such as *beglets* and *bezhenets*, also referred to the act of fleeing. However, a more common term in Soviet usage was *nevozvrashchenets*, or non-returner. A Stalinist neologism, it evoked another perspective: that of a state seeking the return of a wayward citizen. The term appeared in dictionaries in 1938, just as the Soviet Union tightened its borders and toughened restrictions on travel abroad.[19] Most common of all in Soviet legal documents was the word *izmennik*, or traitor, used to refer to defectors. Soviet law even had a special category for those who "betrayed the Motherland" in this fashion: "treason in the form of flight abroad."[20]

Even in the United States, there was confusion over who could be classified as a defector. In no small part, this was because the United States' official defector program—including its formal definition of which migrants could be considered "defectors"—remained a highly classified secret. To make matters worse, the program itself was often one step behind the migrants who chose to abandon the socialist camp. A 1949 US government memorandum noted that "Kravchenko's book," the memoir of Igor Gouzenko, a former cipher clerk who bolted from the Soviet Embassy in Canada, and the dramatic defection of Kasenkina "did more to arouse the western world to the realities of the nature of communist tyranny than anything else since the end of the war."[21] All three fled before a coordinated framework for handling defectors had been created.

Once a formal program was established, it was determined that defectors had to possess two qualities: they had to have "escaped from the control of the USSR or countries in the Soviet orbit"; and they also had to be of "special interest to the U.S. Government," whether as a result of intelligence they possessed or because their defection could "be exploited in the psychological field."[22] Yet even this definition posed problems. For one, it assumed that defection was unidirectional "escape," when in fact some ended up returning home voluntarily. It also assumed that US government agencies had a common definition of what constituted "special interest." Further, it opened the nebulous realm of "psychological exploitation," in which not only state authorities but also journalists and migrants themselves—if they could capture the spotlight—told stories that galvanized a popular audience.[23] Intertwined with the US government's publicly touted Escapee Program, the term "defector" came to be used by reporters, book publicists, ordinary citizens, and even US officials not briefed on its classified definition. Migrants from socialist countries soon seized on it to describe themselves and facilitate their movement across the globe.

The term had counterparts in other countries through which defectors moved. The notion of a defector as one who runs across a border, present in Russian, also existed in French (transfuge) and German (Überläufer); in Finnish (loikkari), the term indicated a leap over a physical or symbolic hurdle; in Polish (uciekinier) it referred to someone who ran away. Reflecting the Cold War's mobilization of ordinary people in a global military contest, languages on both sides of the Iron Curtain often equated defection with desertion, a term typically reserved for soldiers; sometimes defection was distinguished as a political form of desertion, as it was in Spanish (desertor político). Like the Soviet Union, socialist states stood out for using unique legal terms to classify defectors, all of which emphasized illegal movement. In East Germany, defection was referred to as Republikflucht, unauthorized flight from the people's republic.

Despite their various shades of meaning, all of these terms emphasized unauthorized exit and flight across borders. Because defection centered on the notion of illicit departure, it could not really be applied to those traveling from West to East. The fact that most Western citizens could leave their home countries freely made their journeys to Moscow less remarkable. There were a few Western citizens whose relocation to the Soviet Union was described as a "defection." Chief among them was Kim Philby, the British intelligence officer who worked for decades as a secret agent of the Soviet Union before fleeing to Moscow in 1963 when his cover was blown. Yet there were only a handful of cases like Philby's, and these individuals were just as likely to be described as "turncoats." By contrast, the concept of defection was applied to any Soviet citizen who fled, whether that person was a high-ranking KGB officer or a disgruntled sailor, a prominent artist or a humble schoolteacher, an athlete at the Olympics or an unemployed wanderer who evaded Soviet border controls.

Though a numerically small group, defectors had an outsized political importance. They were seen not only as the "elite of the Soviet world," as the US State Department's Policy Planning Staff described them in 1948, but also an elite category of migrants, free to escape (if they could manage to do so) but also freer than most to resettle.[24] The classified document establishing the US defector program, NSC 86/1, granted defectors the possibility of immigrating to the United States "without regard to their former political affiliations."[25] Yet resettlement in America was seen as a last resort. US officials envisioned most defectors either remaining in Western Europe to battle Soviet influence there or being dispatched to Australia, Canada, or Latin America when European allies complained about being burdened with refugees. Defection did not simply mean unfettered mobility. It also meant being rerouted and, in some cases, being stuck in limbo, crossing borders but never reaching one's intended destination.

Even as defection became a global phenomenon after World War II, Western governments, led by the United States, sought to ensure that its pathways followed a logical progression through government-controlled channels.[26] At the inception of the defector program in the early 1950s, all manner of illegal crossings were celebrated. The riders of the Czechoslovak "Freedom Train" were praised for commandeering a locomotive. The US Escapee Program's newsletter heralded the story of a Bulgarian family that crashed through the Greek border in a 1927 Chrysler "reinforced for the journey with steel plates and concrete slabs." The newsletter even touted the hijacking of a Hungarian passenger plane by "seven determined escapees" who "overpowered the communist crew." Such feats were held to be evidence of the "resourcefulness and courage which the love of liberty can create in an oppressed people."[27] Although government officials promoted stories like these, Western journalists sometimes outstripped policy guidelines in their enthusiasm for escape, given the popular interest it commanded. Perhaps the most notorious example was the television network NBC's role in financing and filming an effort by West German students to dig a tunnel under the Berlin Wall to facilitate the escape of friends and family members in the East. When it was ready to air, the Kennedy administration tried to block—unsuccessfully—the television special's broadcast in 1962.[28]

As the years went by, standards were established for admittance, evaluation, and resettlement, with defectors channeled through the same reception centers, asked similar questions at press conferences, and encouraged to write memoirs that all resembled Kravchenko's *I Chose Freedom*. The diplomatic dance between the United States and the Soviet Union that followed a defection also became routinized. Soviet protests kept to a familiar script, with accusations of mental instability and moral failure regularly leveled at those who fled. In 1963, the Escapee Program was formally ended, succeeded by the more generic US Refugee Program, and US officials grew more circumspect when talking about unauthorized flight.

Defectors, however, continued to undermine efforts to regularize their movement. They found new pathways for exit and told stories that did not always conform to the narratives of the Cold War endorsed by the superpowers. Although all were claimed by Moscow, Soviet citizens who fled were a multiethnic group and made varying appeals to diaspora communities abroad. Their unpredictable actions drew the United States and the Soviet Union into refugee camps, border zones, the boundaries of extraterritorial spaces, the seas, and the skies. The Soviet Union's effort to stem illegal emigration and the United States' drive to encourage it shaped the laws regulating refugees more generally. Cases of defection informed the series of maritime treaties brokered at the United Nations in the 1950s, the legal agreements reached in the 1960s to enforce the "inviolability" of embassies and consulates, and the mobilization of international law against airplane hijacking in the 1970s. Admittedly, such agreements made international travel safer and more predictable, but they also bound sailors to ships flying state flags, privileged diplomats over asylum seekers, and domesticated the dream of civil aviation. The way the United States and the Soviet Union responded to defectors produced a version of globalization characterized by limitations on the movement of people, while goods and capital flowed across borders.

SOVIET BORDERS IN GLOBAL HISTORICAL PERSPECTIVE

For all its political importance and popular prominence, defection has been overlooked or under-theorized by most historians. Part of the issue has been a dearth of reliable sources. For decades, the most comprehensive study of Soviet defectors was the one written in 1986 by Vladislav Krasnov, himself a defector. It was based on a copy of the KGB "wanted list" somehow obtained by the National Alliance of Russian Solidarists, a secretive anti-Soviet organization based in Frankfurt that had a history of receiving financial support from the CIA.[29] When the Cold War ended, Soviet archives partially opened, but for years a thorough study of defection remained unfeasible. Access to the central archive of the KGB in Moscow continued to be tightly restricted, with only a smattering of documents released or smuggled out in the form of copied notes.[30] It was only with the mass declassification of KGB records in the Baltic states, Georgia, and Ukraine— the former republics that made up the Soviet state's western border—that a more accurate picture of defection began to emerge. These sources were complemented by the release of a swath of materials detailing the role of Western intelligence services in facilitating defection.

Compounding the problem of sources, the ideological underpinnings of defection have largely been taken for granted. During the Cold War, numerous memoirs were penned by defectors but only a handful of scholarly accounts written, nearly all of them portraying the Soviet Union as a totalitarian society and its citizens as captives. Recent scholars have abandoned the totalitarian framework but still tend to treat the category of defection as a given. Some have taken up the subject as a way of understanding the secretive spying operations of the KGB or the political views of soldiers in the Red Army; others are more concerned with the broader landscape of Soviet emigres and "exiles," including those who fled before the Cold War.[31] A somewhat separate literature follows the established genre of the defector memoir and details the lives of individual defectors.[32] These works have illuminated the history of powerful Soviet institutions, popular attitudes among Soviet citizens, and the biographies of key Soviet figures, but none of them examines defection as a transnational phenomenon coproduced by the opposing powers of the Cold War. They also do not consider its importance as a form of migration that shaped the world's borders in lasting ways.

While borders are sometimes seen as lines fixed on a map, most geographers and political theorists understand them as thick zones of categorization and control.[33] They run inside states and beyond them to filter populations and manage global flows. States draw borders, but borders also constitute states, defining who belongs and who does not. The very same border can be experienced differently by different people, depending on citizenship, class, nationality, race, and gender. Philosopher Étienne Balibar has noted the distinction between migrants for whom the border is a place where their social status is affirmed before they quickly pass through, and those for whom it is a barrier where they risk being trapped.[34] Borders have marked the divide between "citizens" and "barbarians" for centuries, though in the modern era their power has been buttressed by technology and bureaucracy. Yet borders produce paradoxical results: although they purport to eliminate ambiguity between insiders and outsiders, they inevitably cut through communities, leave people in the margins, and create in-between spaces.[35] In some cases, this ambiguity is maintained deliberately, and the border area becomes a "state of exception" where sovereign power operates beyond the bounds of normal legal procedures.[36]

Over time, border enforcement has shifted from a practice mainly observed in wartime to one followed in peacetime with the goal of restraining migrants.[37] In this regard, the Cold War proved a formative period for borders, a time of sustained conflict that often fell short of military engagement but militarized everyday life. The era saw borders reified by the prosecution of unauthorized crossings and the regulation of liminal spaces. Defection was not simply a "rite of passage" from communism to capitalism; it was also what sociologist Pierre Bourdieu describes as a "rite of institution," serving to "consecrate or legitimate an arbitrary boundary" marked on a map.[38] At different points in history, nomads, wanderers, and fugitives have threatened established states by flaunting borders, but efforts to suppress them have served to legitimize the state's presence in border zones. In the name of combating poachers, pirates, smugglers, and terrorists, the world's ungoverned expanses were bounded, claims on the seas and skies extended, and the border backed by lethal force.[39]

Restrictions on leaving that the Soviet Union and most other socialist states imposed were far from an aberrant consequence of their alleged totalitarianism. Rather, they represented a long-term practice of population management that endured into the twentieth century and coexisted, sometimes uneasily, with globalization. Limits on exit often described as inherent to socialism had long-standing histories. In ancient Athens, the "cradle of Western democracy," Plato argued that "no one be allowed to go anywhere at all into a foreign country who is less than forty years of age" to avoid exposing impressionable citizens to dangerous ideas. In neighboring Sparta, laws prohibited travel abroad entirely in order to spare the martial city-state "the infection of bad habits" from the outside world.[40] In the modern age, nineteenth-century European states such as Britain, France, Germany, and Italy alternated between legislating against the emigration of citizens deemed valuable and welcoming the departure of others as a "safety valve."[41] On the other side of the globe, partly in response to the imperial ambitions of these same European states, China under the

Qing dynasty, Japan under the Tokugawa shogunate, and Joseon Korea maintained strict limits on emigration as well as immigration until the late nineteenth century.[42] Even as Western European governments grew more tolerant of population mobility in the name of economic liberalism, Central and Eastern European states remained committed to emigration controls out of concern for demographic loss and a sense—not always unfounded—that their citizens would be taken advantage of beyond their borders.[43] These restrictions on exit provided an important precedent for the closing of the Iron Curtain.[44] Even in the twentieth century, the practice of curtailing emigration was not confined to Europe, nor was it exclusively linked to socialist states; Fascist Italy, Nazi Germany, Haiti under the Duvalier dynasty, the Kingdom of Saudi Arabia, and apartheid-era South Africa all limited exit.[45]

Even as economic liberalization pushed open borders, states gained new methods of controlling populations, thanks to the widespread issuance of passports in the wake of the First World War. With an identification document required for exit as well as entry, states claimed the "monopoly of the legitimate means of movement."[46] In the Cold War, the states that made up "the West" advocated for "freedom of movement" in calling for an end to emigration limits in the socialist bloc. Yet no state allowed unfettered entry. And even the fiercest proponents of free movement, including the United States, occasionally restricted exit by refusing to issue passports to citizens suspected of disloyalty.[47]

To be sure, imperial Russia and the Soviet Union had a longer and more consistent history of limiting exit than most. From the middle of the nineteenth century into the early twentieth century, Russian migration policy selectively chose immigrants for integration but limited emigration for all. Those departing to live abroad were required to renounce their citizenship and faced barriers to returning, though such laws were unevenly enforced.[48] The practice of "holding" citizens carried over into the Soviet period, though not immediately. While the Bolsheviks, having once been emigres themselves, were no strangers to the risks of an emigration composed of political opponents, they allowed the departure of nearly 2 million White Russian migrants, seeing them as people who had no place in the new society they were building.[49] Some fled amid the chaos of the Civil War while others were expelled; most were stripped of their citizenship and left stateless.[50] Until the late 1920s, formal emigration from the Soviet Union remained legally possible.[51] Others left informally, departing on trips abroad never to return.

In response to a string of embarrassing incidents involving officially cleared travelers who refused to come back, Soviet authorities began to adopt a harder line on "nonreturners." Stalin's Politburo declared in 1929 that the failure of a Soviet citizen to return home would be regarded as "defection to the camp of the enemies of the working class and the peasantry and classified as treason." While the measure left the door open to the potential homecoming of those lingering abroad, it could also be applied retroactively to those who had left years earlier. Citizens who refused to return were to be severely punished, with the confiscation of all of their property—a measure that could render remaining family members homeless if their apartment was seized—and a death sentence to be carried out within twenty-four hours of their arrest.[52] The criminalization of emigration was followed by increased surveillance of internal migration through the establishment of restricted zones and passport controls, particularly in the state's western borderlands.[53]

The state's capacity to seal its borders lagged behind decrees issued in Moscow. Well into the 1930s, unauthorized migrants continued to flow across the vast and sparsely guarded boundaries of the USSR, particularly along its southern rim, which stretched from Turkey eastward to Iran, Afghanistan, and China.[54] The Soviet Union may have been established in a territory with a long-standing tradition of limiting emigration, but it was also the latest in a succession of governments overseeing a Eurasian landscape of itinerants and wanderers, difficult to enclose because of its enormous size and unevenly distributed population.[55] The task of enforcing official pronouncements fell to the Soviet Border Troops, established in 1918 at the onset of the Russian Civil War and by 1920 placed under auspices of the Soviet secret police.[56] If the Soviet Union was a fortress state standing against "capitalist encirclement," the border troops were cast as the heroes of the fortress's defenses. Their strength and discipline were celebrated within the Soviet Union and projected abroad in displays of border pageantry meant to repel foes and reassure allies. They patrolled "no man's lands" in border regions and deported populations deemed politically unreliable because of their ties with ethnic groups living outside the USSR.[57]

Soviet borders were tightened further in the late 1930s, as the distinction between foreign and domestic foes blurred amid the Great Terror. In 1937, Nikolai Ezhov, head of the NKVD (the forerunner of the KGB), signed off on a strict set of rules governing the behavior of official travelers, regulating everything from the places they could stay to the newspapers they could read.[58] Around the same time, the system for selecting and monitoring Soviets traveling internationally was standardized and centralized, overseen by a committee on which two high-ranking NKVD officers sat.[59] The following year, a decree formalized the guidelines for stripping citizenship from those who refused to return home.[60] Article 58 of the criminal code of Soviet Russia, dedicated to punishing "counter-revolutionary" activities, had classified flight abroad as a treasonous act since 1934 but mandated stricter sentences for fugitive soldiers. By the late 1930s, civilian "nonreturners" were increasingly punished, like their military counterparts, by death sentences and property confiscation.

Yet even at the height of the Stalinist terror, the fear that the Soviet Union would be infiltrated by hostile foreign agents exceeded concerns about Soviet citizens exiting en masse. A 1938 Politburo decree on "defectors" focused exclusively on potential spies and saboteurs sneaking into the Soviet Union under cover, "allegedly seeking political asylum in the USSR." The decree said nothing about Soviet citizens seeking to leave.[61] In a handful of cases, the NKVD tracked and assassinated prominent former officials and emigre leaders who shared intelligence secrets and collaborated with foreign governments after fleeing the Soviet Union.[62] Like the border policies of most states, however, those of the prewar Soviet Union were primarily focused on keeping external enemies out.

The Second World War turned Soviet border troops into frontline soldiers and made the reestablishment of border controls central to the reassertion of Soviet sovereignty. Those fleeing the Soviet state were treated with even greater severity. Stalin's Order No. 270, issued in August 1941, called for military leaders who showed an inclination to being taken prisoner instead of "fighting to the end" to be "destroyed by all means possible."[63] Even after the German army had been repelled from Soviet territory, Soviet citizens had to be scrutinized for potential collaboration with their former German occupiers. By annexing Estonia, Latvia, Lithuania, eastern Poland, and Moldova, the Soviet Union brought populations with a host of foreign contacts—including ties with large diaspora populations in Western Europe and the United States—into the fold. The war not only produced a borderland full of potential internal opponents but also displaced millions of Soviets beyond state borders. A major effort to repatriate Soviet citizens was undertaken at the war's end and subsequently expanded to include the return of long-standing emigres.

In the war's aftermath, an understandable sense of demographic loss and a determination to prosecute wartime collaboration drove authorities to pursue the return of Soviet citizens from abroad more energetically and to regulate the departure of those within its borders more carefully. With the expansion of Soviet influence, these policies were replicated in countries allied with the Soviet Union, where boundaries were guarded by border troops who resembled—and were supervised by—their counterparts in the Soviet Border Troops. Yet unlike socialist states such as Bulgaria, Cuba,

Romania, and Yugoslavia—which adopted a more flexible approach to emigration or never implemented such strict policies to begin with—the USSR retained legal barriers to exit until the Cold War's conclusion.[64]

Even as the state's borderlands were cleansed of potential opponents, dotted with watchtowers, patrolled by troops with guard dogs, reinforced with high-voltage fences, and buffered by socialist allies whose security services were modeled on those of the Soviet Union, the memory of wartime invasion and displacement loomed large, and the state's borders never seemed fully secure. The efforts of Western intelligence agencies to infiltrate the Soviet Union and encourage defection left Soviet officials wary of loosening border controls, which in turn affirmed the distinction Western policymakers sought to draw between the "free world" and the "captive" socialist camp.

Yet this rhetorical opposition regarding the "freedom of movement" should not be taken at face value. Socialist states were not the only ones to screen migrants based on ideological considerations. Often Soviets who defected found that they had traded KGB minders tasked with maintaining their ideological purity when traveling abroad for CIA handlers who probed their personal biographies while keeping them isolated in "safe houses." Just as the regulation of emigration marked the boundaries of the Soviet state, the question of which immigrants to the United States were considered "legal" and which were deemed "illegal" determined the limits of belonging in the American political community.[65] While the longer-term legacies of serfdom could be seen in the way Soviet policies limited movement and denied passports to rural citizens until the 1970s, the legacies of slavery and segregation linked mobility within and across US borders to skin color.[66] Race, class, and political persuasion remained important in determining who could enter the United States and be accepted as a Cold War refugee.[67]

Like the Soviet Union, the United States pushed its border controls deep into neighboring countries. During the Cold War, US Border Patrol agents ran operations and trained border guards throughout Latin America, and the State Department's network of consular officials managed entry from thousands of miles away.[68] The United States and its allies were under little obligation to grant refuge to migrants they did not want to accept, though the principle of non-refoulement—not returning migrants to countries where their lives would be in danger—became more accepted in the aftermath of the forced repatriation campaigns carried out by the Soviet Union. In many respects, the policies of the superpowers mirrored and influenced each other, the US regime based on limiting entry and the Soviet regime focused on restricting exit.

While it is common to juxtapose a land-based Soviet empire with a more diffuse American empire ruling through economic and cultural influence, both states projected power over movement through territorial and non-territorial means of control.[69] On the Radio Free Europe broadcasts it sponsored, the United States encouraged flight by featuring the stories of defectors "escaping" Soviet control, but it also filtered defectors through its extensive network of military bases and across its own land borders. Soviet foreign policy maintained a buffer zone of allied states in Eastern Europe, but Soviet officials also courted emigres in far-flung corners of the world, took part in international legal debates, engaged in a vigorous program of cultural diplomacy, and laid out new shipping routes and aviation networks. While Soviet ideology emphasized the rootedness of citizens in Soviet territory, Soviet policies created pathways for global mobility tethered to Soviet embassies, ships, and airplanes.[70]

During the Cold War, these parallel empires were unlikely partners when it came to constructing borders. In some cases, the process was unintentional: the Berlin Wall was mutually constituted as the superpowers—and the divided sides of Germany they backed—faced off. In other cases, the building of borders was the result of collusion between the superpowers in the interest of shoring up a status quo that gave them preferential control of global mobility.[71] This collusion was usually tacit and took the form of cooperation for mutual benefit rather than conspiratorial plans.[72] But the resulting global framework made the distinction irrelevant. The situation recalled the prescient words of British writer George Orwell from 1945, when the superpowers first emerged from the Second World War: "unable to conquer one another they are likely to continue ruling the world between them."[73] Although characterized by bipolar rivalry, the Cold War era was also a time when both sides came together to place limits on movement through previously unregulated spaces that neither side could exclusively claim as its own.[74]

Of course, leaders in Moscow and Washington did not determine everything, and other actors were swept up into this process of imperial contestation and collusion around the world's boundaries.[75] Other states, whether in alliance with one of the superpowers or from a position of studied neutrality, exploited defectors for their own purposes. These countries often had to be persuaded to shelter or return them, and sometimes they articulated alternative visions for regulating migration. Ultimately, they had fewer levers of global influence and were sidelined in the meetings that set the framework for international law.[76] Defectors also sought to assert their own agency, finding loopholes in the international order and strategically employing the language of the Cold War to slip through.[77] Though international activists sometimes came to their assistance, such a strategy was not without risks.[78] The imperial authority of the superpowers was dispersed and not always predictable, wielded by Soviet and American intelligence officers, border guards, diplomats, and lawyers operating far from Moscow and Washington and often forced to make snap decisions on the ground. Over time, however, their responses to defection led to an expansion of government authority over borders and movement in a manner that generally suited Soviet and American interests.

Drawing on multilingual sources from over twenty archives in countries on both sides of the Cold War divide, *Defectors* follows the winding journeys of Soviet defectors and reveals the consequences of their travels. The book's first part considers how the superpowers divided the globe into two rival but reinforcing spheres governed by different approaches to managing international migration. Its second part looks at how, after the borders between the camps were drawn, the superpowers colluded to impose a lasting global architecture of migration by regulating the spaces in between. Even after the lifting of emigration restrictions and the collapse of the Soviet state that once enforced them, the dense network of agreements laid during the Cold War to restrain global migration remained in place. These durable limits on mobility, combined with the demise of defection at the Cold War's end, stranded many refuge-seekers. Even if they had gained the right to leave their homelands, they found themselves unwelcome on the international stage once the contest between communism and capitalism concluded.

PART I
Building Borders

1

From Displacement to Defection

Olga Marchenko, an unassuming, middle-aged woman from rural Soviet Ukraine, stood before the judges in the largest chamber of the Palais de Justice in Paris on January 31, 1949. The wood-paneled hall with its three large windows overlooking the Seine was filled with lawyers, diplomats, journalists, photographers, and well-connected French citizens. They had come to watch what was billed as the "trial of the century." Dressed in a plain gray skirt and jacket with a colorful kerchief covering her head, Marchenko was accompanied by an interpreter who translated her testimony from Ukrainian into French. The journalists in attendance hung on her every word, scribbling in their notebooks before dashing off into the adjoining room, where a row of telephone booths had been specially installed to facilitate their dispatches to news desks around the world.[1]

Marchenko seemed an unlikely person to command a global audience, yet she held the attention of the entire assembly as she recounted her tragic dispossession under Stalin as a supposedly wealthy peasant kulak, her forced shipment by the Nazis to work on a German farm, and her decision after the war to remain in the American zone of Germany. As a former kulak she had "no reason to return" to the Soviet Union, she explained.[2] She was the first Soviet displaced person (DP) called to testify on behalf of Victor Kravchenko, the former official with the Soviet Purchasing Commission in Washington who had conspicuously defected to the United States as the Second World War was nearing its end.

On its surface, the trial in Paris was merely a libel case initiated by Kravchenko against *Les Lettres Françaises*, a French communist newspaper, for its portrayal of him as an untrustworthy drunkard who was not the real author of his memoir, *I Chose Freedom*, but instead a "puppet whose clumsy strings [were] 'made in the U.S.A.'"[3] Held in a country with one of Western Europe's most active communist parties, the trial effectively became an international hearing on the influence of the Soviet Union abroad and, relatedly, the place of Soviet migrants in the postwar order.[4] These were by no means abstract issues for the French public. For more than two years after the war's end, the Soviet Union operated Camp Beauregard, the main point for processing displaced Soviets in France, as a small island of Soviet authority outside Paris. The camp was visibly distinct from the surrounding landscape, its walls festooned with red flags and a giant portrait of Stalin hanging over its gate. In November 1947, following the French Communist Party's exclusion from the governing coalition, it was dramatically stormed by police, an infantry division, and two tanks. French authorities alleged that it was a base for kidnapping. Soviet officials claimed that the camp sheltered a recently divorced mother who wished to return to the Soviet Union with her children and denounced the attack as a flagrant violation of international law.[5] In short, France was the perfect place to put Soviet influence on trial.

Ahead of his court date, Kravchenko had sought out witnesses to confirm his memoir's account of life in the Soviet Union by posting appeals in DP camps in the American zones of occupation in Western Europe. At a press conference following his arrival in Paris, he presented the "most recent refugees from the Soviet Union" as truth-tellers "who have found the courage within themselves to come to this trial and to tell the outside world all they know about the Soviet police state and its leader."[6] Marchenko, whom he described as a "simple peasant woman," was chosen to go first because of the "contrast she would make with the array of glittering personalities and notables" called to testify by the Soviet Union.[7] Even those on Europe's left found her trustworthy. The day after she testified, the French socialist paper *Populaire* described the plainspoken Marchenko as "too genuine to falsify anything."[8] She was followed on the witness stand by other ordinary figures transformed into international celebrities by the postwar struggle for Soviet migrants, including a young sailor who had jumped ship in Spain in 1946.[9] Although Kravchenko fled his post in wartime, Marchenko was displaced by the Nazi invasion, and the fugitive sailor left after the war's conclusion, all were grouped together as defectors fleeing the long arm of the Soviet Union.

While it was the editors of *Les Lettres Françaises* who had been sued for libel, the defense enjoyed the full support of the Soviet state. Since Kravchenko's defection, Soviet secret police agents operating undercover had tracked his activities in the United States.[10] A full cast of witnesses was dispatched from Moscow to testify against him, ranging from General Leonid Rudenko, a military official who had headed the Soviet Purchasing Commission, to Zinaida Gorlova, Kravchenko's estranged ex-wife. They were housed at the annex of the Soviet Embassy in Paris, where embassy staff relayed the court's proceedings back to Moscow.[11] As concern grew about the trial's international impact, prominent Soviet public figures were encouraged to denounce Kravchenko. In a scathing article entitled "The Judas Kravchenko and His Masters" published in *Pravda*, wartime novelist and poet Konstantin Simonov claimed that the defector had become a "paid agent of American intelligence" in order to pay off gambling debts and called him a "lowlife, a turncoat, and a traitor."[12]

Kravchenko's opposition to the Soviet Union was likely genuine, motivated by personal, professional, and political grievances against Stalinism. But it was true that he enjoyed the assistance of the US government and advanced America's Cold War aims. His memoir made no mention of the fact that before his defection he had met three times with FBI agents to secure protection and provide information on Soviet activities in the United States. After his flight, he continued his debriefings with the FBI and denounced Soviet policies before the House Un-American Activities Committee.[13] While some American journalists initially described him as a "deserter" in 1944 and even mused that his defection "serve[d] Nazi propaganda," the State Department reclassified him as a "political refugee" following the publication of his book in 1946.[14] The book itself was based on Kravchenko's recollections but ghostwritten by American journalist Eugene Lyons, a former fellow traveler turned strident critic of the Soviet Union, who would go on to head an anti-communist front organization funded by the CIA.[15] While the idea of initiating a case against the editors of *Les Lettres Française* may have been Kravchenko's, the American Military Government in Germany helped him search for witnesses in DP camps.[16] Although he, like Marchenko, was originally from Ukraine, Kravchenko studiously avoided calling any witnesses who advocated Ukrainian independence, hoping to rally Soviet emigres of all nationalities against Stalinism in a way that suited American foreign policy goals of the era.[17] Afterward, State Department officials discussed compensating Kravchenko for a second book based on the trial and oversaw plans for a speaking tour by the defector in the Middle East, South Asia, and Latin America. They also helped Olga Marchenko and her husband relocate from a DP camp in Germany to the United States.[18]

The court case in Paris was but one front in a broader contest between the Soviet Union and the United States over the control of migration in postwar Europe. It seemed to pit two diametrically opposed traditions of managing migrants against one another: the Soviet Union aimed to repatriate its citizens, prosecute those who left, and prevent further exit, while the United States championed the "freedom of movement" and welcomed the immigration of Kravchenko and his star witnesses. This binary formulation, however, obscured a far more complex reality. The Soviet Union had an established history of restricting exit but until recently had also been a known haven for left-leaning political refugees from across the globe; the United States was built on a tradition of immigration but maintained limits on entry that hindered the arrival of Soviet migrants. In the wake of the Second World War, both sides developed parallel systems for classifying, channeling, and competing for the same set of migrants even as each drew rhetorical distinctions between "freedom" and "captivity," as the Americans described it, or "loyalty" and "treason," as Soviet officials would have it.

This process unfolded in postwar Europe's DP camps—extraterritorial outposts initially under the jurisdiction of Soviet and American military officials—and continued in government offices, newsrooms, publishing houses, and film studios as the fate of hundreds of thousands of Soviet migrants displaced during the Second World War hung in the balance. While the United States and its allies initially cooperated in returning Soviet citizens, Western policy shifted to resisting repatriation requests, supporting a politicized refugee system and, ultimately, encouraging flight from the socialist bloc.

Over time, defection supplanted the wartime notion that those like Kravchenko who fled by choice were simply deserters, and those displaced by Nazi Germany's invasion of the Soviet Union were helpless victims of circumstances. While historians studying displacement from the Soviet Union have called attention to the politicization of migrants in the early Cold War, they have generally overlooked the emergence of defection as a distinct paradigm for making sense of migration.[19] Relatedly, the scholarship on defectors has not examined how this paradigm developed in the context of postwar displacement.[20] At first, "defector" was only one of several terms used to classify migrants who fled the Soviet Union and its allies. It later emerged as the dominant one, outlasting "DPs" and "escapees" and enduring until the end of the Cold War. Although its precise definition was difficult to pin down, it transformed migrants from recipients of humanitarian care into brave fugitives who could provide up-to-date knowledge on the Soviet Union, and it offered a path, however treacherous, for those seeking to reach the United States. It was promoted at the top by state directives and the establishment of international organizations to manage migrants. And it was rhetorically deployed at the ground level by emigre

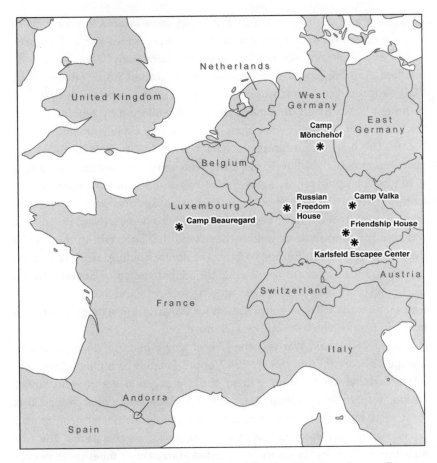

Figure 1.1 DP Camps and Escapee Centers for Socialist Bloc Migrants in Postwar Europe

activists and fleeing Soviets. A focus on defection reveals how the Soviet and American systems for governing migration were shaped not just by prewar pathways and postwar circumstances, but also by their encounter with each other, with consequences for the movement of people across the globe.

DISPLACEMENT AND "DESERTION" BEFORE DEFECTION

On May 10, 1945, the day after Nazi Germany's surrender, the Soviet Union's Administration for Repatriation compiled a list detailing the world-wide diaspora of Soviet-claimed citizens displaced by the war.[21] The results were marked on an enormous map depicting a global network of camps, hospitals, and other institutions. Soviets were clustered in Germany, among different zones of military occupation. They were located in nearly every other Western European country, as far west as France and as far north as Norway. They were present in Palestine, where Soviet Jewish migrants had fled. And they could even be found in the United States, where Soviet POWs captured in German uniforms were held at camps and hospitals.[22] Although it was based on data painstakingly collected by Administration for Repatriation officials since their organization's establishment the year before, the map was incomplete. Its focus on institutions excluded the sizable population of Soviet migrants who were not confined to camps. A full cartographic rendering of Soviet migration would have shown citizens scattered across Europe, squatting in houses and living in crowded apartments. It would have depicted Soviets who fled eastward during the war into Iran and India as well as those who circulated within the French Empire, moving from Europe to French colonial holdings in North Africa and Indochina. After the war's end, the global spread of Soviet citizens continued, with displaced Soviets moving to North and South America as well as Australia.[23] The Administration for Repatriation struggled to map a group of people who were still on the move.

The Second World War was the largest single instance of migration in Europe's history.[24] From 1939 to 1947, approximately 55 million Europeans left or fled their homes; among them, the largest group was from the Soviet Union, numbering over 5 million.[25] The war accelerated global connections even as it wrought destruction: it moved people across borders, spread mass culture, and spurred the creation of global organizations. The war also drew the Soviet Union and the United States closer together than ever before. The Lend-Lease Act of 1941 brought American weapons, trucks, motorcycles, oil, canned meats, and flour into the Soviet Union. Along with these goods came American sailors, who arrived in Soviet port cities on ships bearing Lend-Lease's bounty.[26] The US-Soviet wartime alliance, sealed with American material support and the blood of Soviet soldiers on the Eastern front, saw Soviet pilots train in North Carolina, Soviet delegations move by rail throughout the United States, and the Soviet Purchasing Commission open its headquarters in Washington, DC, with branch offices spread from Fairbanks, Alaska, to Miami, Florida.[27] It was from this organization that Victor Kravchenko fled, at a time when the wartime allies were in daily contact. In his memoir, Kravchenko described a dramatic "flight in the night" through Washington's Union Station and onto a train bound for New York, his hat tilted downward to conceal his face after he "caught sight of a Red Army uniform" in the crowd.[28] Although the incident lent an air of suspense to Kravchenko's account, it also alluded to the fact that a Soviet soldier would not have been out of place in wartime Washington.

During the war, repatriation was generally treated as a matter of logistical coordination rather than ideological confrontation. On April 3, 1944, the very day that Victor Kravchenko told a journalist from the *New York Times* that he was placing himself "under the protection of American public opinion," arrangements were made for a routine transfer of Vladimir Nikolaev, a Soviet POW held at Camp McCain in Mississippi, "to the West Coast for delivery to the custody of the appropriate Soviet authorities."[29] Although Kravchenko would later be regarded as the first defector of the coming Cold War, his flight was at first seen as a minor event. News of it appeared below the fold in the *New York Times*; the main headline that day announced the Red Army's westward push into Nazi-allied Romania.[30] The wartime alliance took precedence, and in seeking the return of Kravchenko, the Soviet government framed its request in military terms. The Soviet embassy's note to the US government stated that Kravchenko, "being in active military service in the Red Army and being temporarily sent to the United States," had "deserted . . . having violated the military laws of the USSR and his military duty." The note expressed "confidence" that the American side would see the "fight against desertion" as "necessary in the interests of both Governments."[31] In response, Joseph Davies, an influential American diplomat who had served as US Ambassador to Moscow, recommended that President Franklin D. Roosevelt turn Kravchenko over to Soviet officials.[32]

Kravchenko's fate remained uncertain. The FBI had all but promised him protection from the Soviet secret police, and the attorney general had been notified prior to his flight, but Roosevelt provided "no definitive instructions."[33] Meanwhile, the president joined British prime minister Winston Churchill in agreeing to the mass repatriation of Soviet citizens "without delay" when they met with Stalin at Yalta in February 1945. Later termed the "secret betrayal," the arrangement was considered a small concession given the outsized role the Soviet Union had played in defeating Nazi Germany. It was deemed necessary for securing the speedy return of American and British prisoners-of-war from Soviet-held territories. It also accorded with the general perception of wartime migrants as people out-of-place who were best served by being sent home.[34] An internal State Department memorandum declared that the United States had "no intention of holding Soviet citizens after the collapse of Germany regardless of whether they desired to return to the Soviet Union or not."[35]

Most Soviets returned home shortly after the war, and many did so by choice. By September 1945, over 2 million Soviet citizens had crossed a war-torn Europe to reenter the USSR; by February of the following year, around 95 percent of all Soviet displaced persons had been brought back home.[36] The Soviet state's desire to reclaim its citizens was understandable. Nearly 30 million Soviets had died during the war, and several million more had fled Nazi occupation or been sent as forced laborers to Germany. For a state that measured its strength in demographic terms, each citizen was a source of labor to be utilized in the rebuilding of cities, roads, and railways.[37] Locating lost citizens was also central to the reassertion of Soviet sovereignty and the reestablishment of border controls. The two processes were closely related: the border's security had been compromised by being overrun by German invaders, and displaced Soviets had been compromised by exposure to Nazi rule. In newly acquired territories, including the Baltic states, western Ukraine, and Moldova, the return of displaced people reinforced Soviet power by shoring up the state's claims to regulate the mobility of citizens throughout the expanded USSR.

Repatriation of displaced Soviets also aligned with the wartime mobility regime of the United States, which remained closed to most who sought refuge there. The interwar period had seen the adoption of strict immigration quotas, including limits virtually barring the entry of Jews, Slavs, and other East Europeans.[38] After the war began, entry into the country became even more difficult, with the closure of US consulates and the implementation of additional restrictions aimed at fortifying the nation's borders.[39] Although the United States emerged from the war with a newfound interest in projecting global power, it remained walled off to most Soviet migrants. Other Western states were also eager to see the swift departure of wartime refugees from the USSR, viewing them as a source of political unrest and an economic liability.

Just as the West was far from an open preserve of "freedom" at the war's conclusion, Soviet borders fell short of a formidable "Iron Curtain." The western boundary of Soviet authority was a confusion of exhausted military divisions, devastated physical infrastructure, uprooted populations, and new lands annexed by the Soviet state. On the ground, the Soviet repatriation process was as chaotic as it was brisk. Even the organization tasked with carrying it out was beset by internal problems: a subsequent audit by Moscow revealed systemic issues in the day-to-day operations of the Administration for Repatriation, with personnel accused of trading in foreign goods, drunkenness, consorting with prostitutes, and failure to follow basic organizational protocols.[40] While those displaced by war were meant to be transported by trucks, vehicle shortages and breakdowns meant that many proceeded on foot. Some traveled in "echelons" organized by the Administration for Repatriation, while others simply arrived at the Soviet border on their own. Many reentered the Soviet Union without passing through checkpoints designated for "filtration," where returnees were supposed to be questioned about potential collaboration with the Germans during the war and, as time went on, investigated to ensure that they had not been recruited by US or British intelligence. Once repatriates crossed over Soviet borders, many found they could freely move into supposedly "restricted" cities such as Moscow, Leningrad, and Kyiv.[41]

Publicly, the Soviet state cast itself as a champion of its displaced citizens and their rights wherever they found themselves. Internally, authorities in Moscow expressed concern about exposure to rising "anti-Soviet propaganda" and pushed for the "speedy transport of liberated Soviet citizens to the Motherland."[42] The United States was generally willing to comply. As late as October 1946, months after the publication of I Chose Freedom, the American Office of Military Government for Germany maintained its policy that Soviet citizens could be forcibly repatriated if there was evidence that they were war criminals, collaborators, or military deserters.[43]

SORTING THOSE WHO REMAINED

Although the number of Soviet-claimed citizens who remained outside the USSR after the end of mass repatriation in 1946 numbered approximately 450,000—less than 10 percent of the total population of Soviets displaced by the war—they soon gained a disproportionate prominence.[44] New techniques introduced to screen and categorize them would lay the foundation for the way migrants were managed across the globe. Organizations established to supervise their care and resettlement became new venues for superpower competition and influence.[45] With their physical location cast as a political choice, they became mobile signposts of influence as Cold War battle lines hardened across Europe. Yet such migrants were difficult to count, let alone control. Some had lost their documents, making it difficult to establish the basic facts of their identity; others concealed their pasts, changed their names, sought to remain stateless by choice, or became experts at telling the stories that states wanted to hear.[46]

Nationality was the most basic criterion for sorting these migrants, though it was far from a straightforward category. Jewish DP camps were placed under the protection of the American military, and Jewish DPs, regardless of their prewar citizenship, were able to claim a unique legal status according to which they could not be prosecuted for crimes by local German authorities.[47] By contrast, ethnic Germans forced to flee East Central European states after the war were generally not seen as worthy of international assistance.[48] The nationality of Poles and Balts from territories recently annexed by the Soviet Union was contested: the socialist state saw those who had fled independent Estonia, Latvia, Lithuania, and the eastern part of Poland during the war as its citizens, while Western governments tended to classify them separately. The situation was further muddled by migrants who deliberately obfuscated their national origins. Some Ukrainians seeking to avoid repatriation sought to pass themselves off as Polish citizens; after the war, the number of Ukrainians claiming Polish citizenship rose from 9,190 at the end of 1945 to 106,549 in the middle of June 1949.[49] They were not the only group to pose as citizens of neighboring countries. At one apartment building in Rome, Soviet officials found an ethnic Armenian from the USSR possessing falsified documents attesting to Iranian citizenship, a Georgian "passing himself off" as a Turk, and one Vasily Belinskii, who was pretending to be Vasily Wangfu, a Chinese citizen.[50]

Postwar migrants were further sorted according to a typology of displacement that had consequences for their future mobility. The definition of a "displaced person"—"civilians outside the national boundaries of their country by reason of the war"—rested on the notion of forced movement.[51] This aligned with the goals of the Soviet Administration for Repatriation, which concerned itself with citizens "who, during the Second World War, had been driven away by the German invaders."[52] With the conclusion of the mass repatriation campaign, Soviet Administration officials subjected those who remained abroad to additional layers of classification based on the manner of their flight from the homeland. They noted which ones were Soviet soldiers who "voluntarily gave themselves over to captivity," and which ones "were injured, and thus taken captive"; among non-military personnel, they determined whether they had been pushed beyond Soviet borders "by force" or had left willfully.[53] This information, based on interrogations, intelligence reports, and document checks, was incorporated into passenger manifests drawn up for those returning home. On one such list, an administrator put red check marks next to the names of those who had engaged in documented "anti-Soviet activities" abroad, indicating that they were to be subjected to further questioning.[54]

Western governments had their own hierarchies for sorting DPs. At first, a special status was granted to those who had been specially targeted by the Nazis, with individuals persecuted by the Germans for their "race, religion, or political activity" labeled "persecutees" and eligible for special benefits.[55] While DPs were supposed to have been forced to flee, the notion of "political activity" opened up the possibility of migrant agency. At the behest of British and American representatives, and against the protests of their Soviet counterparts, the idea of persecution eventually expanded to include experiences under communist rule. DPs seeking to avoid repatriation quickly realized they could assert some control over their destiny by telling stories about resisting communism as well as by telling stories about resisting National Socialism.[56]

These stories were amplified, embellished, and sometimes co-authored by journalists and emigre activists.[57] Western officials had initially been willing to look the other way in particularly brutal cases of forced repatriation. However, several notorious episodes changed public attitudes and cast the entire Soviet repatriation campaign as an operation based on coercion, undertaken with Western complicity. One occurred inside the United States, at New Jersey's Fort Dix, where on June 29, 1945, a riot broke out among Soviets captured in German uniform who were to be transported back to the USSR. US troops responded with tear gas and eventually with gunfire, killing one and wounding eight more. Three more POWs committed suicide.[58] Meanwhile, in Austria, a group of Cossacks who had fought for the German side in the war were beaten and dragged onto transport vehicles by British soldiers and turned over to Soviet authorities despite a prior understanding that British forces would protect them. The event would be commemorated as a martyrdom among anti-Soviet emigres and immortalized in a painting by S. G. Korolkoff entitled "The Betrayal of the Cossacks at Lienz."[59]

Those who had fled Russia and the Soviet Union in previous waves of emigration cast themselves as interpreters of the needs and motivations of DPs. Sometimes they acted in service of Western policies, and at other times they lobbied Western governments in pursuit of their own goals.[60] Anti-Soviet Baltic emigre groups, Baltic governments-in-exile, and sympathetic Catholic organizations were influential in pressing officials in the United States and Western Europe to turn against forced repatriation, especially in the case of Baltic nationalities who were only claimed by the Soviet Union by virtue of the annexation of their countries during the war. In New York, rallies were organized in support of Baltic refugees; in Sweden, the fate of Baltic migrants arriving in makeshift boats became a pivotal issue in the country's politics.[61] Meanwhile, Western officials were flooded with appeals from Ukrainian and Georgian emigre groups, some of whom saw the rescue of "their" DPs as the first step toward national liberation from Soviet rule.

Although its emigre opponents warned of the "totalitarian" nature of the Soviet state, beyond its zone of military occupation the USSR was progressively constrained by international organizations dominated by the United States and its allies. In 1947, the United Nations Relief and Rehabilitation Administration (UNRRA), which Soviet authorities had tolerated but viewed warily, was replaced by the International Refugee Organization

(IRO). The Soviet Union refused to participate, seeing the organization's claims on Soviet "refugees" as an obstacle to the USSR's repatriation mission. Refugees, according to the IRO's charter, included victims of "persecution" regardless of their political affiliation.[62] The Soviet constitution, by contrast, defined refugees as those "persecuted for upholding the interests of the working people and the case for peace"; this meant that those who fled the worker's state or anyone with the slightest taint of wartime collaboration with Nazi Germany could not be considered a refugee.[63] Similar definitions were soon inserted into the constitutions of the USSR's allies. However, without the participation of socialist states in its activities, the IRO's policies shifted further to the right. Soviet authorities viewed it as an unreliable partner, and their perceptions were not unfounded: from July 1, 1947, through the end of 1951, when the IRO wound down its operations, the organization returned only 1,836 people to the USSR.[64]

Despite this setback, Soviet authorities refused to abandon their claims on citizens who eluded repatriation. The state's preoccupation with preventing illegal exit, which preceded the war, demanded it; the postwar Soviet Union's drive to affirm its expanded borders and its status as a superpower lent it additional importance. In fact, the Administration for Repatriation further expanded its mission in 1946 by encouraging emigres in France, Czechoslovakia, Yugoslavia, China, and Japan who had originally fled in the early days of the revolution to receive Soviet citizenship and return "home."[65] Around the same time, the Soviet state endorsed the "repatriation" of the global diaspora of Armenians to Soviet Armenia, a territory in which many had never set foot.[66] While maintaining hardline policies of migration management in Soviet-occupied territory, the Soviet Union launched a "soft" repatriation campaign that employed more subtle forms of influence to reach those who remained in the West.[67] The campaign cast a wide net but targeted migrants from the Soviet Union where they were most vulnerable—the hastily established displaced persons camps that remained in operation for years after the war's end.

THE COLD WAR INSIDE THE CAMPS

DP camps were among the most fiercely contested spaces of the early Cold War. The Soviet government saw them as a place to gather lost citizens and unmask fugitive "war criminals." Kravchenko, his backers in the US government, and a network of Western scholars saw them as a place to find witnesses like Olga Marchenko who could speak the "truth" about Stalinist tyranny and reveal the nature of the Soviet system. Anti-Soviet emigres saw them as a place to strip away the veneer of Soviet influence to recover "true" Russians (and Ukrainians, Lithuanians, Georgians, and others). Aid organizations saw them as a "laboratory" for testing new methods of refugee management. And Western businesses weighed their potential for forging productive laborers and agriculturalists out of Soviet factory workers and collective farmers.[68] Those in the camps were turned into the subjects of government data collection, academic research, "reeducation programs," public health campaigns, and vocational training. They faced competing claims by rival states, intelligence services, emigre groups, and aid organizations.

If there was one commonality among those who laid claims to Soviet DPs, it was that all agreed they were in need of rehabilitation as well as relief. This meant putting them to work. In a brochure disseminated among Soviet DPs, the Soviet Commissariat of Defense claimed that returning home and directing one's labor toward the rebuilding of the USSR was the surest means of shedding the stigma of wartime flight. "Your debt," the brochure explained, will be repaid by "assisting the Motherland with all of your might to help her quickly recover from the serious wounds inflicted by the war."[69] On the other end of the political spectrum, the Tolstoy Foundation, headed by Alexandra Tolstoy, a longtime opponent of the Soviet state, maintained that reeducation through labor was necessary after years of "serfdom" under Soviet rule. US, European, and Soviet intelligence services also put DPs to work as agents and informants. They were tasked with keeping an eye on fellow migrants and subverting the operations of rival governments.

Soviet officials worried that the longer Soviet migrants remained in DP camps, the greater the risk that they would be targeted or turned against them by foreign intelligence. These suspicions only deepened as Cold War tensions grew. When Soviet repatriation officials visited a camp established for Baltic DPs at Blomberg in late 1946, a hand grenade was thrown at their car. It glanced off the vehicle and exploded in the road without injuring them, but they denounced the incident as a "terrorist act" carried out against Soviet officers in the American zone of occupied Germany.[70] At the end of the year, an internal report by the Administration for Repatriation noted numerous instances of American military officials and UNRRA personnel involved in the "recruitment" (a term with clear intelligence connotations) of "Soviet citizens with the goal of moving them to other countries: Brazil . . . Switzerland, Argentina, and others."[71] By 1948, a memorandum written by a colonel in the Soviet Administration for Repatriation warned that even Soviet officers dispatched to assist with repatriation needed to keep their guard up to avoid being coopted by

Western intelligence. They were counseled to limit their interaction with their foreign counterparts, remain "sober" at social gatherings, refuse to attend events alone, and conduct themselves in a "strictly official manner and tone." They were warned about sexual as well as ideological seduction by Western intelligence agents, in the form of the female "guests" who "not so infrequently" appeared at official events. They were also cautioned about hostile emigre organizations whose "anti-repatriation propaganda," expressed in fluent Russian, proved particularly effective at leading Soviet citizens astray.[72]

While emigre organizations like the Tolstoy Foundation were seen by Soviet authorities as operating in coordination with American intelligence, the anti-Soviet attitudes held by emigres often exceeded those of US officials. The youngest daughter of the famous Russian author of *War and Peace*, Alexandra Tolstoy had been repeatedly arrested by Soviet officials over the course of the 1920s before leaving the USSR in 1929. A decade later, she established the Tolstoy Foundation on a farm outside New York to help fellow exiles and refugees from the Soviet Union. For Tolstoy, assisting Soviet DPs was a chance to reclaim Russians from a Soviet government that she saw as an ideologically alien imposition on her native land. Immediately after the war's end, the Tolstoy Foundation began lobbying American officials to resettle DPs from the Soviet Union in the United States. In a note sent to Paul McCormack, an influential member of the War Refugee Board, Tatiana Schaufuss, the Tolstoy Foundation's co-founder and executive director, argued that the "last and only hope" for Soviet DPs was "from America—from *Americans* and Russians in America." She volunteered her organization's services in "channeling" their "cases to other American and international agencies in the field."[73] In collaboration with the lively Russian emigre press in the United States, the Tolstoy Foundation passed allegations on to US officials about strong-armed Soviet tactics, including the alleged "kidnapping of a Russian mother and her daughter by Soviet agents from an apartment building" in the British zone of occupied Germany in January 1946.[74]

Other emigres were even more militant in their opposition to Soviet authority. Konstantin Boldyrev, a leader of the National Alliance of Russian Solidarists (NTS), the stridently anti-Soviet organization that had found common cause with Nazi Germany in fighting against the Soviet Union, pursued the organization's goals as the administrator of a large DP camp at Mönchehof, in the American zone of Germany. His reports on the camp's activities to American military administrators read like a right-wing manifesto. The camp, he wrote, was structured "on the principle of working communities" that aimed at the "reconversion" of DPs through labor. "The first step toward the normalization of relationship between individuals," he explained, was "to put them on a paying basis."[75] Boldyrev's relations with American authorities were sometimes strained. In July 1945, he was arrested by the US military following charges that he was illegally sheltering Soviet citizens from the socialist state's repatriation effort.[76] He was soon released and returned to running the camp, despite continued allegations by Soviet officials that he was providing falsified identity documents to Soviet DPs.[77]

Emigre groups were particularly skilled at helping those averse to return to navigate the overlapping bureaucracies set up to manage migrants. The eligibility officers of the IRO referred to a confidential manual to determine whether displaced persons were "eligible for repatriation," "eligible for resettlement," or "not within the mandate of the Organization." The manual reminded officers that "war criminals," "quislings," "traitors," and "deserters" who fled after the war did not fall within the IRO's mandate. In numerous cases, emigre organizations advised DPs before their interviews with IRO officers on how to frame their stories to avoid such charges. The manual told officers to be on the lookout for imposture and false identification papers, noting that "there have been many cases of Russian Soviet citizens making false statements and producing forged documentary evidence that they are stateless 'Nansen' refugees," a reference to the practice of helping recent Soviet migrants pose as interwar refugees that Boldyrev stood accused of facilitating.[78]

Slowly but steadily, emigre activists recast the displacement of migrants from the Soviet Union as a political choice to leave, linking them to the defectors who followed. A pamphlet published by the Tolstoy Foundation entitled "Who Are the DPs?" boldly stated that "these people left RUSSIA because they DID NOT BELIEVE IN COMMUNISM."[79] In a similar vein, *Thirteen Who Fled*, a popular book by journalist Louis Fischer based on a series of interviews with DPs, framed their fate as a brave decision to seek a new life in the West, even as it downplayed the wartime collaboration with Nazi Germany by several of the book's subjects.[80] Emigres like Tolstoy, who had already made the journey from East to West, promised that they could help Soviet DPs complete their transition from Stalinist subjects to American citizens. In the United States, such assurances played to longer-term convictions about the need to liberate Russians from their own country's "despotism" and "backwardness."[81] Tolstoy placed the latest wave of Soviet migrants within the mythologized American immigrant tradition, noting that though "they are people of different professions, different characters, different classes" they "possess several characteristic traits in common—the yearning for a free, independent life, a strong feeling of hatred toward dictatorships, strong family ties, and a willingness to accept any kind of work."[82]

With Western European governments wary of Soviet migrants becoming an economic burden and the United States barring entry to those at risk of becoming a "public charge," securing work became the key to resettlement.[83] DPs were evaluated as a labor source by representatives from private enterprises, and their capacity for work was also part of the screening process employed by the IRO. Elderly DPs, along with those with mental and physical disabilities, were classified as constituting a "hard core" of refugees who were deemed incapable of productive labor and difficult to resettle.[84] Meanwhile, DPs were employed in the camps and beyond them, making handicrafts, laboring in factories, and working as farmhands, maids, mechanics, and roofers. The drive to turn DPs into a labor source sometimes backfired. In 1947, thousands of DPs—many of them erstwhile Soviet citizens—were sent to Belgium to work as coal miners, an arrangement worked out between American and British officials and representatives of the Belgian mining industry. Once there, however, they began to protest poor working conditions, a development that Soviet officials seized upon to denounce the exploitative use of DPs as a modern form of "slavery."[85] The Soviet Administration for Repatriation, ambitious in its mission and eager to claim the moral high ground, sought the return of all migrants: old emigres and those who took flight more recently, the healthy and those who were ill.[86]

Soviet migrants were also evaluated as a source of intellectual and ideological labor. Emigre groups were among the first to utilize DPs as a source of information on conditions in the Soviet Union. In December 1945, just months after the war's end, the Ukrainian Congress Committee of America published a pamphlet entitled *Plight of Ukrainian DPs*, which provided "a few typical letters" from those "whom the Soviets would forcibly repatriate and doom to enslavement, persecution or death." Copies were sent to President Harry Truman and the State Department.[87] Around the same time, American social scientists, sensing opportunities in the funding landscape of the emergent Cold War, began to see DPs as ideal research subjects. Just as the Ukrainian Congress Committee was recounting the experiences of Ukrainian DPs to Truman, a team of researchers from Johns Hopkins University contacted the State Department to inquire about the feasibility of a large-scale study of wartime displacement from the Soviet Union.[88]

Some studies blurred the line between scholarly research and emigre activism. With the tacit consent of the State Department, one-time Menshevik activist David Dallin, who had originally put Kravchenko in touch with the FBI, traveled to Germany and France in 1948 to question Soviet DPs. Over a three-year period, his interview subjects shifted from those displaced by the war to postwar migrants who were increasingly described as "defectors," including two Soviet soldiers who fled to the West after being stationed in East Germany.[89] The largest interview project by far was the Harvard Project on the Soviet Social System, which received approximately $1 million in funding from the US Air Force and surveyed over 2,000 Soviet migrants from 1951 to 1953. Many interviewees were persons displaced by war, but, once again, special attention was paid to "defectors" who fled in the war's aftermath. The more recent the migrant, it was believed, the more relevant the information they possessed. Among the interviewers were scholars who would become pivotal figures in Cold War Sovietology, including Alexander Dallin, David Dallin's son.[90]

Western governments were not unique in seeing Soviet migrants as a strategic source of knowledge. Soviet secret police officials routinely interrogated returning DPs about conditions in the West as well as the identities, activities, and locations of their fellow citizens who chose to remain there. Soviet agents also operated inside the camps. Whether out of self-interest or sympathy toward the USSR, some DPs willingly cooperated with Soviet intelligence; others were recruited because Soviet spies possessed "compromising material" on them, routinely gathered in interrogations of those who had already returned.[91] Representatives of the Tolstoy Foundation alleged that there was a group of DPs in a camp on the outskirts of Munich who acted as "Soviet-Russian spies and saboteurs." Their activities included falsely denouncing "innocent people" for wartime collaboration to hinder their emigration to the United States. In a dispute between two DPs who had once been neighbors in the Russian city of Stavropol, one denounced the other as a collaborator, while the other responded that his accuser had been an NKVD agent back in the Soviet Union and, to boot, "was known as a 'man-prostitute'" in the neighborhood.[92] Such allegations were difficult to prove or disprove, and it was hard to tell whether they were rooted in long-standing personal grievances or resulted from the work of the Soviet secret police. Either way, they deepened divisions and fostered distrust in the camps.

While Soviet migrants were sorted and labeled by governments and international organizations, beset by rival intelligence agencies, and subjected to the designs of emigre activists, there remained a small space for individual agency in the camps. Most photographs taken of DPs by the UNRRA were posed and showed migrants smiling while undergoing checks for tuberculosis, cheerfully engaging in productive tasks like soap making, and diligently studying in classrooms while sitting in well-ordered rows. Yet the photographs also hinted at less staged moments in everyday life: residents of the camps gathered to eat, drink, and talk into the night; they celebrated weddings with singing and dancing; they exchanged books and shared gossip; they decorated the areas around their beds with cutouts from magazines and homemade embroideries; their children played soccer, made dolls, and ran in between the spaces separating the barracks.[93] Despite the inroads made by competing state and non-state actors, the mandatory medical screenings, and the reeducation and labor programs designed to reform DPs, the camps were never fully places of total "governmentality" or brutal "bare life."[94] Soviet migrants, having navigated the complex terrain that led them to the camps, proved adept at evading those who pursued them.

FROM EUROPE'S CAMPS TO THE GLOBAL REFUGEE SYSTEM

Divisions in the camps shaped and were shaped by the hardening boundary between the American, British, and French zones of occupation and the Soviet one. The exclusion of communist parties from ruling coalitions in Italy as well as France in 1947 emboldened governments in Rome and Paris to clamp down on the activities of the Administration for Repatriation. The United States encouraged anti-communist policies in both countries, and the following year the Marshall Plan gave further definition to Western Europe as a shared economic zone bound to American interests. To the east, the Communist Party of Czechoslovakia, backed by the Soviet Union, seized power in 1948, and communist-led governments friendly to Moscow consolidated their control of Bulgaria, Hungary, Poland, and Romania; all five countries would join the Soviet Union in Comecon, the Council for Mutual Economic Assistance, in 1949, cementing the bloc. The same year, the United States demanded that the Soviet Administration for Repatriation depart West Germany for good. What had once been a unified German nation was formally divided into the Federal Republic of Germany and the German Democratic Republic.[95]

These rival political and economic spheres were also defined by distinct approaches to managing the migration of people, codified in international treaties and domestic laws. The Soviet Union used its influence to track down Soviet citizens in socialist countries and develop a common framework for restraining exit, while the United States redoubled its effort to build a mobility regime governed by international organizations that sorted migrants based on ideological considerations in Europe and beyond. In countries under Soviet influence, the repatriation effort continued apace, with the Administration for Repatriation compiling lists of names, biographical details, and known addresses in coordination with the Soviet secret police and local governments to gather nonreturners.[96] In countries where the Administration for Repatriation was restricted, Soviet officials dispatched letters from relatives remaining in the USSR to urge return. Such letters could be highly personal but sometimes hinted at "coaching" by Soviet officials, with the rosy picture some painted of life on the collective farm back home and the conspicuous references to the positive treatment purportedly received by other returnees.[97] The "Motherland" was interwoven with the threads of family connections.

Relying on family networks to trace and return wayward Soviets was all the more important as the movement of Soviet DPs flowed beyond Europe. The Administration for Repatriation tracked migrants from the Soviet Union to far-flung countries such as Venezuela, leading to American allegations that Soviet authorities were planting "communist agents" among the refugees traveling to the Latin American country.[98] The Soviet state remained reluctant to relinquish its hold even on those tentatively within the bounds of Soviet citizenship, such as Bernadas Chervokas, an ethnic Lithuanian who became a Soviet citizen by virtue of the Soviet annexation of his country. In 1944, Chervokas fled to Germany with a Lithuanian "self-defense" unit, was captured by Allied forces, held in a French POW camp in Strasbourg, and in October 1945 joined the French Foreign Legion. He spent the next five years serving as a soldier for the French in Morocco, China, Algeria, Tunisia, and Vietnam—where he was injured and earned a medal for fighting against the Viet Minh—and subsequently worked as a security guard for the French, British, and American militaries in West Germany from 1950 to 1952. Soviet officials found him in a West German prison after he attempted to cross the border into Belgium without proper documentation. Receiving letters from his parents encouraging his return, in December 1952 he was persuaded to seek repatriation to a state he hardly knew.[99] In coordination with governments in the emerging socialist bloc and through its intelligence networks across the globe, the Soviet state expended staggering resources to locate and return citizens.

The United States continued to push its vision for managing migration through international institutions, in terms that strategically contrasted Soviet repatriation with a system supposedly founded on personal choice. With the Cold War under way, American policymakers saw an opportunity to proclaim themselves champions of the "freedom of movement," which some went so far as to describe as a "fifth freedom," building on Franklin D. Roosevelt's famous State of the Union address in 1941, which had outlined universal values that should be enjoyed "everywhere in the world."[100] This global line of thinking informed the UN's Universal Declaration on Human Rights, adopted in 1948. Although it was an international creation with input from Canada, France, Lebanon, China, and India, Eleanor Roosevelt chaired the commission tasked with drafting the declaration, and it bore an American imprint. Article 13 reflected a particular vision of migration in which "freedom of movement" included the right "to leave any country," phrasing that singled out Soviet restrictions on exit. Article 14 further stated that "everyone has the right to seek and to enjoy in other countries asylum from persecution" but did not require states to offer asylum, thus naturalizing limitations on entry.[101] While the declaration arose from prewar aspirations and moral outrage over Holocaust victims who were unable to flee, it was a Cold War document.[102] It went beyond the original charter of the IRO in securing the rights for Soviets to flee their country; even that organization espoused the idea that when it came to DPs, "the main task" was to "assist in every possible way their early return to their country of origin."[103] Seeing the declaration as an affront to their mission of repatriating citizens, the Soviet Union and its allies abstained from approving it.

Articles 13 and 14 in turn formed the bedrock of the 1951 Refugee Convention, which defined a refugee as someone who had a well-founded fear of persecution based on a range of issues, including "political opinion," and was "unable" or "unwilling to return" to their home country.[104] The convention prohibited "refoulement"—the expulsion or return of a refugee to a country "where his life or freedom would be threatened on account of his race, religion, nationality, membership of a particular social group or political opinion." It also extended protections to those fleeing "as a result of events occurring before 1 January 1951," thus encompassing postwar migrants from the Soviet bloc; these date restrictions were lifted altogether in 1967.[105] Once again, the Soviet Union and its allies studiously abstained from the agreement, which formed the basis for international refugee law.

Privately, the Soviet Ministry of Foreign Affairs described the Refugee Convention as a Western-backed attempt to "legalize" the presence of "refugees and displaced persons" in "capitalist countries" for Cold War aims.[106] Yet rather than publicly denouncing the increasingly popular notion of refugee rights, Soviet officials focused on exposing and exploiting the contradictions of the US-backed refugee system. After all, international agreements promoted by the United States promised rights to refuge seekers while leaving America's restrictive immigration laws relatively unchanged. The United States' 1948 DP Act did reserve 40 percent of its visas for people from "Soviet occupied" territory, which included the newly annexed Baltic states and western Ukraine, but it excluded many other Soviet DPs and effectively barred anyone who had belonged to the Communist Party.[107] The burden to take in migrants was mainly placed on America's allies, even though migrants themselves often hoped to reach American shores.

While Western systems for classifying migrants evolved to privilege the conception of the "refugee" enshrined in the 1951 convention, Soviet officials maintained a vocabulary for describing migrants that was rooted in the sensibilities of the Second World War. They continued to refer to Kravchenko as a deserter. And they were prepared to charge anyone who illegally crossed Soviet borders or refused to return with "treason in the form of flight abroad."[108] Behind the façade of this unchanging lexicon, however, Soviet investigators and prosecutors began developing more subtle ways of evaluating migrant motivations. An opening for return and rehabilitation remained for "nonreturners" who were deemed to have fled during the war through no fault of their own. Internal reports discussing prewar emigres also maintained a distinction between those who left because of their opposition to Soviet rule—the so-called "political emigration"—and those who departed because of better economic opportunities abroad—described as the "economic emigration."[109] The category of "political emigrants" had primarily been used before the war to refer to communists who sought refuge inside the Soviet Union.[110] Its application after the war to those who fled beyond Soviet borders echoed the Refugee Convention's focus on flight as a political choice. Even postwar migrants were often depicted by Soviet investigators as unsuspecting citizens who had been lured by the temptations offered by capitalist societies rather than outright traitors. This view was further reinforced by their understanding of the Marshall Plan as a plot of capitalist infiltration. While the very act of flight immediately suggested treason, prosecutors were sometimes willing to consider mitigating factors, if only to prevent future cases of exit.

THE DEFECTOR PROGRAM AND THE STRENGTHENING OF THE IRON CURTAIN

Drawn by the promise of asylum, postwar migrants continued to wend their way westward, mingling with earlier waves of former socialist citizens in the DP camps. While the United States supported the internationalization of refugee management and leaned on its allies to abide by the 1951 Refugee Convention, the articulation of a distinct set of policies toward defectors, defined as a special class of refugees, allowed it to channel select migrants directly to America. Inevitably provoking a reaction from socialist states, the program ended up reinforcing the borders of the Cold War world it was ostensibly designed to undermine.

The program was officially launched on April 19, 1951, when the US National Security Council approved NSC 86/1, "United States Policy on Soviet-Satellite Defectors." The document stated that "defection of the maximum possible number of persons from all parts of the USSR and from Soviet armed forces" should be encouraged through "conventional and unconventional means." The goal of the defector program was "placing the maximum strain on the Soviet structure of power" by "threatening the regime's control of its population."[111] Going beyond the practice of resettling Soviet migrants uprooted by war or sheltering postwar refugees, it reached across the sovereign borders of the Soviet state to encourage the further flight of Soviet citizens.

The authors of NSC 86/1 built on practices of sorting migrant populations based on their usefulness that had been applied to displaced persons in postwar Europe. Well before hundreds of thousands of DPs had been categorized based on their labor value or potential as research subjects, smaller groups of specialists had been targeted by American forces. Even when the United States was cooperating in the repatriation of Soviet citizens in late 1945, "Operation Paperclip," a program carried out by the Army Counterintelligence Corps, funneled German scientists directly to the United States, circumventing US immigration restrictions as well as concerns about their ties to the Nazi regime. Like the defection program that followed it, the recruitment of Nazi scientists was driven by a sense of competition with the Soviet Union for migrants of high strategic value. As "Operation Paperclip" got under way, the Soviet side launched "Operation Osoaviakhim," which brought thousands of German specialists to research facilities in the Soviet Union.[112]

Even before a coherent policy was set up to deal with them, the United States and its allies were sometimes willing to shelter well-placed migrants sought by the Soviet Union. The US refusal to extradite Victor Kravchenko was communicated on April 12, 1945, the day of President Roosevelt's death. Officially, it was justified to Soviet authorities on technical grounds rather than ideological ones: the United States could not consider Kravchenko a military deserter since he "applied for a visa and came to the United States as an engineer and not as a member of the Red Army."[113] In reality, Kravchenko had come to be seen as an intelligence asset because of the information he provided to the FBI about activities of the Soviet embassy that were "inimical to the United States."[114]

Others like Kravchenko, dispatched abroad as diplomats and soldiers during the war, seized upon the opportunity to remain there after the war's end. Like him, they sought to trade classified information on the Soviet Union for asylum but were stuck in limbo until Western authorities decided what to do with them. Among the most prominent was the cipher clerk from the Soviet Embassy in Canada, Igor Gouzenko, who sought refuge with local authorities in September 1945, just a few days after the war's official conclusion. Although Gouzenko would later shock the world by detailing Soviet spy networks in the West, he was initially met with suspicion and disinterest. After he fled the embassy, he spent two days roaming around Ottawa. He sought help from Royal Canadian Mounted Police officers, approached representatives from the *Ottawa Journal* newspaper, and wandered the halls of the Ministry of Justice seeking a meeting before officials finally decided to grant him asylum.[115]

There was even less coordination in how such cases were handled on the ground in occupied Europe. Disgruntled Soviet soldiers who crossed over to the Allies after the end of the war were sometimes treated as "deserters" or as persons subject to the Yalta Agreement on repatriation, particularly by the American side. It was Britain, with its established tradition of spycraft, that in the middle of 1947 began to formulate policies for dealing with Soviet civilians and higher-level Soviet military personnel, which it classified as "defectors," as opposed to rank-and-file "deserters."[116] Meanwhile, the United States handled runaway Soviets on a case-by-case basis. In 1948, American officials interrogated and then decided to shelter two Soviet air force lieutenants, Piotr Pirogov and Anatoly Barsov, after their surprise landing in the US zone of Austria on a plane commandeered from Ukraine. Brought to the United States, the pair were paraded before the American press, and journalists eagerly covered their amazement with American abundance in the form of automobiles, department stores, and fashion models. The publicity play suffered a stunning setback when Barsov chose to go back to the Soviet Union. In media coverage, the pilot went from being a feted defector to a "deserter," an "extremely confused and pathetic man."[117] US officials wondered if his return could have been prevented with a program to ease his transition from Soviet "captivity" to life in capitalist America.[118]

A formal US policy to encourage the defection of select groups of Soviet citizens and groom them for resettlement began to take shape in 1948 and 1949. In February 1948, the State Department's Policy Planning Staff developed the "Utilization of Refugees from the Soviet Union in U.S. National Interest," which called for a "systematic and combined program." It focused on identifying "social science scholars," "physicists, chemists, and other specialists in the physical sciences," as well as "qualified specialists . . . for use as broadcasters, script writers, translators, etc., by the Voice of America," the US government's international radio network, and for "other propaganda activities." The list of occupational priorities reflected the nature of the Cold War as an arms race, an economic contest, an ideological struggle, and an effort to "know one's enemy."[119] Following the pattern established by prior operations to recruit German scientists, the Policy Planning Staff proposed finding specialists among the current refugee flows from the Soviet Union, though the report's authors also considered ways to encourage the "continued defection of outstanding personalities from the Soviet world."

Defectors were not sought for their skills alone. Their motivations were equally important. A subsequent memorandum written by the Policy Planning Staff in June 1949 specified that they had to have fled for "*bona fide* political reasons" and not for "economic, personal, or other reasons," or "to escape the consequences of a crime or misconduct." Following Kravchenko's example, defectors were people who could be portrayed as having made a principled choice to seek "freedom," no matter the cost. According to the peculiar logic that would underpin defector policy, however, the Iron Curtain needed to grow more restrictive, not less. The memorandum's authors believed that the promotion of defection would undermine Soviet borders by making them so hard they would be liable to break. "Desertions," they observed, "lead to a tightening up and compounding of repressive measures which in turn operate toward a further weakening of Soviet capabilities."[120]

In September 1949, following the conclusion of Kravchenko's trial in Paris, instructions were sent to US diplomatic posts describing defectors as "the best sources of information and intelligence on the Soviet world" and "the most effective agents to destroy the communist myth of the Soviet paradise." Yet, even as the usefulness of defectors was praised, the instructions betrayed a good deal of uncertainty about the extent to which the encouragement of defection was "desirable," especially since US immigration laws made it difficult to resettle these individuals in America.[121] The combination of championing free movement while sealing off US borders recalled the capitalist superpower's uneasy handling of DPs.

Officials debated whether defectors should be cleared for entry to the United States, kept in Europe, or relocated elsewhere. Meanwhile, the US High Commissioner for Germany, at the direction of the State Department, began producing reports based on lengthy interrogations with Soviet defectors in November 1949. These "SPONGE Reports" (an allusion to defectors being "squeezed" for information) offered insight into pressure points in the Soviet Union that could be exploited by US strategists, including "party and government institutions," "the police system," "nationality problems," and "religion and the church." The first report, written up from a string of interrogations conducted from October 18 to October 27, 1949, was based on the account of a Soviet engineer stationed at a large factory in Saxony who had fled the Soviet zone of occupation. It also referred to testimony from his wife, a fellow engineer, who had escaped with him. In total, "SPONGE #1" numbered thirty-three exceptionally detailed pages.[122] In many ways, it mirrored the less classified academic research under way utilizing Soviet migrants as sources. One of the authors was Frederick Barghoorn, a Harvard-educated political scientist, who was dispatched to West Germany, given office space by the State Department's Peripheral Reporting Unit in Frankfurt, and assured the "close cooperation" of "American military authorities."[123] The SPONGE report soon gained the attention of George Kennan, who called it "one of the most interesting ever filed with the Department on Russian matters."[124]

The following year, the US National Security Council made the institutional arrangements necessary for a coordinated defector program. National Security Council Intelligence Directive No. 13 dealt with the "exploitation of Soviet and satellite defectors outside the United States" and gave a leading role to the CIA in "inducing the defection of potential defectors" and "assessing a defector's bona fides." The State Department, for its part, would be responsible for the "overt publicity and propaganda exploitation of a defector."[125] National Security Council Intelligence Directive No. 14 gave the lead to the FBI in the "exploitation" of defectors within the United States for "internal security purposes."[126] To appease an array of competing agencies, an Interagency Defector Committee was established to coordinate work with defectors. It was composed of representatives from the CIA, the State Department, the FBI, the various branches of the military, and the Atomic Energy Commission.[127] With a few modifications, these bureaucratic arrangements for managing defectors would remain in place for the rest of the Cold War.

The National Security Council also established an enduring definition of a defector: a person who had "escaped from the control of the USSR or countries in the Soviet orbit" or was outside its jurisdiction and "unwilling to return to it." Defectors also had to be of "special interest to the U.S. Government" by virtue of their "knowledge of the Soviet world," their "operational value to a U.S. agency," or "because their defection [could] be exploited in the psychological field." Even behind closed doors, American officials saw little contradiction between the program's humanitarian and geostrategic aims. On the one hand, the defector program was linked with the care given to DPs and the Universal Declaration of Human Rights; it was described as "in accord with the best U.S. tradition to endeavor to protect and assist those fleeing from persecution." On the other hand, it was strategically necessary because it was "in the important interests of national security that defectors be welcomed and assisted."[128]

The defector program rested on the assumption that the United States, in coordination with its allies, could assert control over the numbers and types of migrants who arrived. Britain, whose formal policy, instituted in 1950, stated that "defections should be encouraged and defections fully exploited to our advantage," proved eager to cooperate. France did, too, though with less enthusiasm. French intelligence handled cases of defection separately and often declined to share information with its American and British counterparts.[129] Far trickier than managing allies, however, was getting the right people to defect and ensuring that the number of defectors proved manageable. In light of concerns that the number of Soviet citizens seeking refuge in the West was slowing to a "mere trickle" after the consolidation of postwar control by the Soviet Union, the CIA launched Operation REDCAP in 1951, "a systematic and concentrated program of penetration and defection inducement operations" targeting Soviets posted in military, diplomatic, and economic roles outside the USSR.[130]

Yet there were also fears that the number of migrants fleeing the socialist bloc could grow too large. In a calculated move, the National Security Council's defector policy called for encouraging "mass defection" from the Soviet Union with the expectation that it would not actually occur. "Soviet policy and means of control are such," it explained, that the policy "would not result in the defection of more than a few hundred Soviet citizens per year." Furthermore, even if there was "a mass defection by USSR nationals extending beyond immediate United States security and administrative capabilities," the risk was acceptable "in view of the fact that it would represent a substantial accomplishment of United States objectives vis-à-vis the USSR by breaking the Iron Curtain and weakening the Soviet structure of power."[131] Soviets were unlikely to flee in large numbers, American officials reassured themselves, but if they did, the Cold War would be won and the complications sorted out later.

Soviet citizens were seen as more desirable defectors than those from other socialist states, but also less likely to flee. The National Security Council warned that encouraging mass defection from the East Central European satellite states that ringed the Soviet Union could result in "the defection of a larger number of satellite personnel than could be successfully resettled."[132] The governments of socialist satellite states were seen as more unstable and they lay at the edge of the Iron Curtain, whereas Soviet migrants had a longer distance to travel before they reached the "free world"; they were doubly hemmed in by Soviet borders and the migration regime the USSR maintained in East Central Europe.

While the details of the defector program were classified, it was closely connected with the publicly proclaimed "escapee program," approved by the United States in late 1951 and launched in 1952 "in support of US defector policy as set forth in NSC 86/1." The escapee program was used to reassure those fleeing the Soviet Union that they would not be turned away and designed to contrast the West's "freedom of movement" with communist restrictions on exit for the world to see.[133] It also linked defectors to more long-standing Soviet migrants, including some classified as DPs. Phase A of the program focused on the care of the estimated "12,000 persons who fled from Soviet orbit from 1945 to 1951." While the United States would provide funding to assist them, most were envisioned as remaining in Western Europe or being resettled in Latin America, Australia, or elsewhere. The approach allowed American policymakers to champion the 1951 Refugee Convention even as they got to handpick who arrived on their shores. Phase B of the program, which remained highly classified, was designed to encourage further defection, though likely in a targeted manner.[134] Once again, the program's architects were confident that the policy would not result in mass migration. They even suggested that it might end up reducing migration, noting the likelihood that in response to the program "the Communists will increase the severity of repressive measures and that this will reduce the rate of escape."[135] By encouraging flight, the policy cemented the stricter border policies of America's communist foes. The Iron Curtain would have to be strengthened before it could be broken.

STORYTELLING AS A COLD WAR WEAPON

Indeed, the flight of Cold War migrants led socialist governments to tighten their border regimes further to keep citizens in. The stories these migrants told, promoted by American authorities, further reified the perceived divide between a "free" West that enabled mobility and a "captive" East where citizens were chained in place by restrictions on exit and forced repatriation campaigns. These stories conveniently obscured US immigration restrictions while endowing Soviet migrants with a degree of power and prestige—as long as they stuck to the established script. In contrast to the earlier treatment of DPs as a relatively faceless and impoverished mass of people, defectors arrived as individuals or in small groups; their individual preferences and personalities were reported on in news stories, often accompanied by photographs. The widespread coverage they received turned defection into the dominant paradigm for understanding migration from the East to the West.

American policymakers contemplated an array of plans to target the Soviet Union with defectors before recognizing that the most potent weapon defectors possessed was their ability to tell stories. Charles Kersten, a powerful US congressional representative from Wisconsin, attached an amendment to the act funding the Escapee Program that envisioned turning defectors, escapees, and willing DPs into a refugee army that could be used to attack socialist countries.[136] Phase B of the Escapee Program included plans for training armed units of escapees "for appropriate military use in the event of war."[137] The CIA initially saw defectors as spies who could be dropped back behind enemy lines; by 1951, the agency was providing secret funding to Konstantin Boldyrev, who had shifted from running an anticommunist DP camp to boasting about establishing a network of agents that could infiltrate the USSR. Such efforts failed miserably. Betrayed by a lack of training and by Soviet surveillance of emigre groups, most defectors dropped back into Soviet territory were quickly apprehended.[138] When it came to light, the militarization of Soviet migrants was a public relations embarrassment, since it allowed Soviet authorities to level charges of hypocrisy against the United States and its lofty rhetoric about refugee rights.

More promising were the Soviet migrants who could, in the formulation of Phase B, "make a worthwhile psychological contribution either by publicity based on the fact of escape or by participation in psychological programs."[139] Like Kravchenko's memoir, the stories they told were usually a joint production conveyed with the help of a ghostwriter and managed by American officials. The publicity they generated was also a mutual process, driven by official government promotion but also eagerly consumed by public audiences in the United States, for whom tales of dramatic escape resonated deeply and confirmed assumptions of American superiority.[140]

The lines between government policy and private media interests were blurred given the professional backgrounds of those involved in the "psychological utilization" of defectors. Foremost among them was C. D. Jackson, the former managing director of Time-Life International, who became President Dwight Eisenhower's personal representative on the Psychological Strategy Board in early 1953.[141] Drawing on his media experience, Jackson dreamed of spreading a message of mass liberation in the socialist bloc.[142] While the CIA was worried about getting bogged down by migrants with little actionable intelligence, Jackson and the other members of the Psychological Strategy Board pushed to broaden the official definition of a defector. In their March 1953 report, they protested that limiting it to "key individuals" was "too narrow for many psychological purposes." Everyday people who fled from the socialist camp, they argued, would garner broader public interest. Their report extolled the value of telling the stories of "simple peasants, soldiers, or even athletes" who arrived in the West.[143] While the official criteria for labeling someone a "defector" remained unchanged, it was increasingly used in media coverage as a catch-all term for those who fled socialist states.

Ordinary people were viewed with greater sympathy by Western audiences than fugitive KGB officers, and they made for more convincing storytellers. After all, it was a "simple peasant," Olga Marchenko, who had been selected as a key witness at Kravchenko's trial. While she was valued as a Soviet everywoman, athletes could be turned into Western celebrities without the taint of association with a communist regime that former party officials carried. Some fell into the hands of Western authorities even before the start of the defector program, including Marie Provaznikova, the coach of the Czechoslovakian women's gymnastics team, who defected at the 1948 London Olympics after her team won the gold medal. Artists, too, made attractive defectors. Even before the real-life defection of prominent Soviet dancers, musicians, and novelists, the figure of the Soviet artist valiantly struggling against the regime was advanced by the fictional character of Olga Alexandrova, the heroine of the 1949 Metro-Goldwyn-Mayer film *Red Danube*.[144] Played by the glamorous Janet Leigh, Alexandrova was a prima ballerina from Moscow whose return to the Soviet Union had been ordered directly by Joseph Stalin. Brave as well as beautiful, exotic but speaking perfect English with a soft Russian accent, Alexandrova was portrayed as an alluring captive. At the film's conclusion, she chose to jump to her death rather than face repatriation.

Although they provided riveting material for Hollywood films, there were clear political calculations behind the media's production of defector stories. Films such as *Red Danube* were spurred by Hollywood's effort to prove its patriotism amid the House Committee on Un-American Activities' investigation of the film industry; the State Department was involved in managing publicity around Kravchenko's trial; and the Psychological Strategy Board churned out story after story of escape for public consumption. Just as care for Soviet migrants was routed through international organizations and charitable non-profit groups such as the Tolstoy Foundation, the US government sought to manage defector publicity while staying in the background.

US officials packaged and delivered defector stories to different outlets to ensure that they reached the appropriate audience. Some were directed to the Voice of America, which was overseen by the State Department, or

Radio Free Europe and Radio Liberation, which were secretly backed by the CIA, in the hope that their stories would reach audiences in the socialist bloc and draw more defections; some were targeted to audiences in Western European countries where sympathy to socialism remained high; others were passed to the emigre press in order to galvanize anti-Soviet attitudes among the emigration; a few were guided to mainstream American publications such as *Reader's Digest*, which, along with mass market defector memoirs, reminded citizens of the need to remain vigilant against the Soviet threat. The media venues were not always as disparate as they seemed. For example, C. D. Jackson, the former publisher of *Time* magazine, chaired the National Committee for a Free Europe, the CIA front organization that oversaw Radio Free Europe. Joining him on the organization's board was the publisher of *Reader's Digest*.[145] The American Committee for the Liberation of the Peoples of Russia, another CIA front, supervised Radio Liberation, broadcast to audiences in the Soviet Union. One of its founders was Eugene Lyons, the ghostwriter of Kravchenko's memoir.[146]

Press conferences planned by the State Department became a key ritual in launching defectors into the public spotlight. The timing of a press conference was a delicate matter, as it had to be staged while news of a defector's escape was fresh but after preliminary interrogations, vetting by US intelligence, and careful grooming and dressing for the appearance. One of the most prominent press conferences of the era was that of Nikolai Khokhlov, a Soviet KGB officer who had been sent on a mission to assassinate an anti-Soviet emigre leader in Frankfurt but had had a dramatic change of heart. At the event, held in Bonn in April 1954, the State Department gave the appearance of letting the public in on the secrets of spycraft by distributing packets to journalists containing the "consolidated interrogations of Khokhlov made to that date." Naturally, the "interrogations" were edited to feed the press those aspects of the story that the State Department found to be most relevant. Special broadcasts of Radio Liberation, Radio Free Europe, and Voice of America were timed to coincide with the press conference. To generate advance publicity, the Voice of America was provided with a recorded interview with the defector a day before the event.[147] Given Khokhlov's shadowy background as a KGB-trained assassin, stories stressed the role of his wife, who reportedly convinced him to take a "moral" stand against his mission, and her fate in the Soviet Union, where she had been arrested after his defection.

Defectors were not only tellers of stories. They were also a focus group whose reactions were gauged by American officials besotted with the latest methods of media strategy. As part of their debriefings, defectors were asked to complete questionnaires surveying their opinions of Voice of America programs they had listened to before fleeing. Such questionnaires set up a curious feedback loop whereby the testimonies of defectors were broadcast to stimulate further defection, and newly arrived defectors provided advice on the programs' effectiveness before telling their own stories on the air. Sometimes the results fell short of American expectations. A Soviet soldier who fled from the Soviet zone of Germany in December 1953, for example, was asked whether he preferred "straight news," "news commentaries," "political talks," or "feature programs" when he listened to the Voice of America. He replied that he "had no real interest in politics and very little interest in current events."[148] Equally troubling were the batch of surveys revealing that "the most significant stories for utilization behind the Iron Curtain are those involving resettlement outside Germany." Although American authorities hoped to keep most of them outside the United States, defectors were lured by the promise of a safe and prosperous refuge inside the capitalist superpower and were unaware of the immigration restrictions that stood in their way.[149]

A "REVERSE IRON CURTAIN"?

The value of Cold War storytelling was confirmed by the outcome of Victor Kravchenko's trial in Paris. Supported by witnesses who backed his account of the Stalinist system, the defector triumphed in his libel case and scored a decisive victory against the Soviet Union in the court of public opinion. In the end, however, the French Court of Appeals determined that Kravchenko was to be paid only 3 francs, instead of the 50,000 he had originally sought from the editors of *Les Lettres Française*. The court explained that the publicity the defector had gained through the trial was compensation enough, since it had helped him sell thousands of books.[150]

Defection created opportunities for subsequent Soviet migrants who followed in Kravchenko's footsteps, though their deeds and words were expected to further the ideological goals of the United States. Those who evinced "no real interest in politics," such as the fugitive Soviet soldier, were perceived to be of limited use; they were given little time in the spotlight and were more often written about than allowed to speak for themselves. Even more troublesome were those whose politics lay outside the mainstream of Cold War America. Not every Soviet migrant was prepared to denounce socialism altogether.

Kravchenko, though esteemed for his memoir's indictment of Stalinist tyranny and his stand against the Soviet state in Paris, remained a left-leaning social democrat. Although he testified before the House Committee on Un-American Activities in 1950, the next day he denounced the "anti-Communist hysteria" of Senator Joseph McCarthy. After traveling through South America on a book tour later that year, he grew more critical of Western capitalism and turned his attention to a mining venture in Peru aimed at improving local working conditions. US authorities complained, "Why, after all, should this character be listened to on any subject other than Soviet Communism? That is his one value to us."[151]

The defection program sanitized migrant motivations and obscured the wartime migration patterns that had led to Kravchenko's stationing in Washington in the first place. It also deflected criticism of America's initial willingness to return Soviet citizens. A Psychological Operations Board report from March 1953 called for a system to welcome escapees from the socialist bloc that "would overcome the shameful memory of forced repatriation after World War II."[152] Perhaps most important of all, it diverted attention away from US immigration restrictions and emphasized the Soviet criminalization of exit, a practice singled out for criticism in the Universal Declaration of Human Rights of 1948 and the 1951 Refugee Convention. The fact that the encouragement of defection only led to the redoubling of Soviet border controls was privately noted by the program's architects but went unobserved by the general public.

Although encouraging escape became a matter of American policy, uncertainty remained about what to do with those who arrived. The United States was not prepared for a mass influx of refugees; its allies in Europe needed to be coaxed, pressured, and compensated to craft an asylum system to protect and care for them. Even if they managed to flee, many remained isolated, distrusted by earlier waves of emigres because of their association with the Soviet Union, separated from friends and family back home whom they would never see again, and struggling to gain full-time employment in the West.

In the precarious lives of defectors, Soviet authorities saw an opportunity. The experience of Kravchenko's trial had taught Soviet officials that it was unwise to engage defectors in public debates. The trial had only brought greater attention to Kravchenko's claims and elevated the stature of his DP witnesses, who were accorded equal standing to the Soviet military officials in the courtroom. After the prominent defection of a Soviet naval officer a decade later, the head of the KGB division responsible for counterintelligence within the Soviet armed forces explained in a classified memorandum that it was "inexpedient" to make "any statements in our press" in response to the "slanderous speech" the defector made at a press conference. It was a far better policy to "localize" the "clamor" surrounding the defector "inside the United States."[153]

Soviet journalists were instead encouraged to describe the difficulties defectors faced in the West, the joys of returning home to family, and the contradictions of the mobility regime being forged by the United States. They pointed out that the United States banned the immigration of former Communist Party members even as it allegedly sheltered Nazi war criminals. Then there were the restrictions the United States placed on visitors from the Soviet Union, who were barred from many coastal areas, industrial centers, and large sections of the South under Jim Crow, a region that also imposed barriers on mobility for Black Americans. Members of the US National Security Council fretted that American restrictions were being construed by critics as a "reverse Iron Curtain."[154]

Most who fled had little chance of reaching America at all. Even some high-profile socialist bloc migrants, including those who had arrived in West Germany in September 1951 aboard the celebrated Czechoslovak "Freedom Train," complained of being stuck and exploited. By January 1952, the engineer of the commandeered locomotive grumbled that while they earned low wages working at a German firm, "everyone around us is trying to make money on us to this day and we feel we can trust no one."[155] Confronted with a coordinated American program promoting defection, Soviet officials were poised to respond with a psychological campaign of their own, taking aim at those who fled but still felt trapped.

2

Between Intelligence
and Counterintelligence

Vladimir Pronin, a private in the Soviet Army, had to travel east to reach the West. In the spring of 1959, he abandoned his post outside Magdeburg, an East German city close to the border with the Federal Republic of Germany, boarded an east-bound train to Berlin, and, once in Berlin, sneaked aboard a local S-bahn train to the city's Western-controlled half. His journey illuminated the peculiarities of the inner German border, a political and ideological fault line separating Soviet and American influence that still permitted rail and automobile traffic to West Berlin. Two years before the construction of the Berlin Wall, it was easier to travel across the city than it was to brave the main section of the inner border.[1] After informing the police in West Berlin of his desire to seek asylum, he was handed over to American officials and traversed East German territory once again—this time by air to avoid the socialist state's traffic checkpoints—landing in Frankfurt, where the CIA operated its Defector Reception Center.[2] In Frankfurt, Pronin's identity was vetted by officials from the CIA and US military intelligence. Even as the interrogations continued, the procedure for handling defectors called for him to be given new clothes and a haircut, put up in one of the CIA's many "safe houses" in Frankfurt, and assigned a minder from American intelligence.

Even more peculiar than Pronin's circuitous defection to West Germany was his unexpected decision to return several months later. Fleeing American custody, he handed himself over to Soviet officials, who escorted him back to East Germany and then home to the Soviet Union. Grasping for an explanation for Pronin's unexpected reversal, American officials suggested that it could only have come as the result of the "Soviet technique of brainwashing." The notion of "brainwashing" had been popularized a few years before amid coverage of the harsh treatment of American POWs in the Korean War, but the charge was especially troubling because the alleged mind control operation was launched against someone who had fled by choice, rather than a captive. Moreover, it was carried out under the noses of American authorities, in a meeting arranged by the Commander-in-Chief of the US Army in Europe and held inside the carefully guarded IG Farben building in Frankfurt, home of the US Army's V Corps and headquarters of the CIA in Germany.[3]

The Farben building was a short drive from the Soviet Military Liaison Mission. While Frankfurt was the epicenter of American intelligence in Germany, a 1947 reciprocal agreement allowed a small team of Soviet military intelligence personnel to set up an office in the city and keep tabs on their opponent, just as the US Military Liaison Mission did out of its office in Potsdam. On May 5, 1959, the members of the Soviet Military Liaison Mission paid an official visit to the Farben building to discuss Pronin's defection. Protocol dictated that the Soviet authorities could seek a meeting with a defector, particularly a soldier who had deserted his post. The decision to hold the meeting further affirmed the importance of reciprocity between the superpowers, since the United States would want access to any of its soldiers who ended up in Soviet hands.

At the meeting, Pronin, accompanied by the chief of the US Army's Civil Affairs Division and a military translator, sat across from the chief of the Soviet Military Liaison Mission and his staff. The Soviet officials struck a conciliatory tone. They still considered Pronin a "full-fledged citizen of the Soviet Union" and even conjured up an excuse for his actions, claiming that they possessed "documents" showing that he had "accidentally wandered off . . . got [his] orders mixed up . . . and wound up in the hands of the German police." They were prepared to forgive the misunderstanding and "whisk [him] back home." They handed him letters written by his mother and brother urging his return to "those who belong to you and to whom you belong." They contrasted the security of Soviet life with his liminal existence in West Germany, where he remained, in their words, "without documents," "kicking around illegally," unable to find employment, and unlikely to gain American citizenship despite US assurances of asylum.

Pronin showed no outward signs of being swayed. He claimed that he sought asylum of his own "free will," explaining that he was "an ordinary guy, a worker" who simply wanted to "make a living" in the more prosperous West. He rejected the way Soviet officials framed his departure, though his words did not square with American depictions of defection either. In his view, the world was divided not along national or ideological lines but between "two kinds of people: ordinary guys, workers and the top dogs, the bosses . . . who shove them around." He accepted the letters from his mother and brother but refused to read them, explaining: "A mother's a mother. A mother has her opinions, a son has his own opinions." Pronin himself called an end to the meeting and was escorted by an American officer out of the room. After Pronin left, the Soviet colonel heading the delegation remarked curtly, "He'll come back yet."

While the American side blamed Soviet "brainwashing," it is more likely that Pronin's decision to return stemmed from shortcomings in the US defector program. Although the program had been established nearly a decade before, migrants who arrived in the West still found themselves lost in a realm of ambiguous legality, beset by rival intelligence operations. After they were interrogated, those who did not receive the coveted status of "defector" languished in camps and reception centers, where they lived, according to a Psychological Operations Board report, in "penury and despair."[4] Their legal standing remained poorly defined since the 1951 Refugee Convention only covered those who fled before January 1, 1951. Moreover, the convention did not go into effect until April 1954, and key transit countries, such as Austria, France, Greece, Italy, and Turkey, took even longer to sign the agreement.[5] While in limbo, migrants were caught in the cross currents of covert intelligence and counterintelligence operations and subjected to new forms of surveillance, not just of their physical movements but of their mental attitudes. The tools of midcentury psychology and psychiatry were used to provoke defection, induce return, scrutinize migrant motivations, and remake defectors from socialist subjects into capitalist citizens.[6] The American charge of "brainwashing" betrayed a preoccupation with manipulating the minds of migrants that was shared on both sides of the Iron Curtain.

Geographically, this new phase in the construction of rival systems for managing mobility centered on Cold War Europe's most liminal states: Germany, with its uneasy division into east and west, its largest city split in half, and the city's western side divided again into US, British, and French sectors; and Austria, which had been placed under the quadripartite control of US, British, French, and Soviet forces.[7] By 1955, these states had attained sovereignty—Austria on the condition that it would remain neutral, and Germany divided into two states, one in NATO and the other in the Warsaw Pact. Yet even after sovereignty was formally restored, the United States and the Soviet Union maintained a dense overlay of covert networks to monitor and lay claim to the people who continued to cross through Central Europe's borderlands.[8] While US and Soviet policies were informed by the Cold War's increasingly global dimensions, the competition for migrants was fiercest in Europe, and it was in Germany and Austria that the two superpowers came in closest contact with one another.[9]

In this contested but still relatively porous region, the two mobility regimes that had emerged after the Second World War were elaborated and further constituted by their interaction. They competed for the same

Figure 2.1 Soviet and American Intelligence Outposts in a Divided Germany

migrants and sought to influence or undermine the same emigre organizations. Despite their ideological opposition, they often mirrored each other. The United States pressed allies to establish a reliable framework of asylum to shelter migrants from socialist states and dotted the landscape with a series of reception centers and safe houses to screen defectors, gather intelligence from them, and consider their suitability for resettlement. In addition to the US military's "empire of bases," American power operated out of office buildings and nondescript private residences run by intelligence agencies and was manifested through financial support given to private organizations to facilitate flight from the socialist bloc.[10] In response, Soviet authorities coordinated with other socialist states to prevent exit. They used diplomatic and intelligence channels to push for access to escaped citizens in Austria and West Germany, and they proved capable at countering the US-led media campaign touting the flight of defectors to the "free world." While Soviet power in Cold War Europe sometimes took the form of outright coercion, its methods of surveilling and encouraging the return of migrants could be subtle and psychologically savvy.[11] In East Berlin, the Soviet Union established the Committee for the Return to the Homeland, a supposedly non-governmental initiative of concerned Soviet citizens that imitated the philanthropic associations and front organizations funded by the United States.[12]

Arguably, the American side succeeded in setting the terms of the competition. The resources it devoted to encouraging the departure of socialist citizens were never matched by the halting attempts by socialist states to entice capitalist citizens to head east. The United States took the lead in constructing an international architecture for asylum that was directed to support its Cold War aims. US officials were also more enthusiastic about employing psychology and psychiatry to analyze defectors before deploying these migrants in the "psychological war" against the USSR. However, the Soviet Union proved remarkably effective at finding weak points in the asylum regime, undermining the popular notion of Western sanctuary, and using psychological appeals to encourage the return of migrants who found themselves lost between departure from a socialist state and incorporation in a capitalist one.

ENTANGLED INTELLIGENCE NETWORKS IN COLD WAR CENTRAL EUROPE

The IG Farben building, where Private Pronin met with the Soviet delegation, consisted of six massive wings, clad in marble and arrayed in an arc before a reflecting pool lined with willow trees. Constructed as Europe's largest office complex, it had once housed the chemical and pharmaceutical corporation that had produced Zyklon B, the notorious substance used in Nazi gas chambers. After the war, US occupation forces moved in, and it was renamed the Headquarters Building but colloquially known as the "Pentagon of Europe." It became the main base for the soldiers, analysts, and agents tasked with carrying out American intelligence against Soviet targets on the continent. The building's restricted CIA section held a vast card index that catalogued the information gleaned from interrogations with defectors.[13]

The logic of compartmentation underlay the CIA's structure in West Germany and elsewhere: the agency was run out of the Headquarters Building but fragmented its operations so as to conceal the extent of its reach.[14] In 1951, the agency established its Defection Reception Center, a name suggesting it was a stand-alone institution rather than one crucial node in a hidden network of interrogation and intelligence facilities spread throughout Frankfurt. CIA veteran Ted Shackley observed, "The word 'center' in this context was a misnomer, for there was nothing central about it except that all people defecting in Europe from countries of the Soviet bloc were brought here." Defectors were not housed in one building; instead they were placed in "villas scattered widely through the city's environs," staffed and guarded by CIA agents.[15]

Defectors were shuttled from one location to the next. CIA officers, too, shifted locations and made return trips to the Headquarters Building to update files or receive further instructions. In some cases, they might consult with their colleagues in the State Department, which continued to operate a Peripheral Reporting Unit alongside the Defector Reception Center and to gather information from defectors in SPONGE reports. In other instances, CIA officers might travel north of the city to Camp King, a former Luftwaffe detention and interrogation facility that had been taken over by the US military and used for the same purposes. In high-profile cases, defectors could be taken to the safety of the United States, where they could be questioned in restricted interview rooms at Dulles Airport or brought to one of the safe houses the CIA maintained in suburban Virginia and Maryland. In a few instances, defectors might be flown as far as Panama, where the intelligence agency could hold them beyond the reach of the KGB and without recourse to the protections of US law. The Defector Reception Center was linked to an extensive and publicly invisible network of facilities stretching back to the United States and across the globe.

Similarly, the nearby Soviet Military Liaison Mission in Frankfurt was just one manifestation of Soviet intelligence's ability to operate beyond the confines of the socialist bloc. The mission offered a legalized venue for Soviet spies, but more covert networks occasionally surfaced, even in West German cities considered secure. The KGB operated with relative freedom in Berlin and throughout Austria, where occupation lines were easily crossed by undercover operatives who were sometimes hidden in migrant flows and other times posted in an official capacity as diplomats, journalists, and trade representatives. Defector Petr Deriabin testified in 1959 that the Soviet secret police carried out kidnapping operations directed against political opponents outside the socialist camp. Even more common, according to Deriabin, was the KGB's gathering of "compromising materials" and its use of blackmail to pressure people into cooperation as informants and agents, often placed within emigre organizations.[16]

Though its officers called themselves "Chekists," referring to an institutional culture that dated back to the early days of the Bolshevik Revolution, the KGB was no stranger to the principle of compartmentation, which was in fashion among corporations as well as intelligence agencies in the 1950s. Upon its establishment in 1954, the KGB was divided into ten directorates, five special departments, and twelve more divisions responsible for everything from government relations to prisons; the state's border guards were transferred to the KGB three years later. The agency was further divided into republic-level branches, each with their own individual directorates, but all reporting to the central KGB in Moscow. The directorate responsible for counterintelligence had an entire department devoted to monitoring emigre organizations; within it, specialists focused on particular national groups, such as Ukrainian emigres.[17] Like the CIA, the KGB pervaded public institutions as well as supposedly citizen-led initiatives. Every Soviet embassy had a legal "resident" representing Soviet intelligence, but there were also "illegal residents" working under the cover of the Ministry of Foreign Affairs or Soviet press and trade organizations.[18] Similar to the CIA, it was only one part of a Soviet intelligence community. The KGB's military intelligence counterpart, the GRU, oversaw its own intelligence networks, and the KGB and GRU often saw each other as rivals.

The identities of agents pressured into cooperation by the KGB were also compartmented, with their code names often used even in classified reports and their real names carefully guarded. The KGB maintained its own system of internal surveillance. Border guards were monitored by official representatives and informants; higher-ranking officers on sensitive missions might be followed or have their apartments bugged. The KGB's power rested on its panoptic nature: given its official and unofficial forms, extensive informant networks, and domestic as well as international branches, both those inside and outside the secret police organization had to assume they were being watched.[19]

The intelligence networks of the rival superpowers found themselves entangled in Central Europe's borderlands. They operated in close proximity, sought to anticipate the moves of the other side, and sometimes adopted strikingly similar methods. They were drawn into intimate contact in their competition for migrants from socialist states who passed through this contested landscape, since both sides viewed these migrants as valuable for gathering sensitive information, running propaganda campaigns, and shoring up influence. Those who fled the "captivity" of the socialist camp found themselves subjected to novel forms of psychological surveillance aimed at extracting their knowledge, scrutinizing their motivations, and reengineering their political attitudes to suit the demands of the Cold War.

PSYCHOLOGY ACROSS THE COLD WAR DIVIDE

Even as US officials fretted about the machinations of Soviet intelligence, they were confident that modern psychology and psychiatry could be used to attract defectors, glean information from them, and prepare them for life in a capitalist society. The defector program's launch coincided with the postwar rise of Freudian psychiatry in American government, society, and industry. Proponents claimed that its diagnostic potential could be used to understand the susceptibility of populations to all manner of social ills, including racism, poverty, crime, and dictatorial rule. In a phrasing that eerily echoed Stalin's claim that writers were "engineers of human souls," President Truman called psychiatrists "experts in human engineering" when addressing the American Psychiatric Association in 1948.[20] In the Soviet Union, Freudian psychoanalysis was publicly derided as a "bourgeois science," and Soviet psychology and psychiatry were informed by distinct Marxist-Leninist ideological goals. However, notions about the motivations of defectors and their psychological malleability transcended the Iron Curtain.[21] With the minds of migrants at stake, both sides peered across the Cold War divide to study the presumed pathologies and psychological tactics of their opponent.

As psychological subjects, defectors were viewed by American specialists with a mixture of fascination and suspicion. Some, it was alleged, fled mundane personal problems rather than political persecution; others were believed to have made the risky decision to break free from their Soviet lives because they were mentally deranged rather than mentally resilient;

and a handful were scrutinized as potential spies posing as ideologically driven migrants. Midcentury psychology and psychiatry informed the typologies developed to classify Soviet migrants, and it lay behind the effort to cobble together defectors' accounts into a broader understanding of what was referred to as "the Soviet mentality."

The mental world of Soviet citizens was a frequent preoccupation of the SPONGE reports produced by the State Department's Peripheral Reporting Unit in Frankfurt. Summarizing the first ten defector interrogations, lead researcher Dr. Frederick Barghoorn explained that "the mental world of the Soviet man" was "a bewildering composite of traditional Russian, Marxist materialist, and other elements." The Soviet system, he claimed, produced a sort of schizophrenia, in which the Soviet citizen led a "double life" and could not "perceive clearly the line of demarcation between his 'own' ideas and those imposed by authority."[22] Individual SPONGE reports relayed back to Washington elaborated on the idea that the psychological pathologies of Soviet defectors were the product of an aberrant ideological regime. One claimed that Soviet children were "separated from their parents at an early age," "told that Stalin is their real father," and "denied the influence of motherly love."[23] Another concluded that Soviet citizens who defected would suffer attachment issues because of their "hereditary preoccupation with the land" and because they cultivated few positive habits, since "vodka in the great mass [was] the basic Soviet recreation."[24] Such stereotypical claims raised the question of whether Soviets could be rehabilitated at all, suggesting that psychological shortcomings preceded and even played a part in the construction of the Soviet system.

Soviet migrants were not always aware of the psychological framework used to evaluate them, but when they were, they sometimes obliged by providing evidence of the Soviet state's detrimental effects on family relations. However, in one remarkable case, a Soviet defector, referred to only as "Sponge No. 3," pushed back against the diagnosis reached by State Department officials. He took issue with the presumption, popular among Western social scientists, that the practice of swaddling was responsible for warping Russians' mental development.[25] He described the so-called "swaddling interpretation of the Russian character" as "a pernicious oversimplification" that cast "Russians as a peculiar people cut off from the Western world by an impassible cultural barrier."[26] Countering the views of his American questioners, Sponge No. 3, "in his spare time and without the aid of reference works or other literature," went on to write a ten-page statement arguing that the "Russian character," to the extent it existed, was shaped by historical circumstances and environmental constraints, not parenting practices. In making his point, he shifted the focus to the Americans he had met since his defection, noting that though "one could meet Americans from all manner of national backgrounds," they tended to resemble each other more than their respective national ancestors.[27] A State Department representative dutifully summarized Sponge No. 3's retort but dismissed its "tone" as "somewhat defensive."[28]

In most cases, defectors simply told their American questioners what they wanted to hear. When asked about popular support for communist rule, they declared it was faltering; when asked about tensions among Soviet nationalities, they reported they were rising; when asked why they left, they pronounced their staunch ideological opposition to Soviet rule. It is striking how many Soviet defectors, some of them representatives of the state's leading military, diplomatic, and security institutions, quickly swapped their outward affirmation of Stalinist rule for stridently anti-Soviet attitudes. Stalinism had schooled Soviet citizens to adapt their self-presentation to meet state demands, so they may have been particularly skilled at responding to the wishes of state officials on the other side of the Iron Curtain.[29] It is also possible that these sentiments were not only expedient but were voiced with sincerity, since a zeal for personal reinvention and self-improvement pervaded Soviet as well as American society.[30] Barghoorn, however, worried that Soviet migrants were learning "to tailor their line in interrogations."[31]

From a psychological perspective, the most difficult thing to discern was a defector's real motivation for fleeing. Yet doing so was crucial, as the 1951 Refugee Convention had established "fear of being persecuted" for one's "political opinion" as an important criterion to determine who deserved asylum. Plus, the more principled the reason a defector had for leaving, the greater the potential for the "psychological exploitation" of the migrant's story through a US-supported media campaign.[32] Barghoorn called it "among the most difficult problems facing the interrogator," since defection typically resulted "from a combination of long-term and immediate factors" and was often "crystallized by some crisis in the individual's life which causes him to make a break."[33]

The ideal defector was one who had undergone a religious-style conversion and had thoroughly "renounced Communism," in the words of Bernard M. Shanley, Special Counsel to President Eisenhower.[34] The interrogation, therefore, was a spiritual as well as a psychological examination, an inquisition into the subject's very soul, and, when necessary, a means for achieving ideological purification. Though US officials would have been aghast at the comparison, its focus on "unmasking" and obtaining a useful confession recalled the Stalinist interrogations that Soviet citizens had faced in the 1930s.[35] The CIA developed a rigorous process for establishing what the agency referred to as a defector's "bona fides," or true identity and suitability for US intelligence. It entailed an elaborate routine of physical separation, psychological screening, document verification, and assessment of the veracity of the defector's claims. The 1963 edition of the CIA interrogation manual outlined measures designed to prevent the defector from asserting control over the proceedings. Interrogators were advised to collect "as much pertinent information as can be gathered without the knowledge of the prospective interogatee" before beginning questioning; once the interrogation began, they were told to "control the subject and his environment for as long as proves necessary."[36] On average, the process took anywhere from one to four weeks, but in some instances it took longer. In questioning Józef Światło, the deputy director of the Polish secret police who had fled to West Germany, Ted Shackley spent "five hours a day, seven days a week, for three months." In between interrogation sessions, Shackley was busy "cross-questioning, checking, and rechecking" his subject's answers until he was satisfied that the Polish secret police official was telling the truth.[37]

While they underwent questioning, defectors were usually housed in a nondescript room "furnished with a bed, small table, and a dresser," according to an article published in the CIA's classified journal. Next to the bedroom was "an adjoining room for making recordings and visual observations unseen." If space allowed, interrogations took place in a third room, also simple in décor but with a varied array of furnishings, including "a desk and executive chair, one or two easy chairs, a small table, one ordinary straight-back chair, and one uncomfortable straight-back chair." The interrogation room featured a "buzzer to summon the guard" and a "one-way mirror" that allowed hidden "observations from the adjacent room."

Those deemed "obstinate cases" faced far worse conditions. Defectors who concealed information might be moved into a "cell with only a cot and mattress, a small indirect light, and slop bucket."[38] Even more "drastic measures" were reserved for those suspected of being covert agents of Soviet intelligence, a perpetual fear of the CIA, whose interrogation manual claimed that the KGB staged defections "as a means of planting their agents in target countries."[39] A person believed to be working for the KGB might be subjected to "isolation in a dark, sound-proofed room," the "raising or lowering of temperatures to [the] point of discomfort," the limitation of "washing and latrine facilities," "cutting food rations to minimum sustenance," "jostling without actual physical harm," or a "medical examination disclosing [a] fictitious dread disease." If such forms of torture failed, the interrogator could "request permission to use drugs and narco-hypnosis," even if these risked "endanger[ing] the subject's mental and physical health." The author of the article in the CIA's journal was quick to assure readers that "severer methods seldom need to be used." They could usually be avoided if the interrogator was established early on as "a person of authority." It helped if CIA officers possessed "knowledge of the subject's country" sufficient to "evoke respect," command of the subject's language "so fluent as to permit easy, natural conversation," and the ability to convince "the subject of his deep personal interest in his welfare."[40]

The psychological profile that CIA officers developed of the "typical" Soviet defector was at odds with their public portrayal. Considering the cases of eighty-seven Soviet citizens who had passed through the CIA's Defector Reception Center outside Frankfurt in its first seven years, John Debevoise, writing for the CIA's closed journal, quipped, "You *hear* of 'ideological defectors,' but when you deal with Soviets you seldom meet one." In nearly every instance, the migrants had "been in trouble and needed to flee impending exposure or punishment for misdoing." Among the handful of cases characterized by a "comparative purity of motivation," the most notable in his view was a Soviet sergeant who "fell in love with one of the German girls employed by U.S. intelligence in an inducement project" and escaped to West Berlin to be with her. Debevoise advised CIA officers tasked with identifying potential defectors to "look for a Soviet up to his ears in troubles."[41]

Soviet opportunism was understandable, if disappointing, to American interrogators. More concerning were the psychological pathologies from which defectors supposedly suffered. Delmege Trimble, a CIA officer writing in the agency's journal, called defectors "perversities of human nature" and cited a study by researchers with the Massachusetts Institute of Technology, which concluded that 55 percent of the defectors sampled were "severely maladjusted" and 20 percent manifested an "actual acute pathology."[42] According to fellow CIA officer Martin L. Brabourne, defectors were at best "egotistical dilettantes"; at worst, they might never recover from a "warped, emotionally maladjusted personality." While defectors were publicly celebrated as individuals with the mental fortitude to break out of socialist "captivity," Brabourne argued that defection was often motivated by an irrational "fear, hatred, deep sense of grievance, or obsession with revenge far exceeding in intensity these emotions as experienced by normal, reasonably well-integrated and well-adjusted persons." All the defectors he encountered had "manifested some serious behavior problem—such as alcoholism, satyriasis [hypersexuality]," or "morbid depression." "It is only mild hyperbole to say," he concluded, "that no one can consider himself a Soviet operations officer until he has gone through the sordid experience of holding his Soviet 'friend's' head while he vomits five days of drinking into the sink."[43]

These alleged pathologies were blamed on nurture as well as nature, as midcentury psychiatry's emphasis on the former was blended with the racialized thinking used to categorize immigrants to the United States. Stanley Farndon, writing for the CIA's journal, linked "defector behavior patterns" with notions of racial superiority, observing that "Slavs are inclined to be cooperative when confronted by superior authority."[44] Trimble, placing Soviet defectors in a purported hierarchy of immigrant groups, wrote, "Just as immigrants from the UK and Scandinavia became assimilated more rapidly in the United States than those from Southern or Eastern Europe, so the adjustment process is more difficult for a defector who has been exposed to nothing but the Communist system in the USSR during his entire formative life."[45]

The act of fleeing, it was posited, disturbed the troubled psychology of the defector even further. In defecting, according to CIA officer John Ankerbrand, the Soviet citizen "lost his ideals, his 'religion,' his life purpose," and everything else that "heretofore comprised his life, gave him a sense of values, and constituted his standards of judgment." In essence, defection was a kind of social death. Yet those involved in the defector program held out hope that through the prolonged process of interrogation, during which a defector might be subjected to as many as "44,000 distinct questions," the runaway Soviet citizen might be reborn as an individual who could thrive in the West.[46] Their metamorphosis would be physical as well as spiritual. The defector's "Americanization," according to Trimble, might begin "in a barber's chair where a pompadour was reduced to a crew cut," though the defector's "transformation into a worthwhile citizen of the West [was] an involved process stretching into the indeterminate future."[47]

Some defectors even helped American authorities detail the psychological gulf believed to separate the Soviet Union from the United States. In testimony before the House Committee on Un-American Activities in April 1956, former KGB officer Nikolai Khokhlov described a Soviet system based on "thought control," which aimed "to form a kind of psychological shell around every individual in order to separate everybody from everybody, to erect a kind of iron curtain between father and son, mother and daughter, brother and sister."[48] Khokhlov collaborated with US intelligence and eventually completed his doctorate in psychology at Duke University. His warnings about a psychological struggle between the United States and the Soviet Union continued to be heeded, even as his own research drifted into parapsychology. Among the papers he authored was one entitled "Possible

Implications of Soviet Research in Parapsychology for the Aerospace Power of the United States," which alleged that Soviet spies might use ESP to gain classified information on American weapons systems.[49]

While Khokhlov's outlandish claims arguably revealed more about the fears of the American audience to which they were directed than about Soviet realities, there is plenty of evidence suggesting that Soviet authorities also understood defection as a psychological phenomenon. While proponents of defection framed Soviet life as a mentally harmful form of captivity, Soviet officials countered that capitalist societies prioritized economic exploitation over psychological well-being. Responding to defectors who claimed to have found "freedom" abroad, Soviet journalists described the severance of ties with the homeland as a rejection of fellow citizens, friends, family members, and ultimately one's true nature. The KGB's own analyses actually lined up with those of the CIA in linking the decision to defect with professional disputes, personal shortcomings, and problematic personality types, though Soviet intelligence experts stressed the role of pernicious anti-Soviet propaganda in luring those with preexisting psychological conditions.[50] While defectors held that the spiritual transformation they had undergone was irreversible, few souls were lost for good in the view of Soviet officials. Hoping that those who fled would grow disillusioned when the imagined West failed to live up to their expectations, authorities in Moscow held out the promise that those who came back might find redemption upon their return.

American officials were deeply troubled by the notion that a defector might choose to return, their transformation into a full-fledged citizen of a "free" society incomplete. However, persistent worries about supposed Soviet pathologies and Soviet "brainwashing" operations were countered by enduring American optimism concerning the transformative power of psychology and its myriad applications. For defectors resistant to change, one CIA author suggested an approach that combined modern psychology and business: the "hard sell" and "soft sell" techniques described in sales manuals of the era. Although Soviet defectors were believed to suffer from a range of psychological defects, the author was hopeful that they would be receptive to the methods developed by the US National Sales Development Institute. In this way, defectors adjusting to a new life could be "spoon-fed" democracy in "moderate and appropriate doses."[51] This vision of the interrogation process as an educational program designed to teach defectors the "difference between the ideology of unlimited opportunity and that of the totalitarian state" made the CIA's codename for its Germany-based program for housing, debriefing, and resettling defectors, "HARVARD," particularly apt.[52]

A "TESTING GROUND FOR A SORELY TIRED AND BATTERED GROUP OF HUMANITY"

While high-profile defectors were quickly transported to the United States, most traveled from the interrogation room to stay in a resettlement center in Western Europe until a permanent home could be found. Officially, these centers catered to the broader class of emigrants known as "escapees," but since the Escapee Program had been set up to facilitate the exit of more valuable defectors, the boundaries between the two groups were fluid. Some defectors were treated as escapees to emphasize that the West's interest in receiving them was driven by humanitarian rather than geostrategic concerns; some escapees were initially classified as defectors before they were found to be lacking in intelligence value. Resettlement centers stressed their humanitarian mission, but they functioned as places of intelligence gathering while providing housing and care.

In many ways, these centers were modeled on DP camps, which had been designed to house but also psychologically rehabilitate Soviet migrants. Some were even constructed on the grounds of existing camps, yet they sought to move beyond the postwar camps' spartan housing and chaotic atmosphere to offer a more wholesome domestic setting. The emphasis on domesticity served two purposes: it was meant to prepare those who had fled for integration into Western society, and it was designed to encourage more people to defect by showcasing the comfortable conditions they could expect upon arrival. Conveying the spirit of private enterprise and civic involvement claimed to prevail in capitalist societies, resettlement centers received US government funding but were often run by ostensibly non-governmental organizations. Some, such as the American Friends of Russian Freedom, were established with guidance from the CIA and received a direct subsidy from the agency, even though publicly it was claimed that the group was "in every sense a private committee."[53] Others, such as the Tolstoy Foundation, had previously assisted Soviet DPs and received renewed funding, though the emigre activists who ran the organization occasionally had to be reined in by their US government sponsors.

In 1953, the Tolstoy Foundation received the blessing of Secretary of State John Foster Dulles to establish a center for "rehabilitating" escapees from the Soviet Union and socialist bloc countries in a converted military barracks in Karlsfeld, a small town outside Munich.[54] In a Russian-language speech given at the center's opening, executive director Tatiana Schaufuss claimed the initiative came not from the US government, but from the Tolstoy Foundation's leadership.[55] While the way she downplayed government involvement fit the politics of the program, US officials worried that the Tolstoy Foundation might use the center to pursue its own ideological goals. Dulles had approved the project but insisted it should be limited to the "provision of basic services and assistances." He clearly stated that the Tolstoy Foundation should not get involved in the "propaganda field or [in] countering propaganda."[56] Yet two years after Karlsfeld opened, a report written by Schaufuss revealed that the center was carrying out precisely the type of work that Dulles had prohibited, including countering "anti-Western and anti-American propaganda."[57] Dulles was not pleased.[58]

US officials requested periodic reports from Karlsfeld to monitor its operations. They exerted even more control by determining who could live there and, ultimately, who could leave for permanent resettlement. Migrants also exercised their own preferences about where they would live. Some escapees approached by the Tolstoy Foundation chose not to settle there, including one whose "wife refuse[d] to go to Karlsfeld" out of an aversion to living in reconverted military barracks. Others who moved to the center did not fit the notion of a newly arrived defector. One resident had bounced around Europe for years after fleeing the Soviet Union and had recently returned from a work stint in Belgium's mines.[59]

Karlsfeld was only one node in a broader network of centers housing Soviet and East European migrants. Near Nuremberg, Camp Valka, originally established for Estonians and Latvians displaced by World War II, received Escapee Program funding for renovated housing facilities, new "sanitary facilities," a refurbished kindergarten, and a new playground. The camp, operated under the auspices of the German-run Federal Office for the Recognition of Foreign Refugees, was a convenient site for gathering intelligence, since recent arrivals could be brought to the interrogation rooms the US Army maintained on the camp's premises. By 1953, the camp housed approximately 4,000 people, some of them newly arrived escapees, others wartime DPs who had been there since the cessation of hostilities. Despite renewed funding, the camp's conditions remained "substandard" in comparison with those inside the army's neatly furnished questioning office.[60] The Escapee Program's chief noted that the "incidence of petty larceny, assaults, etc." was "still high," and that "persons who give Valka as their place of residence [were] still facing abrupt termination of interviews with prospective employers," since the camp was linked to criminality in the minds of the German public.[61]

An alternative to Valka was the "Russian Freedom House," opened in the southwestern German city of Kaiserlautern in October 1953 by the American Friends of Russian Freedom, the supposedly nongovernmental organization backed by the CIA. The Russian Freedom House promised "a chance for a new life . . . for officers and men who flee to freedom in the

West." Like previous initiatives, it focused on putting migrants to work in the belief that doing so would "give hopeless men a sense of dignity and a chance to reassume economic and moral responsibilities." Its organizers emphasized that "escapees" were to do "all their own work at the center" rather than living as passive recipients of Western aid.[62] Soon after, the CIA-supported group opened another facility, the "Friendship House," outside Munich.

Daily life at these resettlement centers blended labor, vocational and educational training, and recreational opportunities that evoked a summer camp. During the day, residents of Karlsfeld engaged in agricultural work while their children attended educational programs run by the YMCA. In the evenings, leisure options, according to a Karlsfeld report, included "chess, ping-pong, informal dances, volley ball, Russian and American holiday observances," film screenings organized by the American Consulate, lectures by emigre leaders, and cultural events held at the center's "Russian Library," whose most popular titles were the published memoirs of other Soviet defectors.[63] The Russian Freedom House was organized along similar lines, featuring a common room with a radio and an array of leisure activities. Although the ideological content of the programming was stridently anti-Soviet, the emphasis on redemptive labor and "cultured" recreation bore a striking—if unintended—resemblance to Stalinist cultural norms.[64]

The actual conditions at the resettlement centers often fell short of this lofty vision. An internal report on Karlsfeld composed in 1954 by Dean Peabody, a young American with a degree in psychology who worked as the center's director, noted a "general breakdown of internal discipline."[65] Of the "10 House Rules," Peabody observed, "every one has been violated, most of them repeatedly." In Peabody's view, some of Karlsfeld's policies, such as its "regulation strictly forbidding any use of all alcoholic drinks," were "unrealistic." However, the open abuse of alcohol was concerning. He sought to curtail drunken outbursts, such as an incident in which two residents, after a night spent visiting the "neighborhood beer halls," "returned at 2:00 in the morning and, with a borrowed guitar, treated the residents to a drunken serenade."[66]

Other instances of disciplinary "breakdown" at the center were of a sexual nature. Peabody described a twenty-six-year-old Ukrainian woman as a "high-spirited young girl" whose presence was "an unwise experiment . . . in a Center designed for single men," or at least primarily inhabited by single men. He detailed a pattern of "drunken late night entries via the windows" and "surly behavior towards certain of the other residents culminating in a Faschings-party [Mardi Gras celebration] nearby, where her riotous behavior has given the Center a wide-spread notoriety." Linking sexual conduct to notions of domesticity that underpinned the center's organizational vision, Peabody declared that her actions were a far cry from the "housewifely habits" Karlsfeld was supposed to instill among its female population.[67] He added that he could not "presume to know more than around half of the violations" that took place during his tenure, due "to a certain Soviet solidarity among the sinning residents."[68] He blamed the Center's resident supervisor, himself an escapee from the Soviet Union, for tolerating episodes of "drunken rioting and insubordination."[69]

Similar problems plagued the American Friends of Russian Freedom's second facility near Munich. By 1957, allegations emerged that the Friendship House had become a "place of refuge" for "criminal or shady emigres of various nationalities."[70] Camp Valka, which had struggled with a tarnished reputation from the outset, became synonymous with difficult living conditions, particularly after a Czechoslovak defector who had lived at the camp and worked for Radio Free Europe chose to return to his homeland. In a press conference organized by socialist authorities, he painted a grim portrait of life at Camp Valka and claimed that it was no humanitarian refuge but simply an operations site for American intelligence.[71]

At the root of such problems was the fact that the resettlement centers, designed as temporary waystations for certain groups of migrants, were becoming places where a wide array of people were stuck for an indefinite period of time. The centers catered primarily to single men who were supposed to "do all their own work" in residence before finding a stable job and moving out; many, however, were unable to secure employment and, with it, permanent residency. The few jobs that were available were often "with support units of the US Army" rather than local businesses, as originally envisioned.[72] As Peabody's comments suggest, single women were treated like an anomaly, and it was expected that entire families would take up residence only in exceptional cases. In its promotional material, the Russian Freedom House's organizers promised that the sojourn for families in the house would not be a long one and that typically "private homes are found for them after about six weeks."[73] Some remained for years, with provisional housing becoming a permanent home.

In a few cases, Karlsfeld and the other resettlement centers functioned as promised, providing a gateway between the Soviet life migrants had fled and a successful new one in the West. Such was the experience of Valentin Sokolov, an aerospace engineer who served as deputy director of a Soviet-managed airplane construction firm in Berlin. Sokolov abandoned the prestigious posting and sought refuge in the American sector of Berlin in

September 1946. Reportedly he fled because of his opposition to "the deportation of German scientists and their families to the USSR," though he may also have been motivated by his German fiancée, who ran away with him. He was then resettled in the British zone under a new name and a new identity (Walter Dolling, an "ethnic German from Russia"). In August 1953, he sought housing at Karlsfeld and took up residence there several months later. The Tolstoy Foundation helped him apply for resettlement in the United States, where he immigrated in February 1954.[74]

Sokolov's case was unique because he had desirable technical expertise, was readily employable, and had already been vetted by British intelligence. For the most part, Karlsfeld, in the words of Schaufuss, was a "testing ground for a sorely tired and battered group of humanity."[75] Most had little to trade on besides the information they could offer to Western intelligence agencies in exchange for monetary payments or preferential treatment. As early as July 1952, just as the Escapee Program was getting under way, the chief of the State Department's Peripheral Reporting Unit complained in a dispatch to Washington of the "black marketing of information among refugees." Citing the account of a migrant who had "lived for a few weeks in a refugee camp in Berlin," he explained:

> Very frequently the new arrivals are told by the old-timers where to go and what to do with their information. They are also instructed how to play up their stuff to be attractive for a longer period of period of time and to receive their pocket money longer. . . . Newcomers are advised not to release all of their ammunition on the first day. A kind of grading system of information is also supplied. The newcomers must know a little about the military setup in their native countries to be interesting at all. If they do not know anything the old-timers furnish them with all necessary data, after agreeing on the fair share in profits.

The State Department official responsible for overseeing a crucial interrogation unit warned that "people who have lived in the camps longer" had become "good interrogators themselves," able to outwit those questioning them."[76]

The gravest concern of Western officials was the infiltration of resettlement centers by Soviet intelligence. In February 1955 V. M. Denisov, a former major of the Soviet army and the chair of a group that called itself the "Union of Postwar Defectors from the Soviet Union," was arrested upon being caught crossing back from the Soviet zone with a large amount of cash. Upon further investigation, it was revealed that Denisov, who outwardly had been a partner in Western efforts to build a politically active community of defectors to oppose Soviet influence, had in fact been cooperating and communicating with Soviet spies. Denisov would visit a "dead letter box" built into the grave of a deceased Soviet lieutenant in the Oldenburg cemetery, "with flowers in his arms, in order to collect the orders of his bosses."[77]

Particularly alarming was the fact that Denisov had already passed through a careful vetting process. Years earlier he had been described in a report by the American Consul General in Germany as a "mild-mannered, meticulous person" who gave the "appearance of sincerity."[78] It was not clear whether Denisov had been a Soviet plant from the beginning or if he had been enticed—or pressured—into becoming a double agent by undercover Soviet officers.[79] American officials wondered whether disillusionment with life in a US-sponsored resettlement center had left him susceptible to advances from the KGB. As early as 1953, he had complained to a representative of the US High Commission for Germany that the Friendship House, far from being an ideal home in the West, was riven by "denunciation, intrigue, and favoritism."[80] It was as if he had fled only to find himself trapped in a miniature recreation of the Soviet Union at its worst.

BORROWING FROM THE AMERICAN PLAYBOOK: THE COMMITTEE FOR THE RETURN TO THE HOMELAND

Denisov was not the only prominent defector to have a change of heart. Approximately two months after his arrest, the Soviet news service, TASS, called a press conference in East Berlin. Professor Vladimir Vasilaky, a high-profile Ukrainian emigre and the founder of another anti-Soviet organization, the League of Anti-Bolshevik Organizations of the Peoples of the Soviet Union, was ushered out to meet with journalists from the leading newspapers of the socialist camp. Vasilaky recounted how his organization—along with other emigre groups—had been funded by American intelligence, whose agents sought to turn "emigres into obedient and blind tools" of American foreign policy. Disillusioned, Vasilaky decided to seek the most "direct path to a better life amid [his] own people." He called for his fellow Soviet exiles to follow him home.[81] In a letter to Vasyl Dubrovsky, the editor of a Ukrainian emigre newspaper, he wrote of having undergone a "psychological revolution" against the leaders of the emigration and their American patrons. For their part, American officials called Vasilaky's stunning departure a "redefection." Suspicious of the notion that he could have willingly returned, an internal State Department report hinted that he might have been kidnapped by two Soviet "thugs" operating undercover.[82]

In truth, Soviet officials had successfully adopted a strategy employed by their American opponents—the press conference—and started a comprehensive public relations campaign against defection. Initiated in 1955 by the government of Nikita Khrushchev, Stalin's successor, it was a noticeable change of tack for Soviet foreign policy. Since the end of mass repatriation, Soviet authorities had often made the mistake of taking small-scale actions that came across as petty. One example was the lawsuit that composer Dmitry Shostakovich launched against the producers of a film based on the defection of Igor Gouzenko from the Soviet Embassy in Canada. Viewers remembered the 1948 thriller and its resonant title, *Iron Curtain*, but paid little attention to Shostakovich's complaints that his music had been used for the soundtrack without permission. In other cases, Soviet officials inadvertently boosted the prominence of defectors by engaging them directly, as they had done during Kravchenko's trial in Paris. While Vasilaky's press conference reflected the fundamentally defensive posture of socialist authorities—they were not appealing for Western citizens to flee but for their own wayward citizens to return—it proved effective at exposing the struggles of migrants trapped in the makeshift asylum system underwritten by the US government.

Vasilaky's press conference was the first public event of the Committee for the Return to the Homeland. Established just a few weeks before, purportedly as a "private" and voluntary organization of Soviet returnees, the committee's headquarters were located directly across the street from the rear entrance of the Soviet Embassy in East Berlin. Coverage of the Committee's activities in *Pravda* and *Izvestiia* showed that it had the blessing of Soviet authorities, and behind the scenes it operated in collaboration with the KGB as part of a coordinated effort to counter Western intelligence and propaganda.[83] In essence, the enterprise mirrored CIA front organizations such as the American Committee for the Liberation of the Peoples of Russia; it, too, was connected to a radio station targeting migrants, and its leadership had close ties to the state. A Stalin Prize winner, prominent scholars, and figures connected to the Soviet military were among its members.

Heading the committee was Major General Nikolai Mikhailov, the former head of a Soviet tank division who had been captured by the Nazis in a battle outside Kharkiv, Ukraine, in 1942. Mikhailov proved a compelling figure because of his story of finding redemption in captivity. According to the official account, he had refused to join the German army and secretly rallied support for the Soviet Union among the fellow inmates in his POW camp. In the war's aftermath, he was quickly rehabilitated—and likely recruited—by Soviet intelligence and took up work with the

Soviet repatriation mission in Italy, tracking, enticing, and rounding up Ukrainians who had served in the Wehrmacht, a sensitive task that would have required extensive cooperation with the Soviet secret police.[84]

The committee's launch coincided with plans for a withdrawal of Soviet military forces from Austria at a speed that shocked Western observers. Just a few days before Vasilaky's appearance in East Berlin, Soviet officials had cut a deal with the Austrian chancellor for the reestablishment of his country's sovereignty. In the negotiations with the United States that followed, the Soviet Union even agreed to drop one of the provisions of the deal that called for the "voluntary repatriation of displaced persons within Austrian territory" to their homelands on the other side of the Iron Curtain.[85] The American side worried that this language would have given the Soviet Union privileged access to migrants, including those sheltered by the Escapee Program. To the surprise of US negotiators, the Soviet Union conceded the point, a stunning development after a decade of Soviet policy calling for the immediate repatriation of all citizens abroad. Soon after, Soviet authorities entered into direct bilateral negotiations with the West German government and ended up granting diplomatic recognition to Germany's capitalist half.

Political analysts in the United States struggled to understand why the Soviet side was so willing to compromise. They wondered whether the Soviet approach was a cunning tactic to divide the Western alliance or a performance of Khrushchev's policy of "peaceful coexistence" to win over unaligned states around the world. They speculated that it was a practical retreat, with neutral Austria accepted as a buffer even as the USSR cemented control over the socialist camp with the Warsaw Pact, which was signed the same month as the Austria State Treaty.[86] While these were plausible explanations, they ignored the possibility that Soviet authorities were adopting and adapting the tactics of their American opponents by employing more sophisticated forms of psychological influence. Rather than insisting on a state-led repatriation campaign, the Soviet Union encouraged the appearance of spontaneous return to claim that it was a voluntary, bottom-up effort led by socialist citizens disenchanted with the West. Instead of embarking on a costly project to gather all migrants, Soviet authorities selectively targeted prominent defectors to undermine the distinction between a "free" West and a "captive" East.

Soon after the establishment of the Committee for the Return to the Homeland, a broad amnesty for Soviet citizens who had collaborated with the Nazis during the war was triumphantly announced. The idea of an amnesty had been privately proposed by KGB chief Ivan Serov in December 1954 and publicly floated during Soviet premier Nikolai Bulganin's negotiations with the West German leadership in September 1955. Bulganin expressed concern for the more than 100,000 Soviet citizens and "persons without citizenship" who found themselves stuck in West Germany, their repatriation blocked by "certain organizations, hostile to the Soviet Union."[87] Later that month, the Presidium of the Supreme Soviet issued an official amnesty for Soviet citizens "who had collaborated with the occupiers during the Great Patriotic War," whether out of "cowardice" or "carelessness." The amnesty's text observed that it was time to give Soviet citizens who had fled abroad the "opportunity to return to an honest working life and become productive members of a socialist society."[88] It suggested they could exchange their experience of endless waiting for the familiarity of home. Notably, the amnesty offered no specific protections for those who had fled after 1945. Postwar migrants would have to take their chances.

Despite its limitations, the Soviet amnesty was part of a broader push to encourage return throughout the socialist camp, coordinated by Moscow. Soviet authorities oversaw a wave of amnesties and appeals to emigrants in 1955: an amnesty for citizens of Czechoslovakia and the creation of a Czechoslovak committee that resembled the Soviet Committee for the Return to the Homeland; a Hungarian repatriation committee founded in East Berlin, with an office to handle repatriation opened on the Hungarian side of the border with Austria; and a new office to reach out to Poland's diaspora created under the auspices of the new Soviet Embassy in Bonn.[89] All of these organizations employed similar techniques, combining official publications and mass mailings with personal appeals to individual migrants and, occasionally, direct letters from loved ones back home.

The messages these organizations sent to migrants were also similar. All stressed the entwined relationship between one's homeland and one's family. Just as the members of the Soviet Military Liaison Mission had used letters from defector Vladimir Pronin's mother to encourage the errant Red Army soldier to return home, the Committee for the Return to the Homeland was quick to remind Soviet migrants of the connection between one's mother and one's motherland. "A foreign land is the same as a wicked stepmother," one article in the committee's newspaper began, "even if you crawl before her on your belly, she remains your enemy." The "Motherland," by contrast, "is one's own mother, she understands and forgives every one of her children."[90] Such appeals were personalized in the section of the newspaper devoted to letters from relatives and friends in the Soviet Union searching for loved ones abroad. The section featured photographs, alongside emotive headlines such as "Where are you, my son?," "Don't you want to see your daughter again?," and "Come back to your old father."[91] While some of these letters were likely fabricated or written under pressure, they helped the committee's newsletter contrast the tentative existence Soviet migrants faced abroad with a fulfilling life rooted in the land in which they were born, surrounded by loved ones. While the effects of family separation were not put in psychoanalytic terms, they echoed the claims of American intelligence officials, who sometimes blamed the alleged pathologies of defectors on family ruptures.

Faced with a Soviet strategy that undermined their defector and escapee programs, US officials saw the hand of Soviet counterintelligence and sounded the alarm. Tasked with investigating the matter was William Donovan, who had led the Office of Strategic Services during World War II, contributed to the founding of the CIA, and served as a member of the American Friends of Russian Freedom. Donovan completed his lengthy report on Soviet redefection in March 1956, assisted by a commission consisting of members of the International Rescue Committee as well as influential business and media leaders, including the former president of the US Chamber of Commerce and the director of Bell News Corp. Although Donovan emphasized the role of covert KGB operations— suggesting at one point that Soviet agents had stolen "personal files" from a resettlement agency in Frankfurt in order to track down and "victimize" Soviet migrants—his report was candid about the precarious conditions in which migrants lived, which made them susceptible to Soviet appeals. "Many refugees," the report explained, "spend endless days and months waiting for the legal, administrative procedures to grind out their fate." In response, the report's authors proposed that this time of waiting "be made meaningful," turning a "period of stagnation" into a "period of opportunity to learn a new language, trade, occupation . . . and thus make it possible for the individual refugee to indicate his basic acceptability."[92]

Yet while US officials pushed for the transformation of refugees into "acceptable" Western citizens, returning Soviet migrants touted by the Committee for the Return to the Homeland suggested that it was only by going home that one could, in the words of Ivan Ovchinnikov, resume one's "normal life." Ovchinnikov had fled to the West in December 1955 and worked for Radio Liberation. Less than three years later, in October 1958, he reappeared on a Committee for the Return of the Homeland radio broadcast. His account flipped Western accounts of defection on their head by describing a dramatic return flight into East Berlin, pursued by American spies. He spoke at even greater length about his inability to find a place for himself in the West; his plans to attend university or immigrate to an English-speaking country ended in failure. Appearing next to him was Viktor Il'inskii, a former bear trainer from the Moscow State Circus who had defected during the troupe's tour of West Germany in January 1956 but had chosen to return with Ovchinnikov. Il'inskii explained his decision in even more personal terms. His wife, who had been six months pregnant at the time of his defection, had reached out to him and urged him to come home.[93]

While it is tempting to dismiss the Committee for the Return to the Homeland as a cynical counterintelligence effort, discussions within the KGB reveal that Soviet officials held out hope that some defectors could be rehabilitated. Articles in the closed-circulation journal of the KGB's training academy show that the spy agency's experts shared the view of their CIA counterparts that ideologically motivated defection was rare. Instead, Soviet intelligence analysts argued that most defections were the result of an overly impressionable personality type, a "fanatical" obsession with Western material goods, or frustration with working and living conditions in the USSR.[94] Although Soviet law classified illegal exit as a form of treason, other journal articles contended that treasonous behavior had to be committed consciously rather than accidentally, and that prosecution should be put on hold until defectors had been made aware of the consequences of not returning.[95] In contrast to some of the more critical writings of CIA analysts, the KGB did not characterize defectors as psychologically damaged goods but instead as weak-willed citizens who had gone astray. Their emphasis on rehabilitation fit the framework of de-Stalinization, during which many people previously convicted of political crimes were pardoned.[96] It also meshed with the broader Soviet system of crime and punishment, in which even the Gulag was held to be a place of redemption through labor.[97]

The internal records of the KGB and the Soviet Foreign Ministry provide further evidence that most of those who fled were considered potentially redeemable, or at least potentially useful for Soviet foreign policy. Although the Soviet Repatriation Administration officially ceased its operations in 1952, the archive of the Ukrainian KGB's counterintelligence directorate reveals the continued tracking of "nonreturners" through the late 1950s, the tracing of their correspondence to the Soviet Union, and the investigation of their remaining family members to find ways to induce their return. In one representative case, the secret police asked a nonreturner's mother and father to write to their son and urge him to come back home.[98] It is likely that efforts like this one led to many of the letters posted in the Committee for the Return to the Homeland's newspaper. Sometimes, the KGB intervened more directly, dispatching the son of a nonreturner to Vienna to convince his father to return. Most of those tracked by the KGB were not special targets for prosecution but instead were ordinary migrants who were still viewed as Soviet citizens. In cases where nonreturners were suspected of cooperating with Western intelligence, however, punitive arrangements were made, such as the spy agency sending the friend of a Soviet emigrant to Munich to lure him back to his hometown in western Ukraine, where they planned to arrest him.[99]

While it is impossible to determine the overall size of this tracking effort without access to classified materials in the KGB's central archive in Moscow, the materials produced by the Ukrainian KGB give some sense of its scale. The documents assembled on nonreturners for the Drohobych region of western Ukraine alone comprised at least seven volumes of approximately 250–300 pages each.[100] Just as the KGB believed that Soviet migrants were not beyond the reach of the Soviet state, the Soviet Foreign Ministry often referred to emigre organizations—even those fiercely opposed to Soviet authority—as "organizations of Soviet citizens." Through its diplomats, and in coordination with Soviet intelligence, it monitored the activities and meetings of these groups, classifying them as potentially "progressive" allies or as "reactionary" opponents of the USSR.[101]

Operations to infiltrate emigre organizations were sometimes run through Ukraine and other republic-level branches of the KGB, which had the linguistic and cultural knowledge necessary to gain trust among a multiethnic Soviet emigration. The KGB was also quick to exploit personal connections. For example, in 1956 the Estonian KGB dispatched a woman who was officially employed as an accountant at a factory in Pärnu, Estonia, to West Germany to establish contact with her sister, who had fled there years earlier. Taking advantage of her sister's connections, the inconspicuous secret agent was tasked with investigating the "leadership circles" of emigre organizations from the inside, with the goal of undermining them and encouraging return.[102]

For those who did return, the rehabilitation process began with a questionnaire from the Committee for the Return to the Homeland that was handed out when they crossed back into the USSR. The questionnaire encouraged migrants to turn their experience of repatriation into an ideologically useful narrative for the committee's propaganda efforts. They were asked to send a letter to the committee's headquarters in Berlin, contrasting their "former life abroad in a foreign land" with their new "life in the Motherland," including the job opportunities they found upon return and the experience of being reunited with their family. They were also asked to serve as de facto informants, instructed to provide the names and addresses of any "compatriots" they knew of abroad, particularly anyone willing to "assist the Committee's work." Such requests offered returnees an opportunity to write themselves back into Soviet life, suggesting that the stigma of having fled might be overlooked if their return served the goals of the committee.[103] The notion of self-purification through auto-biographical writing was a thoroughly familiar concept, since many educated Soviet citizen kept diaries, and autobiographies were required for applicants to the Communist Party.[104]

Measured in numbers, the results of the committee's campaign were underwhelming. The Donovan Report was written at a time when these numbers made a sharp but brief rise, its authors noting with alarm that 1,158 people had returned to the socialist camp in January 1956 alone, a marked increase from the previous month's total of 829.[105] Yet a mass redefection of socialist migrants never occurred. In April 1958, American officials put the overall total of "redefectors" at only 7,810 since the beginning of 1955. Like their counterparts in the KGB, US officials maintained a vast filing system to track the return of migrants from the socialist camp, overseen by the US Consulate General in Frankfurt and known as the "Central Index of Redefectors." This index revealed a shift in focus for the Committee for the Return to the Homeland—whether by design or as a result of opportunism—from Europe to South America. While 585 Soviet citizens from West Germany and 45 from Austria had gone home since 1955, a total of 3,559 Soviet citizens had returned from South American countries in the same period, many concerned about economic instability and political upheaval in Argentina and Venezuela.[106]

Yet the propaganda value of the campaign was far greater than its numerical results. It undermined the Escapee Program, and it allowed Soviet authorities to advance claims of equivalence: while socialist states maintained restrictions on exit, Western governments actively prevented return; while Western governments promised freedom, socialist governments offered the comforts of family and homeland; while Western officials sounded the alarm about the operations of the KGB abroad, Soviet officials could point to an overseas network of American "spy centers" and "interrogation chambers."[107] For these reasons, the campaign deeply unsettled American officials, who insisted that the American and Soviet mobility regimes were fundamentally different. At a meeting of his National Security Council, President Eisenhower wondered aloud, "What appeal could there be to any rational mind to go back to a life behind the Iron Curtain?"[108] If Soviet migrants were returning, American policymakers assumed that they were being coerced or even kidnapped.

In the words of one of the leaders of the American Friends of Russian Freedom, the committee's activities "entail[ed] almost as much peril to the West as the achievement of Soviet thermonuclear parity."[109] Although the likeness was never acknowledged, the fact that the committee's tactics and structure mirrored the CIA-sponsored front organization may have made it particularly threatening. In response, US officials were prepared to consider drastic countermeasures, even if they meant restricting exit. Hoping to stop "defector kidnappings," Lawrence R. Houston, the CIA's General Counsel, mulled the possibility of having immigration agents detain "defectors who want to redefect" and prevent them from leaving the United States in an August 1955 memorandum. Although he ultimately concluded that "false arrest" posed "obvious problems" in American jurisdiction, he seemed unaware of the irony that such a measure would have replicated the Soviet approach to emigration.[110]

FEARS OF REDEFECTION AND THE CONSOLIDATION OF THE ASYLUM SYSTEM

While they were quick to blame alleged KGB kidnappings, American officials privately acknowledged that the haphazard nature of the international asylum system left socialist migrants vulnerable. Despite the formalization of the UN Declaration of Human Rights in 1948 and the UN Refugee Convention in 1951, the practical details of how migrants would claim and access the protections of asylum still had to be hashed out. The campaign of the Committee for the Return to the Homeland spurred US policymakers to press their European counterparts to construct a stronger architecture of asylum along the western rim of the Iron Curtain. Fears of redefection helped cement the new system.

Because the effort to shore up asylum came just as the United States prepared to withdraw its forces from Austria and turn more power over to officials in West Germany, it was in part a bid to maintain American influence and protect the American intelligence networks bound up with the defector and escapee programs in Europe. While the State Department claimed success for stymying Soviet plans for the Austrian Treaty that "would have jeopardized the security of at least 50,000 refugees from the Soviet orbit in Austria," American diplomats worried that Austria and West Germany might not be able to guarantee the long-term security of migrants from socialist states, thus undermining the idea of a "free" West. After all, the Committee for Return to the Homeland was established after the treaty, launching its alleged "kidnapping" campaign in a neutral Austria. In the view of President Eisenhower's Operations Coordinating Board, the successor to the Psychological Strategy Board, the "regaining of sovereignty by Germany and Austria and the latter's neutrality status [posed] serious problems for the continuation of U.S. Escapee Program operations."[111]

Preserving the distinction between the "free" world and socialist "captivity" would cost a good deal of money. Records of the Operations Coordinating Board show that the United States was prepared to offer significant financial assistance to Austria and Italy to "assist the Free World in the maintenance of liberal policies of asylum." These two countries bore "a disproportionate share of the refugee burden," and Austria otherwise might be "forced to close its borders to Yugoslav refugees contrary to its national policy of asylum."[112] Along with Austria and Italy, West Germany and Greece had been identified by American planners as being "key points of escape" as early as 1951. In the following years, efforts were made to shore up US influence over mobility management in these countries and channel refugee flows through checkpoints and cities identified by policymakers in Washington.[113] By 1960, at the urging of the United States, Greece finally joined the West German, Austrian, and Italian governments in signing the 1951 Refugee Convention. Turkey, Greece's neighbor and the leading destination for Soviet defectors after the construction of the Berlin Wall, signed in 1962, one year after the wall went up.[114] Yet fundamental weaknesses in the asylum system remained.

The care and support given to migrants fleeing socialist states was uneven, inconsistent, and poorly coordinated. The Donovan Report pointed to the "urgent need to coordinate existing programs and equalize the burdens of refugee care, especially in cooperation with such countries of first asylum as Germany, Austria, Greece and Italy."[115] Some countries were overwhelmed with large numbers of migrants, unable or unwilling to live up to the agreements they had signed. An Operations Coordinating Board report warned that the "the resumption of full sovereignty by Germany and Austria [had] resulted in serious questions arising to the character and extent of the asylum afforded." In Germany, there were a "large number of refugees for whom no appreciable reestablishment efforts [were] being made," while in Austria refugees were "the last to benefit from improved economic conditions." Italy was singled out for enforcing an overly stringent distinction between political and economic refugees and was taken to task by US officials for repatriating a number of "economic" refugees to neighboring Yugoslavia. Those responsible for running the defector and escapee programs insisted that asylum for refugees was a "fundamental principle of U.S. policy" and "opposition to forced repatriation" was its "established corollary."[116]

The Cold War battle for socialist migrants pushed US policymakers to reinforce the international asylum regime further. The updated US policy on "defectors, escapees, and refugees from communist areas," approved in March 1957, called upon the United States to "take all feasible action to support the principle of asylum for those fleeing from persecution."[117] However, the mounting cost of this lofty goal caused reservations in Washington. US officials sought to avoid getting stuck with the entire bill, allocating $12.5 million in 1956 to assist countries providing asylum with "basic food and housing," though insisting that the money not make up more than 45 percent of the total cost, with the remainder to be assumed by host governments. Millions of additional dollars in American support were given in the form of payments to the UN Refugee Fund and an array of voluntary agencies, including the Tolstoy Foundation. There were also initiatives aimed at providing refugees with temporary employment, such as the Department of Defense's "Labor Service Units," which employed over 10,000 escapees as guards and drivers in support of the vast American military presence that remained in Europe.[118]

Even as the United States financially supported its allies in caring for escapees from socialist countries, US immigration policies kept most of these migrants far away from American shores. While the United States had pressed European countries to sign the 1951 Refugee Convention, US officials refrained from joining them and only agreed to sign the convention's updated 1967 protocol in 1968.[119] The US vision for asylum involved settling socialist migrants in Europe, promoting third-country solutions in Canada or Australia, or pursuing "land settlement" programs that shipped migrants to Latin America. Yet a sizable number of migrants hoped to reach the country whose propaganda campaign had encouraged them to flee in the first place. With the United States unwilling to take them in, they were left "forgotten and alone," "susceptible to communist redefection appeals," in the words of the Donovan Report.[120] The US Operations Coordinating Board was critical of the fact that around a third of migrants from socialist states in Germany were "unemployed" or "living in poverty" and lambasted Austria for "severely" limiting "the right to acquire citizenship and the right to work." Yet the restrictive American immigration system was at the root of the problem.

The simplest path to America was also the narrowest: the CIA had an annual allotment to bring defectors deemed to be of high intelligence value directly to the United States, but it was limited to only 100 people a year. Another initiative, the Lodge-Philbin Act of 1950, offered a path to citizenship for migrants from socialist states who joined the US Armed Forces, but this fizzled out after plans to organize military units composed of refugees were abandoned. Six years on, the Operations Coordinating Board noted a total of only 976 enlistments through the Lodge-Philbin Act; most of the migrants merely worked as translators for the US military. Then there was the US Refugee Relief Act of 1953. Despite its name, the bill was a compromise between President Eisenhower, who hoped to liberalize immigration restrictions on Southern Europeans to deal with the "surplus population" of rural residents flooding Italian and Greek cities, and influential Nevada Senator Pat McCarran, an anti-communist who wanted to offer refuge for migrants from behind the Iron Curtain but imposed a burdensome requirement that all seeking to enter the United States provide a documented "political history" for the two years preceding their flight.[121]

For most people who fled from socialist states, constructing a verifiable "political history" usually meant starting from scratch in a resettlement center in West Germany or Austria. For two years, their lives were put on hold as they struggled to establish their anti-communist credentials, a task made more difficult by the nearly universal participation in party youth organizations in socialist countries and the fact that some had only managed to reach the border area because of military service. Unless they could convince their American interrogators that they were prominent enough to merit a waiver from the US Attorney General, the Secretary of State, or the Secretary of Defense, they were stuck in a holding pattern, during which time they also had to secure the sponsorship of an American citizen or organization.[122] At best, the system pushed migrants to tell officials and sponsors the stories they wanted to hear; at worst, it led migrants to consider returning home. The authors of the Donovan Report called for the immediate "administrative re-interpretation" of the Refugee Relief Act's two-year political history requirement.[123] In so doing, they employed Cold War rhetoric to lobby for liberalized immigration rules, suggesting that the requirement, designed to filter out communist sympathizers, had become the main "target of Communist propaganda."[124] Seconding their recommendations, the Tolstoy Foundation's Tatiana Schaufuss declared, "Victims of Communism cannot be subject to technical datelines."[125] Yet no major changes to the US immigration system followed the report.

Meanwhile, the defector and escapee programs were propelled forward by their own institutional interests. The Operations Coordinating Board, reporting to the National Security Council in April 1956, argued that the "intensity of the Soviet anti-emigration campaign" was evidence of the "sensitivity of Soviet leaders to the U.S. policy regarding defectors and escapees" and thus confirmed the "continuing basic validity" of programs encouraging exit. By this logic, the greater the pushback they received from Soviet authorities, the more successful the programs were. In a clear sign that the needs of these programs were beginning to overshadow the broader aims of US foreign policy, the report warned that a thaw in US-Soviet relations might lower the risk of nuclear confrontation but could end up harming defection inducement operations. "Any show of friendliness between Soviet and free world leaders," the report's authors cautioned, "is likely to have a dampening effect upon the morale of escapees and their activities."[126]

THE CLOSURE OF COLD WAR EUROPE'S BORDERLANDS

On August 13, 1961, East German security forces began tearing up the streets along the border of a divided Berlin, lining the boundary with barbed wire and, shortly after, concrete barriers.[127] The Berlin Wall would become the most prominent physical manifestation of the Iron Curtain, and the reinforcement of East German border defenses would change the character of defection for the remainder of the Cold War. After its construction, the numbers of migrants fleeing to the West sharply declined, and the contest over defectors shifted from a concentrated battle in Central Europe to a more diffuse struggle waged across the globe. The Wall's solidity could be read as a sign of strength: in the words of East German authorities, it was the "anti-fascist protection barrier"; according to the journal of the Soviet border troops, it defended against the "90 spy centers of Western intelligence, 66 revanchist organizations, and tens of fascist terrorist organizations" located in the city's western half.[128] It could also be interpreted as evidence of weakness, a public admission that socialist states could not otherwise prevent their citizens from fleeing. Returning the following year from a "goodwill tour" to fourteen countries in Asia and Europe, Attorney General Robert F. Kennedy called the Berlin Wall "the most effective argument against the communist system" in a memorandum submitted to his brother, the US president.[129] Once again, American officials privately welcomed the strengthening of the socialist camp's borders as a tactical victory in the broader struggle of the Cold War.

Even before the Berlin Wall went up, the US Escapee Program had begun winding down its operations. Although American planners had envisioned a permanent network of "frontier stations" across Europe to welcome defectors, they slowly backed away from the idea given the problems—and public relations liabilities—that plagued resettlement facilities. The Escapee Program produced too few migrants from the Soviet Union and too many from other countries, exposing the contradiction at the heart of the program: American officials wanted to highlight socialist restrictions on exit, but they were not prepared to facilitate the large-scale entry of socialist citizens to the West. After the 1956 Hungarian Uprising and its brutal suppression by Soviet troops triggered the flight of hundreds of thousands of Hungarians, the National Security Council called for "no action to encourage the departure of large numbers of nationals from countries" besides the Soviet Union and referred to the 170,000 Hungarian escapees awaiting resettlement in Austria as a "problem of great magnitude." Although approximately 30,000 Hungarians would ultimately be allowed to enter the United States through the parole authority of the Attorney General and granted permanent residency through a special act of Congress, American policymakers sought to ensure that the Hungarian case remained an exception and began making a quiet retreat from a broad-based Escapee Program.[130]

Its funding from the US government withdrawn, the Tolstoy Foundation shuttered the Karlsfeld Center a few months before the Wall's construction in Berlin. Around the same time, a State Department task force suggested rebranding the US Escapee Program as a "US Refugee Program," a more generic effort to assist refugees in coordination with the international community. While the United States would maintain its rhetorical commitment to "the principle of international responsibility for refugee problems in the free world," assistance would be rendered only to migrants from the socialist camp "at a level consistent with U.S. national interests." In 1963, the program's name was formally changed with little fanfare.[131]

The end of the Escapee Program coincided with the equally quiet demise of a large-scale Soviet repatriation campaign. In 1959, the Committee for the Return to the Homeland was retitled the "Committee for the Return to the Homeland and the Development of Cultural Ties with Compatriots," which suggested a shift from repatriation to cultural outreach. In 1963 it shed the notion of return entirely and became the "Soviet Committee for Cultural Ties with Compatriots Abroad."[132] With the exception of a few small-scale repatriation efforts, Soviet officials seemed prepared to tolerate a permanent postwar emigration.

Despite the Soviet state's rhetoric about rehabilitation, migrants who did come back were viewed with enduring suspicion. Upon Vladimir Pronin's return, he was charged with "betrayal of the Motherland" and sentenced to imprisonment for ten years.[133] The fact that he had knowingly cooperated with American intelligence in West Germany likely played a role in his sentencing. However, his conduct during the meeting with Soviet officials in the IG Farben building, when he had rebuffed their advances but refused to characterize his flight as anything other than a chance to "make a living," suggested that he may also have been unwilling to mold his story to fit an ideological narrative. This rebellious quality could have been a factor in his punishment as well. Like most other Soviet migrants who crossed Central Europe in this period, his voice can only be heard filtered through documents generated by rival intelligence organizations and emigre leaders. Yet the record of what he chose not to say is nearly as significant as the transcript of what he said.

In Europe, the period of migration unleashed by the Second World War was coming to a close, but the systems of surveillance and networks of intelligence that tracked migrants remained in place. If the immediate postwar period had witnessed an effort by both sides to channel the global chaos of displacement, and the 1950s had seen a more focused battle between competing intelligence services over escapees along the borders of the Iron Curtain, the 1960s marked the advent of routinized and scripted exchanges of migrants supervised and agreed upon by officials on both sides. In Frankfurt, the CIA and the Soviet Military Liaison Mission kept their offices, while in Berlin, the US and the USSR began a series of trades for captured spies and desired migrants carried out at the main crossing points of the divided city—the Gleinicke Bridge along the Havel River (which became known as the "bridge of spies") and Checkpoint Bravo (which spanned the Autobahn shared by both sides). These choreographed exchanges, their details worked out in advance and facilitated by state-authorized middlemen on the eastern side and by the CIA's lawyers on the western side, would continue until the end of the Cold War.[134] While they took on a dramatic air, especially when negotiations grew heated and the two sides squabbled over the minutest of details, such deals were an indication of the advance of state control and the decline of ungoverned migration along what had once been the most porous of Cold War Europe's borderlands.

While the escapee and repatriation programs faded, the US defector program endured, and, along with it, the idea that every crossing of a Cold War border was an ideological choice. Intelligence officers privately regarded this notion with suspicion, and some migrants like Vladimir Pronin refused to play along, but it was publicly extolled for political purposes. Building on its formative experiences in Central Europe, the defector program was institutionalized across the world. The State Department's Peripheral Reporting Program, acting in coordination with the CIA, expanded its operations to Israel, Turkey, and Iran.[135] In the wake of the armistice of the Korean War, the National Security Council decided to encourage defection from North Korea.[136] The defector policy was also promoted in neighboring China and eventually deployed in Vietnam, where Soviet defector Nikolai Khokhlov advised South Vietnamese authorities on covert operations.[137] The program was also expanded within the Western Hemisphere; in September 1960, American officials recommended the inclusion of special language that covered people fleeing Fidel Castro's Cuba.[138]

Soviet officials, faced with a globalized system for promoting defection, were forced to respond. It was no longer sufficient to deny or downplay the departure of socialist citizens in the domestic press, since news reached Soviets via Western-backed radio broadcasts and through expanded economic and cultural contacts between the USSR and the West. Refusing to concede the worldwide contest to control mobility, Soviet officials began searching for new ways to maintain the USSR's borders in a global age.

3

Socialist Borders in a Global Age

While their defection had been prevented, two Soviet citizens, Revaz Mkheidze and Yuri Orekhov, were arrested in the Georgian city of Batumi in September 1962, an incident that provoked panic at the highest levels of the KGB. First, there was the matter of where the pair had been found—on board a boat from Yugoslavia, a socialist country that had refused to sign the Warsaw Pact, docked in a Black Sea port city just a few miles from Turkey, the primary destination for Soviet defectors following the construction of the Berlin Wall.[1] Second, there was the mysterious note Mkheidze had written before his arrest, addressed to an American citizen named George Feifer in Passaic, New Jersey. Third, the pair's personal history exposed deeper levels of disaffection among the emerging generation of Soviet citizens. Despite the opportunities the two young men had been afforded by the relative peace and prosperity of Nikita Khrushchev's "Thaw," both reached their late twenties without completing their university courses and showed little interest in joining the Soviet workforce.

Perhaps most concerning of all, despite prior run-ins with the pair, the KGB had not known of their plan to flee. Four years earlier, Orekhov had had a brush with the Georgian branch of the secret police when he was part of a group of students in Tbilisi who were drawn, in the words of investigators, to "new and repulsive forms of entertainment." The group's pastimes included dancing to "rock-and-roll and boogie-woogie" songs recorded from foreign broadcasts and mixing with "unknown girls of easy virtue and youths without a determined occupation."[2] For his part, Mkheidze had been called in by the Georgian KGB two years earlier for "unseemly conduct" in "meetings with foreigners from capitalist countries."

The young Georgian, who spoke decent English, had struck up an acquaintance with an American visitor in Kyiv in 1956, an American basketball player in Tbilisi in 1958, and a group of participants in the American Exhibition in Moscow in 1959, including George Feifer, a journalist known to the KGB for his "anti-Soviet" reporting.[3] Orekhov and Mkheidze's plan to defect from the Soviet Union was over a year in the making. It involved a stolen map of the restricted Soviet-Turkish border zone, a hand-held propeller custom-assembled in a Tbilisi shop, alleged assurances of American support upon reaching Turkey, and multiple trips to Batumi to conduct reconnaissance beforehand, including visits to the city's Interklub for international crewmembers, where they sought the help of foreign sailors. Yet the KGB only learned of the pair's escape when the captain of the Yugoslav ship decided to call the Soviet border troops stationed in the harbor.

Admittedly, the plan was poorly carried out from the start. Orekhov forgot to bring the copy of the map; the custom propeller proved difficult to transport and was left behind; and the pair missed an earlier opportunity to swim to a British ship where they would have had a better chance of receiving sanctuary. By the time they reached the Yugoslav ship they were exhausted and had no choice but to ask for assistance, even though the crew informed them that they would be turned over to Soviet authorities. Mkheidze later admitted that his claim of promised assistance from Feifer when the pair arrived in Turkey had merely been a boast meant to encourage Orekhov to join him. Feifer had in fact tried to warn him off, considering it too dangerous to flee the Soviet Union illegally.[4]

Despite its failure, the attempted defection invoked the KGB's fears about the weakness of the state's border defenses in the face of new forms of foreign influence in the Cold War. Batumi was known to be one of the most vulnerable points of the Soviet Union's long western border, which touched the tip of Norway, ran alongside Finland, and then reached down from the Baltic to the Black Sea. The northernmost section was less of a concern, since it was sparsely inhabited, and an agreement between Finland and the USSR mandated that anyone fleeing the Soviet state would be returned.[5] The most sensitive stretch of the border was the one between the Baltic and Black seas. It contained restive populations that had been forcibly incorporated into the USSR during World War II, including Estonians, Latvians, and Lithuanians; it divided closely related groups, such as Moldovans and Romanians; and its southernmost portion separated the Soviet Union from Turkey, a NATO member. The multiethnic borderlands between the two seas were also the most susceptible to global flows of information, people, and goods. There, foreign broadcasts could be picked up easily, populations were more likely to have relatives abroad, and black markets thrived in port cities open to foreign sailors.[6]

The fact that socialist states lay on the other side of most of the western border was less comforting than suggested by public affirmations of Warsaw Pact solidarity. In the eyes of the leadership of the Soviet Union's Red Banner Western Border District, based in Kyiv and tasked with enforcing the critical section of the border that ran south from near the Baltic coast to the shores of the Black Sea, socialist neighbors were not always reliable partners. When Mkheidze and Orekhov attempted to flee, Hungary was still seen as unstable in the wake of the 1956 uprising; six years after their

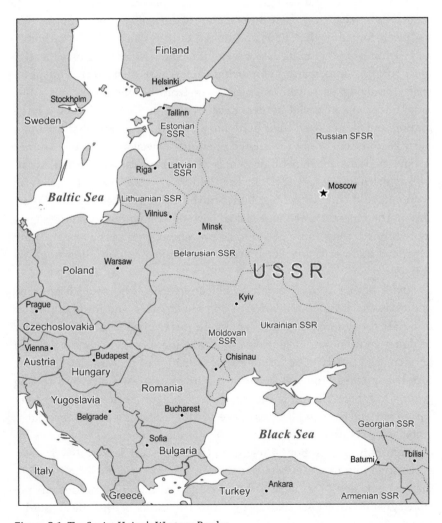

Figure 3.1 The Soviet Union's Western Border

attempted defection, Czechoslovakia would also be seen as a risk because of the Prague Spring. As a socialist country that insisted on non-alignment, Yugoslavia was always viewed warily, and Romania began to go its own way by the middle of the 1960s, allowing for limited emigration, which made it an enticing destination for those hoping to leave the Soviet Union. Even Poland, though it offered little promise as a point of escape to the West, was scrutinized for lax enforcement and potential disloyalty among its security officials.

Overseen by the KGB, the troops of the Western Border District policed a vast domain. Their operations reached outward to maintain a common border regime among the socialist bloc; they also stretched inward to stop the spread of harmful foreign influences and prevent defection before it occurred. In part, they drew on practices of surveillance and control that had been forged in the 1930s and honed during World War II: gathering and wielding demographic data, assembling and weaponizing investigative files, running informants, employing undercover operatives, and physically removing perceived troublemakers from border areas.[7] Yet while most historians of Soviet borders have focused on their Stalin-era consolidation and emphasized their hardening over time, the post-Stalinist mobility regime consisted of regulated openings as well as enforced closures; it governed the movement of people through positive inducements as well as disciplinary coercion.[8] As the Cold War settled into a longer-term economic and cultural contest between the United States and the Soviet Union, the repertoire of those tasked with defending Soviet borders grew more refined. Defection needed to be prevented even as the Soviet Union expanded its international connections and linked its port cities to global shipping routes.

Soviet border troops sought to be gatekeepers who could both open and close the state's boundaries to migrants, goods, and ideas in pursuit of Soviet foreign policy goals. They found increasingly sophisticated ways of doing so in an era of globalization, drawing on new technologies and an increased capacity for "prophylactic policing" to prevent defection before it happened. The state's western borderlands were a critical testing ground for these efforts. It was here that ambiguities of movement were sorted out and the complexities of the USSR's relations with other socialist states were clarified. Behind the façade of a solid "bloc," the establishment of a common socialist border regime in the region was a contested process. It was riven by tensions between the Soviet state and its socialist allies, distrust between Moscow and those living in the USSR's multiethnic periphery, and suspicions that seeped into the ranks of the state's border troops. The Western Border District was a crucial piece of a larger Soviet mobility regime that aimed to rival the United States in its global scope while remaining insulated against US efforts to encourage defection.

SHORING UP THE SOCIALIST BLOC

According to the training manual for its border troops, the Soviet border was doubly exceptional. It was enormous, encompassing the "boundless expanses of our Motherland," and running over 29,000 miles by sea and another 12,000 miles by land. It was also the "most just border in the world." Despite the "aggressive" behavior of its capitalist neighbors, the Soviet Union sought to resolve "any border dispute . . . only through peaceful means." Thankfully, the manual concluded, while the borders between socialist and capitalist states divided "two opposing systems," the borders between the Soviet Union and its socialist allies were "borders of a new, socialist type, with a new class content, borders of solidarity and the friendship of peoples."[9]

The borders of the socialist bloc were meant to channel citizens along new pathways even as they cut off traditional transit routes. Far more variegated than the "Iron Curtain" label suggested, they had filtered openings, differentiated clearances for movement, and zones of mobility and immobility that coexisted in relative proximity. The Black Sea port of Batumi, where the two young men had sought to flee, was a case in point. A bustling area of international shipping activity and seaside tourist resorts, it was located only a few miles from a "forbidden border zone" that was only open to carefully screened local residents and Soviet border troops. The nearby border with Turkey—described in the training manual as an American-backed "base for the organization of subversive activity directed against the USSR"—was reinforced with high-voltage fences, dotted with watchtowers, patrolled by soldiers with guard dogs, and monitored by a *druzhina,* or a brigade of Soviet citizens who vowed to turn potential border-crossers over to the authorities.[10] While Batumi's port was plugged into global maritime shipping routes, a hard line separated Sarpi and Sarp, two halves of a historically unified town on the Soviet-Turkish border just south of Batumi. The only sanctioned means of crossing the divided town required a circuitous 869-mile trip through Tbilisi, Yerevan, and Kars to reach the other side.[11]

Far from being an endemic feature of a "totalitarian" Soviet system, the border regime was an international production. Batumi's bustling port reflected the Soviet Union's effort to establish itself as a force in global shipping in order to take part in global trade on its own terms, reach far-flung allies in the post-colonial world, and save on convertible currency.[12] The nearby Black Sea resorts, catering primarily to Soviet citizens and visitors from neighboring socialist countries, reflected transnational borrowing within the socialist camp, from the architectural style in which they were built to the dishes they served vacationers.[13] The hard border with Turkey was indeed designed to keep socialist citizens in, but its technologies of control were in part borrowed from Western border defenses. By the 1960s, Soviet border troop officials were routinely dispatched to West Berlin, traveling under the guise of tourists to examine the capitalist state's border regime and, where necessary, draw upon its practices.[14] The Soviet border was at once a response to US policies and an imitation of US-sponsored security measures.

These changes in Soviet border enforcement were easy to miss, especially since the training materials of the Soviet border troops so often looked back to the Second World War.[15] Official publications designed for Soviet border troops, such as the closed circulation journal *Pogranichnik*, kept the memory of the war alive for decades afterward, using it to justify the need for continued vigilance. While the Nazi invaders had been repelled by force, the journal's articles suggested that more sophisticated means were necessary to counter the United States, which spearheaded NATO and other "unions of aggression and war," breached Soviet border defenses with covert spying operations and invisible radio broadcasts, and surveilled Soviet citizens through listening stations in neighboring countries.[16] In this rendering, the Cold War was a continuation of the Second World War, waged by other means.

World War II had driven a massive expansion of the Soviet border troops, and the effort to solidify the state's new western border in the Cold War ensured that its personnel was never significantly drawn down. A monthly accounting of border troops carried out by the organization's Political Directorate from 1940 to 1950 indicates that their numbers more than doubled over the course of the Second World War and remained at this size after the war's end.[17] Troop levels would decrease somewhat after Stalin's death but began rising again after the Prague Spring of 1968.[18] The Political Directorate sought to ensure that the contingent of troops was not just large but politically reliable. This was a formidable task and an ongoing source of apprehension. While officers in the border troops had years of specialized training and were likely to be Communist Party members, young conscripts with only a "basic education" made up the rank and file.[19]

Border troops had to guard in two directions, looking inward as well as outward. Seeking to secure the state's newly annexed territories in the war's aftermath, they stepped up the screening of anyone seeking to leave the Soviet Union, with particular attention paid to wartime collaboration, connections to partisan networks, and ties with foreign intelligence.[20] Border troops were also drawn into the socialist state's repatriation effort, called upon to regulate return and prevent those who had been brought back from leaving again. Even after wartime migrants were resettled, border troops continued to monitor their presence, particularly in sensitive border regions, where anyone convicted of illegal border crossing was barred from residing. Intelligence officers attached to the Western Border District continued to surveil the relatives of nonreturners who remained in the western borderlands, monitoring their correspondence well into the 1960s.[21]

These efforts radiated outward through the socialist bloc, where the retrieval of nonreturners helped establish the region as a unified migratory space supervised by Moscow. Georgian secret police records show that SMERSH—the Red Army's counterintelligence operation whose name in Russian was a portmanteau of "death to spies"—had begun apprehending and returning Soviet citizens in Romania as early as 1944, when they caught a man who had swum from Soviet Georgia to Turkey in 1930 and become a participant in anti-Soviet emigre circles.[22] The effort expanded after the war, with the Ministry for State Security's Second Directorate, the division responsible for counterintelligence, submitting a comprehensive list in February 1948 of all residents of Ukraine who had fled to Romania from 1918 to 1941, which the state presumably used in its effort to locate and return them to the Soviet Union.[23] Even as it lost access to Soviet displaced persons in Western Europe, the Repatriation Administration worked closely with intelligence officials and border troops to search for lost citizens and construct a common mobility regime within the socialist camp.

The latter was a particularly challenging task. While concerns about preserving demographic strength after the population losses suffered in the Second World War were shared throughout the region, the various states that made up the socialist camp sought to push migration flows in different ways. If the Soviet Union generally used repatriation and emigration controls to retain a multiethnic citizenry, its allies in East Central Europe were more likely to use them to pursue national homogeneity.[24] In some cases, socialist states negotiated the "repatriation" of Soviet citizens of their titular nationality to their "home" state, as Poland had done in postwar negotiations, and as Hungary did in facilitating the "return" of ethnic Hungarians in the 1950s, even in the face of moderate opposition from the Soviet state.[25] Even as Poland, Hungary, and Romania sought more ethnic Poles, Hungarians, and Romanians, they were inclined to allow the exit of ethnic Germans and Jews. Similarly, Bulgaria allowed the emigration of ethnic Turks to Turkey while making exit difficult for the rest of its citizens.[26]

Confronted with these underlying conflicts, Soviet officials asserted themselves as the managers of the broader mobility regime in East Central Europe. The Soviet Union tolerated some regional variations but also ensured that basic standards were maintained. There were shared policies for preventing exit and a shared terminology that labeled unauthorized emigration as treason. There was also a shared materiality of border construction and border enforcement technology. Border control agencies that had been established under Soviet tutelage, such as East Germany's *Grenztruppen*, gained day-to-day autonomy but were guided by Moscow in a manner that recalled the operation of West Germany's intelligence service, the *Bundesnachrichtendienst* (BND), under the watchful eye of the CIA. By 1955, when West and East Germany gained full sovereignty, Soviet troops were posted directly along the border only in East Berlin and at the Helmstedt-Marienborn Autobahn crossing, which controlled the main route of traffic between West Germany and West Berlin.[27]

Although few Soviet officials could be found along the western edge of the Iron Curtain after the mid-1950s, the stamp of Soviet influence remained in a common set of practices among Warsaw Pact border troop agencies. All of the socialist border agencies used barbed wire fencing, wooden guard towers, anti-vehicle ditches, and observation bunkers designed to keep people in and to keep intruders out. Border troop units walked similarly designed patrol paths along the Iron Curtain, tracing the same geometric arcs outlined in their training manuals. They were sometimes accompanied by dogs to sniff out and chase border violators, and they usually walked in pairs to ensure vigilance and prevent solitary border guards from defecting. Although the terrain varied, the environmental impact of socialist border policing made border spaces look surprisingly homogenous: trees were cleared to make violators easier to spot, steel grating was placed across streams, marker buoys ran across larger bodies of water, and the ground was harrowed in a wide strip on the inside of the border, which made the footprints of would-be escapees visible. If border troops were unable to apprehend an illegal border crosser, they could at least identify the most common exit routes by recording imprints in the loose soil, which were reported to their superiors and used to justify the construction of additional fencing.

All of the Warsaw Pact's border troops wore uniforms that incorporated a green stripe or a green background (borrowed from the Soviet uniform), and all went through training that combined practical patrolling techniques, military skills (especially marksmanship), and a heavy dosage—as much as 50 percent of the curriculum—of political education.[28] All socialist bloc countries relied on a massive level of human effort maintained by conscripting young men who were overseen by an elite stratum of professional officers, party ideologists, and representatives from the intelligence services. Troops were supposed to know the border intimately, yet not be of the borderlands: they were typically rotated to posts far away from where they had grown up and discouraged from residing in the border zone they had been posted to after their service.

Socialist bloc border troop agencies held Warsaw Pact–wide conferences and received regular visits from Soviet officials. While political supervision from the east shaped the institutional culture of these agencies, border control technology sometimes flowed from the west, with the Inner German Border generating new methods of enforcement. The Inner German border was long, at over 600 miles; it was winding, with broad bulges and cul-de-sacs; it divided villages, spread across rivers, ran along a major autobahn route, and even made its way into the Baltic Sea.[29] It was also viewed as the first line of invasion in the event of an all-out war with the West. Given these features, its defenses evolved faster, with updates that later made their way eastward. On land, rickety wooden towers became solid concrete structures equipped with searchlights and connected to telephone lines to report illegal border crossings immediately, and barbed-wire fences became sturdier barriers armed with anti-personnel mines that could be triggered by the slightest movement across tripwires. At sea, the Baltic coast's defenses were transformed by the installation of floodlights and the arrival of high-speed patrol boats. The most advanced technology was employed to monitor the relatively small but sensitive section of the border that ran through Berlin: the wall gained electronic movement detectors and closed-circuit surveillance cameras, and concealed gamma-ray detectors designed to screen vehicles for hidden passengers were used at the Marienborn Autobahn checkpoint.[30]

While technological innovations were shared throughout the Warsaw Pact, Moscow defended the primacy of its claims on defectors. By the 1960s, these claims were more likely to be justified by calls for the extradition of criminals rather than the repatriation of errant citizens, though the difference was slight: any Soviet citizen who fled without authorization or refused to return home was, in a legal sense, an accused criminal. A 1958 agreement concluded between the USSR and its socialist allies established the basis for any member state to extradite criminals from any other member state. However, in a telling sign of the hierarchy within the alliance, extradition from the Soviet Union could be prevented if the individual was also accused of committing a crime on Soviet territory, a loophole that allowed Moscow to hold individuals from neighboring socialist states who entered the Soviet Union without authorization. The Soviet Union's top concern, however, remained controlling the movement of its own citizens, whenever they left and wherever they found themselves.

Coordinated border policies helped make defection from the Soviet Union much more difficult. The case of N. I. Botezat, who repeatedly tried to defect by fleeing into neighboring countries, reveals the Soviet Union's consolidation of control over mobility throughout the bloc. Born in 1920 in independent Romania, Botezat fled the Soviet Union in 1945, shortly after Moldova was annexed and made into a Soviet republic. For the next eleven years he traveled throughout Europe without being apprehended, living first in Romania, then in Hungary, and later Italy, France, Australia, and Canada. Having a change of heart—and perhaps missing his family in Moldova—he approached the Soviet consulate in Canada in 1956 and expressed his desire to repatriate. He returned to the Soviet Union, only to flee again in 1958 to Hungary. This time, however, border controls were tighter, and he was apprehended at the border area of Hungary that abutted Austria and Yugoslavia. Quickly turned over by Hungarian authorities, he was sent back to Moscow and tried and sentenced within a few months.[31] By that time, requests seeking the return of Soviet citizens issued by the KGB to the security services of socialist allies had become routine.[32]

Connections among the border guards of socialist states were affirmed in the Soviet Border Troops journal *Pogranichnik* as well as in companion publications printed in each Warsaw Pact country. These publications emphasized the unity of socialist borders and the friendship that sealed them. A 1964 *Pogranichnik* article, for example, described a visit of Soviet border guards to their "Hungarian comrades." Their bond was affirmed through shared patrols in the snow and a warm gathering at the barracks afterward in which they passed photos of their respective girlfriends and wives back and forth. In the politically pitch-perfect words of a Hungarian officer cited in the piece, "Our friendship with each other, I can say frankly, is fraternal. After all, we guard what is in effect one border—the border of our socialist camp."[33]

In reality, the officers who oversaw the Western Border District were not convinced that their Warsaw Pact counterparts were as thorough as they needed to be to combat pernicious influences seeping in from the capitalist camp. In a series of reports from 1966, Western Border District officials looked with disapproval at the foreign tourists who entered Poland with relative ease and took photographs of the Soviet border from Polish territory; they expressed concerns about a Polish "underground nationalist movement," whose members maintained ties with compatriots living in

"England, the United States . . . and other countries"; and they remarked on uncooperative local residents in Poland and "expressions of dissatisfaction among the local population about border posts."[34] The line separating the Soviet Union from Poland was not only guarded with border posts, but it also featured inward-facing warnings to Soviet citizens who might be tempted to conduct contraband trade across the border. A placard newspaper at the Brest checkpoint, for example, read "Shame on Speculators" and showed photographs of Soviet citizens who had been caught for illegal trading. Such warnings were designed to deter local residents seeking to capitalize on easy access to Polish markets, where Western consumer goods were more readily available.[35] Long feared for its potential to undermine the planned economy, contraband trade was also viewed as a perilous bait that could lure Soviet citizens to defect to the capitalist West.[36]

The suspicions Western Border District officials harbored about their Polish counterparts were significant enough to warrant surveillance operations directed against their "fraternal" allies. In December 1956, Polish state security officers responsible for patrolling the railroad connections between the Soviet Union and Poland arrived in Lviv for a working meeting, bearing what appeared to be promising leads about Soviet-based contraband networks in Poland. The Polish officers expressed hope that the Soviet Union might reciprocate and provide them with information relevant to their own investigations of Polish citizens. Soviet officials, however, remained skeptical of the proposal; instead of pursuing it, they used an undercover agent to tail the Polish delegation around Lviv. At a time of heightened suspicions following the uprising in Hungary earlier that year, they even placed a listening device in the hotel room of their Polish colleagues, which exposed the fact that their "Polish 'friends' were not as devoted to the Soviet Union" as they claimed. The secret recording caught the Polish officials complaining that the Soviets "think we are simpletons" and "only want to use this [material] for their own political purposes." One suggested that they exploit condescending Soviet views by feigning misunderstanding if Western Border District officials asked them questions they did not want to answer.[37]

The troubled Polish-Soviet border was in some ways a best-case scenario. If Soviet officials eyed their Polish counterparts warily, they viewed their Romanian socialist neighbors as outright antagonists. After coming to power in 1965, Nicolae Ceausescu began allowing limited emigration to the West, often in exchange for payment to the Romanian state. By 1969, Romania stopped participating in the Warsaw Pact's military command, though it remained a member of the alliance on paper.[38] Western Border District reports from the period warned that the Romanians were considering "revanchist" claims on the territory of the Moldovan Soviet Socialist Republic and were actively undermining the imperial hierarchies of the socialist camp, carrying out their own spy operations on Soviet border guard posts. By the end of the 1970s, Romania was grouped together with the capitalist countries in the data kept by border troop officials, with those living in the border region screened for relatives "in capitalist countries and Romania."[39]

This unease about the reliability of socialist neighbors trickled down to ordinary Soviet citizens. While Soviet policies permitted citizens to travel with relative freedom within the socialist bloc, Soviet travelers still received warnings before they left on a trip to Poland, Bulgaria, or another allied country. Official guidelines advised Soviet citizens to adopt a degree of noblesse oblige in interactions with their socialist brethren. They were to "respect the national traditions . . . culture, customs, language, literature, and art" of the countries they were visiting, while defending "the interests of the Soviet Union" and remaining aware that there were "enemy elements" present in these countries.[40] Such language suggested that Soviet visitors were not always respectful of their neighbors, nor were they sufficiently vigilant in their dealings with them. Economic, political, and cultural fault lines ran between socialist nations even as the Soviet Border Troops sought to defend the bloc against Western influence and prevent unauthorized exit.

INSIDE THE FORBIDDEN BORDER ZONE

Compared to the lines dividing socialist allies, the borders between the Soviet Union and capitalist states were heavily fortified and unmistakably militarized. Perhaps the most unique feature of these boundaries was the enforcement of "forbidden border zones" that reached several miles into the territory of the Soviet Union, projecting the border regime inward. Movement through these zones required a special pass for visitors or a permanent stamp in the passports of local residents. The presence of any unauthorized person was grounds for suspicion and criminal prosecution. By closing some sections of the border entirely, migration and trade were channeled through authorized crossings that recalled the "filtration" points established for Soviet migrants returning after World War II.

Along the Soviet state's western border, restricted border zones included the area outside of the northern port city of Murmansk that abutted Norway, the Estonian islands of Hiiumaa and Saaremaa near Swedish territorial waters, and the long stretch between the Soviet Union and Turkey.

These areas were often sparsely populated, but when inhabited they were turned into securitized zones by emptying them of groups and individuals whose loyalty was questioned. In the Stalinist era, mass deportations were carried out to cleanse the Soviet-Turkish border region of populations with historic cross-border ties, including Kurds and Meskhetian Turks, who were forcibly removed in 1944, and Laz and Pontian Greeks, who were targeted in operations carried out from 1945 to 1951.[41] These moves fit with a larger pattern of ethnic cleansing pursued in the western borderlands, including the expulsion of Tatars from Crimea and the removal of ethnic Germans and Poles from the state's western flank.[42] After Stalin's death, mass deportations ceased but intelligence officials continued to scrutinize the family connections of local residents and the movement of unauthorized migrants in the border zone. Their efforts were aided by the environmental conditions along much of the border: Arctic temperatures in the north, the frigid waters of the Baltic Sea, and the rugged mountains of eastern Turkey made it hard for would-be defectors to seek shelter.

Equally important was the system of surveillance cast over authorized crossing points, port cities, resorts, and population centers. It was sometimes hidden from view, but pervasive in its reach thanks to the vast network of covert agents and informants maintained by the Soviet secret police. Its goal was to prevent unsanctioned activity while allowing the authorized mobility of people and goods under the state's gaze. The local population was enlisted in this effort. In addition to general "political-educational" efforts by border troop officials to increase the local public's "vigilance" against illegal movement, locals were recruited for *druzhiny*, the specialized brigades called upon to conduct foot patrols, apprehend suspicious people, inform on neighbors who harbored border crossers, and report rumors of people seeking to flee. Despite the supposedly volunteer nature of the brigades, members were sometimes given material rewards for their help.[43] The 1966 work plan for border troops of the Western Border District, for example, indicated that local participants could be paid up to a substantial 400 rubles for apprehending illegal border crossers.[44]

In port cities and seaside resort areas visited by foreign sailors and tourists, informants kept a close eye on interactions between Soviet citizens and visitors from abroad. The KGB was interested in identifying Soviet citizens inclined to "treasonous" behavior, which included harboring plans to flee, but they also welcomed informant reports detailing unauthorized trade of clothing and jewelry, romantic liaisons that sometimes blossomed between Soviets and foreigners, and ideologically suspect remarks overhead in restaurants, clubs, and workplaces.[45] KGB officers believed that petty infractions could lead to more serious crimes, and they were quick to bring people in for questioning. Those caught engaging in such behavior sometimes faced prosecution, or they might be coerced into cooperating with the KGB, further extending the agency's army of agents and informants.

Restricted border zones and surveilled points of exchange operated in close proximity. The international port city of Batumi lay just nine miles from the Turkish border, and a "forbidden border zone" began at the city's southern outskirts.[46] The Soviet secret police hoped to maintain Batumi as a globally connected but tightly patrolled space. Passenger manifests of arriving foreign vessels were inspected by Western Border District troops searching for visiting sailors deemed suspicious because they had relatives in the USSR or possessed knowledge of Russian, which suggested potential ties to "the intelligence services of the opponent."[47] KGB agents and informants reported on the sailors' behavior in the city's restaurants and cafes, including the Interklub establishment designed to cater to them. Some foreign sailors were cultivated as intelligence assets. For example, a Greek sailor who had befriended a young Soviet woman working in the port of Odesa's processing area was identified as having a "loyal attitude . . . toward the Soviet people" and a "dislike of Americans." Recruited under the codename "Olimp" (Olympus), he was used to gather information on the operation of foreign shipping lines. While he seemed like a willing participant, other foreign sailors were recruited by the gathering of "compromising materials" on them, usually related to participation in contraband trade (which typically broke the rules of foreign ships as well as Soviet laws) or sexual transgressions on shore.[48]

As Mkheidze and Orekhov discovered, foreign crews were hesitant to help Soviets defect. Foreign ships could be penalized for harboring fugitives from Soviet justice, and the Soviet criminal code had a special provision allowing Soviet authorities to board ships and seize people in Soviet territorial waters if a crime was committed, including the "illegal exit or illegal entry into the USSR."[49] As a result, ships from capitalist as well as socialist states usually turned would-be defectors over to Soviet law enforcement.[50] Defectors sometimes had better luck bribing foreign crewmembers to look the other way. KGB records suggest that this method for smuggling oneself out of the Soviet Union was not arranged through specialized middlemen but was instead organized on an ad hoc basis, between Soviets wishing to emigrate and foreign sailors. The money involved was not insignificant: in 1979, one Soviet citizen offered 10,000 US dollars and 3,000 Soviet rubles to a Greek captain to spirit him out of the country after he was denied an exit visa.[51] The KGB succeeded in preventing the formation of more permanent smuggling networks by recruiting agents among domestic dock workers, who reported any suspicious activity they observed. Given these restrictions on mobility—imposed by the Soviet state but enforced with the help of informant networks and foreign shipping lines concerned about losing access to Soviet ports—migrants desperate to leave sometimes sought to swim along the Black Sea coast to neighboring Turkey. It was not an easy feat. Petr Patrushev, a professional Soviet swimmer, made it from Batumi to the Turkish shore in 1962, but most others were unsuccessful and, like Mkheidze and Orekhov, left exhausted by the effort.[52]

If Soviet border officials operating beyond the USSR sought to assert their primacy over "fraternal" allies in the Warsaw Pact, within the USSR a predominantly Slavic leadership presided over an agency tasked with enforcing a border that ran along the state's non-Slavic southern periphery. The sensitive border with Turkey was largely patrolled by border troops rotated from the interior of Russia, Ukraine, and Belarus, rather than by Georgian, Armenian, or Azerbaijani locals. *Pogranichnik* ran features celebrating cooperation between the border troops and the local Georgian population, who, according to the journal, "look to border guards with the greatest respect, sign up for voluntary people's guards, patrol roads and population points, and inform border guard stations of the appearance in the border zone of any suspicious persons." In practice, Western Border District troops counted not so much on goodwill as on the fact that many of those seeking to defect in the region were not even from Georgia and thus struck locals as suspicious outsiders in any case.[53]

Central authorities in Moscow had to ensure the support of local officials, party leaders, and police units beyond the control of the border troops. When a young Georgian man defected to Turkey in 1959 after being cleared by local authorities to reside in the border town of Sarpi despite using falsified documents, both KGB chief Aleksandr Shelepin and the party's Central Committee in Moscow blamed failures in Georgia's leadership.[54] Despite the subsequent promise of officials in Georgia to strictly enforce regulations in the border zone, a report nearly a decade later revealed enduring difficulties in monitoring the "mass influx of citizens" visiting nearby Batumi. In the words of the report's authors, Batumi and the surrounding area remained "a base for violators of the border and border regime," particularly those "preparing to flee abroad." From 1963 to 1968, over 50,000 Soviet citizens had been detained in the region, either for not carrying the appropriate documents or for going into the restricted border zone south of the city without the right to be there. The high number likely encompassed locals who flouted the border regime imposed by Moscow as well as potential defectors. Faced with these staggering statistics, the Soviet Council of Ministers approved a tactic that had previously been employed along sections of the western border in the 1930s: the complete "passportization" of the rural population outside of Batumi, with documents to be carried by every adult and regular passport checks sealing the busy port of Batumi off from the sensitive southern border zone.[55]

Regulating contraband trade proved even more challenging, especially in Soviet port cities open to foreign sailors. In the Lithuanian port of Klaipeda on the Baltic Sea, sailors from abroad sold goods directly to dock workers and made deals with Soviet underground entrepreneurs in the city's cafes. In the Ukrainian city of Odesa on the Black Sea, the Soviet state's busiest port, authorities reported contraband trade that exceeded all the Baltic ports combined in its volume and value. During 1960 alone, contraband goods valued at 603,979 rubles were seized in Odesa, likely a small fraction of the overall amount of informal trade.[56] Those tasked with defending the Soviet border were by no means immune; charges against Western Border District troops for participating in unauthorized trade were commonplace.

The state's increased regulation of the border zone produced even more illegality as a wide range of behaviors and patterns of mobility were outlawed. The labeling of everything, from the sale of petty trinkets to larger-scale underground trade operations, as "contraband" heightened the sense that port cities were rife with dangerous goods and people. Anyone the border troops caught in a restricted border area—whether a potential defector, an agent of foreign intelligence, or simply a lost and confused tourist—was deemed a "violator." The term immediately criminalized unauthorized bodies in the border zone, regardless of identity. Although unauthorized migrants seized near the border were often people from the social and economic margins of Soviet society, the border troops' training materials focused on the risk of professional spies and militant emigres sneaking across Soviet boundaries.

The area's security measures paradoxically deepened feelings of insecurity. Policies incentivizing border troops to seize as many "violators" and as much contraband as possible compounded the problem. Quarterly and annual reports gathered from each Western Border District unit detailed instances of illegal border crossing, defection, and contraband trade. Each year, the leadership of the Soviet Border Troops responded by issuing instructions and guidelines for improvement, such as the March 1964 directive, "On Measures for the Improvement of Counterintelligence Work by the KGB Border Troops."[57] Quantifying what was seized along the Soviet border to compare the relative effectiveness of different border units, these directives praised higher performing divisions, such as the troops of the Transcaucasian Border District, and criticized those whose numbers had slipped, including the Western Border District.[58] As a result, there was consistent pressure from above to criminalize any potentially suspicious activity near the border.

The actual motives of those arrested in the border zone were often murky. Judging from the criminal cases initiated against individuals seized along the Soviet-Turkish border, most would-be border crossers were young men, and many had drifted across the Soviet Union without a fixed address or occupation before seeking to flee abroad. Some fled legal difficulties, personal problems, or family troubles; others had a history of drinking or a documented mental illness that made the analysis of their intent even more difficult. For example, twenty-one-year-old Valentin Pozhilov trained as a plumber but then left his home in the northwestern city of Petrozavodsk for Sverdlovsk and Krasnoiarsk in Siberia, before beginning to "wander" without a clear aim in the view of KGB investigators. He turned up twice in the restricted border zone of Batumi, where he was seized and found to be without documents.[59] Others seemed to be running away from their lives in the Soviet Union rather than being lured to the capitalist West. Vladimir Kuziakin, a young man who worked on a steamship in Odesa, stole a bundle of fur hats and fled into the Soviet-Turkish border zone in the hope of avoiding arrest; Nikolai Sergeev, a nineteen-year-old construction painter from Moscow, fled his worksite and a strained relationship with his family and departed for Batumi, journeying southward into the restricted border zone, where he was seized on the banks of the Chorokhi River before he could reach Turkey.[60]

CHANGING TACTICS FOR PROSECUTING AND PREVENTING DEFECTION

Mkheidze and Orekhov were put on trial at a time when the legal framework for prosecuting defection was beginning to change. Western Border District officials still urged their troops to catch ever-greater numbers of border violators. But within the Soviet criminal justice system, more attention was paid to motive, and not just movement, in determining whether treason had been committed. If in the Stalinist era unauthorized movement within the border zone or across the border was almost always interpreted as ideological betrayal and punished severely, in the post-Stalinist period prosecutors were more willing to consider the circumstances of migrants, and courts generally gave shorter sentences. These changes reflected the influence of the Thaw, with its emphasis on the rehabilitation of people who had been incarcerated, the investigation of the deeper sources of social deviance, and preventative policing through "prophylactic" measures to preempt serious crimes. The shift was also a response to negative international publicity labeling Soviet emigration restrictions as a form of "captivity" and likely the result of a pragmatic assessment—drawing on the experience of other, more lenient socialist states—that overly harsh penalties were actually a barrier to the return of Soviet migrants. Though it stopped short of ending the general prohibition on emigration, the state's framework for prosecuting unauthorized migration evolved in dialogue with the world beyond the Soviet Union.

According to the Soviet criminal code, treason encompassed a range of transgressions: crimes of the mind, such as making or circulating anti-Soviet statements; crimes threatening the state's military power, including spying on the Soviet Army for a foreign state; crimes that undermined the planned economy, such as illegal currency trading and theft from state enterprises; and crimes of unauthorized movement, such as planning or undertaking illegal flight abroad.[61] This broad definition of treason had a long pedigree, established in the Soviet criminal code in 1927, expanded in 1934, and subsequently used to conduct mass arrests during the Great Terror. The 1934 definition specified flight abroad as a counter-revolutionary act, to be punished with death and the confiscation of property, which often ensnared the offender's family. The best those arrested could hope for was that prosecutors would find "extenuating circumstances," reducing the sentence to imprisonment for ten years. Death sentences for treason became far less common after Stalin's death, but not until 1960 was the law comprehensively updated. The revision, enshrined in Article 64 of the criminal code, still singled out flight abroad as a crime on par with espionage or switching sides during combat, but it added the "failure to return from abroad" as a legal criterion. This change gave the state leeway in prosecuting defectors by leaving open the possibility of their coming home to avoid full prosecution. Though far from lenient, the punishment for treason became less severe, with a recommended prison sentence of ten to fifteen years, to which might be added a stint in the labor camps from two to five years.[62] In practice, would-be defectors who were caught in the act or those who chose to return to the Soviet Union often served less than ten years.

Granted more flexibility, KGB investigators and members of the Soviet Procuracy paid greater attention to whether flight had been motivated by a conscious choice to act against Soviet interests. In court cases and the lengthy appeals process that often followed them, debates took place about the geographical contours of loyalty for Soviet citizens who were linked to the world in new ways. Many KGB officers took it for granted that these contours were consistent with the boundaries of the Soviet state. Others went a step further, observing that ideological treason could be committed—and defection plotted—within Soviet borders. Reformers operating within the criminal justice system, however, held out the possibility that those who fled beyond Soviet borders might not be traitors and could be tried for lesser crimes, with reduced sentences.

Disputes arose over the culpability of citizens such as Mkheidze and Orekhov found inside restricted border zones but apprehended before they fled abroad. Some investigators and prosecutors emphasized the distinction between conscious flight and flight made under duress or in a state of mental incapacitation. After their arrest, Mkheidze and Orekhov were held and interrogated in the KGB's internal prison in Tbilisi for more than four months. Their prolonged detention may have been part of an effort to coerce a politically useful confession, but KGB investigators seemed genuinely interested in understanding the reasons for the pair's actions. They repeatedly questioned the would-be defectors and their friends and family members, carefully analyzed items seized from their apartments, and filled seven dense volumes with internal discussions about their culpability.

In a verdict reached in January 1963, Mkheidze, the purported mastermind, was given ten years in a labor camp, Orekhov received six years, and their friend, Guram Sulakvelidze, who knew about their plot to flee but did not report it, received two years. The penalties were fairly harsh for individuals who did not even manage to make it across the border, perhaps an overreaction by Georgian authorities due to prior accusations of poor border enforcement along the Black Sea coast, or perhaps because the new legal framework for prosecuting defection as treason remained unclear. Mkheidze quickly appealed, claiming that his scheme to flee had been a case of "stupidity" caused by his "perpetual idleness" rather than a treasonous attitude.[63]

Whether in response to Mkheidze's appeal or because he saw the sentence as excessively severe, Aleksandr Gorkin, the chair of the Soviet Union's Supreme Court, submitted a note of protest concerning the sentence the following year. Gorkin argued that in order to qualify as treason, an act had to be "intentionally committed by a citizen of the USSR to the detriment of state independence, territorial inviolability, or the military strength of the USSR." An attempt to flee abroad, according to this logic, could only be considered treasonous if it was undertaken on the basis of "anti-Soviet motives, with the goal of harming the state interests of the USSR." The fact that Mkheidze's wife had left him, he was having difficulty completing his studies, and his career prospects had evaporated after his contact with foreigners had come to the attention of the KGB suggested to Gorkin that he was running away "from problems and unpleasantries" in his "personal life" rather planning to subvert Soviet interests. The chair of the Soviet Supreme Court argued that Orekhov also needed to be treated more leniently. His inability to find regular employment was chalked up to his poor health and, in a nod to the broader trends of de-Stalinization, it was noted that his father, a newspaper editor, had been wrongfully executed in 1937 only to be rehabilitated in 1956. Gorkin instead placed responsibility on the foreigners Mkheidze met, suggesting that they took advantage of the pair's personal difficulties to lure them to the West. He recommended reducing Mkheidze's sentence to three years and lowering Orekhov's to two years. He also called for their property not to be confiscated, in the hope that they could resume productive lives after they served their time.[64] With the top judge of the Soviet Union arguing on their behalf, the pair's sentences were quickly reduced.

Gorkin, despite his history of presiding over Stalinist purge trials in the 1930s, enjoyed the reputation of being a legal reformer during the Thaw. However, it turned out that even the top officials of the Soviet secret police were growing concerned that defectors were punished too severely and often arbitrarily. KGB officials privately worried that the former tendency discouraged defectors from returning home, while the latter generated negative attention abroad. In August 1965, the head of the KGB, Vladimir Semichastny, wrote to Gorkin complaining about a "lack of consistency" in how cases of illegal border crossing were prosecuted. Some were classified as "treason" and others as "illegal departure," even though the "circumstances" of the cases in question were "essentially analogous." As examples, Semichastny brought up two particularly ambiguous instances of flight beyond Soviet borders: the first concerned a sixteen-year-old student, who, as a result of "childish stupidity," sneaked onto a Soviet ship in Odesa bound for Crete in May 1962, only to return to the Soviet Union several months later; the second involved a Soviet soldier who sought to escape to West Berlin in February 1963 after being brutally beaten by his superiors for a petty theft he did not commit. Since both had been convicted of treason, the KGB chief asked Gorkin's Supreme Court to reconsider their cases and offer "clarification" on how to legally distinguish between defectors who had betrayed the Soviet state and those who had simply strayed across its boundaries. Gorkin promised that the court would "study" the issue.[65] While the laws criminalizing exit remained on the books, such exchanges opened up a space for a more careful consideration of defector motivations.

The notion that defection had to be a conscious decision led to debates about the culpability of migrants who were found to suffer from mental incapacitation. More than a few of the "wanderers" seized by troops in the state's western borderlands appeared to have mental health problems.

In one instance, a young man from Siberia was arrested for vagrancy in 1956 in the Russian Black Sea port of Novorossiisk. After three previous attempts to cross out of the socialist state—along the Finnish border, from the restricted Estonian island of Hiiumaa, and from Tallinn's port—he had taken up work on a refrigerated cargo ship operating out of Novorossiisk but quit after realizing that the ship only ran domestic routes. Although KGB investigators argued that his "repeated attempts to infiltrate the forbidden border zone" were "evidence of intent," his motivations for leaving could not be established and his attempts to flee were haphazard, ill-planned, and ill-fated—after all, he would have been returned had he made it to Finland, and it was fairly obvious that that the vessel he worked on was not used for foreign shipping.[66] A psychiatric analysis commissioned by a Soviet court found that he suffered from a mild "mental deficiency." Citing this evaluation, the Soviet Procuracy pushed back against the KGB's investigators, noting that the young man made no "real attempt to cross the border" and that his mental incapacity made him incapable of "counter-revolutionary thought."[67] Even temporary mental lapses were considered as mitigating factors in prosecuting defectors. In another case, a Russian student at a military academy in Makhachkala told a classmate that he was planning to flee to Turkey. However, it was later revealed that the army trainee made the statement while intoxicated, undermining its credibility as a conscious political choice.[68]

More than a few would-be defectors had previously documented disorders, or they crossed into the border zone while drunk, on a whim, or by accident. The figures gathered by intelligence officers posted to the Western Border District speak to the marginal nature of Soviet citizens seized near the border; few had the clearance or connections to travel abroad, and many were already in desperate straits. Among the 181 people caught trying to flee across the USSR's western border in 1966, for instance, 8 had committed another crime and were running from law enforcement, 10 had traveled to the forbidden border zone out of "curiosity," 21 were found to have got lost and ended up there by accident, and 75 were considered "mentally incompetent" by reason of mental illness or intoxication.[69] Even as the KGB eagerly deployed psychological tactics to entice defectors to return from abroad, prosecutors struggled to comprehend the mentalities of the people they found in the USSR's own border regions, many of them out-of-place young men from working-class backgrounds. In some cases, evidence of mental illness led to a shorter sentence or to confinement in a mental institution rather than a labor camp or prison cell.

Faced with the sometimes inscrutable motivations of those who fled, Soviet officials placed a stronger emphasis on the refusal to return to determine whether the illegal crossing of state borders could be considered politically motivated treason. By the 1970s, a KGB study commissioned after a string of cases initiated by the secret police had been dismissed or downgraded by the Soviet Procuracy observed that, while defection could technically be classified as treason if it harmed state interests, establishing a defector's true motives was far more difficult.[70] The issue came down to evidence. Even in cases where there was a thorough investigation, it was nearly impossible to document a defector's state of mind. While KGB investigations into defection cases routinely ran hundreds of pages in length, it was easier to wait until defectors issued a refusal to return to judge their actions. Since it was standard US practice to allow a "confrontation" between a defector and a representative from the Soviet government, this venue became a critical setting where defectors could make a conscious choice to affirm or disavow their Soviet citizenship, after having been made aware of the consequences by a Soviet representative. In this sense, the final ideological boundary for Soviet migrants lay far beyond the borders of the USSR.

Although it was eagerly sought by Soviet authorities, return was not without its complications. Even if they were cleared of treason, returnees often faced lesser penalties for the crime of illegally crossing Soviet borders. They were barred from living in Soviet border zones and within 100 kilometers of major Soviet cities, which meant that they sometimes had to find a new place to live apart from family members. Even if they were not classified as traitors, they saw their professional opportunities narrow, meaning that they could rarely return to their old jobs. Those who knew them before their defection often kept their distance to avoid the appearance of guilt by association.

Given the difficulty of prosecuting those who left and handling those who returned, Soviet officials concluded that the best course of action was to prevent defection before it happened. Beginning in the late 1950s, Western Border District officials turned to "prophylactic" measures. KGB officers posted to the border employed agents to identify people who considered fleeing or even expressed dissatisfaction with Soviet life. The secret police then approached these individuals and held stern "conversations" with them to encourage them to change their ways. Such methods were less harsh than Stalinist secret police practices, but these "conversations" often involved tacit threats and intimidation tactics.[71]

In its "prophylactic" approach to border enforcement, the KGB cast a wide net, employing agents and other "trustworthy persons" (informants) to gather information on anyone who harbored the "intention to illegally depart abroad." It mattered little whether such intentions were expressed in public, in personal conversations, or in moments of frustration or intoxication. Since the act of treason had not yet been committed, officials could claim a broader mandate to intervene and prevent ideologically dangerous behavior. In August 1966, for example, an inhabitant of a town along the border with Romania expressed his desire to flee—this overheard at the local dining hall by a "trustworthy person." Although the suspect was drunk at the time, the Intelligence Department of the Western Border District still called him in for questioning. They concluded that the underlying causes of his desire to leave were his "political immaturity" and his lack of employment. The latter, it turned out, stemmed from alcohol abuse—he had previously been banned from fishing in the River Dunai for drunkenness after haphazardly entering the boundary waters of Romania in search of his catch. In their annual report, intelligence officials noted that they had conducted several "educational" meetings with the suspect to encourage him to change his ways and that the man was once again employed, though still under the surveillance of the local branch of the KGB.[72]

Other intelligence agents affiliated with the Western Border District patrolled the busy port of Odesa, investigating sailors, dock workers, and even those more tangentially connected with maritime commerce. Prophylactic policing was seen as particularly useful for defending the boundaries between local residents and foreign sailors. In 1969, an undercover agent, codenamed "Birch Tree," reported that a nineteen-year-old woman who worked as a secretary in the port was known to have "liaisons" with visiting Austrian sailors. According to "Birch Tree," some simply gave her presents, while others reportedly engaged her in "intimate relationships." These sexual transgressions were inextricable from ideological transgressions, since the young woman praised living standards in Austria and spoke of her desire to live there. She was flagged by intelligence officials in Odesa for further investigation.[73]

Despite countless reports detailing the KGB's "accomplishments," it is difficult to tell how effective prophylactic policing was in changing behavior. One person called in for a "conversation" in 1966 was a seventeen-year-old boy who had dropped out of school and dreamed of escaping across the River Dunai into Romania, and then on to West Germany. After a meeting with intelligence officers, he disavowed his intention to flee abroad, but three days later robbed his town's dining hall and ended up with a sentence of two years in a labor camp, unreformed by the KGB's intervention.[74] In other cases prophylactic measures were counterproductive. After all, Mkheidze's resolve to flee the Soviet Union had only been strengthened after the KGB called him in to question him about his contacts with foreigners. Following the "conversation," he had been dismissed from his job at the Georgian electric company and assumed—correctly—that his chances at a successful career within the USSR had evaporated. He decided it was better to risk everything to seek a new life elsewhere.[75]

WHO GUARDS THE GUARDIANS OF THE BORDER?

Charged with defending a dynamic border, the Soviet Border Troops placed an ever-greater emphasis on recruitment and self-policing. On the one hand, there was a perceived need to attract more intellectually engaged and culturally sophisticated border officials to respond to new types of external threats seeping into the Soviet Union from the West. On the other hand, the sense of mounting ideological temptation along the western border led to calls for greater discipline among rank-and-file border troops and closer scrutiny of their behavior. The guardians of the Soviet border themselves needed to be better guarded.

The recruitment drive was linked to a larger public relations campaign inside the Soviet Union. Chosen to lead the KGB in 1967, Yuri Andropov turned to film and television to transform the secret police's image from an agency associated with political repression to one characterized by brainy undercover operatives, daring exploits, and foreign escapades. The most famous example of his effort was the massively popular 1973 Soviet television series *Seventeen Moments in Spring*, which centered on a Soviet spy operating undercover in Nazi Germany. It was overseen by the KGB, which assigned consultants to advise during the production process.[76] One of the first productions Andropov's KGB supervised, however, was the 1968 film *The Secret Agent's Blunder*, which targeted a younger audience and celebrated the ideal qualities of a Soviet citizen tasked with defending the border.[77] Since the 1930s, border troops had been celebrated in Soviet art, film, and fiction for their stoic resolve and unflinching bravery in the face of foreign threats.[78] Although the film's young and charismatic hero, Pavel Sinitsyn, was a KGB officer, rather than a rank-and-file border guard, his portrayal updated these virtues for a more globalized age. Sinitsyn was exuberantly masculine but studiously chaste, savvy to contemporary artistic currents but ideologically steadfast. In the film, Sinitsyn stages a false defection to infiltrate an entrenched Western spy network originally established by the Nazis, fleeing across the Soviet border from the shores of a seaside resort. Taken into custody by West German intelligence agents, he is exposed to abstract art, risqué shows on television, an attractive maid who attends to him, and prolonged questioning in a padded cell, where bright lights prevent him from sleeping until his captors are assured that he is not a covert agent. Gaining the trust of the spy network's supervisors, he is secreted by them back across the Soviet border on a ship. Upon his return to the USSR, he successfully apprehends a Russian emigre who had been planted by Nazi intelligence officers to subvert the Soviet Union. Like many other KGB-supervised productions of the era, the episode was supposedly based on "factual" events.[79]

Andropov was aware that he was dealing with a new, postwar generation of border troops. If trained and supervised properly, it was thought, young recruits could be more adept at detecting and responding to new expressions of Western culture, new patterns of contraband trade, and new manifestations of disenchantment among Soviet youth. Who better to prevent the defection of people like Mkheidze and Orekhov, led astray by exposure to Western music, fashion, and foreigners, than their generational peers? The KGB's leadership believed that the right recruits, refined by training, could become reliable "Chekists." At same time, they expanded their efforts to monitor those within their own ranks as they sought to combat subtler forms of foreign influence.

Along the western border, it was never expected that young, inexperienced, and often undereducated conscripts would be responsible for the most sensitive border defenses. That task rested with the Special Department of the KGB attached to the Western Border District, responsible for monitoring military and radar installations along the Black Sea and for carrying out counterintelligence operations among border troops to prevent them from defecting or being recruited by Western intelligence. Those in the Special Department were supposed to have a high degree of ideological purity and educational training. According to a 1972 questionnaire used by the Special Department, its officers were supposed to display "industriousness, honesty, the ability to keep state and professional secrets, modesty, courage, decisiveness, resourcefulness, moral steadfastness, integrity, the capacity to analyze and generalize, and the ability to readily find one's bearings in difficult situations." The KGB sought individuals who were physically fit, but also intellectually engaged in science, art, and culture. Applicants were asked to list and discuss their favorite writers, poets, artists, and films. They were evaluated for their "ideological-political preparation" as well as their grooming habits and hobbies.[80]

Just like the hero of *The Secret Agent's Blunder*, members of the Special Department were expected to employ their skills to guard the border against cunning foreign intelligence operations. In the KGB's view, one of the gravest risks they faced was the potential for defections from the ranks of the border troops. The departure of border troops to the West critically undermined the state's defenses and was also a major political embarrassment. American intelligence officials eagerly questioned Soviet border troops who fled their posts to Turkey and Iran and touted their defection as a sign that those charged with defending the Soviet state were abandoning it. In 1955, for example, the State Department's Peripheral Reporting Unit in Frankfurt composed a detailed report based on the interrogation of a twenty-year-old who fled from Soviet Azerbaijan into Iran. He was questioned at length about security measures along the border and asked to describe patrol methods and the location and effectiveness of trip wires. He also shared details about the monotonous conditions faced by those posted to the border: guards poached grazing cattle to "supplement their otherwise dull diet," smoked cigarettes while they stood guard at night despite regulations prohibiting them from doing so, and shared complaints about their boredom in a rural and remote region of Azerbaijan. Most conscripts, according to the defector, had been drafted from the army, where they were fulfilling their mandatory military service; few were interested in re-enlisting. He had managed to defect after a night of drinking brandy with his fellow guard. After his companion passed out, he waded across the river into Iran.[81] His account signaled to the Soviet Union's opponent that the Iron Curtain was not as carefully guarded as commonly thought.

Instances of defection by border troops were considered so serious that they were reported up the chain of the KGB to the Central Committee of the Communist Party in Moscow.[82] Concerned that low morale in the ranks could lead to flight, members of the Special Department applied the methods of prophylactic policing to the border troops themselves. Some conscripts, like Sergei Savchenko, a nineteen-year-old who served with the Black Sea–based border troops in Ukraine, appeared close to defecting when the KGB stepped in. In 1977, Savchenko was questioned after agents reported that he harbored plans to swim abroad using underwater breathing equipment. He was reassigned to a construction unit of the border troops near Sverdlovsk, far from the border, rather than being sent to prison. In response, he wrote, "I am grateful to the organs of the KGB that they caught me before I committed the gravest of crimes—treason—stopping me before I took the fateful step down this criminal path." Such a statement was clearly made under pressure and probably necessary for avoiding a criminal sentence. Nonetheless, KGB officials described it as a sincere statement of political reeducation, noting in their Moscow-bound report that the impressionable young man had fallen "under the influence of foreign anti-Soviet radio programs" but had been saved by the officials' intervention.[83]

In other instances warranting the KGB's intervention, border troops had not yet made plans to flee but were seen as compromised by pernicious foreign-inspired trends. Prophylactic "conversations" were held when members of the border troops displayed a fondness for "Western music," spoke of wanting to "see the world" beyond Soviet borders, or evinced nationalist sentiments.[84] Agents kept close tabs on individuals like twenty-two-year-old Vladimir Shevchenko, a guard posted on the border between Soviet Armenia and Turkey, who reportedly stated that he would abscond to Turkey if not for concerns about the fate of his parents if he left. In the eyes of the KGB, it was not enough that the fear of punishment kept him in place. Concerned about his ideological steadfastness, officials monitored the music he listened to and the books he read.[85]

A persistent challenge identified by the KGB was the sense of inertia among troops posted to the border, where, except for the occasional apprehension of unauthorized migrants, most days were uneventful. The border troop journal reminded its readers that the "defense of the border is an art form"; the term "formalism" was used to describe the tendency of border guards to simply go through the motions in a job that largely consisted of watching and waiting.[86] The KGB did not limit itself to rhetorical calls for vigilance. The secret police also organized surprise drills in which "educational 'border violators'" tested border defenses. Its undercover officers appeared at checkpoints with forged documents to see if guards would notice, asked about border defenses in sensitive areas to see if local inhabitants would report them, and wandered along rail lines to see if they would be apprehended.[87] Such exercises were designed to generate a greater sense of vigilance, since border troops and local *druzhiny* who failed them were held accountable.

Over the course of the 1970s, concern also mounted about "nationalist and other anti-Soviet manifestations" among the border troops.[88] In the interest of maintaining the state's multiethnic balance, members of the Special Department sometimes scrutinized manifestations of Russian chauvinism against the local population. But the fact that the leadership of the border troops in Georgia, Armenia, and Azerbaijan—the republics that directly bordered Turkey and Iran—remained overwhelmingly Slavic betrayed the imperial dynamics of the border regime and revealed deep-rooted assumptions about who could be trusted to oversee it.[89] By contrast, Ukrainians—at least those with no family involvement in World War II–era nationalist movements and no relatives in the diaspora—appear to have been seen as more loyal. The Western Border District's headquarters remained in Kyiv, and of the four generals appointed to head the border troops from the death of Stalin until the collapse of the Soviet Union, two were Ukrainian.[90] Despite the myriad forms of surveillance and control deployed along the border, the growth of a broad-based Ukrainian nationalist movement inside the Soviet Union would largely take the KGB by surprise.[91]

BEYOND TERRITORIAL BORDERS

In the Soviet Union's final years, the reports of the Special Department of the Western Border District struck an increasingly alarmist tone. A report written in 1987, just as Soviet leader Mikhail Gorbachev's policies were beginning to allow for new forms of international engagement, chronicled a territorial border regime straining against globalization's rising flows. Trade in Western contraband goods in the Black Sea region was rapidly expanding, and more border guards were taking part in it. In a telling sign of the deluge of ideologically inimical Western media, one guard was even caught with videocassettes of two of the decade's leading anti-communist blockbusters, *Rambo* and *Red Dawn*.[92] Worries were also growing about the commitment of the Soviet Union's Polish and Czechoslovak "friends" to defend the borders of the socialist bloc. In eastern Poland, along the border with the Soviet Union, foreigners from capitalist countries traveled with fewer restrictions, photographing sensitive military installations and distributing "harmful" nationalist literature. In Czechoslovakia, the circulation of nationalist literature was blamed on Western intelligence, though it was also hinted that the Czechoslovak border guards were insufficiently vigilant.[93] Aside from a few obligatory references to "perestroika," KGB reports were reluctant to acknowledge that times were changing. Until the end of the Soviet period, these reports continued to identify the United States as the USSR's "main opponent" and equated flight abroad with treason.[94]

Hoping to appeal to fresh recruits and conscripts, the journal *Pogranichnik* went further in embracing the openness of the Gorbachev era, although its underlying messaging remained unchanged. In 1988, the journal was reformatted as a popular magazine, with colorful cover images. It shifted further away from traditional portrayals of border guards to showcase the service as a place where youth culture could flourish. Profiles were run on the handful of female border troops in the service; articles featured favorable discussions of Soviet rock bands like Kino; and one of the covers showed a young coastal border guard looking tenderly at a cat crawling through a porthole, a far cry from the traditional depiction of a stolid border guard in uniform with a rifle in hand and a dog at his side.[95] Yet inside each issue, most of the content stayed the same: strong border defenses were still seen as necessary to prevent foreign infiltration, nationalist sentiment within the USSR was blamed on American propaganda, and the notion that individual Soviet republics could establish their own border policies was openly ridiculed.[96]

In hindsight, the collapse of the Soviet territorial border regime, along with the demise of the broader boundaries surrounding the socialist bloc, might seem inevitable. In East Central Europe, the USSR's partners fell away one by one. Romania had been unreliable since the mid-1960s, Czechoslovakia viewed warily since 1968, and Poland considered problematic since the rise of the Solidarity labor movement in 1980. In 1989, popular protests toppled socialist governments throughout the region and led to the rapid erosion of exit controls, with the mass emigration of East Germans first through Hungary and then over the Berlin Wall, which was torn down by crowds. Within the Soviet Union, the Baltic states drifted toward independence, with Estonia declaring itself a sovereign state as early as 1988. In the same year, violence broke out in the Caucasus over the nature of internal borders surrounding autonomous regions such as Nagorno-Karabakh. Soon after, the border between Soviet Azerbaijan and Iran was overtaken by Soviet Azeris calling for unification with their co-ethnics in neighboring Iran.[97]

It is tempting to see these events collectively as the outcome of a doomed effort to shore up the Soviet border against the forces of globalization. Such a task proved challenging even when border measures were at their most repressive and new technologies traversing geographical boundaries, such as satellite television, had not yet been introduced.[98] The effort had always required the compliance of the Soviet Union's neighbors, who were to serve as a buffer against potential military incursion, a filter for more subtle forms of Western infiltration, and a net to catch Soviet citizens who took flight. Coordinating border policies among fifteen Soviet republics and the eight member countries of the Warsaw Pact was a difficult balancing act. The system required centrally located levers of coercion and a system of internal surveillance patrolled by Moscow; without them, it quickly fell apart.

Yet this line of thinking overlooks the fact that the border system established under the direction of Soviet authorities successfully managed the mobility of hundreds of millions of people for decades. Once the postwar border regime was established, only a handful of Soviet citizens managed to escape abroad each year, a far cry from the larger number of people who spilled across borders in the less regulated period before the Second World War and a stark contrast to the wartime chaos of mass flight and displacement. Along the western edge of the Soviet Union, the border regime was internalized by populations incorporated into the Soviet Union after the war and extended along the territorial waters of the Baltic and Black Seas even as ports opened to international trade.[99] The border endured despite the difficulty of finding qualified troops to guard it. Through new border technologies, prophylactic policing, romanticized media portrayals, positive incentives for those who followed approved pathways for internal mobility, and the demonstrative prosecution of violators who strayed from these pathways, the border kept most people in.[100]

Even as a distinct border regime was maintained around the USSR, to compete in the Cold War the Soviet Union needed to dispatch more of its citizens across the world as diplomats, sailors, performers, and tourists representing the interests and achievements of the socialist superpower. Accordingly, there was another, equally vital dimension to the global competition for Soviet migrants that played out simultaneously but extended far beyond the Soviet Union's territorial borders. This contest was waged around the boundaries of Soviet embassies and consulates, in the international waters through which Soviet ships passed, and on-board civilian airplanes that surmounted border walls with ease. Although it focused on a comparatively smaller group of Soviet citizens, it kept the issue of defection at the fore and allowed the Soviet state to advance claims on mobility from thousands of miles away. In the struggle between the superpowers over Soviet defectors, extraterritorial spaces, the high seas, and the skies formed a second set of Cold War fronts. In a surprising turn, they also became zones of superpower collusion in defiance of the growing global trend toward decolonization. While the Soviet Union and the United States remained ideologically opposed to each other, they found a common interest in setting the rules governing movement for the rest of the world, narrowing the avenues open to refuge seekers everywhere.

PART II

Governing Global Mobility

4

Soviets Abroad

For one brief moment on an August afternoon in 1948, a Soviet school-teacher, falling from the third floor of the Soviet consulate, found herself in midair, between the reach of the socialist superpower and the jurisdiction of the New York City Police Department. In the two years leading up to the incident, Oksana Kasenkina had spent most of her time inside the compounds that the Soviet Union maintained on Manhattan's Upper East Side: the mansion that served as its consulate, where she made her dramatic exit, and the Russian-language school several blocks to the north, where she educated the children of Soviet diplomats. She was one of around 2,000 Soviet citizens who held diplomatic visas and lived in the United States but whose lives were largely limited to buildings that felt like outposts of the homeland, from their staid Stalinist décor to the smells of cabbage soup in their kitchens. In the summer of 1948, the sense of isolation among this group of Soviets abroad grew with the start of the Berlin Blockade and the hardening of Cold War borders in Europe.

A tangle of telephone wires below broke Kasenkina's fall and probably saved her life. With a crowd of journalists, activists, and pedestrians looking on, a team of New York police officers breached the Soviet compound, engaging in a "brief tussle" with consular staff before loading her onto an ambulance bound for Roosevelt Hospital. Soon after, she gave a filmed interview from her hospital bed proclaiming that she had been held "prisoner" inside the consulate. Soviet consular officers, barred from her hospital room, complained that they were being denied access to a "sick Soviet citizen." The Soviet ambassador, Aleksandr Paniushkin, delivered a furious note to the US State Department claiming that the NYPD had "violated the extraterritoriality" of the Soviet consulate.[1]

Kasenkina's dramatic jump was proclaimed a "leap to freedom" in the American press. Yet this narrative belied a much more ambivalent story. Even setting aside the allegation, made by Soviet consul Iakov Lomakin, that Kasenkina was mentally unwell and her leap had been a suicide attempt, the fact remained that she had already fled the consulate once before and publicly returned of her own free will. Less than two weeks earlier, with the Soviet school set to close and a ticket home booked for her on the Soviet ship *Pobeda*, she had sought refuge at the Tolstoy Foundation's Reed Farm outside the city. Yet she immediately felt uncomfortable at Reed Farm, resenting the chores she was given in the farm's kitchen and surrounded, she later alleged, by White Russian monarchists who regarded her as an "object of instant curiosity."[2] She posted a frantic letter to Consul Lomakin asking to be picked up, and, according to the account provided by Alexandra Tolstoy, willingly entered the black car dispatched by the consulate, which "started with a roar and left the premises at a terrible speed."[3] Shortly after, she appeared alongside Lomakin at a press conference, claiming she had been "rescued" from an attempted kidnapping by reactionary emigres. Anti-Soviet activists argued otherwise. They surrounded the consulate and obtained a writ demanding that Kasenkina appear in a New York courtroom on the grounds that she was being held against her will. The day she was due to appear in court she instead leaped from the building's window.

Although Kasenkina claimed that her decision to jump had been inspired by the Hollywood movie *The Iron Curtain*, she was far from the model defector.[4] Unlike Igor Gouzenko, the cipher clerk with access to secret documents heroized in the movie, Kasenkina had no intelligence value and a confusing backstory. Her appearance was harshly judged, especially her heavy use of makeup, and she was soon outshined in the press by the so-called Swedish Kasenkina, a Soviet defector in Stockholm several decades younger and a "music prodigy" to boot.[5] While diplomats, like defectors, commanded the public's attention because they were believed to represent their home country's aspirations, Kasenkina was a bit player in Soviet diplomatic circles and it was unclear what she stood for. The most compelling thing about her was her desperate leap. Given the attention the case generated, President Truman, in the midst of a tough electoral campaign, conceded that she deserved asylum following an initially tentative response by the State Department.[6] In a dramatic escalation that played to an American audience but caught Soviet officials off guard, the president expelled Consul Lomakin for his role in the drama, setting in motion the

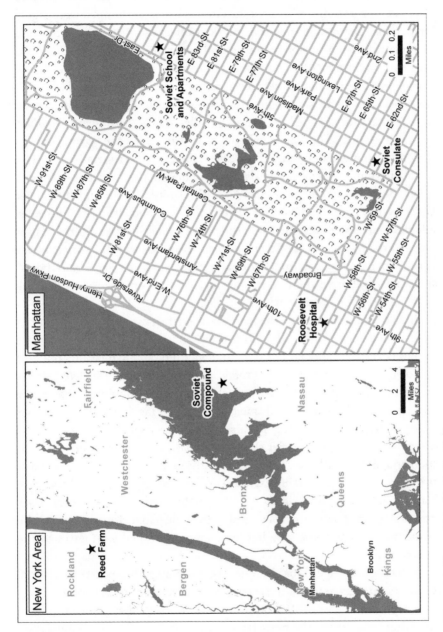

Figure 4.1 Oksana Kasenkina's New York

closure of Soviet consulates in the United States and US consulates in the Soviet Union for the next twenty-four years.[7]

Just as Kasenkina was a more ambivalent figure than her "leap to freedom" suggested, the borders she crossed when she jumped were highly ambiguous. The boundaries that marked off embassies, consulates, and diplomatic missions rested on norms and assumptions rather than codified international law. By 1948, Ambassador Paniushkin's open appeal to the notion of "extraterritoriality" seemed anachronistic. The idea that diplomatic residences were the sovereign jurisdiction of a foreign state transposed onto the territory of the host state had fallen out of favor decades earlier, seen as a vestige of European colonial expansion. Even the Soviet guide to diplomatic immunity published in 1949 called extraterritoriality merely a "symbol," and a "harmful and dangerous" one at that, since it infringed upon the rights of the host state.[8] Yet the United States and the Soviet Union were in a competition for global influence, and although both sides adopted anti-imperialist rhetoric, their actions recalled the efforts of past empires to lay claim to far-flung outposts across the world. Both countries carved out exceptions in international law and employed "legal black holes" in ways that allowed them to operate as sprawling empires while denying that they were being imperialist.[9]

The control of mobility through extraterritorial means was practiced by both states. A 1965 textbook for the KGB's Higher School argued that extraterritoriality applied not only to Soviet diplomatic missions but also to Soviet citizens journeying abroad.[10] The socialist state insisted, in its guidelines for state-sanctioned travel to capitalist countries, that every "Soviet citizen located abroad must be an active facilitator of the foreign policy of the Soviet Union."[11] In this sense, any Soviet abroad was seen as a representative of the Soviet state and carried the state's interests—and its boundaries—with them. American officials were less inclined to make pronouncements supporting extraterritoriality as a principle, but they still claimed extraterritorial rights for their global network of military bases and diplomatic posts, and they used both to dispatch citizens around the world and to determine whether local migrants would gain entry to the United States.

Defection brought the borders surrounding these extraterritorial outposts into sharp focus. If Soviet embassies sometimes served as points of escape, embassies of Western countries functioned as potential places of asylum. In perhaps the most famous case, the dissident Cardinal Jozsef Mindszenty of Hungary sought sanctuary in the US embassy in Budapest following the Soviet invasion in 1956 and remained there for fifteen years.[12] There were many others: "walk-ins" who showed up unannounced at Western diplomatic missions behind the Iron Curtain, and political and artistic figures from the socialist world who sought refuge in Western embassies while on state-authorized trips and tours abroad.

While Kasenkina's story has been recounted as a formative episode in American media portrayals of Soviet defectors, it also illustrates how the Soviet Union advanced its extraterritorial claims even as increasing numbers of Soviet citizens traveled abroad.[13] The resulting debates concerning embassy borders, diplomatic immunity, and diplomatic asylum reveal the unexpected emergence of a shared set of interests—and a level of tacit collusion—between the Soviet Union and United States. Ultimately these common grounds shored up diplomatic law against the coming wave of decolonization, the subsequent proliferation of embassies and consulates, and the mounting demands of post-colonial migrants. Just as Kasenkina's multiple flights to and from the consulate can be read as an effort to find a place for herself before she was finally hemmed into a Cold War narrative, decolonization involved the search for new forms of political expression but in the end saw post-colonial populations bound to a state system presided over by the superpowers.

THE END OF EUROPEAN EMPIRES AND THE PERSISTENCE OF EXTRATERRITORIAL PRIVILEGES

Kasenkina made her "leap to freedom" at a time when debates about international representation and sovereignty were gathering force across the globe. While most American and European observers assumed that post-colonial nations would eventually become nation-states organized according to Western models, many post-colonial leaders imagined a future in which their countries were not necessarily confined by national borders.[14] Some sought to articulate new forms of transnational solidarity that united post-colonial populations in regional and cross-regional groupings. These efforts were in evidence at the 1955 conference of African and Asian states held in Bandung, Indonesia, where attendees laid the groundwork for a non-aligned bloc of nations that would serve as an alternative to NATO and the soon-to-be-established Warsaw Pact. According to a statement adopted at the conference, the military alliances on either side of the Cold War divide served the "interests of the big powers" and were essentially new manifestations of imperialism.[15]

Yet post-colonial countries found it difficult to escape the framework of the Cold War and an international system that accorded legitimacy to nations as individual member states of the United Nations. In theory all nation-states were equal within the international organization, but its Security Council accorded a preponderance of power to two waning empires, Britain and France, and the two postwar superpowers, the United States and the Soviet Union. The council's sole Asian seat, belonging to China, was held by nationalists in Taiwan rather than communists on the mainland.[16] The structural logic of the UN was consistent with the notion that post-colonial nations would be ushered into the international community as discrete nation-states under the guidance of established powers.[17]

Post-colonial migrants, too, sought to build lives across national borders. The French Union, established in 1946, recast France's empire as a federation. Although it was guided by leaders in Paris, many Africans took advantage of the possibility of free movement between Africa and France as citizens of a common union.[18] Similarly, in 1949, the British Commonwealth of Nations became simply the "Commonwealth of Nations," in which all states, though united by the legacy of British imperialism, were supposed to be "free and equal."[19] For a time, migrants from Commonwealth nations could move with relative ease to Britain, though concerns about the "influx . . . of coloured workers from other Commonwealth countries" drew the concern of officials in London by 1955.[20] It was not long before racially defined limits on international migration were proposed to restrict post-colonial mobility.

International law, long intertwined with the efforts of European empires to govern the world, was also entering a new era. Since the nineteenth century, international law had been dreamed of as a tool for "civilizing" nations and permanently eradicating armed conflict. In the aftermath of the Second World War and in the face of the Cold War, its proponents scaled back their aspirations, believing international law incapable of reshaping the balance of geopolitical power and arguing instead for more pragmatic applications that served the interests of established states.[21] The United States and the Soviet Union both took up the mantle of international law, but on their own terms: the Soviet Union used the International Military Tribune at Nuremberg to punish Nazi leaders while avoiding retribution for its own involvement in the Katyn Massacre; the United States supported an international refugee regime that aligned with its defector and escapee programs without substantially altering its own immigration system.[22] One of the most important figures when it came to America's engagement with international law in this period was Hans Morgenthau, a German Jewish emigre who became the primary proponent of foreign policy "realism" and influenced US officials responsible for dealing with the Soviet Union, including George Kennan. Writing in 1948, Morgenthau made the case for a more limited international legal regime that dealt primarily with issues such as "the limits of territorial jurisdiction, the rights of vessels in foreign waters, and the status of diplomatic representatives."[23] Scholars have argued that Morgenthau and other legal experts of the postwar era relegated international law to insignificant matters "outside the key issue of foreign policy."[24]

In fact, the resolution of legal questions concerning borders on land, at sea, and around embassies was crucial to shaping the postwar global order and had profound consequences for migrants. While the Soviet Union and the United States remained locked in conflict over a host of issues, they found common cause in enclosing the global commons around embassies, at sea, in the air, and even in outer space, creating a shared framework that regulated other states even as it carved out exceptions for themselves.[25] Among the efforts that brought the two Cold War opponents together, the Vienna Convention on Diplomatic Relations, agreed to in 1961, has been described as "the most successful product . . . of the United Nations' 'legislative process'" and a "cornerstone of the modern international legal order."[26] The rules it established affirmed the inviolability of embassies and upheld immunity for diplomats but left diplomatic asylum the unregulated prerogative of states strong enough to enforce it, thus enshrining a crucial instance of superpower collusion.

Diplomatic asylum, like diplomatic immunity, rested on the presumption of extraterritoriality: by entering an embassy compound, one essentially claimed sanctuary in a foreign country without traveling abroad.[27] Its practice emerged in early modern Europe, but over time, criticism mounted over abuses of extraterritoriality by powerful embassies that flouted local laws; claiming *franchise du quartier*, diplomatic missions sheltered criminals and dodged taxes. Attacks on extraterritoriality grew in late nineteenth-century Europe as the notion gained traction that state sovereignty needed to be set within clearly defined limits.[28] Yet around the same time, extraterritoriality was extended by European powers in their imperial dealings on the other side of the world. In China and Japan, commercial treaties granted Europeans almost complete immunity from local laws, protected Christian missionaries, and regulated the operation of European-controlled ports and railroads.[29] While reciprocity was expected among European states, relations with states in Asia played out unequally. Even as British merchants in China operated with impunity, the Chinese legation in London was charged with the "abuse of diplomatic privilege" in 1896 for apprehending the Chinese revolutionary Sun Yat Sen.[30] The embassies of powerful states could exercise wide authority within and even beyond their walls; the diplomatic missions of less powerful states were far more restricted.

The decline of European empires raised the question of whether the ability to offer migrants refuge in a foreign embassy was a generalizable right enjoyed by all states or a privilege claimed by a dominant few. Latin American countries had long been at the vanguard of a more universal approach. In 1889, Peru joined Argentina, Bolivia, Brazil, Chile, Paraguay, and Uruguay in recognizing the right of diplomats to grant asylum to political dissidents in a treaty signed at Montevideo and bolstered in the 1920s and 1930s. Although the codification of diplomatic asylum was limited to Latin America, it took on global dimensions during the Spanish Civil War, when thousands sought asylum in the diplomatic missions run by Latin American countries in Madrid.[31] The notion of formalizing the practice of diplomatic asylum among all states was discussed but not resolved at the League of Nations in 1936 and 1937.[32]

These debates were rekindled after World War II, as the right to seek asylum was affirmed in the 1948 UN Declaration of Human Rights and refugee protections were detailed in the 1951 Geneva Convention. For many asylum seekers, entering a foreign embassy was the easiest means of seeking refuge, since it did not require international travel or a dangerous journey through a remote border region. In discussions on the UN Declaration of Human Rights, Bolivia and Uruguay both sought to add amendments establishing the right of asylum in embassies, but they were opposed by a majority of countries, including the Soviet Union, whose representative commented that it might "provide a pretext for misuse of the principle of extraterritoriality."[33] The 1951 Refugee Convention was similarly silent about diplomatic asylum, despite a recent decision by the International Court of Justice in 1950 concerning Victor Raúl Haya de la Torre, a Peruvian political figure who was granted asylum in the Colombian Embassy in Lima after his opponents seized power. While the court found no evidence supporting Colombia's argument that the principle of diplomatic asylum could be "accepted as law," it refrained from explicitly prohibiting the practice, noting that its "legal basis" had to be determined "in each particular case."[34]

Those responsible for drafting the 1951 Refugee Convention chose to refrain from resolving the ambiguity that surrounded the Haya de la Torre decision. This legal uncertainty left a narrow opening for those hoping to gain asylum in a diplomatic mission. It also made for compelling journalism, as each asylum seeker's fate hung in the balance, subject to the whims of a particular set of states and their diplomats. The explosive growth of new embassies and consulates operated by post-colonial states in Asia, Africa, and the Middle East further complicated debates about diplomatic borders. Even as the superpowers lent rhetorical support to the aspirations of post-colonial nations, they took up some of the same tools their imperial predecessors had used to claim extraterritorial authority. US diplomatic missions worked with European allies to construct an international asylum system built to advance US goals by funneling certain classes of migrants to the West, although it remained unclear whether American embassies might grant asylum to defectors and escapees, let alone shelter post-colonial populations. Meanwhile, Soviet embassies staked out claims to extraterritorial privileges in the post-colonial world while using diplomatic missions to shield Soviet citizens abroad from American advances.

SOVIET "COLONIES" AND THE REGULATION
OF CITIZENS ABROAD

Lynchpins of a global mobility regime based on restraining exit, Soviet embassies differed from their American counterparts in some important ways. The American system relied on its embassies and consulates to limit entry to the United States by "remote control," using them to screen potential immigrants long before they reached American shores. The regime maintained by the Soviet Union tethered traveling citizens to Soviet diplomatic missions, which directed and monitored their movements. Soviet embassies were less likely to function as places of sanctuary since those hoping to reach the USSR could usually do so legally, whether by traveling there directly or by going through a neutral country such as Finland. As a result, it was rare for a Western person to "defect" to the Soviet Union via one of its embassies, though in a few cases foreign communist party members fleeing political persecution sought refuge there.[35] Generally, US embassies functioned as a gateway for potential arrivals, while Soviet embassies were entrusted with guarding those who had departed Soviet borders and reclaiming them if necessary.

As Cold War competition shifted to the sphere of culture, both superpowers treated athletes, musicians, dancers, and tourists as instruments of foreign policy; Soviet authorities went further by insisting that all travelers remained subject to the state's extraterritorial claims.[36] Soviet travelers were screened before they were permitted to leave, accompanied by official minders, and urged to rely on Soviet diplomatic missions for a host of situations. For example, if they had any unplanned contact with foreigners, they were to contact an embassy, and they were supposed to use diplomatic channels if they wanted to send a postcard to family members back home. The screening process could be a harrowing and unpredictable experience, as individual ministries lobbied to send delegations abroad in pursuit of trade deals and scientific exchanges, while security officials insisted on scrutinizing each traveler. In approving foreign travel, authorities balanced the trip's potential to advance foreign policy goals against the risk that Soviet citizens might not return. In the words of the KGB training manual outlining the rights and responsibilities of Soviets abroad, dispatching delegations beyond Soviet borders was vital for the "expansion of the economic, scientific, and cultural ties of the USSR with other governments," yet Soviet travelers would be exposed to the "intelligence organs of imperialist governments" and the "anti-Soviet organizations" that cooperated with them, both of which were allegedly bent on inciting Soviet citizens to defect.[37] The Soviet state did all it could to ensure that a journey abroad did not turn into a permanent emigration.

The Stalinist era process for approving Soviet citizens for travel evolved in response to the demands of the Cold War. The system had first taken shape in 1937, coinciding with the Great Terror that targeted perceived internal enemies and their alleged foreign backers, another way of fortifying the USSR's ideological borders.[38] For a state that championed centralization, a unified screening system was also seen as a way of standardizing a patchwork set of preexisting procedures. Nikolai Ezhov, head of the NKVD, took the lead in establishing guidelines regulating Soviet citizens abroad. With war on the horizon, the 1937 rules called for militaristic levels of discipline among Soviet travelers. In the face of "capitalist encirclement," they were prohibited from having "friendly conversations about political or everyday topics" with foreigners and even forbidden from carrying Soviet newspapers with them, as if periodicals with a circulation in the millions were classified state documents.[39]

With the start of the Cold War, these prohibitions were leavened with positive exhortations. There was a dawning sense that insisting on the complete isolation of Soviet citizens abroad was neither feasible nor desirable. As early as 1947, an update encouraged travelers to learn from foreign production techniques and technology.[40] A broader post-Stalinist revision came in 1955, though the Soviet turn to greater openness was tempered by fears that it would be exploited by the United States.[41] Originally launched in 1951, the CIA's Operation REDCAP systematically targeted Soviet embassies, military bases, and official delegations and sought to encourage defections. CIA officers were advised to take advantage of the same shortcomings Soviet officials screened for in selecting citizens for foreign travel. They were instructed to study Soviets abroad carefully to learn their "characteristics, habits, weaknesses (whether sex or alcohol), places of residence, restaurants they frequent, shops they patronize," and the "names and addresses of their secretaries and mistresses."[42] The CIA's closed-circulation journal advised officers to exploit the marital problems of Soviet officials overseas and to monitor their "wives' personal chatter" for "flashes of irritation, frustration, and anger, for identifying persons who are disliked and isolated." Soviets "already chafing at the restricted and highly organized Soviet embassy existence" were believed to be ripe for recruitment.[43]

While Soviet counterintelligence may not have known the precise details of REDCAP, the evolution of the Soviet guidelines for those heading abroad—"The Basic Rules of Conduct for Soviet Citizens Traveling to Capitalist and Developing Countries"—reveals that they were familiar with the CIA's methods. The rulebook became more entrenched in response to the activities of US intelligence. Soviet travelers were warned to be on guard against the operations of the "intelligence organs of capitalist countries" bent on compromising Soviet citizens abroad, "even to the point of inciting treason," which included defection. Some rules emphasized the need for internal discipline, noting that capitalist spies sought to exploit any "personal weakness," such as "a propensity to drink alcohol, to have casual relations with women, or to gamble." Both sexual and ideological deviance were seen as closely related: Soviets abroad were prohibited from visiting places of "dubious entertainment" (brothels and strip clubs) and watching "anti-Soviet or pornographic films," just as they were forbidden from mixing with Soviet emigres. While some of these venues were easily avoided, Soviet travelers needed to stay vigilant without coming across as "closed-off or aloof in their relations with the citizens of another country."[44] Every Soviet citizen lucky enough to obtain an international passport had to learn and agree to these guidelines. Although they were officially classified, the guidelines' general thrust was widely known, as was their practical impact; the famous Soviet bard Vladimir Vysotskii lampooned them in his 1973 song, "Instructions Before Traveling Abroad," which poked fun at Soviet citizens' lack of knowledge about foreign life.[45]

While Soviet foreign policy was supposed to advance revolutionary goals, the historic logic of extraterritorial authority coursed through its framework for managing citizens and diplomatic missions abroad. Internal KGB documents referred to diplomatic posts and compounds as "Soviet colonies" and warned that "separation" from them increased the likelihood that Soviets would be recruited by foreign intelligence.[46] Moreover a broad array of Soviet travelers were accorded diplomatic protection, which became a matter of contention in 1949 when a Soviet TASS journalist accused of libel in the United Kingdom claimed immunity from prosecution on the grounds that the press agency was "a department of the Soviet state."[47] For the Soviet Union, protecting its "colonies" became a way of policing its citizens and defending its interests in capitalist host nations. While critics in the West tended to judge this approach as evidence of "totalitarianism," Soviet policies followed imperial precedents for managing the mobility of citizens, albeit with a greater focus on controlling exit and a leading role given to the KGB.

Operating undercover inside Soviet "colonies," the KGB kept tabs on diplomats and reported cases of misbehavior back to Moscow; among traveling groups of athletes and performers, minders connected to the KGB tracked interactions with locals, maintained curfews, and checked hotel rooms; on Soviet ships, members of the vessel's "political department" performed a similar function, while also offering mandatory lectures on ideologically sensitive issues that sailors might encounter on their voyage. The KGB seeded foreign delegations with agents tasked with spying on fellow citizens and foreign targets alike. While overall statistics are hard to come by, a secret report by the Lithuanian branch of the KGB indicated that 102 counterintelligence agents were hidden among the republic's scientific, cultural, and athletic delegations to capitalist and developing countries in 1977 and 1978, and another 159 agents were placed in the ranks of Soviet tourist groups in the same period.[48] Surveillance networks were reinforced by a sense of collective responsibility; if anything went wrong with an individual Soviet traveler, their entire group would come under scrutiny.

Soviet diplomats posted abroad for long periods of time faced even tighter restrictions on their behavior and sometimes felt as if they had never left the Soviet Union. Arriving in Burma's capital in 1957 for the first overseas posting of his career, Aleksandr Kaznacheev, a recent graduate of the Moscow State Institute of International Relations, felt a creeping sense of familiarity as he drove past the Soviet compound's creaky gate and saw clothes hanging haphazardly on lines. Later he would sarcastically observe that "our people had been able to re-create so well the dear, drab untidiness of Soviet life." He felt that he and his colleagues were "captives of the Soviet colony," separated from their surroundings by an "invisible curtain," with nearly "every minute" of their non-working time taken up by meetings, study groups, and official events.[49] His description echoed that of defector Victor Kravchenko, who described the Soviet Embassy in Washington as a place that "looked and even smelled remarkably Soviet," as if it had been "torn loose from the banks of the Moscow River and deposited intact on the shores of the Potomac."[50] Kasenkina similarly described the entire Soviet diplomatic mission in New York—from the consulate's atmosphere of secrecy, to the Russian school's "inevitable portraits of Lenin and Stalin," to the "dachas" maintained by high-ranking officials at the mission's compound at Glen Cove in Long Island—as "Soviet America . . . a hothouse variety of the Soviet Union."[51]

Despite strict guidelines and the KGB's methods of surveillance, there was always a gap between the rules established for Soviet citizens and the way these rules were navigated by people thousands of miles from home. Even in the accounts of Kravchenko, Kasenkina, and Kaznacheev— defectors invested in portraying Soviet diplomatic missions as bastions of totalitarianism—there were numerous instances of Soviet citizens skirting official procedures. Kravchenko noted that embassy officials "were forbidden to visit night clubs, to see 'counter-revolutionary' films or plays," or "to listen to radio commentators considered 'unfriendly' to the Soviet cause." "Being human," he added, they in fact "did many of these things."[52] In her application to work abroad, Kasenkina falsely reported that her husband had died in 1927—a decade before he was arrested during the Great Terror—and officials believed her, a telling example of Soviet bureaucrats not being able to manage the information Soviet intelligence so carefully collected. Despite official prohibitions, Kasenkina went to see markedly anti-Soviet films, including *The Iron Curtain*. She also recalled lots of unofficial shopping and trading. In fact, one of the first things she was told upon her arrival in the United States was how she could sneak more than the allotted six pairs of shoes in her return luggage.[53] In Burma, Kaznacheev described how the wives of Soviet diplomats ran an illicit trading operation through diplomatic channels, investing the pay of their husbands—who were compensated in local currency—in consumer goods, such as "ladies' wrist watches," "Italian carpets and bedspreads," and "nylon blouses." These items, purchased in Europe during their return trip home, were then sold at a substantial markup in the Soviet Union, netting a handsome profit.[54]

Kaznacheev found numerous ways to subvert official rules. When he began work for the embassy's intelligence section—planting anti-American stories fabricated in Moscow in the local press—he was given a personal car and allowed to live outside the embassy compound. While he still reported to the embassy every morning, he spent the rest of his time with Burmese people as "'Mr. Alex,' a Burmese-speaking European who concealed his Soviet origins:

I visited their homes or hostels, I ate, and slept with them. On week ends we usually went by a river steamer or by a car out of Rangoon to small Burmese towns and villages. . . . On my own I visited the Buddhist monasteries and made the acquaintance of Buddhist monks, especially the younger men. They gave me my first lessons in Buddhism—a teaching I found to be the most humanitarian and appealing, and which I think I was ready to accept wholeheartedly in spite of my strictly materialistic upbringing. I became so deeply absorbed with Burmese life that at times they even forgot I was a European and not one of them.[55]

His account read like a case study of the political and ideological transgressions that worried Soviet authorities: intimacy with locals, religious conversion, and the abandonment of Soviet identity. It was also reminiscent of the foreign emissaries of past colonial powers who "went native" upon assignment abroad and lost their connection to the tight-knit "colony" and the distant homeland.[56]

A subsequent investigation by the KGB and the Communist Party's Control Commission linked Kaznacheev's ideological break with a rupture in his family. His wife, unmentioned in his memoir, sought to join him in Burma but he sent her back home. "Spending a long time . . . without his family," the report noted, he ended up engaging in a series of "intimate relations with Burmese women."[57] Kaznacheev's father, a prominent technical specialist affiliated with the Soviet Academy of Sciences, was taken to task for not informing officials about his son's marital troubles, which allegedly precipitated his split from his Soviet compatriots abroad.[58] If guidelines were abandoned and KGB surveillance networks failed, it was believed that family connections in the Soviet Union were the final cord connecting Soviets abroad to the socialist motherland.

For American intelligence, the stifling sense of isolation that Soviets such as Kasenkina, Kaznacheev, and Kravchenko felt presented a recruitment opportunity, especially since all had also lost or been estranged from family members back home. Yet by the late 1950s, the scope of the REDCAP program was diminished, and the operation would formally end in 1965.[59] Its demise was due in part to the withdrawal of Soviet forces from Austria and the construction of the Berlin Wall, which reduced Americans' access to Soviet targets. There were also indications that the program was becoming a public relations liability. In 1961, the KGB circulated a fabricated State Department document detailing the ways US intelligence allegedly encouraged Soviets abroad to defect, which received front-page coverage in the UK's *Daily Express* and generated global controversy.[60] Although the document was fake, it bore a striking resemblance to the actual methods employed as part of REDCAP, such as targeting vulnerable Soviet officials, threatening blackmail, and enticing them into compromising situations with prostitutes.[61] A final issue with the program underlined the reciprocal relationship in which the superpowers found themselves: if Soviet diplomats were targeted, American diplomatic emissaries were likely to be singled out for countermeasures.

In the rhetoric of US officials, outward-looking American embassies were contrasted with restrictive Soviet "colonies." They were also distinguished from the diplomatic missions of waning European empires. Seeking to draw a line between the foreign policy of the United States and the imperialist practices of its European allies, a State Department memorandum from January 1956 argued that "extraterritorial jurisdiction has, for a long time, been a symbol of colonialism." It added triumphantly, "The United States has renounced its right of extraterritorial jurisdiction in all other countries of the world where it possessed them (China, Korea, Japan, Egypt, Turkey, et cetera)." Drafted in response to the emergence of an independent Morocco freed from French colonial rule, the memorandum argued that the United States should relinquish the extraterritorial claims it held on the North African country because the United States could not "afford to lag behind by hanging onto this vestige of colonialism," which was ripe for "being pilloried by Soviet propaganda."[62]

The extraterritorial authority of the United States, however, did not simply come to an end, nor was it mainly expressed in the types of claims relinquished in Morocco. The United States maintained a global "empire of bases," which expanded rapidly during the Cold War even as the country recognized the independence of the Philippines, granted statehood to Alaska and Hawaii, and cast itself as an advocate of decolonization.[63] Many of these bases were on land that was leased rather than annexed, a distinction that allowed the United States to avoid being labeled as an empire while doing little to diminish American power on the ground.[64] Even as the United States recognized the formal independence of post-colonial nations, it secured a range of extraterritorial privileges for its military bases, some of them hidden from public scrutiny. Such was the case in Libya, where a public agreement officially granted the Libyan government broad jurisdiction over an American base in the newly independent nation, while a secret exchange of notes following the agreement ensured that the Libyans would cede jurisdiction in most cases connected to the base.[65] The agreements US officials reached with foreign governments often recalled colonial-era hierarchies. Although NATO members were granted concurrent jurisdiction when it came to American military bases, countries with a history of being dominated by Western imperial powers, including Japan, the Philippines, Taiwan, Iran, and Turkey, were pressured into ceding a greater degree of control to the United States.[66] The racial and post-colonial hierarchies that underpinned these arrangements were taken for granted by many American officials. While "we acknowledge Philippine independence," one US diplomat casually remarked in 1977, thirty years after independence had been granted to the Southeast Asian country, "we still think of bases extraterritorially."[67]

US authorities were more circumspect when it came to claiming extraterritorial rights over embassies, since diplomatic arrangements relied on carefully constructed reciprocal agreements supposedly made by two equal states. Privately, however, American officials had little doubt that US embassies deserved special treatment. America's military empire was linked to its diplomatic presence by the posting of US Marines to defend its embassies. Speaking privately to Chinese premier Zhou Enlai in Beijing in 1973, Secretary of State Henry Kissinger stated that "our position has always been that the Embassy is extraterritorial and we can put anyone in there we want as guards."[68] The belief that some foreign embassies were entitled to claim more extraterritorial authority than others was an assumption that their Soviet counterparts shared. A classified article advising CIA officers on the recruitment of Soviets abroad acknowledged that "no Soviet is going to consider seriously defection to nationals or intelligence services of small powers," since doing so would leave them unprotected.[69]

Such attitudes were especially striking when they were expressed by State Department officials posted to post-colonial countries, where American diplomats often occupied the physical and social spaces previously inhabited by European colonial rulers. In Burma, for example, US diplomatic representatives lived in a manner reminiscent of the British officials who governed the Southeast Asian country until 1948. Posted there in the early 1950s, Donald Wilhelm, a CIA officer embedded in the US embassy, lived with his wife in a sumptuous five-bedroom house with nine servants, who polished the floors every morning; the pair made regular trips to the capital's "whites-only swimming pool," which had been established by the British and continued to enforce racial segregation even after independence.[70]

Like their Soviet rivals and their British predecessors, US officials worried that those posted abroad might "go native" if they failed to maintain boundaries between themselves and the local population. Such fears were not limited to post-colonial contexts but also surrounded Americans working in socialist countries. In 1948, when Annabelle Bucar, an employee of the Cultural Information Section of the US Embassy in Moscow, stated her intention to remain in the Soviet Union and support "its fine people who are doing their utmost toward making the world a better place to live in," her decision was chalked up to the fact that she had fallen in love with a Russian operetta singer. Diplomatic cables and American media reports focused on the seduction of an American woman abroad; some even suggested that she had been the victim of an entrapment operation ordered by the Soviet secret police.[71] Anxieties about personal relationships undermining political loyalty were present on both sides of the Cold War, as this particular episode unfolded in the aftermath of Stalinist legislation outlawing marriages between Soviet citizens and foreigners.[72]

Tasked with encouraging defection but wary of local populations, US officials were unsure how to handle Soviet citizens who appeared at American embassies seeking asylum, particularly if they had not previously been on the CIA's radar. Some showed up at the US Embassy in Moscow, where the staff sought to determine whether they were defectors who had made a premeditated choice to flee, impulsive individuals who had entered on a whim, or Soviet KGB agents operating undercover. Even after that determination had been made, US diplomats worried that sheltering a defector in their embassy might lead Soviet officials to revoke their diplomatic status.

While gaining asylum by entering a US embassy in a socialist bloc state was thus extremely rare, Soviet migrants had a slightly better chance of finding refuge at an American embassy in a neutral country. In those countries, the United States offered sanctuary to Soviet citizens on a case-by-case basis, often operating on very little information. These conditions sometimes led to embarrassing incidents for American authorities, as occurred when V. B. Lukashevich, second secretary of the Soviet Embassy in Cambodia, defected in March 1958, only to be subsequently diagnosed by American experts as "emotionally and mentally unstable."[73] Just months after seeking refuge in the US Embassy in Cambodia, he claimed that he had been "forcibly removed" to the United States and sought to return to the USSR.[74] Ultimately, he had to be handed over to Soviet officials in Berlin.[75] US officials struggled to process Soviet defectors who unexpectedly appeared at American embassies in such locations as Beirut, Karachi, Lagos, and Tokyo. Some were suspected of being KGB "plants"; others simply exaggerated their importance; many, like Lukashevich, had second thoughts about their decision to flee.[76]

Faced with a motley assortment of Soviet migrants and forced to make ad hoc decisions in far-flung diplomatic posts, the United States sought to establish guidelines for handling the people arriving at its embassies. Under international law, it was difficult to classify someone who showed up at a US embassy in a socialist country as a political refugee, since the person technically remained in the country where the embassy was located. However, a special exception was made for individuals who were considered desirable as defectors. The guidelines noted that "a foreign national requesting political asylum may walk into a U.S. Government establishment and through this overt act may be considered a defector, if he has intelligence value to the United States, or a refugee, if for humanitarian or other reasons he would be helped by the refugee program." Being categorized as a defector offered far more security than being designated as a humanitarian case. A classified set of instructions on handling defectors deemed to be of "value for intelligence purposes" was sent out to embassies and consular posts on August 19, 1958; it gave leeway for the CIA to process this select set of people and, presumably, spirit them out of the country. The treatment of socialist bloc refugees deemed to lack "intelligence value" was more ambivalent. Another set of instructions issued on January 21, 1959, seemed to scale back the embassy's promise of extraterritorial protection, claiming that "U.S. officials abroad of course cannot grant the right of asylum on foreign soil to an escapee."[77]

Although they promised clear-cut instructions, these policy statements papered over broader ambiguities. An official summary issued a little over a decade later admitted that there was not so much a general US policy as a loose set of procedures, with each asylum seeker, "whether a defector or refugee . . . dealt with on a case-by-case basis."[78] While a blanket policy of embassy protection for citizens from socialist countries might have threatened the operation of American diplomatic missions in the socialist camp, fear of Soviet reprisals was not the only factor limiting the scope of US diplomatic asylum. American officials wanted to select defectors rather than be selected by them, to maintain their regime of screening potential immigrants remotely, and to maximize their flexibility. Being a superpower meant projecting extraterritorial authority when it was needed but also withdrawing its protections or even denying its existence when it was desirable to do so.

Whatever guidance US diplomats received remained secret, so Soviet migrants were left guessing whether they would be eligible for protection upon entering an American embassy. This dynamic was evident on September 12, 1959, when Leonid Markovskii, a Soviet citizen from Kyiv, entered the grounds of the US Embassy in Moscow by "walking in behind a vehicle with diplomatic plates." Although staff members encouraged him to leave by telling him that "the Embassy was closed," he "ensconced himself in the ninth-floor reception room saying he had a very important story to tell." The "story" concerned the fate of his father, executed during the purges in 1937, and his own fate following his attempt to cross the Soviet-Finnish border illegally in the mid-1950s, after which he was subjected to "18 months' imprisonment as a psychiatric patient." Markovskii's faith, whether desperate or naïve, in the promise of American sanctuary was demonstrated by his decision to send a registered letter addressed to President Eisenhower through the Soviet postal system, in which he requested asylum in the United States before he even reached the embassy.

Embassy officials judged that Markovskii was not a defector "of intelligence value," and his "signs of psychological imbalance" made them even more reluctant to shelter him. He was merely asked to sit for a photograph before embassy officials sought to spirit him away in a Soviet taxi. Even this effort was compromised after Soviet police officers posted outside the embassy approached the taxi. In the end, Markovskii was simply "walk[ed] to the gate with an Embassy officer" and was left standing in the streets of the Soviet capital.[79] While American sources went silent about Markovskii's case after he was ushered from the compound, he appeared two years later in the records of the Soviet Procuracy, with a warrant issued for his arrest for fleeing across the Soviet-Turkish border near Batumi. Despite his prior record and the fact that he had likely been watched by the KGB as a potential defector, he found the "forbidden border zone" to be more porous than the walls of the US embassy.[80]

Yet Soviet citizens, urged to "escape" Soviet rule by US-funded radio programs, kept showing up. Two months after Markovskii's unscheduled visit, Eduard Baks, a Soviet citizen of Polish descent, came running into the apartment of a Marine Corps member stationed at the US Embassy in Moscow. A subsequent report noted that Baks had eluded "the militiamen [Soviet police officers] outside the embassy entrance, ran up the stairs and into the first apartment whose door he found open." Although Baks was determined to "emigrate either to Poland or the West," the Marine told him that "nothing could be done in his behalf." After approaching another person in the embassy courtyard and still finding no assistance, Baks left the compound and was quickly stopped by Soviet police outside the gates.[81] Still, the walk-ins continued. On January 14, 1964, a young woman strolled in through a "little-used side door," claiming to be facing expulsion from the journalism department at Moscow State University because of her "bad attitude toward the Komsomol." She was told that the "United States does not recognize political asylum in its embassies abroad (with very few exceptions), and the policy of the Embassy in Moscow is not to grant asylum." Escorting her to the street, embassy officials noted that while she was not immediately stopped by Soviet police officers, "in the past persons have been allowed to get a half a block or so away before being picked up."[82]

The handling of those deemed "defectors" by US diplomatic missions remains a largely classified subject. However, the case of Aleksandr Kaznacheev is illuminating. After months of disillusionment with the government he represented, the young Soviet diplomat chose to defect in June

1959 by walking into the US Information Service Library in Burma. Despite a mild rebuke from the Burmese government for not being consulted beforehand, American officials were able to hold Kaznacheev in a safe house and grant him a level of "protection" akin to asylum while they vetted his "bona fides." He was even allowed to hold a press conference disclosing alleged Soviet spy efforts in Burma before leaving on a US Air Force plane. He reappeared in the United States as a guest on "Meet the Press."[83] The CIA subsequently asked Kaznacheev to write letters to his former colleagues in the Soviet Foreign Ministry encouraging them to flee as well. One such letter, sent to an attaché of the Soviet Embassy in Thailand with whom Kaznacheev had studied in Moscow, was intercepted by the KGB.[84] The CIA continued to carry out recruitment efforts focusing on high-level Soviet diplomatic targets even as everyday Soviet citizens were turned away from the US Embassy in Moscow.

AN UNEXPECTED ALLIANCE IN VIENNA

In many ways, US efforts to promote the defection of Soviets posted abroad—and the Soviet state's use of its diplomatic missions to restrict the mobility of citizens overseas—reproduced the Cold War divide around embassies across the globe. The lack of a comprehensive international diplomatic treaty left each side to assert broad claims of immunity in its own embassies and to complain about the other's embassies overstepping their bounds. Considering the American targeting of Soviets abroad and the Soviet scrutiny of American diplomatic missions within the socialist bloc, it seems perplexing that by 1961 the two sides would cordially agree to the terms for the Vienna Convention on Diplomatic Relations, the most sweeping codification of diplomatic law in history. The process by which this landmark agreement was reached, even as Kasenkina remained sheltered in the United States and Mindszenty holed up in the American Embassy in Hungary, reveals that, when it came to diplomatic missions, the divide between East and West was perhaps not so great as the one between the global North and South.[85]

Given the fierce competition between the superpowers for influence in the post-colonial world, it initially appeared that the politics of the Cold War would jeopardize any agreement on diplomatic representation. At meetings of the UN, the USSR decried the "imperialist" ambitions of the United States and cast itself as the defender of new states emerging from British and French colonial domination, and it regularly decried the absence at the UN of the People's Republic of China, the world's most populous nation. In response, the United States was quick to label the Soviet Union an empire for the influence it claimed in East Central Europe and joined non-aligned countries estranged from the USSR, such as Yugoslavia, in denouncing Soviet foreign policy.

When a Yugoslav representative, Veljko Vlahovic, first proposed codifying an agreement on "diplomatic intercourse and immunities" at the October 29, 1952, meeting of the UN General Assembly's legal committee, he did so by singling out the bad behavior of the Soviet Union and its allies. He claimed that "the states of the Soviet Bloc had been pursuing a policy of aggressive pressure for several years." Vlahovic detailed "physical attacks" on Yugoslav diplomats and "illegal entry" into Yugoslav diplomatic residences, and he described an alleged "kidnapping" incident in which Bulgarian security officials had entered the Yugoslav Embassy in Sofia to arrest a Yugoslav citizen who planned to flee."[86] Vlahovic's remarks were quickly taken up by the United States, whose delegate noted further violations of diplomatic norms by states aligned with the USSR.[87] Predictably, the Soviet representative angrily responded to the claims of his Yugoslav and American counterparts, and the Soviet Union's ally, Poland, denounced them as "slanderous accusations."[88] The following year, the United States continued its alliance of convenience with Yugoslavia, supporting the appointment of a Yugoslav candidate to the UN's International Law Commission.[89] American authorities were willing to overlook the fact that Yugoslavs faced similar, if less severe, restrictions on exit and were even welcomed as "escapees" by the US Escapee Program.[90]

At the time, Soviet leaders dismissed the United Nations as an American-dominated organization and were little inclined to consider an international agreement that appeared to target restrictions on exit. Just two years before, Iakov Malik, the Soviet ambassador to the UN, had stormed out of the UN Security Council after its failure to recognize the People's Republic of China as the legitimate holder of China's seat, leading to a months-long boycott by the Soviet Union of the council's proceedings.[91] The Soviet relationship with the UN began to change after 1953, with the death of Stalin and the appointment of Dag Hammarskjöld as secretary general. Seen by Soviet authorities as a more neutral leader, Hammarskjöld asserted the international organization's independence early on by barring FBI agents from carrying out investigations on its premises.[92] With the vast wave of decolonization approaching, the UN was seen as an important forum for the USSR to bolster its international image and appeal to the so-called Third World.[93] Yet even as it championed the recognition of newly independent nations at the UN, the Soviet Union sought to preserve its privileged authority—and its veto—on the Security Council.

Soviet attitudes also began to shift in response to signs of increasing unrest engulfing embassies across the globe. In 1953 the Soviet Embassy in Tel Aviv was attacked, and in February 1955 emigres seized the Romanian mission in Bern, Switzerland, holding the staff captive and killing the chauffeur. The Soviet Union and its allies came to understand that an unregulated diplomatic environment that left embassies and diplomats unprotected posed risks for socialist as well as capitalist states. Their concerns were shared by US authorities, particularly following attacks on the American embassies in Taiwan and Turkey in 1957 and 1958. Even more unrest swirled around British and French embassies in the post-colonial world, with diplomats concerned about missions being stormed by protestors or overrun by post-colonial subjects with claims to British and French citizenship.

A few glimmers of cooperation between the Soviet Union and the United States began to appear at the UN. After years of bickering over the admission of new member states prompted by fears that the organization's ideological balance could be tilted in favor of one side or the other, a deal brokered by the superpowers in 1955 allowed sixteen countries to join; twenty-three more states were permitted to join by 1961.[94] In 1956, the superpowers cooperated in pressing for the withdrawal of British, French, and Israeli troops from Egypt amid the Suez Crisis, and the United States showed restraint at the UN as the Soviet Union violently suppressed the uprising in Hungary.[95] The superpowers also began to make headway in discussions that would lead to the Vienna Convention. Although the superpowers had helped hasten the end of British and French imperial rule during the Suez crisis, they would find common cause with the fading powers of Europe in the regulation of diplomatic missions.

Britain, France, and other European states in the process of shedding colonial holdings were wary about the unrestricted mobility of former colonial subjects and eager to wall off their diplomatic missions from unwanted migrants. Debates about which migrants were deserving of diplomatic asylum invoked race, often directly. When Sir John Lomax, the UK ambassador to Bolivia, wrote with concern about upheaval in La Paz and asked for guidance on providing sanctuary in the British embassy, he specifically had in mind the country's "white population" endangered by Bolivia's "unceasing political unrest."[96] When British embassies were faced with a wave of asylum seekers in newly independent Ghana and Nigeria, they expressed concern that they might be expected to shelter not only the "local British community" but also Ghanaians and Nigerians, seen as less desirable even though they had similar claims to Commonwealth citizenship.[97] Such views reflected deep-seated racialized anxieties about post-colonial migration more generally. In 1956, a secret report by a committee appointed by Prime Minister Anthony Eden of the UK warned of the long-term consequences of the growth of the population of "coloured people from the African and Asiatic territories of the Commonwealth and from the West Indies," identifying the risk of "inter-breeding" and "race riots" and calling "coloured immigration" an "ominous problem which cannot now be ignored."[98] In the wake of the 1958 riots in the London neighborhood of Notting Hill precipitated by attacks on its West Indian residents, British officials began to discuss legislation to restrict Commonwealth immigration and allow for the deportation of "undesirable immigrants."[99]

Although the United States was quick to establish relations with post-colonial countries, it, too, was wary of post-colonial migrants. Its immigration system already imposed far greater restrictions on migration from Africa and Asia than those being considered by Britain, and its embassies buffeted themselves against the pressures of unauthorized migration from the Global South. Even as several Latin American states agreed to the Convention on Diplomatic Asylum, which strengthened the rights of those seeking refuge in embassies, State Department officials assured the British ambassador in Mexico in 1954 that the United States had "no intention of opening the doors of its Embassies to the host of political refugees whom Latin American politics engenders." "Latin American politics," of course, was not so easily separated from US foreign policy. The United States, long a destabilizing force in the region, would back a coup in Guatemala less than two months after the Convention on Diplomatic Asylum was signed.[100] The informal nature of America's empire made it easier for US officials to look the other way when the region's migrants sought refuge.

The Soviet Union's willingness to broker a deal with its superpower rival did not mean a ceasefire on rhetorical attacks against American "imperialism" in Latin America and elsewhere. With civil conflict brewing in the newly independent Congo, Soviet premier Nikita Khrushchev personally headed the Soviet delegation to the Fifteenth Session of the UN General Assembly in the fall of 1960. In the session, the Soviet side put forward a measure supporting immediate decolonization that seemed designed to put the United States in an uncomfortable bind. The plan called specifically for the "liquidation of foreign bases" and pressured Washington to choose between its clients in the Third World and its European allies who remained resistant to a firm deadline for granting colonies independence.[101] The Soviet proposal encouraged a coalition of twenty-six African and Asian countries to pass the Declaration on the Granting of Independence to Colonial Countries and Peoples in December 1960, from which the United States was forced to abstain.[102] Even in 1961, the year the Vienna Convention on Diplomatic Rights was signed, Soviet officials supported a resolution of the

Afro-Asian Bandung Conference denouncing Western embassies as "active agents of neocolonialism" that functioned as "centers of espionage and exert pressure on African and Asian governments."[103]

Behind such rhetoric, Soviet officials worried about the erosion of their state's preeminent position in a changing world. Ultimately, they were prepared to do whatever was necessary to shore it up, even if doing so meant cooperating with their ideological opponent. While contemporary observers predicted that the International Law Commission's 1957 session on diplomatic privileges and immunities would be beset by the same Cold War divisions that had plagued earlier discussions, it quickly made strides toward an agreement.[104] The draft text that emerged from forty-nine meetings held that year in Geneva, chaired by Jaroslav Zourek of Czechoslovakia, set forth rules meant to "reproduce the actual practice of States as it has existed for a very long time." The draft enshrined the principle of embassy inviolability but sidelined diplomatic asylum as a practice that did not enjoy universal protection and was potentially "incompatible with the functions" of a diplomatic mission.[105] Based on the available documentation, the draft was not the result of a conspiratorial agreement between the superpowers, but instead the product of tacit collusion guided by mutual interest.[106]

This shared interest of the superpowers was not altogether new. Even amid the showdown over Oksana Kasenkina in 1948, the American side had been wary of contesting Soviet claims of extraterritoriality out of a desire to protect its own diplomatic missions.[107] Moreover, Soviet diplomats and intelligence officers proved just as suspicious as their American counterparts of uninvited "walk-ins" showing up at their embassies. A guide written by Ivan Serov, who led the KGB from 1954 to 1958 and the GRU from 1958 to 1963, warned of "imposters" and sympathetic but misguided individuals who offered "'important' documents which, when checked, prove to be of no value."[108] Neither state wanted its embassies overwhelmed by asylum seekers, and both staunchly opposed the codification of diplomatic asylum as a universal legal right. The superpowers saw the advantages of upholding an international system that allowed special privileges for strong states like them even as it tolerated the formal representation of new but less powerful ones from the post-colonial world. Although it was the willingness of the United States and the Soviet Union to reach an accord that made a comprehensive agreement on diplomatic law possible, European states were willing to go along, hoping to protect what was left of the global status quo.

It helped that the United States and the Soviet Union had international law experts whose intellectual networks spanned the Iron Curtain and who could communicate with relative ease across the Cold War divide.[109] Even in the xenophobic atmosphere of High Stalinism, David Levin, the leading Soviet specialist on diplomatic law, published books and pamphlets that incorporated the findings of foreign law journals. In his 1949 book, *Diplomatic Immunity*, he argued that "all representatives of the discipline of international law" agreed that refuge in an embassy could not be granted to someone facing criminal charges; he cited recent conferences at Harvard and Columbia as well as the Soviet criminal code, according to which anyone seeking to emigrate without permission was committing a crime. He noted that while Britain and the United States had violated this norm by sheltering fugitives from Soviet law after World War II, the Soviet Union more consistently upheld international law, since "in Soviet doctrine" the right to diplomatic asylum was "denied completely."[110] Despite Levin's criticism, British legal experts with the Foreign Office, reviewing a series of asylum cases connected to embassies in 1951, tended to agree with him on principle and even cited his book in their report.[111] US officials concurred that the practice of diplomatic asylum "except in a very limited sense" was dangerous and destabilizing. They worried about giving small countries broad latitude in advancing extraterritorial claims, emboldening them to shelter opponents of US influence in Latin America and elsewhere.[112]

The superpowers ushered their respective blocs through the process of turning the commission's draft into a durable agreement; Britain and France sought to do the same with their former colonies. Proceeding in a manner that revealed the endurance of colonial-era hierarchies, Britain first consulted with the "settled monarchical members of the Commonwealth"— Canada, Australia, and New Zealand—to reach a consensus before broaching the matter with countries such as Ghana and Pakistan. Such a delineation reproduced racial divides and the divide between the global North and South. France, too, was interested in preserving the vestiges of its imperial order. In meetings with their British counterparts, French negotiators sought to preserve the "special arrangements" France's diplomatic representatives enjoyed in former colonies such as Morocco.[113] Nearly all these discussions took place behind closed doors and through classified correspondence, with little press coverage and many post-colonial states excluded from the conversation.

When the foreign delegations gathered in Vienna in the spring of 1961 to give final approval to the legal framework on diplomatic representation, there was remarkably little acrimony, even though the meeting occurred amid renewed Cold War tensions surrounding the Congo crisis, the shooting down of an American spy plane in Soviet airspace, and the US decision to cut off relations with Castro's Cuba. Except for a pro forma complaint by the Soviet delegate about the absence of representatives from East Germany, Mongolia, and the People's Republic of China, both superpowers showed their readiness to work together. Despite US concerns that the Soviet side would raise the issue of Cardinal Mindszenty, still in refuge at the US Embassy in Budapest, Moscow's delegates did not mention the matter.[114] The decision, supported by the United States, to hold the event in the Austrian capital also pleased Soviet officials. The choice of Vienna met Soviet demands for a neutral location and bolstered Soviet prestige by encouraging comparisons with the Congress of Vienna of 1814–1815, where the codification of diplomatic immunity had first been discussed under the watchful gaze of Russian Tsar Alexander I. Perhaps most important, the convention itself was something of a staged ceremony, since the International Law Commission had already established the basic framework for codifying the inviolability of embassies. Officially, the Vienna Convention was a meeting of thirty-four independent nations, including states such as Ghana, which had established an independent government only the year before, and populous countries in the developing world, such as Brazil.[115] In practical terms, it was a glamorous venue for rubber stamping an agreement brokered by the superpowers and supported by Europe's old empires.

British representatives were impressed by the spirit of cooperation they saw across the Cold War divide. A confidential report from Vienna remarked that "the United Kingdom delegation and the Soviet delegation were both active in preventing many of [the] new additions" proposed by the "smaller countries, and even some of the larger ones" at the meeting. The Soviet side even seemed willing to go along with the British effort to reserve privileges for its High Commissioners; although "in private the Russians told the Americans they thought High Commissioners a vestige of colonial days . . . in public no derogatory word was spoken." In the British view, the meeting in Vienna "was remarkable for the absence of political divisions between East and West on normal United Nations lines." "If anything," the reported concluded, "on the more important issues the division was between the major and the minor Powers."[116]

In the Vienna Convention on Diplomatic Relations adopted in April 1961, states on opposite sides of the Cold War agreed that their diplomatic personnel should be protected from prosecution but also prepared for dismissal if they were declared persona non grata; they were to enjoy free communication between their mission and the home country; and their diplomatic premises were not to be entered without permission and were not to be searched or have their property seized. Two years later, another UN conference in Vienna extended these protections to consulates.[117]

Although the Soviet Union had championed the diplomatic recognition of new states, it was prepared to work with its capitalist opponent to rein them in, tie them to the established state system, and co-author the rules that governed their behavior.

Yet superpower collusion did not fully explain the extent to which the states of the Global South went along with the agreement. After all, states of Africa, Asia, the Middle East, and Latin America, most with a recent past of colonial rule, made up sixteen of the thirty-four original signatories of the convention; with the support of neutral Austria and Switzerland—or Albania, which was in the process of distancing itself from the Soviet Union—these states would have had a majority at the conference. In effect, the conference exposed another divide: the gulf between those leading the states of the Global South and the populations they governed. While enthusiasm for Third World solidarity was at its height, post-colonial elites were eager to see their countries join the international community by opening new embassies and becoming full-fledged members of the modern state system. In the final analysis, post-colonial states shared with their former colonial rulers a distrust of migrants, and they were not keen on having their citizens emigrate, especially to the former metropole. East joined with West to turn the debates into a discussion between North and South, but ultimately states—both old and new—banded together against more spontaneous forms of migration and more porous forms of citizenship.[118]

The Vienna Convention on Diplomatic Rights was significant for what it did not include and what it left unsaid. In the interest of walling off embassies and regulating migration, the proposal of Latin American countries to codify the right to diplomatic asylum was repeatedly beaten back, both by the United States and the Soviet Union. The practice was neither codified in the Vienna Convention nor was it explicitly prohibited. This exclusion was maintained in the name of "flexibility," giving strong, established states the ability to determine what constituted an "exceptional case" of asylum that merited diplomatic protection.[119] Established states—with the superpowers leading the charge—retained the right to decide what was allowed and not allowed in this deliberately ambiguous corner of international law.[120] Meanwhile, migrants approaching embassies received no guarantees, and less powerful states lacked a set of universal rules to which to appeal. The same course of action was subsequently taken in regard to consulates, which were held to be inviolable but left undefined as potential sites of asylum.

The two Vienna Conventions may primarily have been diplomatic arrangements with a secondary focus on the rights of asylum seekers in and around embassies and consulates, but they marked the beginning of a bigger shift toward curtailing post-colonial migration. The sealing off of foreign embassies from asylum seekers was soon followed by limits imposed by European states on migrants from their former colonies. In 1962, Britain passed the Commonwealth Immigrants Act, which restricted free immigration to those who held United Kingdom passports, were the spouses or children of UK passport holders, or had earlier resided in the United Kingdom. These rules were further tightened in 1968, in part because of fears that large numbers of people of Indian origin fleeing Kenya would take up refuge in Britain.[121] Between these two pieces of legislation, Britain issued new guidelines regarding "asylum in diplomatic presences" to its overseas missions in 1966. The document made it clear that there was "no general right in international law" to grant asylum in an embassy and that "refugees" in a diplomatic mission should be "surrender[ed] . . . to the territorial authorities upon their request."[122] France similarly retreated from its offer of French citizenship and free migration for residents of its former colonial territories and protectorates. The French Union was dissolved in 1958, and its successor, a watered-down French Community, largely ceased functioning by the early 1960s. By 1964, post-colonial migrants needed employment contracts to work in France; in the late 1960s, cumbersome medical checks were introduced; and by the early 1970s, residence and work permits were required. Post-colonial states generally agreed to these restrictions and even instituted their own efforts to control the movement of migrants. For example, fearing the unconstrained outflow of its citizens and their labor power, Senegal instituted an exit visa for Senegalese hoping to travel to France.[123]

Even in this more tightly enclosed global commons, stronger states still retained the right to wield extraterritoriality in and around their embassies. The fact that American embassies would continue to offer sanctuary to Soviet defectors when deemed desirable was made clear in March 1967, when Svetlana Allilueva appeared at the US Embassy in New Delhi to request political asylum. The daughter of former Soviet leader Joseph Stalin, she had traveled to India following the death of her long-time partner, Brajesh Singh, and her presence in the South Asian country was known to American authorities. She was immediately whisked out of India on a plane bound for Rome, accompanied by an embassy official. While State Department officials debated whether she could be cleared to travel on to the United States without causing a rift in Soviet-American relations, she was moved to neutral Switzerland, where George Kennan, the former ambassador to the Soviet Union, personally debriefed her.

Allilueva's defection occurred just as the US Congress, following the agreements in Vienna, was ratifying a convention with the Soviet Union to reopen the two countries' consulates, which had been closed since the Kasenkina affair.[124] Kennan recommended downplaying the role of the US government in helping her defect, believing it important to establish plausible deniability that "she was in the 'United States Government's pocket.'"[125] This approach was in line with the guidance of the CIA, which was concerned about the "political repercussions" of the case.[126] Turning to private connections instead of government contacts, Kennan arranged for a New York law firm to help Allilueva obtain a visa to the United States. He also put the defector in touch with American publisher Harper & Row to discuss the publication of her memoir.[127]

America's allies, too, sought to exploit Allilueva's defection while claiming to have no part in it. In the words of an internal communication of the British Foreign Ministry, "It is our deliberate policy to have no policy about the Svetlana story."[128] Indian authorities—seeking to maintain good relations with the USSR—lodged a minor protest against the fact that Allilueva had been taken out of the country without notifying them; more quietly, they dispatched an official to Switzerland to meet with her.[129] Soviet authorities made formal complaints, but mainly chose to cast aspersions on Allilueva's character in the press, depicting her as mentally deranged, egotistical, and motivated by greed.[130] After a private meeting with Soviet deputy foreign minister Nikolai Firiubin, an Indian official reported that the Soviet Foreign Ministry was "relatively mild about the episode."[131] Allilueva's defection through the US Embassy in India was only a temporary setback for the consular agreement; consular relations between the USSR and the United States were finally reestablished a few years later, in 1972.

Given the publicity that Allilueva's defection generated, it is little surprise that a rash of Soviet citizens followed her example in seeking asylum, both at the US Embassy in Moscow and the embassy in New Delhi. One potential migrant, arriving at the entrance of the US Embassy in Moscow in May 1967, told officials that "everyone in Rostov [the Russian city where he lived] knows about Svetlana" and how she "had received political asylum in the free United States." In this case, as in most others, the embassy "walk-in" was turned away.[132] American authorities insisted that they had not granted diplomatic asylum in Allilueva's case, which was technically true, though they had used the embassy in New Delhi to channel her to Switzerland and then the United States, where she was given asylum and, eventually, citizenship. In 1970, the State Department reminded all US embassies that "it remains the policy of the United States not to grant refuge in any except extraordinary circumstances." The updated instructions urged embassy staff to "exercise extreme caution" and await "instructions from Washington."[133]

Meanwhile, Cardinal Mindszenty remained in residence at the US Embassy in Budapest until 1971, when he was allowed to depart Hungary to resettle in neutral Austria.

The Soviet government continued to protest cases of defection publicly but was privately reassured in the aftermath of Allilueva's flight by the US State Department, which promised that Soviet authorities would be notified in future instances of defection and allowed to meet with defectors held by US officials before they were granted asylum.[134] The Soviet Union, like the United States, continued to insist that it did not recognize the principle of diplomatic asylum, though it shared with its rival a tendency to make exceptions when it was politically expedient to do so. Following the coup against socialist president Salvador Allende in Chile in 1973, Soviet officials supported the right of around 8,000 Chileans to seek refuge in sympathetic diplomatic missions and helped resettle some of them in the USSR.[135]

EMBASSY WALLS GROW TALLER

Oksana Kasenkina spent her last years living in seclusion in a Miami hotel under an assumed name, writing a novel that would remain unpublished. She died in July 1960, less than a year before the Vienna Convention on Diplomatic Rights was signed.[136] Although her name went unmentioned during the proceedings, the accord was an attempt to resolve the issues of diplomatic extraterritoriality raised by her dramatic escape. While she was a Soviet citizen rather than a post-colonial migrant, her experience bore more than a passing resemblance to those whose lives had been uprooted by empire and who, after imperial rule ended, were left stranded by new limits on their mobility. Long before she jumped from the window of the Soviet consulate, Kasenkina had been forced to flee her native Don region in Ukraine for Moscow twice, first during the Russian Civil War and again during the Second World War. Her family had been consumed and scattered by larger historical events: her sister fled to Britain during the Civil War; her daughter died during the famine unleashed by collectivization; her husband, a former officer in the tsar's army, had been caught up in the Great Terror; her son, called up to Soviet military service, had been missing in action since January 1942. Displaced to Moscow, she worked her way up to the position of school inspector and earned a coveted posting to New York, but she felt isolated among her compatriots, treated, by her own account, as an unsophisticated bumpkin by the consulate's staff.[137]

After the publicity surrounding Kasenkina's defection had dwindled and her ghostwritten memoir had been rushed to press, Kasenkina's American handlers distanced themselves from her. The Soviet government also found her perplexing and expended little effort in trying to secure her return. Before she died, she reached out to the Soviet embassy, perhaps hoping to find out more about the fate of her son, but she would only speak through the hotel door to the man dispatched from the embassy, who left shortly after.[138] She had taken advantage of the ambiguity of extraterritorial borders to evade Soviet authority, but she remained disconnected and out of place. After the Vienna Convention reaffirmed the inviolability of diplomatic premises, future defectors were less likely to receive the assistance she had briefly enjoyed from US authorities.

While the United States and the Soviet Union cast themselves as champions of decolonization, both saw the advantages of upholding the international system that they had inherited from European empires. Their interests coincided with those of European states, and collectively they overcame resistance by post-colonial states by offering them the trappings of diplomatic representation to domesticate the more revolutionary strands of post-colonial nationalism.[139] Some post-colonial states went along eagerly, worried that they might otherwise lose the citizens needed to develop their economies, fill their armed services, and build the new societies planned by their leaders. The solidification of borders around embassies privileged states over migrants, and strong states over weaker ones; it sealed off a small but notable opening in the global commons. The willingness of the United States and the Soviet Union to collaborate in closing pathways to movement proved a harbinger of détente, when the superpowers would draw even closer together to impose order on a changing world.[140]

The Vienna Convention's approval also coincided with a new phase at the United Nations, where the East-West divide over ideology was gradually superseded by a North-South division over the international organization's structure and goals. From the outset, post-colonial states such as India had looked to the UN as a vehicle for a more equitable global government.[141] While they remained fierce guardians of their own sovereignty, post-colonial nations were more inclined to urge the UN to intervene within states as well as between them, to address underlying issues rather than simply keeping the peace, to promote a more democratic global order rather than upholding the privileges of established powers.[142] Although the Soviet Union continued to court the non-aligned movement and lend rhetorical support—and sometimes financial and military assistance—to clients in Africa, Asia, Latin America, and the Middle East, its leaders shared with their counterparts in the United States a sense that the world ought to remain divided into spheres of Soviet and American influence.

Over the course of the 1970s, smaller and less powerful states, particularly those in Latin America, continued to push for a more comprehensive agreement on asylum in general and the codification of diplomatic asylum in particular. In 1974, the issue of diplomatic asylum was raised again in the General Assembly, but the only fruit of this effort was a lengthy report on its history produced by the secretary general, which nodded to the historical practice of diplomatic asylum by Latin American countries but noted significant objections voiced by the United States, the Soviet Union, and the countries that made up their respective blocs. While the General Assembly promised to give the issue further consideration in "a future session," the notion of diplomatic asylum as a universal legal right was essentially abandoned and received little attention from the International Law Commission for the remainder of the Cold War.[143] The freedom of more powerful countries to accept or reject asylum seekers at their embassies as they saw fit was preserved.

Deliberate legal ambiguity could be useful, but the United States, the Soviet Union, and other states took additional steps to wall off their embassies in a time of growing unrest. Over the course of the 1970s, forty-eight embassies were taken over by force.[144] Once again protecting their basic interests, the Soviet Union and the United States quickly agreed to terms for the Convention on the Prevention and Punishment of Crimes against Diplomatic Agents and Other Internationally Protected Persons in 1973, even as efforts to codify diplomatic asylum stalled. The scope of "exception" for diplomatic missions was deliberately restricted: anyone who stood accused of attacking an embassy or harming or threatening a diplomatic representative was deemed ineligible for asylum and had to be prosecuted or extradited to face justice. The real or perceived threat of "terrorist acts" against foreign missions led to the adoption of additional security measures around embassies and consulates, making the cases of migrants walking in behind a diplomatic car or coming in through a side door a thing of the past.[145]

In this same period, human rights advocacy created a new, if narrow, opening for migrants.[146] With the growth of transnational advocacy networks, some Soviet citizens were able to use extended stays in American embassies to gain popular support and pressure US officials to admit them. Such was the case with the Siberian Seven, a family of Soviet Pentecostals who stayed in the US embassy from 1978 to 1983, before being allowed to leave for the United States via Israel, thanks in part to the lobbying of American evangelicals, who elevated the case to a matter of national political attention in the United States.[147] Although these seven individuals were able to gain protection and eventually asylum in the United States, many more were turned away. In several instances, Soviet citizens attempted to breach the US Embassy in Moscow by driving through its gates at high speeds in a desperate effort to gain asylum; all were handed over to Soviet police.[148] Despite the rise of human rights rhetoric, states generally refused to offer a clear definition of what constituted "humanitarian grounds" in diplomatic asylum cases and gave few guarantees.

Such an approach generally allowed the United States to intervene where it chose. The defection of high-level diplomats was still welcomed. In 1978, Arkady Shevchenko, the UN under-secretary general for political affairs, was granted asylum by US officials while on duty in New York, after several years of supplying intelligence to the CIA.[149] The United States was even sometimes supportive of mass asylum seeking, though usually when it came to embassies that were not its own. In 1980, after thousands of Cubans sought asylum by gathering on the grounds of the Peruvian Embassy in Havana, the United States agreed to accept them among the many other Cuban refugees who arrived in the Mariel Boatlift. Toward the end of the 1980s, the United States again looked sympathetically at the crowds of East German citizens who massed on the grounds of West Germany's embassies in Prague and Budapest in an effort to cross the Iron Curtain.[150] And in 1989, the US Embassy in Beijing sheltered pro-democracy activist Fang Lizhi in the wake of the crackdown in Tiananmen Square before granting him political asylum in the United States. Yet asylum seekers who did not enjoy the support of the American government were abandoned; one of the most prominent cases involved the so-called Durban Six, a group of anti-apartheid activists in South Africa refused sanctuary by the US Embassy in Pretoria.[151]

Embassy extraterritoriality, while largely abandoned as a formal legal principle, remained a recognizable phenomenon in practice. The lack of codified rules for diplomatic asylum meant that sanctuary could securely be given by larger states but would remain an insecure promise when offered by less powerful ones. The world envisioned by the superpowers remained one of imperial ambitions and hierarchical relations. The Cold War rivals would continue to extend their influence and preserve their prerogatives wherever they could and however they could, even if it sometimes meant working together.

5

International Waters

On May 24, 1954, the tanker *Tuapse* sailed from Odesa, as the strains of Soviet crooner Leonid Utesov's love song to the USSR's largest port city blared over the ship's loudspeakers.[1] The tanker—with its sparkling white deck and towering red and black-striped funnel—had been built the previous year in the shipyards of Copenhagen. The bulk of its crew was composed of young men, many of whom had never before left the Soviet Union. The ship's journey was international, but the major stops on its itinerary were confined to the socialist world. The tanker was scheduled to travel to the nearby Black Sea city of Constanta in Romania to pick up more than 10,000 tons of kerosene and then deliver the fuel to Shanghai, the largest port of the People's Republic of China.[2] On its way to Shanghai it would sail through the Bosporus, the Suez Canal, the Arabian Sea, and the Indian Ocean, and would stop briefly to refuel in Singapore. Upon reaching the Asian city-state, a group of sailors wandered through its bustling marketplace, where they were propositioned by a White Russian emigre who invited them to spend time with her two teenage "daughters." Though forbidden by Soviet law and contrary to Marxist-Leninist ideology, engaging in petty commerce and consorting with prostitutes were part of life at sea for many Soviet sailors.[3]

Leaving Singapore, the *Tuapse* entered the South China Sea, one of the world's busiest shipping lanes but also the most contested maritime region of the early Cold War. The sea's territorial waters were disputed between the communist People's Republic of China and the nationalist Republic of China, whose Kuomintang authorities had retreated to Taiwan in 1949.

Claims were also advanced by French Indochina, the newly independent Philippines, and other neighboring states, which projected their sovereignty into the sea by staking out the islands and reefs that speckled its waters.[4] In the wake of the Second World War and the Korean War, there was also an unmistakable American imprint on the entire Pacific region that extended into the South China Sea. America's presence took the form of air- and sea-based patrols conducted by the US Navy that aimed to protect what remained of the Kuomintang's rule. When the *Tuapse* reached the South China Sea, US Navy planes had standing orders "to conduct shipping surveillance" and "photograph all merchant ships" passing through.[5] The tanker's sailors reported seeing US aircraft in the skies above them.[6]

Nearly a month after it had left Odesa, amid the "haze of a tropical night," the *Tuapse* was surrounded by naval destroyers operated by the Kuomintang.[7] While the risks of sailing through the South China Sea were known, the incursion on the Soviet merchant vessel came as a surprise, since it occurred in the international waters between Taiwan and the Philippines. The tanker's captain, Vitaly Kalinin, decried the seizure of the *Tuapse* as a "violation of the rights of navigation." In defiance, his crew launched a hunger strike, but soon realized they had little chance of holding out against a military opponent. The next day, the *Tuapse* was brought into the southern Taiwanese port of Kaohsiung. The Soviet Union, which did not recognize the Chinese nationalist government in Taiwan, submitted a sharp protest note to the United States, alleging American participation, describing the ship's seizure as a "gross violation of the freedom of navigation in the open seas," and calling for the "immediate return of the ship, its cargo, and crew."[8] In a press release two days later, Kuomintang authorities insisted that they had discovered the *Tuapse* in Taiwanese waters and claimed that the ship's cargo of kerosene was meant for jet fuel and thus among the "strategic materials banned by the United Nations for shipment to the Chinese Communists."[9] Left unresolved was the fate of the ship's crew, Soviet citizens captured in international waters and held in a maritime borderland fragmented by Cold War divisions.

Even as land borders more thoroughly filtered migrants and land-based extraterritorial spaces were walled off to would-be asylum seekers, the high seas remained a zone of contestation. The seizure of the *Tuapse* triggered international debates over the nature and delimitation of maritime borders in a post-colonial context. For centuries, a handful of European empires, led by the British, had dominated the world's waterways and set the rules governing mobility at sea.[10] Such rules were rarely codified, but they were backed by the force of gunships and came to be accepted as customary, creating a durable, if never entirely stable, legal regime. Yet technological advances in fishing, oil exploration, and shipping spurred changes to maritime law that unfolded against the backdrop of super-power rivalry. Immediately after World War II, President Truman extended American jurisdiction beyond the traditional limits of the country's territorial waters through a proclamation laying claim to the resources of its continental shelf, spurring other nations to follow suit.[11] Across the globe decolonization threatened the maritime supremacy of European states, as the number of countries with claims on the sea proliferated. With maritime borders in flux, the United States and the Soviet Union energetically competed to extend their global shipping networks and sought to set the rules that governed movement on the seas. The South China Sea was at the center of this contest, since it linked the issue of maritime borders with the question of the diplomatic recognition of China, in a region with a centuries-long history of European colonialism.

While the United States and the Soviet Union built up their naval fleets, commercial shipping was an equally vital arena of Cold War competition, crucial to building connections and spreading influence in the post-colonial world. The United States held the edge in this contest, but the Soviet merchant fleet was on the cusp of a dramatic expansion. Between 1959 and 1975, the Soviet merchant fleet nearly quadrupled in size, becoming one of the largest in the world.[12] Commissioning bigger and faster ships, the Soviet Union took advantage of having the world's longest coastline and consolidated control over most of the Baltic and Black Seas. Its growing fleet supplied the Soviet economy and brought goods, fuel, and weapons to allies in Asia, Africa, and Latin America.

Participation in global shipping meant increased contact with the capitalist world. Soviet authorities strove to gain entry to the world's busiest ports: Singapore, Antwerp, Rotterdam, Lagos, and Tokyo, among others. Soviet officials even sought access to ports in the United States, where they vociferously protested the "discriminatory" searches of Soviet vessels that slowed down travel times.[13] At research institutes throughout the Soviet Union, planners pursued technological advances pioneered in the West that promised to open up new trade routes and fishing areas and unlock the ocean's depths for oil exploration.

At sea, the Soviet Union sought to construct a legal framework that reflected its ideological views but also asserted the state's geopolitical and commercial interests. Some policies were aimed at maximizing sovereignty, with Soviet officials calling for the closure of the Baltic and Black seas to foreign warships and asserting that Soviet commercial ships, unlike those sailing from Western countries, deserved full immunity and extraterritorial privileges, since they were owned and operated by the state rather than a private corporation. In other cases, the Soviet state downplayed Marxist ideology to champion the freedom of navigation and extend its shipping networks into capitalist ports.

The *Tuapse* incident and its aftermath epitomized the aspirations and contradictions of the maritime expansion of the Soviet Union. Soviet authorities sought to use the *Tuapse*'s seizure to pry open the South China Sea, promote the international recognition of the People's Republic of China, and tar the United States and its allies in the region as supporters of "piracy." At the same time, they nervously viewed maritime zones as places of ideological transgression and strove to police the behavior of Soviet sailors and preserve the Soviet ship as a "floating piece" of sovereign territory.[14] These concerns grew alongside the expanded merchant fleet, as the phenomenon of Soviet sailors "jumping ship" in international waters and foreign ports only increased.[15] The state's campaign for free navigation never envisioned the unregulated movement of Soviet citizens.

Sailors were seen as a uniquely troublesome group of Soviet citizens abroad. By necessity they were often less groomed by educational and ideological training than other official Soviet travelers and moved across borders in greater numbers. The Soviet Union was not the first maritime state to regard its sailors suspiciously and curtail their movement; the British Royal Navy had a long tradition of forced recruitment and widespread desertion among its crews.[16] In the context of the Cold War, however, jumping ship was understood as defection, and efforts to prevent it shaped the way the Soviet Union defined borders at sea. Although they took great risks and swam great distances to seek refuge on capitalist ships and in foreign ports, Soviet sailors paradoxically served as a vehicle for advancing Moscow's legal goals. The state's claims on them were written into international agreements reached at the United Nations that established the boundaries of territorial waters and created a framework for governing the high seas for the first time in history.

The sailors of the *Tuapse* were at the center of this struggle for the seas and the minds and bodies of those who sailed across them. While Kuomintang authorities encouraged their defection and the United States promised them asylum, the Soviet Union mounted an international campaign to bring them home. The stranded sailors offered Soviet officials a unique opportunity to wield international law, counter the narrative of defection promoted by the United States, and push their distinct vision for governing mobility at sea.

In extending its power at sea, the avowedly anti-imperialist Soviet Union followed in the wake of past European empires built on the water and replicated, to some extent, its tsarist predecessor. The development of the imperial Russian navy had entailed the adoption of foreign shipbuilding and navigational techniques in service to Russia's great power ambitions.[17] This process was not without its risks, since it inevitably exposed rank-and-file Russian sailors to foreign lands and new ideas. When the revolution came, the radicalized crew of the battleship *Potemkin* in 1905 were among its first proponents; sixteen years later, an uprising led by sailors stationed at the naval fortress of Kronstadt challenged Bolshevik rule. The Soviet navy grew slowly in the 1930s, with authorities carefully monitoring the behavior of Soviet sailors, though the institution was less important to the state's military effort in the Second World War than it was for the United States and Britain. It took the outbreak of Cold War competition and the establishment of new alliances beyond Europe to spur the rapid postwar growth of the Soviet navy as well as the commercial fleet.

Concerned about the rise of Soviet maritime power, the United States sought to counter it whenever possible. As the Soviet state looked to expand its merchant fleet, the United States requested the return of the vessels it had transferred to the USSR as part of Lend-Lease.[18] By 1949, US officials worried about the creation of a Comintern shipping company, led by the Soviet Union, with an office in the busy port of Hamburg, West Germany. The company, warned officials, had the potential to become a global force in maritime shipping that would make inroads in the West and dominate routes to India and China.[19] State Department reports show that the United States monitored the construction of new vessels for the Soviet fleet, including the *Tuapse*, whose technical specifications were secretly relayed to Washington on its completion in 1953.[20] While records show that the US Seventh Fleet declined to take an active role in the Soviet tanker's seizure, the United States gave Kuomintang officials information about the ship's location in the South China Sea, and CIA officials subsequently praised the incident's potential to "disrupt bloc ocean traffic" in remarks before the National Security Council.[21] US officials were prepared to go to great lengths to maintain their country's maritime supremacy.

The sea allowed for the global circulation of information, people, and goods to advance the Soviet state's mission but at the same time was a space of ideological peril.[22] Just as the British Empire mobilized racial and ethnic minorities in its maritime expansion but viewed the participation of such groups warily, the Soviets drew heavily on non-Russian populations who lived in the state's coastal areas—among them Lithuanians, Ukrainians, and Georgians—to staff their merchant fleet but worried about their susceptibility to nationalist tendencies.[23] Official Soviet publications proudly observed that many sailors came from worker and peasant backgrounds; indeed, serving on a merchant ship was one of the few ways that Soviets without a higher education, party membership, and official connections could travel abroad. Yet their experiences on the high seas and in foreign ports raised concerns that they might elude state control. Despite strict policies to police Soviet sailors' behavior, authorities in Moscow worried that the sea served as a site of foreign contamination, exposing citizens to capitalist goods, habits, and ideas. Perhaps most concerning of all, the state's opening to the sea brought a greater risk of defection.

To combat this risk, Soviet sailors who showed any evidence of "treasonous intent" or made "treasonous statements" were banned from sailing abroad.[24] These were broad categories for defining dissent and could include anything from expressing dissatisfaction with life in the Soviet Union to demonstrating an appreciation for American fashion. As on land, the KGB relied on political officers to explain what was acceptable and placed informants on ships to report bad behavior. However, sailors often found creative ways of avoiding the scrutiny of their ship's political officer and skirted the restrictions placed on them while on shore leave. While they were supposed to enter foreign ports in groups of four or five with an "elder" Communist Party member as a chaperone and officially restricted to a brief visit to the local marketplace and some window shopping, many managed to buy blouses, scarves, nylons, chewing gum, and jewelry that they sneaked into the Soviet Union to sell. Others eluded their "elder" and wandered off to entertain themselves in the bars and brothels found in port cities across the globe.[25] The KGB scrambled to piece together what transpired during these unsupervised periods, and violations could place the entire group of sailors under scrutiny; this reinforced mutual accountability but sometimes meant that infractions were not reported out of fear of punishment.[26]

While it remained a dangerous endeavor, fleeing in a foreign harbor or swimming from a Soviet ship was sometimes a better prospect than defecting across a land border, since Soviet authorities lacked clear legal jurisdiction in maritime spaces. One sailor to take advantage of the shortcomings of Soviet control in foreign ports was Vladislav Tarasov, a twenty-four-year-old crewman from Ukraine. He set sail on the tanker *Chernovtsi*, bound for Calcutta, in the fall of 1962. On the way, Tarasov ran afoul of the ship's political officer. After Tarasov skipped a string of mandatory political meetings required of crew members, the officer searched his personal items, finding notes Tarasov had written complaining of life on board the Soviet ship. The officer hinted that the voyage would be Tarasov's last. In response to this threat to his livelihood, Tarasov crawled through a porthole when the *Chernovtsi* arrived in Calcutta, jumped in the water, and swam to a nearby US merchant ship, requesting asylum.

The Soviet Consul in Calcutta accused Tarasov of having stolen 700 rupees from the Soviet vessel's cash box, a charge that appears to have been concocted after his flight. Tarasov was held in a jail cell while his case was heard in an Indian court. Since theft in Indian territorial waters was not grounds for extradition, Soviet officials claimed that the alleged robbery took place before the ship's arrival, in international waters. The evidence Soviet authorities provided, however, was not convincing, and the court found that some of the documents presented by the Soviet side had been fabricated.[27] Tarasov was released and allowed to emigrate to the United States. The following year he testified before the House Committee on Un-American Activities on the restrictions Soviet sailors faced on board ships, suggesting that many more would defect if they were able to do so.[28] In the case's aftermath, the KGB conducted interviews with the ship's crew as well as Tarasov's wife, who remained in the Soviet Union, to see what might have been done to prevent his defection.[29]

Where it could, the Soviet state sought the return of wayward sailors. In the case of Akram Gindulin, a radio operator who defected in September 1956 while his ship was docked in Denmark, Soviet authorities were successful, but reliant on the sailor's unhappiness abroad. In Denmark, Gindulin was forced to serve a brief prison sentence for illegal entry and then moved from place to place by representatives of the anti-Soviet emigre organization NTS, which sought to use the story of his "swim to freedom" for propaganda purposes. Feeling exploited, he fled from a New Year's party in Copenhagen organized by NTS members to the Soviet embassy, where he requested safe passage back home.[30]

Gindulin's decision was welcomed by the Committee for the Return to the Homeland, which rendered his story as a cautionary tale of a sailor's disillusionment with life in the West. In a front-page article in the committee's newspaper, he confessed the mistakes leading to his "fall." After the failure of three successive marriages, he reported that he "began to abuse alcohol and drank especially heavily on his last journey at sea." Despondent, he "naively came to believe that fleeing abroad would resolve the problems in [his] personal life." Returning to the Soviet Union meant confronting his personal problems and accounting for his actions. He wrote, "I am proud of the fact that I found the courage to acknowledge my shortcomings and honestly express my guilt before the Motherland."

In closing, he expressed hope that his story would serve as a "warning" to other Soviet sailors.[31] Unmentioned was the fact that Gindulin was held in the internal prison of the KGB when the article was published. Despite his voluntary return and public confession, he still faced charges of treason for deserting the ship.[32]

While the KGB's prosecutorial powers within Soviet borders were formidable, the government's legal options were far more limited at sea. Authorities insisted that ships flying the Soviet flag were the same as a piece of the USSR as they sailed the globe, but Soviet sailors in international waters or foreign ports found themselves in spaces of contested sovereignty. As the experience of the crew of the *Tuapse* would attest, sailors remained the most vulnerable component of the Soviet Union's rise as a maritime power.

THE *TUAPSE* AT THE UNITED NATIONS AND
THE SUBSEQUENT JOURNEYS OF ITS CREW

Following their ship's seizure, the sailors of the *Tuapse* found themselves at the center of an international debate over the borders of sovereignty and citizenship at sea. Their captivity was protested by Soviet authorities, who sought their return and hoped to use the incident to undermine the Kuomintang and expand socialist shipping networks in the South China Sea. In Taiwan, the crewmembers' potential defection was seen as a way of thwarting Soviet ambitions and, at the same time, getting a group of Soviet citizens to recognize the legitimacy of communist China's archrival.[33] The capture of a brand-new commercial ship by what Soviet authorities referred to as the "Chiang Kai-shek remnant clique" highlighted the regional uncertainty caused by the competing claims of Taipei and Beijing.[34]

Kuomintang efforts to interdict shipping along the coast of mainland China began in 1949, the year the People's Republic of China was founded. The Soviet Union's decision to swiftly recognize communist China was viewed as a personal affront by Chiang Kai-shek, who had signed the Treaty of Friendship and Alliance with the Soviet Union just four years earlier. Though nationalist in its ideological orientation, the Kuomintang's ties with the Soviet Union went back several decades: Chiang Kai-shek had studied in Moscow, and his government in Taiwan arguably resembled a "quasi-Leninist party-state."[35] Chiang was viewed warily by the United States, which recognized his authority but refused to commit to defending Taiwan against a potential attack by Chinese communists until the outbreak of the Korean War in June 1950, after which the US Navy's Seventh

Fleet entered the Taiwan Strait at the northern end of the South China Sea to "neutralize" the body of water. The following year, a coalition led by the United States passed a UN resolution endorsing a trade embargo of the People's Republic of China that banned the shipment of weapons as well as "petroleum, transportation materials of strategic value, and items useful in the production of arms."[36] In February 1953, President Eisenhower issued an order "deneutralizing" the Taiwan Strait, which ended the Seventh Fleet's blockade of the waterway but exposed commercial vessels to aggressive patrols conducted by the Kuomintang, largely on decommissioned ships provided by the United States. In October of that year, the Kuomintang seized the *Praca*, a Polish tanker, confiscating the ship and bringing its crew to Kaohsiung; in May 1954, they captured a second Polish tanker, the *Gottwald*.

Kuomintang patrols threatened communist China's allies, but they also disrupted Western shipping companies seeking to resume trade with the Chinese mainland following the armistice in Korea.[37] According to data collected by the National Security Council, the interception of British ships heading to Chinese ports and the strafing of one by Kuomintang aircraft caused insurance rates on British cargo bound for China to quintuple. Britain, which had long supported the notion of freedom of navigation undergirded by its own naval power, responded by instituting a regular naval patrol in the Taiwan Strait to protect its merchant vessels.[38] Meanwhile, tensions continued to mount between Taipei and Beijing, culminating in the outbreak of the First Taiwan Strait Crisis in August 1954. Months-long armed disputes between Chinese nationalists and communists over islands in the strait ended with the United States threatening a nuclear strike against the People's Republic of China.[39]

Rather than getting directly involved in the military confrontation in the Pacific, the Soviet Union made its case for the opening of the South China Sea and the Taiwan Strait at the United Nations. The fact that the *Tuapse* sailors were being held in Taiwan enabled Soviet authorities to call for the free movement of ships in the Pacific and around the globe while maintaining a firm position on the jurisdiction of Soviet vessels and the rights of Soviet sailors. As the Soviets pressed their case in New York, Chinese nationalists in Kaohsiung stepped up their campaign to coerce all forty-nine crewmembers of the *Tuapse* to defect and seek asylum rather than return home. The effort was part of Chiang Kai-shek's campaign of "White Terror" against communist sympathizers in Taiwan.[40] It also paralleled communist China's efforts to induce the defection of American soldiers captured in Korea, using similar methods to discredit another superpower seeking influence in the region. The Kuomintang kept American intelligence apprised of their efforts, though the level of the CIA's involvement remains unclear.[41] Regardless, the defection of Soviet citizens, initially welcomed by Washington, took on new dimensions as it was pursued by a troublesome American ally with domestic goals in mind.

At first, the Kuomintang's interrogators employed material incentives: the Soviet crew was brought from the ship to an elaborate banquet, and a Russian-speaking officer in the Kuomintang's employ appealed to them to sign a petition requesting asylum. Those who did so were given new clothes, paid a monthly stipend, and housed in a hotel. As a special reward, some were granted a stay at a resort on picturesque Sun Moon Lake. Those who held out were subjected to harsh interrogation tactics, confined to individual cells, and told that the rest of the crew had defected and that they alone remained incarcerated. By the fall of 1954, twenty-one people, nearly half of the crew of the *Tuapse*, had requested asylum from Chiang Kai-shek's government. The extent to which their defection represented a sincere ideological break was questionable. According to a secret State Department memorandum, when one of the defectors "recanted" and decided to withdraw his request for asylum, he was subjected to electric shock treatment to "restore his mental stability."[42] Remarkably, he held out and joined the majority the ship's crew—twenty-nine of them in total—who insisted that they be returned to the Soviet Union.

Most of the sailors who requested asylum hoped to move on to the United States, but American authorities were not convinced that they could truly be considered defectors. Even if US officials set aside the questionable validity of the coerced asylum requests, the country still lacked a clear policy for dealing with fugitive Soviet sailors. Article 11 of the 1951 Refugee Convention called merely for "sympathetic consideration" of asylum for sailors, and only for those serving as crew members on a ship registered in the country where they hoped to resettle.[43] Given the convention's ambiguity, the National Security Council repeatedly debated the procedures for handling "asylum for seamen from communist ships."[44] In addition to legal questions, there were logistical impediments to consider, since sailors sometimes jumped ship far from any US diplomatic mission.

These issues initially arose in discussions over the resettlement of the twenty-three Polish sailors who had defected from the first two socialist ships seized by the Kuomintang, the *Praca* and *Gottwald*. While the secretary of state and attorney general authorized their entry into the United States and a congressional resolution gave them the "right to make application to regularize their status," restrictive US immigration regulations prompted Joseph May Swing, the commissioner of immigration and naturalization, to suggest an unusual means of crossing America's borders. On

October 21, 1954, Swing called upon US authorities "not to issue any visas, passports or anything else and to have the Navy or Airforce pick them up in Formosa [Taiwan] and bring them to an agreed point in California where they would be paroled by the Immigration Service as though they had been shipwrecked and picked up in the open sea."[45]

Even when socialist sailors managed to enter the United States, questions remained about their desirability. Without permanent residency or US citizenship, they were unable to travel abroad and could no longer be employed in long-distance shipping, making them an economic liability. Moreover, American authorities were skeptical about whether they could be categorized as political refugees. Although their escape was often dramatic, most seemed to be motivated by a desire for a better life or a lust for adventure—or, in the case of those seized by the Kuomintang, they were pressured into making a political choice. They did not easily comport with existing understandings of refugees, let alone defectors of "special interest," since many were relatively uneducated and possessed little in the way of sensitive intelligence. Although Soviet sailors had a slightly better chance of reaching American shores than those from other socialist states, officials in Washington were concerned that an open-ended commitment to granting asylum to crewmembers would harm the naval and shipping operations of the United States. Such a commitment, they feared, might encourage the Soviet Union to seize American ships in disputed waters and could threaten access to American sailors who ran into trouble in socialist states. In this regard, the American stance resembled the cautious approach to uninvited asylum seekers at US embassies.

The *Tuapse*'s seizure presented even thornier problems when it came to law and America's entanglements abroad. Privately, Secretary of State John Foster Dulles conceded that he knew of "no grounds recognized by international law on which [the] tanker could be confiscated." In classified reports, US intelligence analysts acknowledged that the *Tuapse* had been seized beyond the territorial waters of Taiwan and confirmed that the kerosene on board was unsuitable for jet fuel and was indeed meant for lighting, as the Soviet side had claimed.[46] While the National Security Council was gleefully briefed on the "tie-up of valuable vessels and cargos" owned by the Soviet Union in the wake of the ship's seizure, and the CIA received reports on the interrogation of its crew, the prolonged detention of the Soviet sailors was becoming an international relations liability for the United States.[47] Yet Chiang Kai-shek proved unshakable in his pursuit of the crew's defection. He even rebuffed a personal request from President Eisenhower in the fall of 1954 to return the ship and its sailors.[48] Although the United States retained an overwhelming naval advantage in the Pacific, its reliance on a stubborn ally with its own designs on the South China Sea created an opening for the Soviet Union.

On December 13, 1954, nearly six months after the seizure of the *Tuapse*, Soviet diplomat Iakov Malik stood before the United Nations General Assembly and denounced the detention of the ship and its crew as an "act of piracy on the high seas."[49] Although his speech was framed as an appeal for "international peace," Malik drew on a long tradition of using anti-piracy campaigns to advance state-backed legal regimes at sea. Centuries earlier, European empires had claimed the right to pursue pirates and used the discourse of international law to extend their jurisdiction over disputed maritime areas.[50] With European imperialism fading, the Soviet Union sought to rally opposition to the "state piracy" practiced by Kuomintang authorities and backed by the United States.

Malik's remarks reflected the emphasis on "socialist legality" inside the post-Stalinist Soviet Union and the deployment of international law beyond its borders. The latter's public face, at least initially, was Andrei Vyshinsky, the jurist who presided over the Moscow Trials of the Great Purge but also supervised the Soviet delegation at Nuremberg and saw international law as an institution that could stabilize the interstate order and secure Soviet interests. As the permanent representative of the Soviet Union at the United Nations in 1953–54, Vyshinsky argued that the Soviets should press the issue of the seizure of the *Tuapse* at the UN even if its resolutions had little chance of passing. In a note to the Communist Party's Central Committee before Malik's speech, Vyshinsky stated that "the very discussion . . . of the *Tuapse* will possess political significance since it will once again allow us to expose a gross violation by the government of the United States of widely recognized norms of international law and one of its most important principles: the freedom of navigation."[51] Vyshinsky called for a coordinated international press campaign to accompany the Soviet Union's appeal at the United Nations.[52] In the articles of sympathetic journalists, appeals to international law were used to portray the United States as an imperialist actor claiming the seas of Asia and beyond, unfettered by any rules.[53]

While he placed the blame squarely on the United States, Malik framed the governance of the high seas as an issue of concern to all states. He chronicled the "systematic attacks of Chiang Kai-shek's forces, acting under the protection and authority of the United States," against "ships flying the flags of the USSR, Poland, the United Kingdom, Denmark, the Netherlands, Italy, Panama, and various other states." Among these, he noted that "there had been 141 such attacks on British ships alone." His primary focus, however, was the fate of the *Tuapse*, which "had been seized, its cargo looted, and its crew subjected to violence." He detailed sightings of US fighter jets in the area, Eisenhower's support for Kuomintang naval patrols, and US financial assistance as evidence that the United States was ultimately responsible. Citing Western legal scholars, he declared that "the principle of freedom of navigation had been confirmed in all international treaties on the subject for centuries." The resolution presented by Malik condemned the "violations of freedom of navigation in the area of the China seas" and called upon the United States to stop them.[54]

The proposal garnered some predictable responses. China, represented at the UN by the nationalist government in Taipei, denounced it as "outright propaganda." The Polish representative, supporting his Soviet allies, called for an expanded definition of piracy that would include the actions of the US-backed Kuomintang. The US representative viewed the complaint as simply "another maneuver in the cold war" and denied accusations of direct involvement.[55] Yet Secretary of State Dulles had to work harder than expected to rally American allies, including Britain, to oppose the measure.[56]

The context of decolonization proved crucial, as it was for the discussions on diplomatic immunity and asylum. Given their experience with the coercive maritime tactics of Europe's empires, post-colonial states were interested in establishing new legal norms at sea that would secure their claims to territorial waters and ensure that maritime boundaries would not simply be defined by American and British warships. The Soviet campaign cleverly affirmed solidarity with post-colonial states dreaming of controlling their waters—and the resources in them—even as it aimed to open the world's waterways to the growing power of Soviet shipping. A classified CIA report warned that "American responsibility for the *Tuapse* incident" would be "taken for granted in most quarters" throughout Asia and could have broad appeal in Vietnam, where Ho Chi Minh had just defeated French colonialists in the battle of Dien Bien Phu.[57] Even close American allies were forced to admit their support for the "freedom of navigation" while dismissing Soviet charges of direct US involvement. Although the Soviet resolution faced little chance of passing because of adamant US resistance, a group of post-colonial states, led by Syria and including Egypt, India, and Indonesia, gained backing for a slightly more neutral resolution calling on all countries to refrain from acts "considered contrary . . . to the principle of freedom of navigation on the high seas." With Soviet support, the resolution was approved and referred it to the International Law Commission for further consideration.[58] It was no small feat that Soviet diplomats had managed to champion the freedom of navigation without relenting on their claims to Soviet sailors.

The fate of the sailors of the *Tuapse* remained at the forefront of international attention. By the time Malik raised the case at the UN, a group of crew members who had defected in Taiwan were seeking admission to the United States, hoping to follow in the footsteps of the Polish defectors from the *Praca* and the *Gottwald*. The stakes were clear as the Soviet Union expanded its maritime presence: the issue of defection at sea was not going to disappear, and so the Soviet side sought to establish a clear precedent by launching a major campaign to return the *Tuapse* crew, while also working to build a sustainable legal framework that would maximize Soviet power over its ships and sailors.

Viacheslav Molotov, the Soviet minister of foreign affairs, spearheaded efforts to repatriate the tanker's sailors. In a meeting held in San Francisco in June 1955 with John Foster Dulles, he asked his American counterpart to urge the Taiwanese authorities to release the crew and their ship.[59] The Soviet Union, in a move that was both strategic and pragmatic, had already approached France for assistance in fall 1954. For France, taking on the task of negotiating the sailors' release gave the fading empire a prominent regional role after its embarrassing loss at Dien Bien Phu. France offered the services of its consulate in Taiwan, though its involvement undermined the unity of NATO. In a secret telegram, Dulles expressed concern "lest [the] French through cases such as *Tuapse* should come to view [them]selves as impartial meditators [in the] East-West conflict." Noting the "wobbly stand [of the] French in [the] past on [the] voluntary repatriation issue," he cast doubt on the "advisability" of encouraging them to "act as arbiter . . . on crew member defections."[60] Dulles feared that in cooperating with the French side, the Soviets might establish an international precedent on the return of wayward socialist sailors, just as they had done with the repatriation of Soviet citizens after World War II.

Nonetheless, the French established themselves as the primary intermediaries between the Soviet government and the authorities in Taiwan. In October 1954, the French chargé d'affaires was permitted to visit the crew before reporting back to the Soviet government.[61] The following month, Soviet officials appealed to the French government to take a more active role, passing along stipends, Soviet newspapers, and letters collected by the Soviet Ministry of the Maritime Fleet.[62] With French assistance, the twenty-nine crew members who had refused to defect were allowed to depart for Hong Kong and then traveled overland through mainland China. Flying from Beijing to Moscow, they reached the Soviet Union in August 1955, more than a year after the ship's seizure.[63]

Despite a heavily publicized appeal by the newly returned sailors for the release of crewmembers still in Taiwan, their repatriation was not forthcoming. Soviet officials blamed the French for their reluctance to press the issue further, noting "France's dissatisfaction with the position of the USSR in regard to the Algerian question before the UN," which signaled tensions in the two countries' opportunistic partnership.[64] Even if France had been willing to assist, it seemed that several of the sailors of the *Tuapse* no longer wanted to return home. It remained less clear who would take them. Of the twenty crewmembers remaining in Taiwan, US authorities decided to resettle nine determined to be "*bona fide* defectors of intelligence value" in the United States. Their purported intelligence value and, more important, their significance as people who had been sympathetically covered by major American media outlets like *Time-Life* outweighed concerns that their admission to the United States would cause Soviet charges of "piracy" to be "heard more sympathetically than last year in the United Nations General Assembly."[65]

The case appeared to be conforming to a familiar Cold War script: the United States welcomed a high-profile group of Soviet defectors while the Soviet Union vociferously protested. Just months after their arrival in America, however, five of the nine Soviet sailors dramatically redefected to the Soviet Union with the help of Soviet officials posted to the United Nations. Their decision to return, occurring in the midst of the broader Soviet "redefection" campaign, stoked fears among American policymakers that the Soviet Union was not only expanding its influence at sea but also within the territorial borders of the United States.

Initially, the Soviet Foreign Ministry had instructed its ambassador, Georgi Zarubin, simply to seek a meeting with the sailors in the United States, sending him letters from their family members and authorizing him to give assurances that they would not be prosecuted upon their return but would instead get their old jobs back in Soviet shipping.[66] However, after an official request by Ambassador Zarubin to meet with the sailors was rebuffed by the State Department in February 1956, the Soviet side resorted to more nefarious measures. According to a subsequent report of the US Senate Judiciary Committee, KGB officers, operating under the cover of the Soviet delegation to the United Nations, systematically tracked the sailors down, accosting two of them on the New York subway, and later approaching the same pair at a local dancehall, where they delivered letters from the sailors' relatives.[67]

While the Senate report may have been biased and the details of the KGB's operations abroad are still classified, it is worth noting that the same letters had earlier been provided to the Soviet ambassador, along with photographs of the sailors to help identify them. It would not have been the first time that the KGB's foreign operations were entwined with those of the Soviet Foreign Ministry.[68] According to the Senate committee, representatives of the Soviet UN delegation next appeared in the room of another one of the sailors at the George Washington Hotel in New York in the afternoon of April 5, 1956, bearing letters from the sailor's mother and asking him to come to the residence of the Soviet ambassador to the United Nations. The same evening, two more of the *Tuapse*'s sailors were visited in Paterson, New Jersey, by the same Soviet officials. The officials told the landlord to leave, purchased three bottles of vodka and several bottles of beer, and stayed in the apartment until 6:00 the following morning, when they departed with the sailors. The landlord came back to find that pictures "had been broken" and "records had been smashed." He also reported finding "a bloody shirt," evidence in the eyes of the Senate committee that "force, and even violence, had been committed."[69] It is also possible that the dogged ability of the Soviet state to track their whereabouts may have intimidated the sailors and convinced them that return was their best option.

Whatever transpired, when Immigration and Naturalization Service officials caught up with the five departing sailors as they prepared to board a Scandinavian Airlines flight at New York's Idlewild Airport the next day, all attested they were leaving of their own free will. In the wake of their departure, the two Soviet representatives from the UN delegation accused of accosting them, Aleksandr Gurianov and Nikolai Turkin, were told that their presence in the United States was "no longer desirable."[70] Returning to the Soviet Union, Gurianov and Turkin would later provide testimony on the behavior of the sailors in the United States to the KGB; it is likely that they were employed by the secret police during their entire American posting. The crew members were given a public welcome, and the Soviet press explained that they had escaped "threats, torture, and systematic abuse" in Taiwan only to end up trapped in the United States, "surrounded by agents and persons hostile to the Soviet Union."[71] Officially, it was reported that they would receive three months' paid leave before returning to their jobs. In reality, they soon faced prosecution for treason behind closed doors.

Meanwhile, the sailors from the *Tuapse* who were still in Taiwan found themselves with a dwindling set of choices. In 1958, four of the eleven sailors were permitted to relocate to Brazil after the United States turned them down. Their transportation costs were quietly covered by US Escapee Program funds, but American authorities kept them at arm's length despite the fact they had hoped to resettle in the United States.[72] It was feared that they, too, might redefect and generate further negative publicity, although the decision to send them to a third country backfired. After arriving in Brazil, the sailors traveled to Uruguay, located the Soviet embassy, and

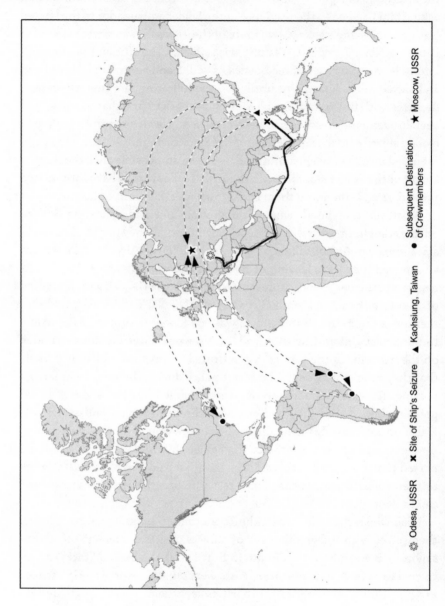

Figure 5.1 The Voyage of the *Tuapse* and the Subsequent Journeys of Its Crew

✳ Odesa, USSR   ✖ Site of Ship's Seizure   ▲ Kaohsiung, Taiwan   ● Subsequent Destination of Crewmembers   ★ Moscow, USSR

returned home.[73] The four sailors remaining in the United States became permanent residents through a special act of Congress but lived under assumed names and worked odd jobs in lumberyards, factories, and restaurants. As the decade came to a close, seven crew members remained stuck in Taiwan under house arrest.

COMPROMISES AND CARVE-OUTS IN GENEVA: SUPERPOWER POLITICS AND THE LAW OF THE SEA

With the sailors of the *Tuapse* scattered across the globe, Soviet representatives were dispatched to Geneva in February 1958 to codify a legal regime for the seas and advance the Soviet Union's maritime agenda. Those meeting in the Swiss city sought to define maritime borders comprehensively for the first time in history. Past efforts to do so, such as the one undertaken by the League of Nations at the Hague in 1930, had been derailed by bickering among European empires and disputes over how far state authority extended beyond coastlines.[74] While the Cold War seemed like an unlikely time to find international consensus on such a contentious issue, the decline of European naval power, the rise of new states, and the participation of blocs led by the United States and the Soviet Union raised hopes that one might be reached. Adding to the sense of optimism was the fact that concurrent discussions at the UN on diplomatic immunity and asylum had taken a surprisingly productive turn.

The 1958 United Nations Conference on the Law of the Sea was the culmination of years of debate among the UN's International Law Commission. The need to establish a "regime of the high seas" had been identified as a priority in the commission's very first session in 1949 and prioritized over more controversial issues, such as a broader right to asylum.[75] Composed of representatives from capitalist and socialist countries alike, the commission had to steer a difficult course. One of its first reports, a memorandum composed in 1950, cited President Truman's postwar claim to the continental shelf of the United States as a major "turning point in international law." The memorandum sought to balance the proliferation of similar claims by other states against the need for the freedom of navigation, which, its authors optimistically wrote, had "lost the absolute and tyrannical character" it once had as a tool of imperial expansion. The commission was at least united in its commitment to punish piracy—portrayed as a threat to all states at sea. Even if committee members were divided on how to define the practice, the shared concern with piracy revealed that the legal regime at sea, though global in its reach, was to be state-based in its design. Ships flying the flags of old and new states alike were to be protected, while those who operated beyond the bounds of state authority were subject to punishment.[76]

Yet the case of the *Tuapse* was a reminder that the international recognition of post-colonial states was a protracted process, with two sets of actors claiming to represent the maritime interests of the world's most populous nation on the international stage. Charges of piracy, first leveled against the Republic of China by Soviet diplomat Malik at the UN General Assembly, became a way to undermine the legitimacy of Kuomintang claims on the South China Sea. The following year, Jan Balicki, the Polish representative on the International Law Commission, explained that while Kuomintang naval patrols flew the state flag of nationalist China, their seizure of foreign ships, cargo, and crewmembers revealed "the intent to plunder for gain" and "qualified as piracy"; as such, it needed to be "prosecuted by all states."[77] Although the International Law Commission, whose structure left socialist states in the minority, declined to expand the definition of piracy to include acts committed by government-authorized warships, the Soviet Union and its allies were whittling away the maritime ambitions of the government in Taipei.

Socialist bloc representatives had better luck arguing a second point, that socialist merchant ships deserved immunity as state-registered vessels. After much discussion, the International Law Commission agreed to grant state-owned tankers the same "complete immunity from the jurisdiction of any state other than the flag state" enjoyed by government warships.[78] Not only did this framework offer socialist sailors protection against potential attacks by Kuomintang "pirates," but it also made the path easier for socialist states to prosecute sailors if they attempted to jump ship, since it placed socialist ships firmly under the jurisdiction of the state in which they were registered. While a wider definition of piracy would have undermined the international legitimacy of nationalist China and exposed other maritime states to prosecution, safeguarding the immunity of government vessels was in the interests of all states. However, it benefited socialist ones—whose merchant vessels were state-owned—more than their capitalist counterparts.

A broader point of disagreement, especially worrying to post-colonial nations, concerned the limits on territorial waters that states could claim as their own. While the United States had been the among the first to assert commercial claims to its continental shelf, its leaders wanted to limit territorial waters to areas within three miles of the coastline. In essence, America's leaders wanted to maximize commercial exploitation off the US coast while preserving the right of their ships to move through the world's waterways and along the shores of other states. The proposal was fiercely resisted by its neighbors in the Western Hemisphere, as many Latin American states saw wider territorial claims as essential to safeguarding their sovereignty as well as their access to the sea's resources. Some states, such as Chile, Ecuador, and Peru, claimed a significantly wider berth for territorial waters, leading State Department officials to label them "200 mile extremists."[79] Realizing that states with a history of being dominated by larger foreign powers were inclined to support broader territorial claims on the sea, the US strategy was to keep discussions out of the General Assembly and confined to the International Law Commission. When the International Law Commission's draft was passed to a preparatory committee for the 1958 conference, US officials worked behind the scenes to oppose "excessive" Latin American representation while forging agreements with "moderate" Latin American partners.[80] Meanwhile, Britain assured its American partners that it could nudge the Commonwealth countries, along with France, Burma, Turkey, and Iraq, toward an agreement.[81]

Yet it soon became clear that Britain's lingering imperial influence and US lobbying were insufficient to secure the Anglo-American vision of a strict three-mile limit on territorial waters. Smaller states with less developed navies rightly assumed that a narrow limit would only serve the interests of more powerful maritime states. In this instance, the Soviet Union aligned itself with post-colonial countries, proposing a more amenable twelve-mile limit. President Eisenhower was forced to admit to British prime minister Harold Macmillan that "we probably will not be able to halt the mounting momentum for Conference approval of a twelve-mile territorial sea."[82] Britain's lead negotiator in Geneva, Sir Alec Randall, worried that the United States and Britain risked being labeled "great power obstructionists" if they refused to compromise.[83]

Compromises and carve-out exceptions were essential for reaching the four Geneva Conventions on the Law of the Sea, which were finalized on April 29, 1958. Superpower politics, and the issues raised by the *Tuapse*'s seizure, set the boundaries of what was possible. Since it remained contentious, the definition of territorial limits at sea was ultimately postponed for a future conference. Instead, the Convention on the Territorial Sea and the Contiguous Zone floated the twelve-mile figure as a maximum and recognized state power to "prevent infringement" of its regulations, including those governing migration, within its "contiguous zone."[84] The question of whether all state-operated ships would enjoy immunity was also left without clear resolution. The United States, Britain, most Western European states, and even a handful of Latin American countries opposed the International Law Commission's draft agreement applying immunity to all government ships. The final text of the convention restricted immunity to "government ships operated for non-commercial purposes," but the Soviet Union and its allies were successful in codifying the "right of innocent passage" for all ships through territorial seas, including "straits which are used for international navigation between one part of the high seas and another part of the high seas or the territorial sea of a foreign State."[85] The detention of the *Tuapse* and its crew, disputes over the South China Sea, and the First Taiwan Strait Crisis lurked in the background of the phrasing. The USSR also used its power to declare an exception for itself and the entire socialist bloc: in a series of nearly identical signing declarations, the Soviet Union and its allies reserved the right to claim immunity on their state-run shipping vessels.[86] Another article in the convention strengthened the power of the flag state to regulate actions on board the ship.[87] In effect, the Soviet Union wrote restrictions on the rights of its sailors—and special preferences for its commercial ships—into a document of international law.

The second document agreed to in Geneva was the Convention on the High Seas. Once again, the *Tuapse* episode informed the Soviet agenda, which advocated an expanded definition of piracy. Although Soviet language broadening the definition of piracy to encompass "unlawful actions by state vessels" on the high seas, a reference to the *Tuapse* incident, did not make it into the convention, Soviet diplomats issued an official signing statement noting that the document's definition of piracy "does not cover certain acts which under contemporary international law should be considered as acts of piracy and does not serve to ensure freedom of navigation on international sea routes."[88] Similar statements were issued by the remaining signatories from the socialist camp.[89]

The Soviet side was quick to score political points and express solidarity with the "Third World" even as it affirmed some points of common interest with the First World. While Soviet representatives in Geneva argued for broader claims on territorial waters and spoke up for the interests of the People's Republic of China, they ultimately agreed to a framework that ensured the freedom of navigation for established maritime powers. Randall, the British representative, looked beyond Soviet rhetoric and perceived a convergence of East-West viewpoints at the conference, noting that "the Cold War situation, while it may have made some problems practically impossible to solve, has introduced in other directions a tendency to compromise instead of insisting on absolutely rigid positions."[90]

Both conventions on the law of the sea, like the Vienna Convention, preserved ambiguity and, hence, latitude for stronger states. A similar dynamic played out in the other two conventions forged in Geneva, which dealt with fishing rights and the exploitation of continental shelf areas. For the Soviet Union, ambiguity had clear benefits: its signing statements asserted the state's sovereign control over its ships and sailors even as the language on free navigation affirmed the right of Soviet ships to sail where they pleased. They reflected a broader Soviet effort to embrace selective aspects of globalization without relinquishing Moscow's hold on its citizens.

While some observers compared the extraterritoriality of embassies to vessels on the high seas, there were features of maritime borders that made them more difficult to define. Although a ship was sometimes described as a "floating territory," international waters were characterized by the absence of clear-cut state sovereignty, whereas embassies were permanently bound by claims of the host state and the sending state.[91] Embassies thus rested more firmly on the principle of reciprocity, whereas the high seas featured a shifting set of claims advanced by multiple sides, all of which rested on their ability to mobilize maritime power. While the international agreements reached in Geneva began the process of formally codifying maritime law, sea borders remained "liquid."[92] Even as Moscow pledged support to a global legal regime that reinforced its claims to Soviet sailors, officials concluded that the surest means to police a ship's borders was to shore up disciplinary measures inside the Soviet state.

TELLING THE STORY OF THE *TUAPSE* TO DEFINE LOYALTY AT SEA

Within the Soviet Union, the fate of the crew of the *Tuapse* was refashioned into a didactic tale about the ideological steadfastness of socialist sailors in the face of foreign pressure to get them to defect. Such a story, designed to edify the Soviet public and inoculate those preparing to set sail against Western tactics and temptations, was based upon scrupulous investigations by the KGB.[93] As crewmembers returned home, the KGB either held them up as representative examples of good behavior at sea or prosecuted them for having transgressed ideological borders while they were abroad. The experiences of the ship's crew became the focus of a series of criminal cases; they were also the subject of a wildly popular Soviet film, numerous articles in the Soviet press, and two literary accounts. The issue of maritime law was dramatized in these cinematic and literary representations, which depicted the diplomatic maneuvering of the Soviet government on the world stage. Yet these popular accounts went beyond strictly legal arguments to examine the essence of loyalty and treason at sea.

The Soviet state began determining whom to prosecute and whom to hold up as an instructive example even before the sailors returned home. The freed sailors were interrogated upon their arrival in mainland China by representatives from the Ministry of the Maritime Fleet as well as the Soviet embassy—some of whom were likely undercover KGB officers.[94] Crewmembers were kept in Beijing from July 28 until their flight to the Soviet Union on August 5, 1955. The delay was attributed to concerns about the sailors' health after a lengthy period of captivity, but that time was also used to question them about their experiences and begin grooming them for public appearances. Shortly after they touched down at Moscow's airport, Viktor Bakaev, the minister of the maritime fleet, wrote a top-secret memorandum to the party's Central Committee summarizing the preliminary findings on the crew's behavior in Taiwan. Bakaev detailed the pressure the sailors faced to defect from the Soviet Union and the methods Kuomintang authorities had used against them, including threats, beatings, and solitary confinement, but also material rewards given to those who cooperated. Even at this early stage, the Soviet state sought to determine who among the crew remained unwavering, why those who defected did so, and how the case might be used publicly to inculcate a sense of loyalty among other sailors.

Bakaev's report introduced elements of the sailors' story that would later resurface in popular artistic representations: a cunning Kuomintang officer named Li, who led the interrogations as a master of psychological torture; Sokolov, a Russian emigre who worked as a "provocateur" for the authorities in Taiwan; and the coercive practice of photographing the sailors with scantily clad women, a form of blackmail meant to convince them that, if they returned home, the pictures would be made public and they would be punished by Soviet authorities. The individuals and themes described in the report fed into preexisting concerns about the psychological, ideological, and sexual threats that Soviet sailors faced at sea.[95]

Those who had not wavered were celebrated at an initial press conference after their return. However, their remarks at the event were limited to expressions of gratitude to Soviet officials for securing their release and returning them home. The official story of their experience was still being revised by the KGB and the Ministry of Foreign Affairs, both of which were involved in directing publicity around the *Tuapse* case. When the details of their extended stay in Taiwan were disclosed several months later, some elements from the secret report to the Central Committee were preserved, others were reframed, and a few were removed. Appearing at a meeting with leading Soviet artists and writers on November 2, 1955, meant to inspire state-sanctioned literary and cinematic productions, the ship's captain,

Vitaly Kalinin, and its first mate and political officer, Dmitry Kuznetsov, relayed an account that remained artistically compelling but was clearly designed to instruct Soviet citizens about the risks of sailing the high seas in the Cold War.

Smartly dressed in a suit and tie, with his hair freshly cut, Kalinin commanded the audience's attention as he recounted his harrowing experience.[96] He recalled the sense of promise he felt as his gleaming new vessel, outfitted "with the latest technology," set sail from Odesa, though he remained cognizant of the threat that foreign travel posed, with "capitalist countries doing all they could" to turn Soviet sailors "into traitors of the Motherland." At first he demurred to go further, saying it was "shameful" what the Kuomintang "pirates" did to coerce the defection of Soviet sailors, but the crowd audibly begged him to go on. The account he then provided incorporated elements of the Soviet Union's appeals to international law, noting the ship's position 125 miles from Taiwan when it was seized. It also cast blame on the United States, whose intelligence officers reportedly oversaw attempts to get the crew to defect. He emphasized the crew's resistance, first in preventing the nationalist Chinese forces from lowering the ship's Soviet flag, then in going on a hunger strike, and finally in resisting the Kuomintang's interrogation tactics. For the first time, he introduced a few heroic figures among the crew who represented the bravery befitting Soviet citizens: Kolia Fedorov, a seventeen-year-old on his first voyage who remained "steadfast" in captivity; and Olga Panova, the ship's buffet operator and the sole woman on board, who was held in solitary confinement for seventy-two days, then dropped off in a military barrack, where she was taunted and threatened, but through it all, the Kuomintang "could do nothing to break her will."

Gone from the story were the sailors who gave in to the Chinese nationalists' demands. Speaking of the twenty crewmembers who had not yet returned to the Soviet Union, Kalinin claimed that "not a single one had committed treason"—allegations to the contrary were simply a "provocation" by the Kuomintang and their American patrons. An aesthetic innovation in Kalinin's account was his effort to cast the experience as an "Oriental captivity" narrative, specially designed, it would seem, to counter popular accounts of American POWs held in Korea and "brainwashed" by communist forces.[97] Kalinin spoke of the use of "Asiatic methods" of torture: confinement in aluminum sheds in extreme heat, starvation, threats of execution, and even sleep deprivation by prolonged exposure to screaming children, though he was careful to contrast the Kuomintang with the "good" communist Chinese despite the fact that both shared the same "physical appearance."[98] The fact that the captain's account was intended for popular consumption was reinforced by his participation in a radio broadcast for Soviet sailors several weeks later. Again he told his story and reminded listeners that the Soviet ship was a "small but sacred piece of Soviet territory." Following the captain's account, the famous Soviet opera singer Maksim Mikhailov concluded the broadcast by remarking that Kalinin's resolve in captivity placed him in the pantheon of Soviet heroes, alongside celebrated Red Army soldier Vasily Chapaev in the Civil War, the martyred partisan Zoya Kosmodemianskaia in the struggle against the Nazi invaders, and the tsarist-era patriot Ivan Susanin, whom Mikhailov was famous for portraying on stage in *A Life for the Tsar*.[99] The process of mythologizing the sailors' difficult experiences abroad was under way.

A few months later, in March 1956, the Young Communist League's publishing house released *The Tanker Tuapse: A Documentary Tale*. The book's title acknowledged that it was a mixture of fact and fiction. Although the authors listed were Kalinin and Kuznetsov, the narrative was in the third person and the plot structured around a tale of survival on a hostile tropical island that evoked *Robinson Crusoe*.[100] The novella opens with the seizure of the *Tuapse* by a ship flying the "pirate flag" of the Kuomintang, followed by the captivity of the crew on Taiwan.[101] The island's tropical conditions are at once oppressive and alluring; when the sailors begin their hunger strike, their Taiwanese captors taunt them by throwing bananas, pineapples, and papaya through the ship's portholes. These exotic fruits—unavailable in the Soviet Union—tempt the sailors, but even seventeen-year-old Kolia Fedorov, cast as the novella's sympathetic hero, resists.[102] As a bastion of Kuomintang rule propped up by American patronage, Taiwan and its temptations also have a Western flavor. The crew is brought to sumptuous restaurants, where impeccably dressed waiters attend them in a "cool" dining room that offers a respite from the tropical heat.[103] Their captors represent the island as a gateway to the West: if the sailors simply sign the request for asylum, they will be resettled in the United States and given houses, cars, and good jobs. Young Kolia is even promised work as an actor in Hollywood but defiantly proclaims that he would rather return home to the collective farm where he grew up.[104] In addition to the steadfast Kolia, a slightly older figure, Misha Boltunov ("Bolt"), embodies the ideal Soviet sailor. As the son of collective farmworkers from central Russia, he is grounded in the soil, but as an educated person who sagely cites Jules Verne upon meeting the French consular officer, he is a capable representative of the socialist state abroad.[105] Although his character was based on an actual crewmember, the novella's production notes indicate that the chapter on "Bolt" was added later to provide an aspirational role model.

While the ship's sailors are rooted in the Soviet Union, the captors are depicted as nationally indeterminate people with no homeland. "Mister Li," the main interrogator, is described as a "half-Chinese, half-Yankee" who speaks fluent Russian. According to the novella, he was born in the eastern Russian port of Vladivostok, studied in the United States, and subsequently lived around the world in "parts unknown."[106] The other interrogator in the story, also based on an actual figure, is the Russian emigre Sokolov. He invites Kuznetsov, the first mate, to join him like a true "Russian sailor" in drinking a bottle of vodka with a label that reads "Comrade."[107] Sokolov, however, is unmasked as a shape-shifting CIA officer by Kuznetsov, who says, "You are not Russian, 'Mister Sokolov,' and you're not Sokolov."[108] A third figure, Lena, is identified as the half-Russian, half-Chinese wife of one of the interrogators. She attempts to seduce "Bolt" by visiting his cell and speaking to him in "a most tender voice." Rather than falling for Lena, "Bolt" ends up pitying the young woman, who was born in Moscow but spirited by her wealthy parents out of Russia after the revolution.[109] Even while she is imprisoned on a distant island, Olga Panova, the ship's buffet operator, laments the tenuous position of emigres such as Lena and Sokolov, people who "were Russian by language and by birth, but were not citizens of their own country."[110]

The Soviet state eventually reaches the loyal sailors. In a final scene, the crewmembers, freed from solitary confinement, gather around a table in their shared quarters. At the center is a Soviet flag fashioned out of scraps of paper pasted together with breadcrumbs. The reader is solemnly reminded that this is the "real government flag of the USSR, because the people surrounding it, despite everything that happened, remained citizens of the Union of Soviet Socialist Republics."[111] Through such embellishments, combined with actual incidents culled from interrogations, the story of the *Tuapse* was refashioned into a tale that encapsulated the Soviet vision of maritime mobility, in which Soviet sailors, no matter how far they traveled, remained bound to the Soviet homeland.

Approximately three years later, the film *Emergency*, produced in Ukraine, was released, generating more ticket sales than any other Soviet movie in 1959.[112] In the film, the ship is renamed the *Poltava* but still carries kerosene to communist China and is seized by the Kuomintang. In place of Kolia and "Bolt," the film's hero is Viktor Raiskii, a charming young man from Odesa played by Soviet heartthrob Viacheslav Tikhonov; as Raiskii's love interest, the film introduces the equally fictional Rita Voronkova, an attractive young woman who works as the ship's secretary, in lieu of the real-life Olga Panova. Reflecting the relative openness of the Thaw, the film shows Soviets sailors in strikingly realistic terms: one has a tattoo of palm trees across his chest, another alludes to small-scale contraband trading. Once the ship is seized in open waters, however, the film uses clear visual language to make its political points. When the crew is taken to shore, the American military personnel who orchestrated their detention lurk by the docks in front of a container reading "made in USA." Held on an island of tropical temptations, the crew are bombarded with pineapples while on a hunger strike; later, they are taken to jazz clubs. When these methods do not work, the captors try to break their will through brutal interrogations. Once again, a contrast is drawn between clear-eyed Soviet citizens and a cast of morally compromised and nationally ambiguous villains. Sokolov, the Russian emigre, tempts the crew to defect in exchange for whiskey and women.

Unlike the novella that preceded it, the film addresses the issue of defection head on. One of the men on board, a difficult person who had poor relations with his shipmates, requests asylum. Yet he remains behind barbed wire as a plane takes off for the Soviet Union carrying the majority of the sailors at the film's end. In this sense, the film presents the "emergency" the crew experienced as a test of character and ideological loyalty. Raiskii, the film's hero, passes this test through bravery but also cunning, convincing his captors that he has defected in order to reach the French consulate, where he secures assistance in returning home. The film introduces the possibility that not all Soviet citizens were prepared to withstand the temptations that Soviet sailors faced in the Cold War.

In the three years between the novella's publication and the film's release, the Soviet state had interrogated and investigated nine additional crew members of the *Tuapse*: the five sailors who came back from the United States in 1956, just one month after the publication of *The Tanker Tuapse*, and four more crewmembers who arrived from Brazil in July 1958. Publicly, the return of these wayward sailors was trumpeted as proof that Soviets struggled for their own repatriation. The front page of the Committee for the Return to the Homeland's newspaper claimed that the sailors coming from the United States had sought to return earlier but were delayed because they were monitored by American intelligence and were so isolated that they had no idea the Soviet embassy was trying to reach them. The newspaper showed the young men smiling at the press conference following their arrival in Moscow. The photographs were contrasted with one taken in "free" America, where the faces of the homesick sailors in a drab room "spoke for themselves." Coverage of the story shifted the blame away from Soviet emigration restrictions, instead criticizing the United States for blocking the return of Soviet citizens.[113]

When four more sailors returned from Brazil in 1958, the same newspaper proclaimed "Another Four Are Saved." The accompanying article explained that the men had been coerced into requesting asylum in Taiwan after two months of "brutal beatings." Their choice was described as an elaborate subterfuge meant to help them return. While in exile, they were temporarily forced "to follow the orders of American intelligence, giving the impression that they were slandering the Soviet government." As soon as they could, they sought out the assistance of Soviet diplomats in South America. Back home at last, the newspaper reported that they would be welcomed back into the "friendly family of Black Sea sailors."[114]

The records of the KGB, however, reveal that the state's prosecution of the errant sailors was just beginning. Among the five returning from the United States, Nikolai Vaganov was charged with being the first to accept Sokolov's proposal to request asylum at a banquet in Taiwan. The crew members who returned with him provided testimony that resulted in Vaganov being sentenced to ten years in prison.[115] Those who arrived from Brazil were also held and interrogated for months, three of them in Moscow's infamous Lefortovo Prison and another in a separate KGB prison.[116] All faced charges of treason, and all were pressed to establish a precise accounting of the transgressions that occurred at sea, in captivity, and in resettlement abroad. The cases were as much about meting out punishment as they were about investigating the circumstances that led the sailors to defect.

Based on the evidence available, there is no indication that those sailors in the first group to return to the Soviet Union from Taiwan in August 1955 were prosecuted. Among those who came back from the United States, Vaganov, seen as a defector motivated by self-interest, was the only one formally charged. No information is available about the fate of those who returned from Brazil. Given the Soviet Procuracy's more lenient approach to prosecuting defectors during the Thaw, it is likely that they were punished but spared the death penalty allowed in cases of "treason in the form of flight abroad." Vaganov was credited for time served in the KGB's custody. After a "heartfelt admission of guilt" in which he confessed that he had "consciously decided on a criminal path," the state declined to confiscate his property and home.[117]

Soviet officials were more severe in prosecuting the ship's sailors who refused to return. The trials of those remaining abroad, conducted in absentia while the film *Emergency* was screened in theaters, were part of an effort to project Soviet justice beyond Soviet borders and into maritime spaces, even if the accused could not physically be brought to trial. Search warrants were issued for the four sailors still in the United States—Mikhail

Ivan'kov-Nikolov, Venedikt Eremenko, Viktor Tatarnikov, and Viktor Solov'ev—even though the Soviet state knew that they were beyond the practical reach of its laws; this legal act signaled that the men would continue to be judged as Soviet citizens.[118]

The primary target of the state's prosecution in the United States was Ivan'kov-Nikolov, who was seen as the original instigator of the crewmembers' betrayal. Even before the seizure of the *Tuapse*, he stood out from the other sailors as something of a misfit. Born in 1920, he was in his mid-thirties at the time of the ship's capture, while the other sailors who refused to return from the United States were much younger. While all four came from working-class backgrounds, Ivan'kov-Nikolov was the only one with advanced education, having studied radio operation at the Merchant Marine's technical institute in Odesa. However, according to a subsequent psychological analysis conducted by the KGB, he had also suffered a series of difficult setbacks. His father died in 1922 of typhoid, and his mother had also passed away by the time the KGB launched its case against him. After serving in the USSR's communication troops during the Second World War, he planned to continue his studies, but his department at the Higher Maritime School was disbanded, leaving him without a degree. For several years after, he seems to have drifted, working as an itinerant laborer around Odesa, leaving his first wife to marry another, and suffering from a bout of gonorrhea before finally joining the crew of the *Tuapse*. While there was a demand for experienced sailors like Ivan'kov-Nikolov in Soviet shipping, in hindsight KGB investigators saw that he fit the profile of someone who might flee.[119]

Investigators found evidence that Ivan'kov-Nikolov's ideological wavering began even before the ship's seizure. In Singapore, Ivan'kov-Nikolov was the one who spoke to the White Russian emigre who approached the sailors in the marketplace, and he later thanked his crewmates for not reporting the conversation to the ship's political officer.[120] When the ship was seized, he allegedly delayed reporting its capture to Moscow. Instead, he willingly served as a translator from English to Russian for the troops who boarded the ship and accepted new clothes from the Kuomintang in exchange for his services. Even seemingly petty details were catalogued by investigators, such as the fact that Ivan'kov-Nikolov refused to share his cigarettes with the crew in the early days of their captivity, stockpiling seventeen packs until the captain ordered him to divide them up.

Just two weeks after the ship's seizure, Ivan'kov-Nikolov was the first crewmember to formally "betray the Motherland," leaving his shipmates to live in a separate house with a Kuomintang officer. Because he obediently followed his captors' instructions and wrote a request for asylum personally addressed to Chiang Kai-shek, he received "privileges" denied the other sailors. KGB investigators were particularly interested in the precise nature of these privileges, which included a monthly stipend, more new clothes, and English lessons with an American teacher named Rebecca Van.

At this point, Ivan'kov-Nikolov began to voice distinctly anti-Soviet views. Encouraging his crewmates to join him, he praised the stores in Taiwan with their shelves full of products, comparing them to empty shelves in the Soviet Union. He spoke about his desire to move to the United States, the country with "the highest standard of living" in the world.[121] As he socialized with representatives of Russian emigre organizations, his statements grew more and more outrageous. At a banquet organized by the National Alliance of Russian Solidarists (NTS), he falsely described himself as the scion of a "noble family."[122] In another conversation, he claimed that "blue blood" ran through his veins.[123] Defection, it would seem, allowed Ivan'kov-Nikolov to reinvent himself as an aristocrat.

Yet the accounts given to KGB interrogators revealed strains behind the defector's aspirational self-fashioning. His crewmates noted that Ivan'kov-Nikolov spent a good deal of his stipend on alcohol and was frequently drunk, at one point falling from his balcony.[124] Such accounts fit the KGB's assumptions that moral dissolution accompanied unauthorized flight. The interrogations of the sailors who had returned from Brazil reinforced these assumptions; Leonid Anfilov, one of these sailors, reported that they drank heavily, slept with prostitutes, and used narcotics while in Taiwan.[125] The defectors who remained in the United States were described as particularly transgressive: Solov'ev reportedly came down with a bad case of syphilis; Eremenko dreamed of joining a Russian Orthodox monastery; and Tatarnikov allegedly began to speak to his captors in Chinese, while at the same time suffering from paranoid hallucinations and believing that his room was filled with spiders.[126] Poring over foreign news accounts of the defectors' lives abroad, investigators concluded that these psychological shortcomings were more likely a consequence of defection rather than its cause.

Prosecutors declared that the four sailors still in the United States were mentally competent to stand trial, as they had all defected "voluntarily" and "consciously." Ivan'kov-Nikolov was singled out, however, as someone who had plotted to work on "ships headed abroad" and "waited for the opportune moment to stay abroad and refuse to return to the Soviet Union," defecting mentally before departing physically.[127] On March 11, 1959, all four were given the most severe sentence possible: on the basis of the Stalinist-era order "On the adoption of the death penalty for traitors to the Motherland," they were to be shot and their property confiscated.[128]

Soviet officials probably did not imagine that they would be able to enact the sentence. However, a little over a year later, in October 1960, a man going by the name of Michael Nichols showed up at St. Elizabeth's Hospital in Washington, DC, displaying signs of schizophrenia. Since he spoke fluent Russian and talked about the Soviet Union, the local police contacted the Soviet embassy. When embassy representatives visited the man, they discovered that he was Ivan'kov-Nikolov. Although they suspected that he was suffering from a "psychiatric illness," they proceeded to encourage his repatriation. While he told them that he longer considered himself a Soviet citizen, the diplomats convinced him to complete an official repatriation certificate. American officials allowed the repatriation to proceed, perhaps seeing Ivan'kov-Nikolov as an unpredictable liability. On November 13, 1960, *Izvestiia* ran an article, "The Fate of a Traitor," using Ivan'kov-Nikolov's story as a cautionary tale of the mental degradation of a defector who had been promised wealth and fame in the West but suffered a psychological breakdown after being abandoned by his American patrons.[129] The following month, he was arrested upon his arrival in the Soviet Union. An updated account published by Kalinin, his former captain, in 1961 described Ivan'kov-Nikolov as a "weak-willed" Judas who had sold out his crewmates for "thirty pieces of silver," only to end up discarded by his American backers "like an unneeded, useless object."[130]

Within the Soviet criminal justice system, Ivan'kov-Nikolov's culpability remained the subject of debate. Although he had been cast as the Kuomintang's cunning collaborator, he was transferred from prison to medical care, and his death sentence was suspended. KGB investigators concluded that he had likely been suffering from schizophrenia since 1956; they released him to a regular hospital in 1977 and allowed him to return home to the care of his second wife in 1982.[131] Although Soviet authorities sometimes used psychiatric medicine to discredit and suppress dissent, the fact that Ivan'kov-Nikolov had been found in an American hospital suggested that he was indeed suffering from a severe mental illness. The decision to release him should not be seen as a purely humane action, however. He had already played his part in the cautionary tale Soviet officials had fashioned from his life.

The fate of the seven sailors still stuck in Taiwan remained obscure. After being featured in debates over maritime law and recounted to audiences in the Soviet Union, the story of the *Tuapse* was of declining political use. The remaining seven were scarcely mentioned by the Soviet press, and when Loren Fessler, an American journalist, located them in the suburbs of Taipei and sought to write about them for the *Washington Post* in 1967, the US State Department successfully pleaded with him to postpone the article. State Department officials worried that if the stranded sailors were brought to the United States, they might immediately seek repatriation to the Soviet Union. In fact, the Soviet Union ignored a direct repatriation request from them a few years later, concerned that proceeding would provoke an international incident of little political benefit. The crewmembers of the *Tuapse* had already served multiple purposes: in captivity, as the cornerstone of the Soviet state's effort to claim passage through the South China Sea; in emigration in the United States, as a deviant group of escapees from Soviet rule; upon their return home, as exemplary Soviet sailors or psychologically damaged defectors. Those remaining in Taiwan after so many years did not fit any clear-cut Cold War narrative. As Walter McConaughy, the US ambassador in Taipei, coolly remarked, "The seamen are ciphers now."[132]

THE UNCERTAIN FATE OF SEAGOING DEFECTORS

Even as the last group of sailors of the *Tuapse* were left stranded, state power was extended at sea, with the superpowers taking the lead. In the decades that followed the ship's seizure, shipping networks expanded, and governmental and commercial claims enclosed over 40 percent of the world's oceans.[133] Although the Soviet Union continued to contrast its "peace-loving" approach to maritime law with the "aggressive" and "imperialist" policies of the United States, it quietly backed away from the notion of "state piracy," drastically expanded its fishing fleet, and saw its shipping networks grow more entwined with those of its capitalist adversary.[134] The Second Law of the Sea Conference, held in Geneva in 1960, made no progress toward an agreement on the limits of territorial waters, but the United States and the Soviet Union began a series of bilateral talks at the decade's end to avoid "incidents at sea" between their ships.[135]

By the 1970s, the Soviet Union had achieved its goal of becoming a dominant force in naval operations and global shipping. It tended to view the sea like the traditional "great powers," seeking to maximize freedom of movement and brush aside local claims that encroached on its global maritime operations. The distinction between "capitalist" and "socialist" shipping operations, though never clear-cut, became even blurrier: capitalist ships traded in socialist ports, and socialist ships, some of them chartered by private operators, carried cargo from capitalist states.[136] By 1977, a classified American intelligence briefing observed that Soviet ships, despite "inferior service," offered shipping at lower rates than their Western competitors.[137]

By 1982, when the third and most sweeping UN Convention on the Law of the Sea was signed in Jamaica, the international framework regulating navigation, shipping, fishing, and territorial boundaries was firmly established.[138] It allowed states to claim territorial waters up to twelve miles from shore, a long-time Soviet demand, but also established exclusive economic zones of up to 200 miles. Soviet officials left Jamaica assured that the immunity of the state's vessels would continue to be protected by the convention's guarantee of the "right of innocent passage," though in a signing statement the Soviet Union refused to accept the convention's compulsory procedures for disputes over boundary limitations or any other matter that fell under the purview of the UN Security Council, where it retained veto power.[139] The United States declined to sign the convention altogether, noting that it would accept most of the provisions but remain unbound by the guidelines on seabed mining and oil exploration, which American policymakers and corporate leaders described as unnecessarily restrictive. In both cases, the superpowers made deliberate exceptions for themselves. They were not alone in doing so; most industrialized nations did not formally accede to the convention until a more favorable agreement was reached regarding the exploitation of deep seabed resources. Such an agreement was finally forged in 1994, leading the vast majority of the world's states—168 in total—to sign on, including post-Soviet Russia. Asserting its exceptional status as a superpower, the United States agreed to abide by the updated convention but refused to ratify it.[140]

The codification of maritime law during the Cold War advanced the claims of powerful states, sanctioned the extraction of resources, and protected shipping networks, but it virtually ignored migrants on the seas. The series of UN conventions wrote migrants out even as they wrote states in: governments gained the right to enforce immigration and emigration laws within twelve miles of their coastline; ships had to fly the flags of recognized states; and those deemed "pirates" could be seized and prosecuted by any state.[141] The fate of seagoing defectors and refuge seekers remained ambiguous, as they lacked many of the protections of international law. Their tenuous position recalled that of migrants seeking refuge in and around embassies but finding themselves without the protection of asylum. At sea, this arrangement suited the Soviet Union and its allies, which sought to engage globalization without loosening control of their citizens' mobility. It was largely accepted by the United States and other capitalist countries, which were primarily interested in protecting their maritime commercial interests and hesitant to accept renegade sailors who jumped ship.

Occasionally, the defection of a Soviet sailor brought the limitations of this arrangement into focus, as occurred in November 1970, when the United States and the Soviet Union met off the coast of Massachusetts to discuss fishing rights. Convened in the spirit of détente, the meeting began as a business-like discussion in which fishing industry representatives from both countries sought to strike a deal on the volume of flounder available along the US coast. Because of bad weather, they agreed to move the meeting from international waters to the territorial waters of the United States. Nearing the shores of Martha's Vineyard, the Soviet ship *Sovetskaia Litva*, carrying Soviet fishing specialists, moored alongside the US Coast Guard's *Vigilant*, carrying their American counterparts.

In the middle of discussions, Simas Kudirka, a Lithuanian sailor on the Soviet ship, jumped onto the deck of the *Vigilant*. Unsure what to do, its captain made repeated calls to the Coast Guard, which was not in the habit of handling asylum claims, and the State Department, which warned that the sailor's actions could be a Soviet "provocation." As a sailor who had jumped directly from one ship to another, Kudirka's legal status was unclear: according to the State Department, had he instead been found in the frigid waters below, he could have been "treated as a mariner in distress and rescued in accordance with the long-standing traditions of the sea." Meanwhile, the *Vigilant*'s captain was informed by the Soviet side that Kudirka was merely a "deserter" who had stolen $2,000 from the Soviet ship and was likely "drunk or mentally disturbed." In the end, the leadership of the Coast Guard, wary of undermining cooperation with the Soviet Union at sea, allowed a group of Soviet officers to board the *Vigilant* and drag Kudirka back to the *Sovetskaia Litva* against his will.[142]

After the incident on the *Vigilant* provoked an outcry among the American public and influential members of Congress, both the Coast Guard and the State Department revised their policies. They declared that "under no circumstances should the person seeking asylum be arbitrarily or summarily returned" before "determination of his status."[143] Yet over a decade later, in 1985, when Miroslav Medvid, a sailor on the Soviet merchant ship *Marshal Konev*, swam to shore near New Orleans, he was forcibly returned to Soviet authorities after two US border patrol officers concluded that the fleeing sailor had entered the country illegally.[144]

Defecting suddenly, often without any form of identification, sailors themselves helped maritime spaces remain zones of instability. Even after Mirsolav Medvid was returned to the Soviet ship, rumors spread that the man sent back to the *Marshal Konev* was not the same one who had swum to the Louisiana shore days earlier.[145] Others made journeys which so drastically diverged from the itineraries of oceangoing vessels that they raised suspicions. In 1974 Stanislav Kurilov, a thirty-six-year-old oceanographer from Leningrad, was found gripping the side of a fishing boat off the coast of the Philippines. He claimed to have jumped overboard from a Soviet cruise ship with only a snorkeling mask and fins and swum the long distance toward shore. Kurilov was initially thought to be a spy: his story seemed incredible, and State Department reports emphasized that he was "a former Soviet Air Force Lieutenant."[146] He was held for six months in the Philippines before he was finally allowed to emigrate to Canada.[147]

Some who swam to capitalist shores seized the popular imagination precisely because they were "ciphers" on whom all manner of desires could be projected. In September 1971, Sergei Kourdakov jumped from a Soviet trawler off the coast of British Columbia. The handsome young man claimed to have "found God" in the cold Canadian waters and became a popular speaker for Evangelical Christian audiences. They saw his defection as an inspirational case of spiritual transformation, even as questions swirled around the accuracy of his account.[148] Another kind of sensationalism surrounded the defection of eighteen-year-old Lillian Gasinskaia in Australia's Sydney Harbor in 1979. A crew member on the Soviet cruise ship *Leonid Sobinov*, she reached the wharf wearing only her swimsuit; photographs of the "Girl in the Red Bikini" appeared on the front pages of newspapers around the world. Gasinskaia's hasty flight conveyed a story of conversion to the desires of Western popular culture. Months after she claimed asylum, she became the first centerfold in the newly launched Australian *Penthouse* (under the headline, "Lillian: The Red Bikini Girl— Without the Bikini").[149]

Not all fleeing Soviet sailors were so welcomed. Few were as photogenic as Kourdakov and Gasinskaia. Most were uneducated laborers rather than eccentric oceanographers like Kurilov. Almost none had any real intelligence value. More typical were Vladimir and Grigory Talyshev, brothers who jumped ship in Tokyo and requested asylum at the US embassy. According to the State Department's evaluation, the brothers had "almost no money," "very few documents," "very little knowledge," and "slight education."[150] Low-ranking merchant sailors like the Talyshevs had little to offer US authorities, besides the risk that they might cause a public relations scandal by returning to the Soviet Union, which is what the brothers ultimately did.[151] The State Department warily tracked the rising number of incidents that occurred as Soviet shipping and tourism expanded and the sea became the closest thing to a pathway to emigration for many ordinary Soviet citizens. A sampling of incidents from the 1960s reveals their global spread: Tofik Kozunov, a Soviet sailor, sought asylum at the West German

Embassy in Japan; Bronislavas Kulbeskis, another sailor, jumped ship in Cameroon; Olga Farmakovskaia, a Soviet tourist, jumped from a cruise ship in Lebanon; and another tourist, Nikolai Maslokovets, jumped ship in Greece. Placed between the United States, which did not have a solid commitment to shelter defecting sailors, and the Soviet Union, which strove to maintain control over its citizens abroad, many third countries simply turned away these would-be defectors.[152]

Refuge seekers who arrived in larger numbers from countries besides the Soviet Union faced far less favorable odds. Among those fleeing Vietnam by boat following the fall of Saigon, it is estimated that thousands died at sea; many who managed to make the crossing were confined to makeshift camps in Indonesia and Malaysia.[153] Hoping to stem the arrival of Vietnamese "boat people" in British-ruled Hong Kong, in 1979 Prime Minister Margaret Thatcher directed her legal advisers to investigate the grounds for refusing "Vietnamese refugees taken on board vessels on the high seas."[154] The high seas remained open for commerce even as they became increasingly treacherous for migrants.

In the end, the last group of sailors from the *Tuapse*'s voyage were not brought home until 1988, more than three decades after they had left. They were probably only allowed back in support of Soviet premier Mikhail Gorbachev's efforts at improving relations with longtime adversaries like Taiwan. When they appeared on a Soviet television program following their arrival in Odesa, news commentators referenced the well-known film *Emergency*, which the sailors themselves had never seen. Strikingly, having been all but abandoned by the Soviet state and forced to live most of their lives in Taiwan, only three ultimately chose to come back. Four stayed in Taiwan, two passing away from illness, one committing suicide, and one becoming a full citizen of the Republic of China.[155] Despite the attempts of diplomats, prosecutors, and legal experts to apply state-backed law and order to the sea, sailors remained unpredictable and borders on the water remained fluid.

Cold War Airspaces

The plane carried vacationers returning from resorts on the Black Sea, families traveling to meet relatives, an enterprise manager making a connection for a flight to Moscow, and a merchant marine reporting for duty. Aeroflot Flight 244, one of many regional flights operating within the Soviet Union, covered the state's southern coast and was scheduled to run from Batumi to Sukhumi in the Georgian Soviet Socialist Republic before going on to the Russian city of Krasnodar. Among those boarding the plane in Batumi on October 15, 1970, were Pranas Brazinskas and his teenage son Algirdas, two Soviet Lithuanians who traveled widely across the USSR. The father earned his money shuttling between the Baltic republics and Central Asia, buying and reselling furniture, spare car parts, and carpets. Born in independent Lithuania in 1924, Pranas Brazinskas spoke Lithuanian as his native language, but his Russian was good enough to find opportunities in the burgeoning informal economy. After he separated from his Lithuanian wife to marry a Ukrainian woman and relocated to Central Asia, Russian was the language he spoke at home. Algirdas, born in 1955, more than a decade after the Soviet Union's annexation of Lithuania, was educated in Soviet schools and knew little of life beyond Soviet borders.[1]

On that October day, the pair had a plan that diverged from the plane's state-sanctioned itinerary and would take them across one of the most heavily guarded boundaries of the Cold War. Approximately five minutes after takeoff, the elder Brazinskas handed a note to the flight attendant, nineteen-year-old Nadezhda Kurchenko, ordering the pilot to change course and cease radio transmissions. When the alarmed flight attendant ran to the front of the plane and tried to lock the door of the cockpit,

Brazinskas and his son stood up and charged forward, armed with pistols and a hand grenade. The pilot sought to neutralize the hijackers by making a quick and sudden descent. Thrown to the floor, the hijackers began shooting; Kurchenko was killed and two members of the flight crew, including the captain, were wounded. After the firing stopped, Brazinskas and his son successfully occupied the cockpit. The crew had little choice but to follow their instructions.

On the ground, Soviet troops posted to the "forbidden border zone" between Georgia and NATO-member Turkey could do nothing as the plane passed over the observation towers and high-voltage fences constructed to prevent the unauthorized exit of Soviet citizens. Just thirty minutes later, the plane made an unscheduled landing in the Turkish Black Sea city of Trabzon. When the plane touched down, the passengers managed to exit through the side door, while Pranas and Algirdas Brazinskas remained in the cockpit. After some negotiation, they turned themselves over to Turkish officials, who agreed to consider their case for asylum. Political unknowns rather than active dissidents, the unlikely pair had carried out the first successful hijacking of a Soviet airplane.

Across the globe, the jet age was riven by a central contradiction: although the rise of civil aviation was fueled by government subsidies and took place during the Cold War, air travel promised a world without borders.[2] From the air, land borders that had been carefully fortified for decades were all but invisible, and oceans could be crossed in a matter of hours. Route maps produced by an American airline company in the 1960s depicted the globe as an interconnected network of cities set against a white background undivided by national boundaries.[3] In many ways, this optimistic vision transcended the Iron Curtain and was shared by civil aviation enthusiasts in socialist states. The Soviet air carrier Aeroflot was among a handful of companies at the forefront of the global aviation industry; its routes not only crisscrossed the Soviet Union and bound socialist countries to Moscow but also preceded US carriers in offering a regular jetliner service to London.[4] As had been the case with Soviet shipping, US officials warily regarded the expansion of Soviet air service before acknowledging that it was better to work with the Soviet side to build a jointly regulated framework. As late as 1963, the Kennedy administration considered it a matter of policy "to persuade other countries, particularly in Latin America and other underdeveloped countries, not to permit Soviet Bloc countries to provide air services."[5] Three years later, however, American policy had shifted away from direct competition, and the United States and the Soviet Union signed a civil air transport agreement to establish direct air service between the two superpowers.[6]

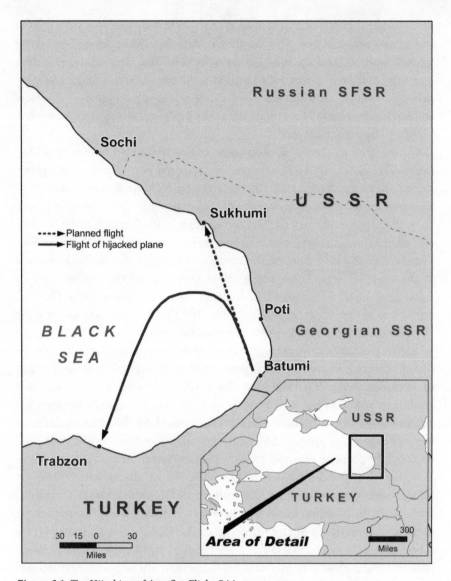

Figure 6.1 The Hijacking of Aeroflot Flight 244

The era's dream of global mobility was by no means accessible to all. An entry visa, contingent on one's citizenship, was needed upon arrival, and most socialist states still required an exit visa as a way of screening the ideological reliability of citizens traveling to the capitalist camp and ensuring their return home. Border controls were tightened at airports.[7] Airfare remained expensive, and even for those who could afford a ticket, planes were carefully ordered spaces with clear hierarchies of class and gender expressed in their seating arrangements and the prescribed roles of captain and crew.[8] Dreams of flying captivated the public in capitalist and socialist countries alike, but for most civilians unfettered air travel remained solely in the realm of the imagination.

For a time, hijacking was a powerful, if dangerous, tool that was used by marginal people on both sides of the Iron Curtain to reorder the hierarchies that governed airspace and challenge the prevailing borders of the Cold War. It grew into a global practice that spanned the political spectrum; in the late 1960s and early 1970s, protestors decrying US "imperialism" diverted planes to Cuba; the Popular Front for the Liberation of Palestine (PFLP), the Marxist branch of the Palestine Liberation Organization (PLO), sought international recognition by forcing aircraft to land at the "Revolution Airport" it established at Dawson's Field in the Jordanian desert; and disgruntled citizens in the Soviet Union pursued emigration by seizing Soviet airliners.[9] The practice tested the power of state sovereignty in the later decades of the Cold War and turned airspace into a borderland of competing jurisdictions and conflicting claims of citizenship.

The history of hijacking illustrates how states reasserted themselves in response to the global circulation of people, goods, and ideas in the jet age.[10] Responding to an outbreak of aircraft hijackings like that of Aeroflot Flight 244, the Soviet Union and other states devised new ways to patrol their borders and regulate the global mobility of people, even as they contended with new technologies, the emboldened networks of transnational activists, and the increased movement of capital. Just as decolonization had been accompanied by the walling off of embassies to migrants and the proliferation of maritime shipping networks paired with the enclosure of the high seas, the hijacking of Aeroflot Flight 244 reveals a more uneven history of globalization, in which expanded global flows of information and advocacy coincided with the extension of state jurisdiction in the skies.

Despite ideological divisions and heated disagreement over the fate of the Brazinskases, both the Soviet Union and the United States ultimately worked together to advance an international legal framework that redefined hijacking as an act of terrorism and turned the hijacker into a global pariah figure.[11] As they had done in extraterritorial zones and on the seas, the superpowers tacitly colluded to regulate Cold War airspaces when it suited their interests, even as their rhetorical attacks against one another continued. On both sides of the Iron Curtain, civilian airports and airplanes were militarized as states fought to retain the power to include or exclude people traveling by air based on established notions of citizenship. The experience of Pranas and Algirdas Brazinskas demonstrated that the "perils of statelessness" that had plagued displaced persons in the immediate postwar period remained relevant across the globe decades later.[12]

Even as it was integrated into the global economy and pressured by transnational advocates, the Soviet Union maintained control over the exit of citizens and sought to retrieve those who unlawfully crossed state boundaries by air. While the United States and its allies continued to criticize the limitations the Soviet Union and other socialist states placed on emigration, they tightened restrictions on the entry and the granting of citizenship to hijackers. The bid by the Brazinskases to defect by hijacking a plane, which tested the limits of Cold War claims about the freedom of movement, would be debated in a series of court cases in Turkey, the Soviet Union, and the United States that, along with agreements limiting diplomatic asylum and projecting governance onto the seas, helped the superpowers prop up their global mobility regimes in a rapidly changing world.

AIR PIRACY ACROSS COLD WAR BORDERS

Decades after he and his father carried out the first successful hijacking of a Soviet civilian aircraft, Algirdas Brazinskas sought to make sense of the dramatic event that marked the beginning of what he described as his "long search for freedom" beyond Soviet borders. He likened the episode to past instances of Cold War defection and explained that they had decided on hijacking only after other means of exit were closed off. His father dreamed of "escaping by walking through the deserts into Afghanistan, walking through the mountains into Iran, walking through the forests into Finland or sailing through the Baltic Sea into Sweden."[13] The younger Brazinskas, after "studying history books and maps of the Soviet Union and the surrounding countries," advised his father that they should escape to Turkey "because it [was] a member of NATO and [had] a long history of wars against the Russian Empire."[14] Their decision to hijack an airplane was inspired by the series of hijackings carried out by the Marxist PFLP at Dawson's Field just one month earlier. "If the Soviet-supported Palestinians can divert Western passenger airplanes and get worldwide publicity for their cause," they reasoned, "so must Lithuanians divert a Soviet passenger airplane and get worldwide publicity for the cause of Lithuanian independence and the struggle for liberation from Soviet occupation."[15]

Hijacking was not entirely new, but it gained prominence with the expansion of civil aviation in the 1960s and held the promise of transcending Cold War boundaries.[16] Unlike the more long-standing practice of Soviet military pilots absconding with their own airplane, the first instance of which dated back to 1934, hijacking involved the violent seizure of a plane, its crew, and its passengers. It could be carried out by ordinary citizens, even those not cleared for foreign travel.[17] A string of aerial hijackings had accompanied the Cold War's onset: in 1948, Romanian officers hijacked a flight to Turkey, a Czechoslovak flight was diverted to West Germany, and a Yugoslav plane made an unscheduled landing in Italy. All were cases of planes taken across socialist borders in pursuit of political asylum, though none of them were launched from inside the Soviet Union. Because hijacking was still an uncommon occurrence affecting a mode of transportation used only by a few, sympathetic observers in the West who welcomed the "escape" of socialist citizens likened it to the commandeering of other modes of transport on the ground and at sea. They compared instances of aircraft hijacking to soldiers driving stolen jeeps across postwar Europe's zones of occupation, sailors commandeering naval vessels, and the rerouting of the Czechoslovak "Freedom Train" to West Germany. A 1958 US Escapee Program newsletter went so far as to cite "three anti-communist Czechoslovakian citizens" who forced the pilot of an internal flight "at gun point" to cross into Austria as an example illustrating "the means which ingenious escapees employ in their efforts to gain freedom." "It is people like these," the newsletter concluded, "that the United States Escapee Program and the voluntary agencies stand ready to help in their rapid assimilation in the Free World."[18]

The liminal zones of airspace and airports drew increased attention as aviation technology grew more advanced and air travel more widespread. The issue of airspace came to the fore with the launch of secret US reconnaissance flights over the Soviet Union in the mid-1950s. These flights provided information about Soviet military capabilities but became a public relations embarrassment when an American U-2 plane was shot down and its pilot, Gary Powers, was captured. In an open letter to the United Nations, Soviet Foreign Minister Andrei Gromyko denounced the "policy of intrusion of U. S. military aircraft into USSR airspace," which "grossly violate[d] generally recognized principles of international law."[19] On the ground, airports became the scene of several prominent defections. Awaiting a flight at Le Bourget Airport in Paris in 1961, Rudolf Nureyev, the principal dancer of Leningrad's Kirov Ballet, eluded his KGB minders and dashed into the arms of a pair of French gendarmes, requesting asylum. In a reference to Nureyev's acrobatic abilities that also recalled Oksana Kasenkina's jump from the Soviet consulate, the ballet dancer's defection was described as a "leap to freedom" that occurred in an airport's international terminal.[20]

While airplanes, like ships, were generally believed to be subject to the territorial jurisdiction of their flag, when they were on the ground and physically connected to airport gates, it was less clear how much extra-territorial protection they were to be accorded. After the Bolshoi Ballet's principal dancer, Aleksandr Godunov, defected while on tour in New York, his wife, the Bolshoi's leading ballerina Liudmila Vlasova, was placed on a plane bound for Moscow. US authorities detained the plane for three days at John F. Kennedy Airport to make sure Vlasova was not being returned against her will. Since there were questions about the legality of boarding the Aeroflot plane, US negotiators met Vlasova in a "mobile lounge" devised by the CIA's counsel, Jeffrey Smith, as a neutral meeting spot between the Soviet aircraft and the American airport.[21] Although Vlasova ultimately decided to leave her husband and return home, the impromptu structure's back door was left open in case she chose to descend to the tarmac below and claim asylum.[22]

In contrast to incidents featuring prominent defectors and the legal loopholes created to accommodate them, hijacking often involved non-elite individuals and entailed unpredictable itineraries that were unsanctioned by any state. By the end of 1960s, hijacking had burgeoned into a widespread global phenomenon and US authorities began looking for ways to prevent it—even when it occurred in the socialist camp. The practice peaked in the late 1960s and early 1970s, when "skyjacking" became a rather common occurrence. According to one social scientist, who argued for the "contagiousness of aircraft hijacking," from 1968 to 1972 there were 326 hijacking attempts around the world, or on average one attempt every 5.6 days.[23] Confounding the notion that the freedom of movement was restricted only by socialist states, the greatest number of hijackings during this period involved planes steered from the United States to Fidel Castro's Cuba, which US citizens were legally barred from visiting.[24] US officials were initially at a loss as to how to thwart hijackings. Having armed guides ride planes was deemed "insufficient for guarding all flights," using metal detectors at airport gates was seen as intrusive and not "promising as a rapid solution," and "supplying stewardesses with knock-out drops" rested on the hopes that hijackers "could be persuaded to have coffee or champagne."[25]

As hijacking proliferated and crossed political divisions in every possible direction, its initial definition as a flight to freedom collapsed. In the United States, the public watched as the two technologies many believed would bring about global unity—the jet airplane and satellite television—instead conspired to produce dramatic hostage situations that unfolded on the nightly news.[26] Seeking to make sense of the phenomenon, readers eagerly consumed mass market publications authored by hijacking "experts." In one book, a Freudian psychiatrist suggested that most hijackers suffered from inner ear impairments during childhood, leaving them with a sense of helplessness that was only transcended when they seized control of an aircraft; in another, the former public relations director of Pan American Airways described hijackers as "sky pirates."[27]

The comparison between aerial hijacking and maritime piracy proved especially salient. In popular usage, it cast the hijacker as a romanticized outlaw; in a historical sense, it evoked the way some governments tolerated hijacking if it advanced their aims, just as past empires relied on privateers; in legal terms, it raised the possibility that the hijacker, like the pirate on the high seas, might be deemed *hostis humani generis* (enemy of humankind) and thus subject to prosecution by any state across the globe.[28] The criminalization of hijacking as piracy was made easier by the UN Conventions on the Law of the Sea agreed to in Geneva in 1958: the Convention on the High Seas gave states the right to pursue and detain pirates, and the Convention on the Territorial Sea and the Contiguous Zone extended state sovereignty "to the air space over the territorial sea" as well as above its land mass.[29]

Though likened to lawless "piracy," hijacking was not yet firmly associated with terrorism. In terms of dramatic genre, it could be portrayed as grave tragedy, as in the 1972 film *Skyjacked*, in which a routine flight to Minneapolis, piloted by Captain Hank O'Hara (played by Charlton Heston), is hijacked to Moscow by a disturbed Vietnam veteran. Perhaps because casualties were still relatively uncommon—airlines typically had a policy of acceding to hijacker demands—hijacking was also the subject of numerous political cartoons and two Monty Python sketches. In some cases, actual events bordered on the farcical. When a plane carrying Allen Funt, the host of the television series *Candid Camera*, was hijacked to Cuba in February 1969, a number of passengers initially thought the episode was a prank organized by Funt and began guffawing and pointing at the celebrity. After safely returning from Havana, Funt stated, "The biggest joke for me was how much the whole thing looked like a bad movie."[30]

Jokes told about hijacking could be heard on both sides of the Iron Curtain. West Berliners liked to say that LOT, the Polish airline, stood for "Landet Ooch in Tempelhof" (Landing Also at Tempelhof), a reference to the high number of Polish flights successfully hijacked to West Berlin's Tempelhof Airport.[31] In the socialist camp, there was initially less media coverage of hijacking attempts, the outcome of a policy that aimed to contain the "contagion," but news of aircraft hijackings still spread through informal channels, and the phenomenon became a part of popular humor among socialist citizens. Many jokes hinged on the nationality of the perpetrator. One, likely inspired by the Brazinskases' escape, told of an airline crew member who inquired whether there were any Lithuanians on board the plane. When one Lithuanian passenger spoke up, the captain approached him and politely asked "Where to, sir?"[32]

Even as hijacking came to be viewed as a threat to public safety, anti-communist groups in the West, many of them made up of emigre activists, continued to claim that hijackers arriving from the socialist camp deserved asylum on political grounds and insisted that hijacking was yet another form of defection from the "Captive Nations" of socialism. Yet if ordinary defectors were sometimes seen as having questionable motives, hijackers were regarded with even deeper suspicion, since their actions blurred the distinctions between political activism and criminal violence. They might claim to be terrorized "captives" from behind the Iron Curtain seeking refuge, but their actions threatened to terrorize civilian travelers and undermine international stability. In response, socialist as well as capitalist states sought to control, restrain, and ultimately eradicate the practice, asserting their sovereignty in the liminal realm of airspace.

AERIAL BORDERS ON TRIAL

The seizure of Aeroflot Flight 244 was initially perceived as a minor incident that the governments of both the United States and the Soviet Union could exploit for short-term gains. When President Richard Nixon heard about the hijacking, he caustically remarked that it was "good that it happened." National Security Advisor Henry Kissinger agreed, saying that it showed that hijacking was "a universal problem." These statements reflected the administration's interest in pressing the Soviet Union to join it in taking a tougher stance on the practice.[33] A little more than a month earlier, on September 11, 1970, Nixon had issued a stern directive to combat the "menace of air piracy" following the hijacking of four jet airliners by the PFLP that saw American citizens held hostage at Dawson's Field in Jordan. After years of resisting such measures, the president deployed armed guards, surveillance cameras, and baggage screening, and called upon the international community to "take joint action to suspend airline services with those countries which refuse to punish or extradite hijackers involved in international blackmail."[34] In his statement, Nixon affirmed his support for the 1963 Tokyo Convention against hijacking and the efforts of the International Civil Aviation Organization (ICAO) to coordinate anti-hijacking measures among member states.

The Soviet Union's resistance to these international efforts against hijacking had undermined their effectiveness, especially beyond the capitalist camp. While the post-Stalinist leadership in Moscow had pursued a policy of engagement at the United Nations and sought to direct the development of international law to their country's advantage around embassies and at sea, civil aviation remained an area where the Soviets eschewed multilateralism. The Soviet Union had declined to join the ICAO upon its creation in 1944, publicly objecting to the inclusion of Franco's Spain. Privately, it is likely that Soviet leaders resisted joining the organization—and continued to do so even after Stalin's death—because, although it was a UN agency, the ICAO was established in Chicago, its headquarters was in North America, and it used English as the international language of civil aviation. In addition, the ICAO, while affirming that states had sovereignty over the airspace above their territory, allowed for overflights and stopovers without advance permission. Serving the interests of countries that already had the capacity for international air service, it laid the groundwork for the dramatic expansion of US air carriers into foreign markets and the development of national airlines in the developing world under US supervision.[35] The Soviet Union, by contrast, first sought to develop domestic air networks within its vast territory, then strove to forge international linkages through bilateral agreements with its socialist allies, and only then attempted to match the growth of Pan Am and TWA, something its state-run airline, Aeroflot, eventually achieved.[36]

The Soviet Union had also refused to sign the 1963 Tokyo Convention against hijacking, partly because it had been prepared by the ICAO and partly because Soviet leaders wanted to preserve their right to determine what exactly constituted "air piracy," having conceded in their efforts to redefine piracy at sea in Geneva a few years earlier. The Soviet stance made some sense in the early 1960s, when planes were most frequently hijacked from the United States to Cuba; in essence, hijacking could be dismissed as a sign of discontent in capitalist societies. Furthermore, the Soviet Union maintained ties with radical groups involved in hijacking, including the PLO.[37] Indeed, Soviet press coverage of the Dawson's Field episode in September 1970 downplayed what it blandly described as "incidents involving airplanes," claiming instead that alarmist depictions of the hijackings in the "reactionary press . . . only served to help pro-Israeli propaganda divert attention" from the occupation of Palestinian territory.[38] While the Soviet Union refrained from openly endorsing forms of "air piracy" that fit its ideological worldview, some of its clients in the Middle East publicly praised hijacking as a useful tool to pressure more powerful states. In 1969, Syria even released a postage stamp commemorating the illegal diversion of TWA Flight 840 to Damascus by Palestinian hijackers.[39] Belief in hijacking's potential to transcend political limitations and challenge the stateless position of Palestinians was not unfounded. Looking back, the PLO's chief observer to the United Nations reflected that "the first several hijackings aroused the consciousness of the world and awakened the media and world opinion much more—and more effectively—than twenty years of pleading at the United Nations."[40]

Yet the Soviet Union had begun to change its view of hijacking even before the Brazinskases' unauthorized flight to Turkey, seeing the practice as a potential threat to socialist countries. In June 1970, Soviet authorities had arrested sixteen "refuseniks," most of them Soviet Jews who had been denied exit visas to Israel, for conspiring to hijack an airplane in Leningrad in order to flee the Soviet Union.[41] While the KGB had monitored the group of refuseniks, knew about their plans in advance, and arrested them at the airport, Soviet authorities were surprised by the level of international sympathy the would-be hijackers inspired among Western and Israeli audiences. For foreign activists who opposed restrictions on Soviet Jewish emigration, the escape plan seemed like a heroic, if desperate, effort to fly to freedom.[42] Concerned that hijacking as a form of defection could proliferate in the socialist bloc, the security services of the Warsaw Pact states met in Poland in October 1970 to discuss the adoption of special measures to combat the unauthorized seizure of aircraft. These measures were reaffirmed in a memorandum circulated soon after "the pirates' assault and kidnapping aboard the Soviet An-24 aircraft in Turkey," a reference to Aeroflot Flight 244.[43]

Compared to the case of the Jewish refuseniks—a group of intellectuals and dissidents who had been arrested before they could even board their plane—the hijacking of Aeroflot Flight 244 was violent and politically murky, involving a father with a criminal record for illicit trading and his underage son. It marked a turning point in the Soviet Union's approach to international civil aviation agreements and provided the superpower with an opportunity to publicly change its position on hijacking and link unauthorized attempts to leave the socialist bloc with criminality and murder. On the very same day of the hijacking, the Soviet Union noted its adherence to ICAO standards and Soviet Foreign Minister Andrei Gromyko sent a telegram informing William Pierce Rogers, US secretary of state, that the USSR planned to join the Chicago Convention on International Civil Aviation that underpinned the ICAO.[44] A few weeks later, on November 14, 1970, the Soviet Union officially became an ICAO member.[45] The USSR also joined the United States in signing the Hague Convention against hijacking that December. Notably, none of these multilateral agreements required extradition; the Hague Convention called hijacking an "extraditable offense," but stopped short of demanding it.[46] Despite Nixon's sharp rhetoric, neither the United States nor the Soviet Union wanted to cede control over people who entered their respective spheres of influence. The lack of clarity surrounding extradition created a loophole that helped the Brazinskases remain in Turkey, a NATO country with which the Soviet Union had no extradition treaty. However, it also allowed the Soviet Union to claim the moral high ground and accuse the United States of shielding the Soviet perpetrators from justice.

Although Nixon sought to maintain his firm stance against hijacking, the United States was hemmed in by its long-standing support for defectors from socialism as well as the rapid political mobilization of the Lithuanian diaspora. Composed of emigres who had fled Soviet rule, their children, and the descendants of people who had left Lithuania in earlier waves but retained an emotional connection to their homeland, the diaspora was a small but tightly networked community. Its members proved skilled at turning the hijacking of Aeroflot Flight 244 into an international incident that would draw attention to Soviet restrictions on emigration and also cast Soviet rule over Lithuania as illegitimate.

Even as Nixon declared his intention to stay out of the incident, Lithuanian activists in the United States began demanding that the United States and Turkey resist Soviet calls for the extradition of Brazinskas and his son. According to the US Embassy in Turkey, representatives from US-based Lithuanian diaspora organizations began arriving in Turkey just three days after the hijacking. Among them was Anthony J. Rudis, the head of an engineering company with a range of government contracts, the host of the "Lithuanian Radio Forum" on Chicago's WXRT-FM, and a fervent activist who had expressed his devotion to freeing "communist-enslaved" Lithuania in letters to US presidents since the mid-1950s.[47] In meetings with embassy officials, Rudis affirmed his longtime commitment to anti-communism and said that he hoped to make arrangements to bring the hijackers to the United States with the help of a Turkish "business associate"; soon after, Rudis hired a Turkish attorney to represent the Brazinskases.[48] On October 21, 1970, a Turkish newspaper reported that Turkish president Cevdet Sunay had received "thousands of cables" from Lithuanians in the United States, urging that the hijackers not be returned to the Soviet Union.[49] Scores of letters were also sent by Lithuanian Americans to members of the US Congress, pressing their representatives to secure political asylum for Pranas and Algirdas Brazinskas.

In consultation with his National Security Council, Nixon agreed to fight against the return of the Brazinskases to the Soviet Union, though he also made it clear that the father and son should not be granted asylum in the United States. While US authorities still maintained the defector program and still prioritized refugees fleeing from the socialist camp, they had grown wary of ordinary, non-elite socialist citizens who breached the nation's embassies, jumped ship, or otherwise appeared on America's doorstep unannounced. This wariness was heightened by the sense that the government needed to draw a hard line when it came to hijacking. A telegram authorized by Nixon and sent to the State Department on January 18, 1971, stated that the pair were ineligible for admission to the United States, explaining that granting asylum to the Brazinskases, though a position "strongly supported by [an] already active US ethnic group," would be "inconsistent with US policy" and have "severe implications for success in [the] anti-hijacking campaign."[50] The Nixon administration's position— that the United States did not want to grant the hijackers asylum but it also did not want them returned to the Soviet Union—was communicated to Turkish officials.

The Turkish government was caught in a dispute between its primary NATO ally and its immediate neighbor. Although Soviet-Turkish relations had been undergoing a minor thaw at the time of the hijacking, the United States was in a privileged position when it came to issues concerning Turkish airspace. The US military operated Turkey's massive Incirlik Air Base, and US experts had helped develop the country's civil aviation system by supplying aid for pilot training, airport construction, and airline management.[51] Turkey's response to the dilemma was to seek a middle path by expeditiously returning the plane's other passengers while holding the hijackers until they could be tried in a Turkish court. Yet even as they awaited trial, they received special treatment from Turkey's National Intelligence Organization: they were housed in a spacious villa, food was ordered for them from restaurants, and they were even brought by intelligence officers to the center of Trabzon to view Turkey's Republic Day parade on October 29. Reflecting on this period, Algirdas Brazinskas described it as "the happiest time."[52]

The initial trial of the Brazinskases, held in Trabzon in November 1970, found that the hijackers had lived in a country, Soviet Lithuania, where "a regime came to power that was not in accordance with their wishes." The pair may have been Soviet citizens, but the legitimacy of Soviet authority over their homeland was questionable; at the time of the hijacking, the United States and many of its allies did not recognize the Soviet Union's annexation of Lithuania, which arguably gave the pair political grounds to seek an escape from Soviet rule. The court considered the hijacking to have been a criminal act with a "political character" and noted that the hijackers did not have any ill will toward those they injured. The judge, Ahmet Selim Teymun, was swayed by Pranas Brazinskas' argument that he "had to commit a crime in order to emigrate" because of the Soviet Union's closed borders.[53] Privileging the pair's motive over their violent methods, Teymun ruled on November 21 that they would not be extradited. Yet while they were freed, their legal status remained uncertain. Unwilling to grant them Turkish citizenship, Turkish intelligence officers temporarily housed them in another one of their villas in Istanbul.

The Soviet side had taken a conservative approach to the hastily organized trial in Trabzon, probably not expecting that the state's sovereignty would be called into question by a minor hijacking incident. In the midst of the trial, in a move that appealed to established Cold War standards of reciprocity, Soviet authorities handed over two US Army generals and a Turkish colonel who had been seized for crossing into Soviet airspace while surveilling the Turkish-Soviet border less than a week after the hijacking of Aeroflot Flight 244.[54] Soviet officials, expecting "a similar act of goodwill from the Turkish side," anticipated that the Brazinskases would be returned. Meanwhile, the Soviet Ambassador to Turkey believed that getting overly involved in the trial would legitimize the court's proceedings and wrongly signal that the Soviet Union had conceded jurisdiction over its runaway citizens.[55] In the trial's wake, the Soviets continued to favor high diplomacy, with Nikolai Podgorny, chair of the Presidium of the Supreme Soviet of the USSR and the second most powerful leader after Leonid Brezhnev, pressing the case with Süleyman Demirel, the Turkish prime minister.[56]

Soviet diplomacy seemed to have succeeded when Turkey's Supreme Court of Appeals annulled the Trabzon court's decision on March 8, 1971. However, just four days later, a coup staged by the Turkish military resulted in an abrupt change of government.[57] Political upheaval in Turkey served as a reminder that domestic politics could undercut international unity in the US-led bloc and leave migrants fleeing the Soviet Union exposed. For the Brazinskases, the change of government caused a great deal of uncertainty. The National Intelligence Organization guards at their Istanbul villa informed them that they would soon be free to depart for the United States, while the head of the Turkish intelligence agency expressed concern that they might instead be "turned over to the Soviet Union."[58] Indeed, in a conversation held in Moscow, the Turkish ambassador to the Soviet Union indicated that his government would consider a request for their extradition "after the remaining legal formalities."[59] For the time being, the Soviet Procurator's Office was optimistic about its chances in the second trial, which began shortly after the annulment of the first verdict.[60]

Making its case through a Turkish lawyer, Tevfik Arasly, to avoid inserting itself directly into the Turkish judicial system, the Soviet Union affirmed its position that the hijacking and the murder of the young flight attendant took place in Soviet airspace, on a Soviet aircraft, and among Soviet citizens. The Soviet Procurator's Office submitted post-hijacking interviews conducted by the Georgian KGB with passengers on the plane attesting to the fact that the shooting occurred on the Soviet side of the border.[61] The passengers' testimonies, given immediately after their return, emphasized the dangers that their unplanned Turkish sojourn posed to them as Soviet citizens. According to their reports, while in Trabzon, they insisted that their Turkish hosts house them in one hotel; mirroring the practice of official delegations dispatched beyond Soviet borders, the group even delegated authority to two "elders" among the passengers—a senior fishing enterprise manager and a Communist Party member—who took the lead on negotiations with the Turkish side and patrolled the halls to make sure that no one spoke with the foreigners until officials arrived from the Soviet embassy. Such claims may have reflected what the passengers thought Georgian KGB interrogators wanted to hear, but they were consistently affirmed among the passengers questioned. Moreover, the entire group, with the exception of the hijackers, willingly returned to Batumi the following day on a special flight.[62] The interrogations set the stage for what was to come inside the USSR. The mobilization of popular support for the Soviet border regime and the harnessing of public outrage by Soviet citizens at the hijacking would later emerge as crucial components of the USSR's campaign against the Brazinskases.

Soviet authorities claimed the right to prosecute the Brazinskases even as they portrayed the pair as outcasts who had violated the norms of Soviet citizenship. At the trial, the Soviet Procuracy spared no effort to cast the hijackers in an unflattering light. It submitted a history of Pranas Brazinskas's past criminal offenses for unauthorized private trading and details of his failed first marriage to portray him as an untrustworthy opportunist.[63] Arasly reminded the court that disputes over the status of Lithuania were for the United Nations to solve, while the court's job was to decide if the hijackers were guilty or not guilty for their actions.[64] Attempting to draw a line between air piracy and other forms of defection, he argued that hijacking was a threat to "peaceful relations" among countries and "could not be considered a political crime." Citing the title of Kravchenko's memoir, which had become shorthand for describing ideologically-motivated defection, he argued that it mattered little whether Brazinskas proclaimed "I chose freedom." The Hague Convention still called for prosecution or extradition. In Arasly's view, giving special treatment to "murder with a political motive" would essentially be a "means of sanctioning murder."[65] The Turkish appeals court, while conceding that the hijacking was a criminal offense, noted that the episode had "a relationship to an act of a political character." Furthermore, it reaffirmed that there was no legal basis for the hijackers' extradition. In the end, both father and son were convicted of manslaughter for killing flight attendant Nadezhda Kurchenko. The father received a thirty-eight-year prison sentence, the son was handed down a twelve-year sentence.

The decision was a setback for Soviet officials, who had been intimately involved in the details of the second trial, to the point of editing Arasly's closing argument.[66] Internal correspondence suggests that the Soviet Procuracy really did expect extradition, and Arasly's repeated assurances over the course of the trial did nothing to dissuade them of this opinion.[67] In a subsequent conversation with Soviet officials, Arasly accused the Brazinskases' lawyers of paying bribes to sway the ruling.[68] However, the Soviet Union may have simply been outmaneuvered by the legal team assembled to defend the Brazinskases, which had an impressive set of international connections. Joseph Valiunas, head of the US-based Supreme Committee for the Liberation of Lithuania, met regularly with the US ambassador to Turkey throughout both trials and employed three "prominent Turkish lawyers," one of whom, Nihat Erim, later became the prime minister of Turkey, while another, Celal Yardımcı, was the former minister of justice.[69] After the second trial, the Turkish side politely dismissed Soviet protests concerning the case, insisting that all communication regarding the Brazinskases be conducted through the Soviet embassy and reminding Soviet officials that, while they held them in the "highest esteem," there simply was no agreement on legal assistance between the countries that could force extradition.[70] Imprisoned in Turkey, the hijackers were beyond the reach of Soviet authorities.

The unfavorable outcome led to a shift in the Soviet Union's approach. Keen to redirect attention away from emigration restrictions and toward the dangers of hijacking, Soviet officials chose to prosecute their case through dramatic legal proceedings, public relations campaigns, literary and cinematic productions, and high-profile diplomatic complaints. Directed at international as well as domestic audiences, these efforts aimed to reassert the ideological boundaries of Soviet citizenship and push back against the transnational networks of emboldened activists advocating free emigration from the USSR. While the Soviet state had not initially reported the arrest of the group of largely Jewish refuseniks for their hijacking attempt in Leningrad in June 1970, in the wake of the Brazinskases' flight to Turkey, the Leningrad hijackers were very publicly tried in a Soviet court.

The December 1970 trial claimed to expose larger networks of "Zionist" conspirators involved in plotting the Leningrad hijacking.

While the trial may have succeeded in associating efforts to leave the Soviet Union with a Jewish "fifth column" within Soviet borders, authorities were unprepared for the international backlash caused by the spectacle.[71] Allegations of a vast underground conspiracy running through secret Jewish study groups and aided by shadowy foreign sponsors reeked of anti-Semitism. The defendants, a group of ten men and one woman who refused to be cowed by the court, drew sympathy. The death sentences two of them received provoked outrage. Salvador Allende, Chile's socialist president, and Golda Meir, the Israeli prime minister, called for clemency, and public protests were held in Stockholm as well as Jerusalem.[72] Some even credit the episode with mobilizing international support for unfettered Jewish emigration from the Soviet Union, leading Western leaders and international Jewish organizations to take a much more strident position.[73] Although Soviet officials continued to voice allegations of a "foreign conspiracy," the level of international protest appeared to register with them: the death sentences were overturned, the prison sentences the other plotters received were reduced, and a subsequent trial in May 1971 hewed to a more "legalistic" line. Its proceedings were also closed to foreign journalists.[74]

The Brazinskases were a comparatively easier target, given the violent nature of their actions and the father's criminal past. The state-led publicity campaign against them and their subsequent in absentia trial in a Soviet court were used to demonstrate to Soviet citizens that hijacking would not be tolerated. These efforts also served to sow divisions between Lithuanians in the USSR and Lithuanian activists in the diaspora who railed against Soviet "captivity." Growing aware of the role played by global advocacy networks, Soviet leaders turned to ostensibly independent civil society organizations to rally international support for their legal demands. In November 1970, the Committee of Soviet Women wrote an appeal to the Society of Turkish Women urging them to "raise [their] voices" against the "barbarous murder" of Kurchenko, the young flight attendant killed by the hijackers.[75] Soviet officials responded to claims that the USSR was a "prison-house" for non-Russian nationalities by encouraging the state's Lithuanian and Ukrainian citizens to speak out against the Brazinskases. They widely publicized a protest in Pranas Brazinskas's hometown in Lithuania that denounced the pair as "traitors."[76]

Officials in the Soviet Ministry of Foreign Affairs believed that the Brazinskas case could be used to drive a wedge between "reactionary" Lithuanian organizations abroad that were assisting the hijackers and the more "progressive" members of the diaspora who believed that they should be returned to the Soviet Union to face justice for their violent crime in the skies.[77] A few years later, the Soviet foreign ministry, along with the KGB, the head of the Soviet news agency TASS, and the party's central committee approved a letter signed by Aeroflot's pilots calling for the extradition of the "criminal Brazinskases."[78] Such efforts were sanctioned at the top but also demonstrated and in turn generated genuine popular anger over the incident. Several letters addressed to the Council of Ministers expressed frustration at the inability of Soviet officials to bring the Brazinskases home to face trial. One letter-writer from Moscow upbraided the authorities, writing, "They killed one of our own, and we remain silent."[79]

Recognizing the ubiquity of hijacking stories in the international media and acknowledging that such accounts could no longer be suppressed, Soviet authorities broke with their past practice of muting reports of aircraft hijackings. Kurchenko's funeral was covered in dozens of Soviet newspaper articles, and, less than a year after the hijacking of Aeroflot Flight 244, a Soviet film, *The Applicant*, was commissioned; it presented a lightly fictionalized account of the event with a love story at the center (the heroine in the film was engaged to be married when she was killed).[80] A subsequent novella, *The Death of a Stewardess*, cast Pranas and Algirdas Brazinskas as odious villains and affirmed Kurchenko's status as a Soviet martyr of the late Cold War.[81] In death, Kurchenko became ubiquitous: a museum at the Soviet flight academy was built in her honor; city streets and parks throughout the Soviet Union were named after her; and her name was attached to a mountain, a tanker, and an asteroid. Through such efforts, the authorities reminded Soviet citizens that Kurchenko had died in a noble attempt to defend the Soviet border in the skies.

Although the Brazinskases' purported villainy was central to Kurchenko's martyrdom, the subsequent Soviet prosecution of the pair was almost an afterthought to the state's full-throated media campaign. In 1974, the Brazinskases were tried in absentia; to the crimes of hijacking and murder, authorities added charges of treason, equating their unlawful crossing of Soviet borders with the "betrayal of the Motherland."[82] The formulation was by now well established in Soviet law, but as the USSR began to ease some restrictions on emigration during détente, the hijacking case reaffirmed the criminalization of unsanctioned exit. After years of serving defectors with lighter sentences, a Soviet court sentenced the father to death and the son to ten years in prison. While the death sentence the Soviet court handed down in absentia to Pranas Brazinskas made his extradition even less likely, it demonstrated to Soviet citizens that hijacking would not be tolerated.

In 1974, only three years into their prison sentences, the Brazinskases were suddenly released under a general amnesty commemorating the fiftieth anniversary of the Republic of Turkey. Yet the international state system's hardening stance against hijacking made them unwanted guests. While father and son had dreamed of finding a new political community abroad, they discovered that statelessness awaited them on the other side of the Cold War divide. Their situation recalled that of the remaining crew of the *Tuapse*, but while the lost sailors were seen as unfortunate victims and all but forgotten, the Brazinskases were international pariahs thanks to the Soviet Union's campaign against them. Facing jail and execution if they returned to the Soviet Union, and denied political asylum in the United States and Turkey, the hijackers were sent to a place reminiscent of the early days of the Cold War: a displaced persons camp in Yozgat, about one hundred miles east of Ankara. Even more than the wartime refugees from the Soviet Union for whom the camp had been established, the Brazinskases found themselves confined to its barracks-like housing, under virtual house arrest as a condition of their release.[83] However, by asserting their Lithuanian nationality, they continued to find support among a global Lithuanian diaspora that, since the end of the Second World War, had acquired more political clout and was poised to link established Cold War rhetoric to new forms of political mobilization.[84] The case of the Brazinskases pitted state-led efforts to enforce aerial borders against an advocacy network that operated across state boundaries and was willing to be more assertive in pressuring US authorities.

With the pair's consent and participation, anti-communist Lithuanian activists in the United States and elsewhere worked to fashion the Brazinskases into romanticized freedom fighters. This was neither easy nor straightforward, since the son was a minor at the time of the hijacking, and the father had a checkered criminal past. In 1973, a Lithuanian publisher in New York addressed the former issue in his introduction to a collection of poetry attributed to Algirdas Brazinskas. Although the publisher noted that the boy had not yet reached eighteen years of age, he expressed his hope that the book would "show our young people" that the "creative word" can be uttered not just in conditions of "freedom and abundance" but also amid "captivity, exile, and imprisonment." Featuring a headshot of the handsome teenager, the book of poetry decried the tyranny of Soviet rule over Lithuania and expressed Algirdas Brazinskas's longing for freedom. One poem, entitled "Victory," was supposedly written on the evening of the hijacking; it denounced the "Russian bloodsuckers" who kept Lithuania in captivity and prophesized that the "gates of slavery" surrounding the Baltic nation would soon come crashing down.[85]

As for Pranas Brazinskas, his imprisonment in the Soviet Union was linked to his anti-communist views rather than his wheeling and dealing in the informal economy. Lithuanian activists cited his assertions, made at the second trial, that he had in fact been a secret member of an established "Lithuanian anti-communist organization" and that there had been armed Soviet "secret police agents" involved in the melee on the plane.[86] The former claim burnished his credentials as a dissident while the latter called into question his culpability for Nadezhda Kurchenko's death. The Soviet KGB's own records, marked "top secret," do not offer any evidence to support either claim.[87] As with Algirdas Brazinskas's poetry, it was difficult to determine whether Pranas Brazinskas's allegations were the result of coaching by allies in the diaspora or were simply reflecting a canny understanding of Western rhetoric in the Cold War. It may have been both. By the time of the pair's hijacking, diaspora networks were more emboldened and years of international travel and exchange, as well as continued Western-backed radio programming, had widely disseminated Cold War notions of captivity and freedom. Either way, the globalization of advocacy as well as the global spread of ideas about the freedom of conscience helped these erstwhile Soviet citizens frame their story in a politically resonant manner.

Both father and son received sympathetic coverage in the Lithuanian American press, particularly in *Draugas* (*The Friend*), published in Chicago by the Lithuanian Catholic Press Society and distributed in Lithuanian communities around the world. Even as they were held in the DP camp, the pair was visited by politically connected supporters from the Lithuanian diaspora, including Joseph Valiunas, whose organization gave the Brazinskases a radio, a typewriter, some cash, and correspondence written by Lithuanian supporters.[88] By this point, the son had learned English with the aid of a dictionary and study guide, helping him argue for his case abroad.[89]

Traveling to Turkey, Lithuanian activists also pressed officials at the US embassy. Some in the State Department may have been sympathetic to their views, but embassy cables give the impression of US policymakers being pulled back into the case despite their desire to be rid of it. Embassy officials had to make sense of diverse and sometimes competing Lithuanian organizations advocating on behalf of the Brazinskases; some arrived in Ankara with the backing of elected officials in the US Congress while others had to be investigated for potential ties to Soviet intelligence.[90] Sensitive to concerns that Soviet agents might forcibly seize the Brazinskases and return them to the USSR, the US embassy monitored security measures at the DP camp. Housing only nine refugees in total, the camp had five Turkish police officers assigned to it, far more than would ordinarily have been needed.[91] These safety concerns may not have been unfounded: the former chief archivist of the KGB's First Directorate later alleged that Soviet intelligence had sought to assassinate the Brazinskases, only to call off the operation when the task proved too difficult.[92]

Supporters in the Lithuanian diaspora pressed for the Brazinskases to be resettled in the United States, even though their case for asylum was all but closed by the 1971 US National Security Council decision and rejected again by immigration officials in 1974. In a move that recalled the shuttling of un-wanted migrants to third countries and the utilization of private agencies in the early years of the Cold War, Henry Kissinger advocated resettlement outside the United States and insisted that the matter should remain in the hands of the Brazinskases' "private sponsors" and not involve US gov-ernment officials.[93] Yet events on the ground forced the US government's hand. In 1976, the pair somehow managed to escape from the DP camp; a guard was accused of accepting a bribe for their release, though he later claimed it was the result of a decision made by his superiors.[94] The pair soon turned up at the US Embassy in Ankara, where they began a sit-in protest demanding asylum.

Their odds of gaining asylum seemed lower than ever. The Hague Convention, backed by the United States, discouraged the granting of asylum to hijackers. With the solidification of diplomatic borders that followed the Vienna Convention, US embassies were less well disposed to "walk-ins" than they had once been. Even the Organization of American States, whose membership included the most vocal supporters of the right to diplomatic asylum, had banned the granting of sanctuary to those ac-cused of terrorism, a charge with which hijacking was increasingly asso-ciated.[95] Yet the pair would not be deterred. During his protest, the elder Brazinskas slashed his stomach with a penknife, a shocking demonstration of his desperation to leave and perhaps further evidence of his willingness to do what was necessary to draw the attention of global media.[96] The case had become a diplomatic headache for both the United States and Turkey, and embassy officials had to turn to Lithuanian diaspora activists to spirit the pair out of the embassy and ultimately out of the country. Once again, US authorities took advantage of ambiguities in international law: the pair were not granted asylum, but they were given protection. While US officials wanted them out of their hands, they concluded that extraditing father and son to the USSR would risk a massive backlash among anti-communist activists in the United States.

While the Brazinskases sat in the embassy, Mary Rudis, the wife of Anthony J. Rudis and president of the Lithuanian Relief Fund of America, arrived in Ankara to help them. Rudis cited the support she had received from US senators and congressional representatives and renewed calls for the pair to be resettled in the United States. Embassy officials refused but described her in a cable as a "very determined person."[97] US officials finally requested that the Turkish government provide the necessary documents for the Brazinskases to leave the country with Rudis. Among Rudis's contacts in the Lithuanian diaspora was a "senior friend" in the Vatican, Monsignor Ladas Tulaba, who offered to shelter the Brazinskases at the Pontifical Lithuanian College of St. Casimir, an institution established in 1944 to educate Lithuanian clergy in exile following the Soviet annexation of Lithuania.[98] State Department personnel helped coordinate the group's travel arrangements from Turkey to Italy, seeking to avoid the possibility of Soviet extradition while allowing for plausible deniability on the part of the US government.[99] Departing Turkey under the assumed names of Mr. and Mrs. Benjamin Nill and Mr. Thomas Foster, Rudis and the Brazinskases arrived in Rome on July 11, 1976.[100]

While the hijackers were given temporary shelter in Vatican City, Rudis obtained documents from the UN High Commissioner for Refugees (UNHCR) that cleared the pair to obtain permanent residency in another country, but by this point no state wanted to be associated with them. They were forced to remain in seclusion, even as Soviet officials suspected their presence and senior Italian political figures who learned about their location sought to have them leave as soon as possible. Expressing their concern to the Deputy Chief of Mission of the US Embassy in Rome, two officials from the Italian foreign ministry worried about attacks from the Italian left "in support of the Soviets who wish the return of "airplane hijackers," as well as criticism from the Italian right that the government was "turning back fellow Catholics."[101] US embassy officials further feared that political controversy over the hijackers could jeopardize the legal transit of Jewish refugees from the Soviet Union and Romania through Italy, which was by then occurring on regularly scheduled flights. On July 30, Kissinger sent the following notice to the US Embassy in Rome: "There is no rpt [repeat] no thought of issuing US visas to the Brazinskas [sic]. The US considers this case to be a matter for the UNHCR and the private sponsors now to resolve without further USG [US Government] involvement."[102]

Under pressure from the United States and her requests for the Brazinskases' entry refused by more than thirty other countries, Mary Rudis finally obtained tourist visas for them to travel to Venezuela, a nation with a long-standing tradition of offering asylum—both territorial and diplomatic—to political refugees.[103] While the United States had pushed back against the liberal asylum policies of Latin America a little more than a decade earlier, in this case US officials seemed relieved by the offer of their South American ally. On August 9, State Department officials in Turkey received a report that Rudis and the Brazinskases had arrived in Caracas and made arrangements to deliver the Brazinskases' personal effects left in the embassy in Ankara. The State Department singled out Rudis for "special praise" for her role in resettling the hijackers, though in another cable officials referred to the Brazinskases' saga as "the case that won't go away."[104]

Indeed, what happened next showed that, despite their vulnerability as stateless people, the pair still had the power to create problems for states by exploiting ties with non-state actors and generating publicity. In contrast to the early Cold War, when most of the publicity that migrants generated was stage-managed by State Department officials, the Brazinskases and their backers had the power to make their own news and were not so easily controlled. While officials—and Rudis—assumed that the Brazinskases would remain in Caracas, the two had other plans. According to the son, the pair felt that Rudis had "deeply disappointed them" when she told them they should abandon their efforts to enter the United States and stay in Venezuela.[105] Falling out with Rudis and boarding a flight from Caracas to Toronto, they managed to evade immigration authorities during a stopover in New York and enter the United States illegally. It is difficult to prove whether they had assistance from other supporters in the Lithuanian diaspora in executing this plan, though the idea of having them seek asylum in Canada after a stopover in the United States had been floated more than two years earlier by Lithuanian American activists.[106]

The US Immigration and Naturalization Service soon located the pair, but it was not so easy to expel them from the country. After arriving in New York, Algirdas Brazinskas had hastily married a US citizen of Lithuanian descent with whom he had corresponded while in prison, perhaps hoping to bolster his claim for asylum.[107] The bigger issue for US authorities, however, was that there was nowhere to send the Brazinskases. Returning the pair to the Soviet Union to face jail time and execution was seen as too costly in political terms, particularly in an election year. While the Cold War rhetoric of Soviet "captivity" had long resonated on the American right, calls for freedom of emigration from the Soviet Union united a peculiar coalition of human rights activists and anti-communists, as well as Jewish, Catholic, and Pentecostal groups.[108] The return of Lithuanian defectors was a particularly sensitive topic, one that had garnered popular attention after the US Coast Guard returned Simas Kudirka, the Soviet Lithuanian sailor who defected off the coast of Martha's Vineyard, to Soviet authorities in November 1970. Years later, the case was still referred to in a popular book by a Cleveland-based Lithuanian American activist as the Coast Guard's "Day of Shame" and dramatized in 1978 in an Emmy award–winning television special.[109]

Yet even as the pair's case was framed as another instance of escape that evoked earlier journeys by land and sea, they were stranded by the hardened stance against hijacking adopted by states across the political spectrum over the course of the 1970s. While the PFLP's hijacking of an El Al flight in 1968 has been described as the start of "modern, international terrorism," hijacking was initially viewed in a variety of ways.[110] Although always involving the threat of force and the coerced movement of the crew and passengers away from their intended destination, hijacking was at the outset more likely to be a way of getting to where one could not otherwise go, and it rarely ended in violence. Even the PFLP, which turned hijacking from a getaway strategy to a vehicle for hostage-taking, refrained from killing passengers in 1968 and again in 1970—though at Dawson's Field they blew up the empty planes when their demands were not met. The link between hijacking and terrorism was more solidly established in 1972, when the Black September Organization, which also had ties to the PLO, killed eleven Israeli athletes during the Summer Olympics in Munich; later that year, Black September sympathizers forced a Lufthansa flight to change course and threatened to kill the passengers until three perpetrators of the bloodshed in Munich were released from prison, allowed to board, and given a hero's welcome on the hijacked plane's arrival in Libya. These events were televised to a global audience and generated public outcry over the inability of governments to protect their citizens, especially those traveling by air. The sense of international crisis and the corresponding demand for "law and order" measures were further heightened by a series of bombings carried out across West Germany that same year by the Red Army Faction, a group of left-wing German radicals with global ambitions who had trained in Jordan with the PLO.[111]

State authority was reasserted and the prosecution of aerial piracy used to advance governmental control over a world of potentially destabilizing global connections. If states could not control the publicity around migrants to the same degree they could in the past, they could at least control their physical movement. The militarization of airspace by state security organizations followed. After Munich, Nixon, who had first dispatched armed guards on airplanes following the Dawson's Field hijackings, established the Inter-Departmental Working Group on

Terrorism; in 1973, West Germany established the tactical unit GSG 9 (*Grenzschutzgruppe Neun*) to deal with hijacking and hostage situations. The following year, the USSR formed the Alpha Group, a special forces unit within the KGB that became known for applying extreme force to suppress hijackings, including an infamous episode in Georgia that resulted in eight deaths after Alpha Group members with assault rifles stormed the plane.[112] As the tactics used by hijackers grew more violent, so too did the measures taken by states to prevent them. By the late 1970s, the leadership of the PLO, which once saw hijacking as a tool to raise international awareness about the plight of the Palestinian people, largely eschewed the tactic to avoid negative publicity. At the same time, potential allies in the post-colonial world were more cautious about granting hijackers asylum.[113] When Venezuelan officials were asked to give the Brazinskases sanctuary again in October 1977, they rebuffed a high-level US request, citing their government's new "anti-terrorist" position.[114] Airspace had been transformed into a highly regulated environment protected by airport screenings and in-flight security measures, and air pirates had become politically undesirable terrorists.

The hijacking of Aeroflot Flight 244 turned out to have been a transitional case that laid the groundwork for tightened regulations by state authorities across the world. Strict anti-hijacking measures, even when they risked harming innocent bystanders, were deemed preferable to allowing unfettered movement across air borders. When Ivan Vitiuk, a Soviet man with a criminal record, attempted to hijack a plane from Leningrad to Sweden in April 1973, threatening to blow up the plane with an explosive device if his demands were not met, the pilot, after communicating with the ground crew, grounded the plane in Leningrad anyway. Even though the pilot would later be praised in a report to the Central Committee for his "bravery and flying mastery" in executing a sudden landing and attempting to trick the hijacker into believing they had touched down in Helsinki, Vitiuk quickly saw through the ruse and triggered his bomb, killing a crew member as well as taking his own life.[115] The Soviet Union even used the anti-hijacking framework to address another long-standing problem: the occasional defection of its pilots, who sometimes fled in their state-issued planes to sanctuary abroad. Even as the Brazinskases faced deportation from the United States, Soviet authorities persuaded the Shah of Iran to turn over Lieutenant Valentin Zasimov, a Soviet mail pilot who landed his plane in northern Iran. Although Zasimov had flown solo and there could be no specter of coercion without other passengers on board, he was extradited back to the Soviet Union to face justice under the terms of a hijacking treaty between the two countries agreed to in 1973.[116]

Even in West Berlin, a longtime haven for defectors, authorities struggled with the question of how to treat a group of East Germans who commandeered a Polish flight from Gdansk with a starting pistol in the late 1970s. While West Germany had a history of welcoming those fleeing the socialist bloc, anti-hijacking agreements demanded criminal prosecution. Because the plane landed at the US Air Force Base at Tempelhof, the State Department decided to try them under US law in the "United States Court for Berlin," which granted the American side extraterritorial jurisdiction over US-occupied Berlin but had never before been convened. Herbert Jay Stern, the US district court judge for New Jersey, was flown to Berlin to preside over the trial. Charges against one of the defendants were dismissed, while the other was convicted of a lesser charge but sentenced only to time served.[117]

Back in the United States, with sovereignty over the skies more clearly demarcated, a judge allowed the Brazinskases' case to stall by exploiting one last legal gray area. Despite accepting the post–World War II borders of the Soviet Union in the 1975 Helsinki Accords, the US government still did not formally recognize the authority of the Estonian, Latvian, and Lithuanian Soviet Socialist Republics.[118] Accordingly, when a US court ruled that the Brazinskases were to be deported to "Lithuania," they could not be delivered to an unrecognized political entity, nor would the Lithuanian government in exile issue them a passport for the purpose of deporting them to Soviet-controlled territory.[119] After their decade-long effort to disassociate themselves from the hijackers, US authorities had little choice but to allow the father and son to remain in the United States. While government officials publicly denied knowledge of their whereabouts, the Brazinskases were quietly given US passports that extended the protections of citizenship, though under assumed names. Despite the relative safety of their new home in California, they avoided public attention and reportedly stockpiled weapons out of fear that Soviet agents might still find and kill them.[120]

For their part, Soviet authorities never ceased calling for the pair's extradition and seldom hesitated to use the case to remind international audiences of the hypocrisy of the United States and its allies. After all, the United States had spearheaded international action against hijacking and ended up sheltering two violent hijackers. By the end of the 1970s, the Soviet Union had taken the lead in pushing for tougher anti-hijacking measures, including one that would have required countries to extradite hijackers to their country of origin to face trial.[121] As had been the case in their approach to unsanctioned movement around embassies and at sea, the two superpowers agreed that airspace needed to be jointly governed, though this international consensus did not stop the rhetorical battles waged over the Brazinskases' fate. Soviet emissaries continued to lodge diplomatic protests about the matter well into the 1980s, and Washington's decision to shelter the Brazinskases was among the reasons the Soviet press cited in justifying the USSR's boycott of the 1984 Olympic Games in Los Angeles.[122] Even though the Soviet boycott was more likely a reciprocal measure taken in response to the United States' decision to withdraw from the games in Moscow four years earlier, the armed hijacking remained a controversial case and a politically useful one for the Soviet Union. Although it had lost the battle to extradite its escaped citizens, the Soviet Union arguably won the contest to exploit the episode for political gain.

TRAPPED IN THE MARGINS OF THE COLD WAR

For a brief historical moment, hijacking held the promise of allowing ordinary people to move spontaneously and forge new ties of solidarity across the borders of the Cold War world. It mobilized the latest technology, generated wall-to-wall news coverage, and seemed to surmount the limitations that had hindered past migrants. Hijackers were assisted by transnational activists, who appropriated the rhetoric of socialist "captivity," pressuring the Soviet Union to allow free emigration and compelling the United States and its allies to let migrants in.

Once they had fled the socialist superpower by air, the hijackers of Aeroflot Flight 244 leveraged their ties with non-state actors outside the Soviet Union. The importance of their diasporic connections is revealed by a comparison with another hijacking to Turkey undertaken by two ethnic Russians, Nikolai Gilev and Vitaly Pozdeev, just one week after the Brazinskases' flight. Even though Gilev and Pozdeev did not injure anyone on board, they received little assistance, lacking ties to a mobilized diaspora community with a global reach like the Lithuanians who assisted the Brazinskases, or the American and Israeli Jews whose political activism ultimately secured the release of the refusenik hijackers in Leningrad.[123] In despair, Gilev and Pozdeev chose to return home after less than two years in Turkey.

While the hijacking of Aeroflot Flight 244 led to a confrontation between the Soviet Union and the United States, the case only temporarily disrupted a consensus that air piracy needed to be eliminated. Hijacking was a commercial threat that undermined massive state investments in aviation infrastructure. Moreover, the practice gave too much power to hijackers with unpredictable political agendas. Just as the threat of maritime piracy had been used to justify the expansion of state power on the high seas, culminating in the UN agreements of the Cold War era that enclosed the world's oceans with law, the proliferation of hijacking led to clearer and more stringently enforced lines of jurisdiction in the air.

Even as state power over economic activity and information waned, it was asserted in new ways to govern the movement of people on planes. By the end of the 1970s, airlines in the United States may have been transformed by deregulation, but airports and airspaces remained tightly controlled by government agencies.[124] Aerial borders could be opened by states, as they were for select groups of Soviet Jews permitted to emigrate in the wake of the Leningrad hijacking attempt; they could just as easily be closed to those who did not travel with the proper documents, sometimes leaving passengers stranded within the confines of an airport.[125] Even this possibility was closed off in the 1980s as West European states adopted stricter transit visa rules targeting those seeking asylum in air terminals.[126]

A broader change was under way when it came to defection. While non-state actors seized upon terms like "defector" and "Captive Nations" to advocate for those fleeing from the socialist bloc by airplane, Western governments seemed less enthusiastic than ever about accepting unsanctioned migrants, particularly those like the Brazinskases who came from a non-elite background and possessed no translatable skills but had ample political baggage. And socialist governments, led by the Soviet Union, seemed more inclined than before to let some people go. The competition for defectors had begun as a way for governments to assert control over the global migration flows unleashed by the Second World War. It promised to turn those rendered stateless by mass displacement into citizens, reclaimed by the country they left or welcomed by their country of refuge. In the wake of decolonization and in the aftermath of the Brazinskases' hijacking, it was clear that statelessness had returned—if it had ever gone away in the first place. Certainly, in comparison to other stateless groups of the era, such as the "boat people" fleeing Vietnam who were neglected by many foreign governments and remained relatively anonymous on the international stage, the act of hijacking temporarily granted the Brazinskases access to influential connections abroad and garnered them global media attention as individuals.[127] Yet they remained confined to the margins of established political communities.

Their sense of being people out of place would only increase after the end of the Cold War, when they were shunned even by the Lithuanian Americans who had advocated for their freedom. Although their hijacking remained the subject of occasional press coverage, the two perpetrators all but disappeared from view, only to resurface on January 5, 2002, when police in Santa Monica, California, arrested Albert Victor White for bludgeoning his father to death in their two-bedroom apartment. Press coverage soon revealed that Albert Victor White was the name given to Algirdas Brazinskas upon his receipt of US citizenship and that his father was Pranas Brazinskas. To those who would listen, Algirdas Brazinskas, now Albert White, continued to frame his story as a winding journey from "Soviet occupation" to the "free world."[128] When put on trial for his father's death, however, he defended himself against charges of murder by claiming self-defense and testifying about his father's violent past. Abandoning his stance that the hijacking had been a heroic effort to break through the Iron Curtain, he told the court that the event was simply an example of Pranas Brazinskas's rash behavior, one that he was dragged into as a fifteen-year-old boy.[129] Although he would be found guilty of second-degree murder, his testimony confirmed the transformation of hijacking from a romanticized bid for freedom to a senseless act of terror.

While the identity of the father and son had been an open secret among members of Santa Monica's Lithuanian community, its leaders further drew a line between their actions and the fight against Soviet "captivity." Interviewed in 2002, Regina Oslapas, head of the Santa Monica chapter of a Lithuanian community organization, explained that her group "did not consider Brazinskas a patriot because of the violence in his past."[130] The 2002 incident received a good deal of coverage in the Russian press as well, especially after Albert Victor White was found guilty. In an article that alluded to the hijackings of September 11, 2001, one Russian newspaper sardonically pointed out that the United States had harbored the Soviet Union's "first hijackers" and remarked that the story of these "terrorists" had ended "ingloriously," but with a rough sense of justice.[131] Although the murder of Pranas Brazinskas by his son could be interpreted as the final manifestation of an innate pattern of violence, the pair's fate also spoke to the profound sense of marginalization that followed their defection. Their experience of being stranded and all but abandoned presaged defection's eventual demise and the corresponding rise of statelessness.

Conclusion

After Defection

At the station in Vienna, the passengers shuffled onto the train under the escort of armed guards, each carrying the two suitcases allotted for their remaining possessions. Later, in an Italian field, they were told to disembark to be counted, the men separated from the women and children. Following their arrival in Rome, they struggled to find housing, supported themselves by selling trinkets as well as family heirlooms, lived in cramped communal arrangements in a run-down beach town outside the Italian capital, and congregated around the fountain in the town square to trade rumors about the best way to reach the United States.[1] During the previous year, 99 percent of Soviet migrants had been granted refugee status by American authorities, but in 1989 many fleeing the USSR saw their applications rejected and were denied entry, leaving them stateless.[2] This was the situation facing the thousands of primarily Jewish Soviet emigres stranded in the heart of Europe as the Cold War waned.

Unlike the Soviet-claimed citizens displaced by the Second World War, these migrants flowed westward as the Soviet Union eased emigration restrictions. After years of encouraging unauthorized flight, Western leaders, when faced with mass migration from their longtime rival, began rethinking their policies. Just two years earlier, US vice president George H. W. Bush had called upon Soviet premier Mikhail Gorbachev to release hundreds of thousands of "refuseniks" who had been denied exit visas, proclaiming, "let's not see five or six or ten or twenty refuseniks released at a time, but tens of thousands, hundreds of thousands, all those who want to go." The latest in a long line of American leaders to criticize Soviet limits on emigration as a form of captivity, Bush scolded Gorbachev, then in the midst of his campaign of glasnost and perestroika, by telling him that "openness begins at the borders."[3] Yet as president, Bush wearily reminded reporters that the United States could not accept an unlimited number of refugees from the Soviet Union. Americans, Bush explained, needed to keep "the control of our demographics in our hands."[4] In the period between Bush's conflicting statements, the number of Soviet emigres arriving in the United States had increased more than tenfold. The total number of those leaving the Soviet Union was far greater still.[5]

Defection, a paradigm for understanding and managing migration, faltered as the Cold War ended and then collapsed altogether with the Soviet Union's end. The fact that the Soviet Union was allowing its citizens to leave made it harder for Soviet migrants to demonstrate the "well-founded fear of persecution" they needed to gain refugee status. As tensions eased, long-standing problems surrounding America's defector policy were exposed. Bush's reference to "demographics" pointed to an enduring contradiction of the defector program: from the beginning, escape from the Soviet bloc had been encouraged with the tacit understanding that it would not result in mass migration from East to West.

Even as the United States pushed its vision for an international asylum system to welcome Soviet defectors, first in Europe and then across the globe, it kept sharp restrictions on immigration. The US Immigration and Nationality Act of 1952 maintained quotas based on national origin even as it created a small opening for Soviet "escapees." The Immigration and Nationality Act of 1965, while ending formal limits restricting migration from beyond Europe, still privileged migrants with particular skill sets, even as it disadvantaged migrants from more populous countries and preserved barriers for people with physical disabilities as well as those deemed "mentally defective," a broad category that included LGBTQ migrants.[6] The system was designed to funnel in certain classes of migrants and keep out those considered undesirable.

Large-scale migration from the Soviet Union revealed the fractures in the international asylum system the United States had helped construct. West Germany, soon to be reunited with its eastern half, primarily wanted ethnic Germans from the Soviet Union. Israel's government, seeking a demographic infusion to preserve a majority Jewish state, sought Soviet citizens of Jewish ancestry, even if some had little identification with Judaism and did not see Israel as an ideal homeland. Austria, which had functioned as a neutral waystation for Soviet Jewish emigres since the 1970s, insisted that Soviet migrants be given the choice of their final destination as long as they did not remain in Austria. Many spilled into Italy, but in Ladispoli, the "down-at-the-heels resort town" where stranded Soviet migrants were housed, locals griped about being outnumbered by Russian speakers.[7] The last wave of Soviet migrants was free to leave but did not necessarily have a place to go.

It was also unclear what term could be used to describe them. Many did not consider the final wave of Soviet migrants to be defectors because they had left legally. Some even painted the migrants in an unflattering light. In Israel, those who came only to leave were disparagingly referred to in Hebrew as *yordim* (those who go down). Among earlier waves of emigres who had fled following the Bolshevik Revolution and World War II, or who had openly protested emigration restrictions in 1960s and 1970s, those abandoning the faltering Soviet Union were sometimes derisively called a "sausage emigration," as they fled a country with stores emptied of basic goods—including sausages—for a more comfortable life abroad.[8] The people who left received little coverage in the Soviet press; when they did, were depicted as opportunists who were disappointed when they encountered the realities of social isolation and economic precarity rather than the "good life" in the West.[9]

Although they faced an uncertain future, Soviet emigres were just one of many groups seeking refuge around the globe at this time, and their odds of securing asylum were better than others. Their "Italian holiday," as they sardonically called their sojourn outside Rome, came to an end because of an amendment by US Senator Frank Lautenberg to an immigration bill; this amendment allowed Soviet migrants to claim refugee status on the basis of belonging to a minority religious group, opening US borders to Jews, Evangelical Christians, and Catholics from the Soviet Union. Although the amendment included a provision for religious minorities from Southeast Asia, an acknowledgment of those stranded by America's haphazard withdrawal from Vietnam, it excluded most of the world's refuge-seekers.

Globally, the number of people classified as refugees by the United Nations continued to rise: figures doubled from a low of 1,656,664 in 1960 to 3,251,850 in 1972, more than tripled by 1982 to 10,319,353, and almost doubled again by 1992, when the number reached 17,838,020. Refugees from the former Soviet Union made up only 4 percent of this total. Far more came from post-colonial countries in Africa, Asia, and the Middle East. The situation eased somewhat as refugees were resettled or returned home over the course of the 1990s, but the numbers shot up again amid the "refugee crisis," mainly from the post-colonial world, in the mid-2010s. Aid workers, human rights activists, and legal advocates pushed the United States and other Western countries to shelter previously excluded categories of migrants, including victims of trafficking and criminal violence as well as those persecuted because of their gender identity or sexual orientation. In its fundamental design, however, the asylum system that migrants encountered was the one that had been established in the Cold War, with its narrow definition of a "political" refugee and scant regard for the economic or environmental factors that helped drive migration.[10] Still more migrants were forced to flee but encouraged to remain in their own country, where they were counted separately as Internally Displaced Persons (IDPs).[11]

The United States officially maintained its defector program, which granted entry to migrants of special intelligence value, until the Soviet Union collapsed. One CIA analyst even described the arrival of "hundreds of Soviet citizens offering to trade secrets in return for an escape from their crumbling empire" as "the greatest wave of Soviet defectors in the history of the CIA."[12] Right up until the Soviet Union's dissolution, Western journalists continued to celebrate the arrival of certain Soviet specialists as "defectors" even as those showing up in larger numbers in Italy and elsewhere were scorned. A prime example was hockey player Sergei Fedorov, whose 1990 defection before the Goodwill Games in Portland, Oregon, was celebrated as a cloak-and-dagger spy operation, even if his journey from the back door of a restaurant to a private jet bound for Michigan had been orchestrated by the Detroit Red Wings rather than the CIA.[13] Fedorov followed in the wake of earlier celebrity defectors, such as Mikhail Baryshnikov, who requested political asylum while on tour with the Bolshoi Ballet in Canada in 1974. Baryshnikov at first insisted he was a "selector" not a "defector," but he later embraced the role of a Cold War refugee on screen in the 1985 dance thriller *White Nights*.[14] The "defector" term masked the fact that athletes, ballet dancers, musicians, and scientists were members of an emergent group of highly skilled—and mobile—migrants in an era of globalization. Some arranged their "defection" beforehand, in discussions with American ballet companies, sports teams, orchestras, and corporations.

The closure of pathways to non-elite migration had been quietly under way for decades. While the two superpowers saw migrants as markers of influence, drew on their respective historical legacies of migration management, and disagreed about the relative importance of immigration and emigration restrictions, their mobility regimes had taken shape in dialogue with each other. It was impossible to imagine the US-guided construction of an asylum system, first across Europe, and then across the globe, without the Soviet-led system of exit restrictions it targeted. Similarly, without the capitalist West's encouragement of escape, these restrictions might not have been so fervently enforced. Sometimes setting aside direct

competition to secure their position as superpowers in the face of decolonization, the Soviet Union and the United States also engaged in self-
interested acts of inter-imperial collusion. They used the resources at their
disposal to mutually reinforce borders around embassies, at sea, and in the
air. They deployed international law to render human mobility governable
and hamper the unexpected arrival of migrants who resorted to unruly
methods, such as hijacking.

In addition to public agreements brokered at the United Nations, there
were private bilateral arrangements that revealed the extent to which the
superpowers were prepared to work together. In 1968, just as the Soviet
Union began to allow limited emigration, the United States secretly altered
its defection policy to ensure that the Soviet government was notified of
the arrival of Soviet defectors on American shores. The policy formally
affirmed the practice of permitting Soviet representatives to "confront"
defectors in meetings hosted by US officials.[15] Tolerating small-scale emigration allowed the Soviet Union to rid itself of troublesome activists;
granting Soviet officials access to defectors ensured that the United States
would not be burdened with ambivalent migrants who might seek to return home. Five years later, US and Soviet officials went further, discussing
measures to facilitate the return of Soviets in the United States who wished
to repatriate as well as Americans in the Soviet Union who wished to do the
same.[16] Changes like these occurred in incremental steps and out of public
view, even as a handful of defection cases gained widespread publicity.

While the Cold War's conclusion was thought to usher in a globalized
world in which the freedom of movement was universally accepted, it primarily ended restrictions on exit that the Soviet Union and its allies no
longer found feasible to maintain. At the same time, privileges for post-
socialist migrants evaporated, and entry, in most cases, remained gated.
Although defection disappeared as a way of framing mobility, it had played
a crucial role in fashioning a system of globalization in which goods, culture, capital, and certain classes of people flowed across borders with ease
but the movement of the masses was tightly controlled. Its unmistakable
imprint on the international migration system long outlasted the Cold War.

DEFECTION IN DOUBT

Ironically, the 1980s had begun with grand dreams about the renewed
promise of defection in the West. The CIA was still basking in the success
of having secured the defection in 1978 of Arkady Shevchenko, the UN
under-secretary general and the highest-ranking Soviet official ever to flee

in the Cold War. Following Reagan's landslide election, the CIA's new director, William J. Casey, was given autonomy to develop covert operations against Soviet interests across the globe.[17] In Afghanistan, Casey provided support to the mujahideen and welcomed the defection of Soviet soldiers. Some deserted their posts while others were captured by Afghan forces and requested asylum as POWs. A US House of Representatives resolution sponsored by politicians from both parties called for a more extensive "defector pipeline" that would bring additional Red Army soldiers to the United States.[18] The cause rekindled the advocacy network of the Tolstoy Foundation, whose leaders likened Soviet POWs in Afghanistan to Soviet DPs in postwar Europe.[19]

Yet with renewed attention, the problems that had plagued defection from the very first days of the Cold War resurfaced. Foremost among them was the issue of redefection, which caused officials on both sides to question the benefit of competing for unreliable migrants. In 1984, Svetlana Alliluyeva, nearly two decades after seeking asylum, renounced her American backers and chose to return to the Soviet Union. At a press conference organized by the Soviet Women's National Committee, Stalin's daughter complained of being treated as "a favorite pet of the CIA" and distanced herself from the authorship of her best-selling memoir, which she described as a "collective production" co-authored by the American intelligence community.[20] The next year, Vitaly Yurchenko, a high-ranking KGB officer who had originally defected at the US Embassy in Rome, strolled out of a French restaurant in Georgetown, telling his CIA minder he was going for a short walk. He resurfaced in Moscow, claiming that he had not really defected but had been kidnapped and held by US intelligence until he finally managed to elude his captors.[21] Like many defectors before them, the Soviet soldiers from Afghanistan had difficulty adapting to their new lives in the United States and received little support after their initial debriefings. By 1988, twenty-two Red Army defectors out of a total of approximately 250 had decided to go back to the Soviet Union.[22] The vaunted "pipeline" meant to funnel them to freedom seemed like a dead end.

Concerns about these high-profile instances of redefection were so great that in 1987 the US Senate held what was billed as Congress's "first comprehensive public overview of the handling of defectors." Opening the hearings, Senator Sam Nunn praised defectors as a "tool" to "pierce" the "all-encompassing veil" of the socialist bloc's "state security apparatus."[23] The hearings, though, would unintentionally pierce another veil—that surrounding the decades-old defector program run by America's intelligence agencies. Beneath the secrecy that shrouded the program, there was still confusion over which Soviet migrants could be classified as defectors.

Speaking at the hearings, John F. Sopko, deputy chief counsel responsible for leading Congress's investigation into Yurchenko's disappearance from the Georgetown restaurant, observed that the term "defector" was "not legally defined anywhere" in American law. Pressed for a definition, Sopko deferred to William H. Webster, the recently appointed CIA director.[24] Webster, however, only obfuscated, claiming that the "nature and extent of our work is, of course . . . classified and cannot be discussed in specifics."

Among the classified items was the agency's very definition of a defector. Questioned by the senators, Webster offered evasive answers: a ballerina who took flight would probably not be considered a defector, but she could be if she were renowned enough that her defection would send "a signal to the rest of the world about the differences between our free society and their closed society"; a "Jewish refusenik" would probably be a "resettlement case" unless "his background and work history" allowed the potential emigrant to "be brought within the category of defectors."[25] While the CIA director hinted that classified rules guided these decisions in a rational manner, the agency's secrecy concealed subjective criteria that were often applied inconsistently.

In truth, the American intelligence community wanted to pick and choose its defectors; the CIA's founding legislation, Public Law 110, had granted the agency 100 slots for defectors each year, and the CIA wanted to use these as its leadership saw fit. The law allowed the agency to circumvent US immigration procedures, give defectors cover stories, and provide them with economic support with little oversight.[26] CIA officers helped determine who was of "intelligence value," though the value of defectors in general was a contentious matter inside the agency. While some in the CIA welcomed the arrival of defectors, others preferred to rely on new sources of intelligence gathered by reconnaissance satellites and electronic surveillance equipment. Most believed that it was better to keep informants inside the Soviet Union as "defectors in place" rather than facilitating their exit, since the value of the information they possessed began to decline the moment they left.[27] Meanwhile, the other part of the agency's definition of a defector—a person of "propaganda use and value"—was even more nebulous.[28] In some cases, Soviet migrants seized control of their own propaganda "use and value" by defecting in a dramatic way, earning them the special treatment typically accorded intelligence targets even if they had little useful information to provide. Such was the case with Oksana Kasenkina, the first group of sailors of the *Tuapse*, and Pranas and Algirdas Brazinskas. The vagaries of the defector program could be exploited in unpredictable ways by migrants, even when their actions ran counter to national strategic interests.

The range of migrants from the socialist camp invoked or called on to testify at the hearings further betrayed the confusion swirling at the defector program's center. They included former intelligence officers, soldiers, and ambassadors, but also "farm boys," sailors, Jewish and Pentecostal activists, and Soviet hockey players. The one thing they had in common was their place of origin. At hearings focused on "Soviet and communist bloc defectors," among the seven individuals selected to provide extensive testimony, six were from the Soviet Union and one was from Czechoslovakia. No defectors from China, North Korea, Vietnam, Cuba, or other socialist countries were invited to speak. This casting revealed the tacit hierarchy of the defector program: Soviet citizens were relatively privileged, followed by those from socialist countries in East Central Europe, and, below them, migrants from socialist nations in Asia and Latin America. Such an arrangement may have fit with the identification of the USSR as the chief rival of the United States in the Cold War, but it also reflected the long history of racialized limits on immigration to the United States. One influential senator, William Cohen, did ask why the United States should prioritize Soviet defectors over "Haitians, or Mexicans, or others from Latin America," though he did so only in the role of "devil's advocate" to clarify the defector program's justification.[29] If there was one point of consensus at the hearings, it was that defection entailed illicit flight from one's country. With the Soviet Union poised to allow freer emigration, defection's future was in doubt.

THE DELIBERATE OPENING OF SOVIET BORDERS

In meetings held behind closed doors in Moscow, top Soviet officials and party leaders had been loosening exit restrictions since the 1960s, though at such a sluggish pace that some failed to notice the creeping change over time, while others grew infuriated at its slowness. At first, emigration was begrudgingly tolerated only for those with stated ties abroad, such as Soviet citizens married to foreigners and those seeking reunification with family members. It was then considered for those classified by Soviet officials as having a "homeland" beyond Soviet borders: Jews and Germans whose loyalty to the Soviet state was questioned and whose departure was seen as a minor concession in the pursuit of larger geopolitical goals. These groups were followed by disenchanted Armenians who had "repatriated" to Soviet Armenia after World War II, largely from countries in the Middle East, and Pentecostals, viewed as a dangerous "sect" with foreign ties.[30]

While US officials dreamed of a "defector pipeline" that would deposit desirable defectors onto American shores, Soviet officials hoped to filter emigrants and allow only unwanted elements to pass through the state's border controls.

The notion of sorting migrants based on nationality was not new, having been employed on both sides of the Cold War. It had been a key criterion for screening and channeling postwar DPs, with Jews given relative autonomy in their camps and Baltic nationalities more likely to be granted refuge in the West. The emphasis on nationality continued in subsequent decades. The US-led Escapee Program targeted the nationalities of East Central Europe, except for Germans, and encouraged mass departures only among Soviet citizens. Diaspora activists, for their part, emphasized the experience of national minorities in calling for an end to emigration restrictions. As early as the Eisenhower administration, American Jewish leaders made appeals loud enough for the American president to raise concerns about discrimination against Soviet Jews in a meeting with Nikita Khrushchev at Camp David in 1959.[31]

Faced with mounting international pressure as well as growing calls for *aliyah* among Soviet Jews in the wake of the Six-Day War of 1967, Soviet leaders decided to begin allowing limited Jewish emigration. They agreed to tolerate a level of exit calibrated to "contain the slanderous assertions of Western propaganda concerning discrimination against Jews in the Soviet Union." In June 1968, KGB chief Yuri Andropov and Soviet foreign minister Andrei Gromyko submitted a memorandum to the party's Central Committee calling it "expedient" to allow up to 1,500 departures a year. In addition to setting an exit quota, the memorandum made the case that selective emigration could in fact advance Soviet goals: the state would avoid losing its most productive citizens by giving preference to visas for elderly persons without a higher education, and the KGB could use the emigration "channel in its operational goals," most likely by recruiting or placing agents among those cleared for exit.[32]

Around the same time, the Soviet state also began expelling troublesome citizens even before they made the choice to leave. One of the first to be expelled was Ukrainian dissident Valery Tarsis, whose 1962 story *Bluebottle*, a satirical send-up of Soviet society, had landed him in a psychiatric ward.[33] After his release from forced hospitalization, Tarsis drew the ire of Soviet authorities again by writing an autobiographical novel about his time in psychiatric care. The novel, *Ward No. 7*, circulated underground and was published abroad, calling attention to Tarsis's predicament.[34] In 1966, Soviet officials decided that the best way to undermine

Tarsis's claim of being trapped inside the Soviet Union was to permit him to travel abroad and then deprive him of Soviet citizenship to prevent his return. After the author's departure, KGB chief Andropov and Soviet procurator general Roman Rudenko smugly noted that "among the organizers and encouragers of the anti-Soviet hype raised on behalf of Tarsis . . . the very fact of his being allowed to leave the Soviet Union has caused noticeable confusion." As proof, they cited a *Daily Mail* piece, which claimed: "In the West, [Tarsis] will attract interest for five minutes, and then be lost among the rest of the emigres in Paris or somewhere else."[35] In the event that Tarsis was not forgotten, he could be defamed. Party leaders were assured that the KGB would "continue to further discredit Tarsis abroad as a mentally ill person."[36]

After Tarsis, prominent dissidents were dumped abroad by Soviet authorities: in 1972, the poet Joseph Brodsky, rebuffing official pressure to emigrate, was put on a plane to Vienna; in 1974, the author Aleksandr Solzhenitsyn was arrested and deported to West Germany; and in 1979, the Leningrad hijackers, imprisoned since the start of the decade, were exchanged for Soviet spies and allowed to emigrate to Israel.[37] All were stripped of their citizenship under the 1938 law allowing revocation "for actions defaming the title of citizen of the USSR." Though the law was several decades old, its proactive application by the KGB was new, since it had previously been used against defectors who refused to return home or had long resided abroad, and then only with approval from the Ministry of Foreign Affairs, the KGB, and the Supreme Soviet's Presidium.[38] In a few prominent cases, such as that of Svetlana Alliluyeva, a person whose citizenship was revoked could have it restored.[39] Otherwise, revocation was a form of political death. Grouping dissidents with defectors who had "betrayed the Motherland," it equated departure with disloyalty.

While it may have seemed surprising that the push to encourage selective emigration came from the same intelligence service tasked with defending Soviet borders, the KGB's approach to defectors had shifted over time. As early as 1948, in the wake of Oksana Kasenkina's flight from the Soviet Consulate, Soviet intelligence agents in the United States criticized Consul Lomakin's decision to stage a public press conference with Kasenkina before she jumped. The press conference, they argued, had drawn undue attention to her case; without it, they believed, there would have been no crowds around the consulate and no "leap to freedom."[40] While their remarks were only an isolated note of protest, by the early 1960s Soviet intelligence officials had come to the conclusion that it was better to impugn the reputations of Soviets who defected—or to coax their return—than it was to give them a public platform by loudly contesting their right to leave. A more subtle approach was deemed especially prudent when it came to those whose only claim to fame was having fled beyond Soviet borders. Without publicity, their "propaganda use" in the West quickly deflated.

The punishments meted out to defectors also lessened over time. Following the embarrassing defection of KGB officer Bogdan Stashinsky in 1961 and his stunning public confession to killing two Ukrainian emigre leaders, Lev Rebet and Stepan Bandera, at the KGB's behest, Soviet intelligence grew more reluctant about physically targeting those who fled.[41] According to the records of KGB archivist Vasili Mitrokhin, plans were floated to maim ballet stars Rudolf Nureyev and Natalia Makarova to prevent them from dancing after their refusal to return to the USSR, but the KGB decided to damage their reputations instead by promoting slanderous rumors.[42] When it came to chess grandmaster Viktor Korchnoi, who fled the USSR in 1976, Western observers fretted about the KGB's alleged use of undercover operatives, including a parapsychologist with "eyes . . . like burning coals," to distract the defector in his 1978 world championship match against the Soviet-backed Anatoly Karpov in the Philippines.[43] Yet the KGB retained other, more effective weapons in its arsenal. Korchnoi's defection had left his wife, Bella, and son, Igor, trapped in the Soviet Union. On the eve of the 1978 match, KGB chief Andropov urged that Korchnoi's wife and son not be allowed to emigrate. While some exit restrictions had been eased, Andropov argued that allowing the relatives of defectors to leave would establish a dangerous "precedent" that could be "exploited by other nonreturners and traitors to the Motherland."[44] Immediately after the championship, Andropov went further, calling for the chess player's son to be drafted into the Soviet army, or, if he refused, sent to prison. Igor Korchnoi spent the next two years behind bars and was only allowed to leave with his mother in 1982.[45] Soviet intelligence also remained committed to tracking down defectors from its own ranks, who were referred to as "particularly dangerous traitors" and typically sentenced to death in absentia. While the vast majority, sheltered by Western intelligence services, remained physically unharmed, a few suffered mysterious accidents and poisonings. Many more lived out their days in hiding, wary of being found.[46]

Shifting Soviet tactics were anticipated and accompanied by changes in other socialist states that opened the door even wider to exit. Yugoslavia, which remained outside the Warsaw Pact, began relaxing exit controls in 1962, allowing Yugoslav migrants to work in capitalist countries to alleviate domestic unemployment and generate remittances.[47] Other socialist countries more closely aligned with the Soviet Union used emigration to allow—and even encourage—the departure of national minority groups. Starting in 1948 and continuing through the mid-1950s, Poland reached agreements with Israel that swapped Jewish emigres for trade incentives. In 1968, Poland allowed its Jews to depart for Israel if they gave up their Polish citizenship; the offer, accompanied by an officially sanctioned campaign of anti-Semitism, led to an exodus of more than 13,000. Two years later, Poland concluded an agreement with West Germany to allow for large-scale ethnic German emigration as well.[48] While these moves aligned with efforts to establish a more homogenous Polish population, Poland, Bulgaria, Czechoslovakia, and Hungary, in comparison with the Soviet Union, were generally more tolerant of citizens traveling abroad. Romania was even more permissive, launching a series of cultural, scientific, and technical exchanges with France in 1959 and again in 1965.[49] Under the leadership of Nicolae Ceaușescu, Romania allowed Jews to emigrate in exchange for cash, loans, and military equipment from Israel.[50] East Germany, too, went from seeing emigration as a demographic threat to perceiving its economic potential. From the middle of the 1960s until the fall of the Berlin Wall, 33,755 individuals held in East German prisons were traded with the West for "ransom" payments made through West German charitable organizations and Stasi-backed shadow brokers. During the same period, an additional 215,019 were allowed to leave in the name of "family reunification."[51]

On the other side of the Atlantic, the Cuban government, confronted by the spectacle of thousands of citizens seeking asylum on the grounds of the Peruvian Embassy in Havana, announced that anyone in the crowd who wanted to emigrate could do so. The ensuing exodus, the Mariel Boatlift, brought well over 100,000 Cubans to Florida in 1980, overwhelming the US immigration system and leading to inflated allegations—stoked by Fidel Castro—that many of the migrants were hardened criminals.[52] The Cuban leader essentially called the bluff of his American rivals, who had long criticized him for limiting emigration.

Yet socialist countries were unwilling to remove all barriers to emigration until the very end, with the Soviet Union lagging behind most of its allies. Soviet officials had not always been so cautious about exit from the socialist camp. Early in the Cold War, Stalin had adopted a fairly tolerant attitude toward flight from East Germany, perhaps willing to allow the demographic decline of a country that had invaded Russia in two world wars. The Berlin Wall, by most accounts, was an initiative proposed by East Germany's leaders and only approved by Moscow after much deliberation.[53]

However, as a sprawling superpower, the Soviet Union faced a unique set of external and internal pressures that led to a hardening of its borders. Soviet citizens, unlike their East Central European, Asian, and Latin American comrades, were more aggressively targeted for mass defection by the United States. Soviet leaders, unlike authorities in Poland, ruled an explicitly multiethnic state; even though they saw Soviet Jews as potentially disloyal citizens, they did not envision the complete loss of their Jewish population or any other national group that made up the "fraternal union and unbreakable friendship of the peoples of the USSR."[54] A vast state buffered by subordinate allies, the Soviet Union remained the most committed to creating and maintaining a distinctly socialist sphere of international mobility.

There was also the weight of institutional inertia to contend with when it came to changing Soviet border policies. Permitting free exit beyond a trickle meant overturning decades of border restrictions and surmounting a historical legacy of limiting emigration that stretched back into the imperial period and was more extensive than similar traditions among the Soviet Union's East Central European neighbors. Well into the 1980s, even as Soviet leaders permitted lawful emigration, cases of unlawful exit continued to be prosecuted: those fleeing to Finland were extradited based on the long-standing agreement with the USSR's neighbor, and ethnic Armenians who had the prospect of leaving through legal channels were treated as "traitors to the Motherland" if they circumvented official procedures.[55]

The framing of unauthorized exit as treason in Soviet culture also proved resistant to change. A 1984 book, ominously titled *Inevitable Retaliation*, offered a true-crime style account of defection "based on the trial materials of traitors to the Motherland, fascist executioners, and agents of imperialist intelligence," lumping the nonviolent dissident activist Anatoly Sharansky together with Nazi collaborator Andrei Vlasov and American spy plane pilot Gary Powers and implying that all were equally treasonous.[56] Two years later, a 1986 episode of *The Camera Looks at the World*, a Soviet television series covering international news, used select footage from a US-produced documentary to convey the situation of "former Soviet citizens" in the United States. It portrayed their plight in the same way the Committee for the Return to the Homeland had three decades before. Viewers saw that those who fled the Soviet Union hoped for prosperity but found unemployment. Although they "chose freedom," the emigres were homesick for their native land and the friends and family they had left behind.[57]

Yet evidence was mounting that restrictions on exit were harming rather than helping the Soviet state. In 1985, dozens of members of the French Academy of Sciences signed an open letter calling on the Soviet Union to allow all "refuseniks" to emigrate, including the imprisoned Sharansky. The denial of exit visas was depriving the socialist superpower of support even among left-leaning French intellectuals, whom it had courted in the years since Kravchenko's trial in Paris. Sharansky was finally released the following year in exchange for Czech, Polish, East German, and Soviet spies held in the West.[58] Soviet officials were also cognizant of the economic benefits of liberalizing the rules governing international travel. In 1980, soccer star Anatoly Zinchenko was permitted to play in Austria, with the Soviet government receiving his salary; and in 1985, pianist Andrei Gavrilov, who had spent years living under house arrest at Andropov's orders, was allowed to venture beyond Soviet borders and sign a contract with a foreign impresario, as long as the Soviet Ministry of Culture could seek a share of his earnings.[59] Perhaps most important, Soviet officials wanted to travel more freely. Even Soviet intelligence agents became more assertive in advocating for more open borders, at least for themselves. In 1986, the KGB requested that the Central Committee allow the spy agency to send agents abroad for up to one year, rather than the six-month limit previously in place, and to pay agents in local currency.[60]

Finally, in 1988, Soviet foreign minister Eduard Shevardnadze submitted a secret report to the Central Committee calling upon the Soviet state to abide by the "norms of the international agreements signed by the USSR," including the Helsinki Accords' final act, which called for freedom of emigration.[61] After years of debate, it was decided that ending emigration restrictions would help Soviet diplomats bolster the state's reputation abroad. At the same time, it was believed that Soviet spies could more easily do their job and that alluring international economic opportunities beckoned with the opening of borders. Although international activists and internal dissidents had succeeded in pressuring the Soviet state to act, when changes were ultimately made to border policies, they were made with assent at the top.

The collapse of the Soviet Union was not preordained nor directly caused by the limits it placed on emigration. However, demands for unfettered exit proliferated as Soviet institutions faltered in the subsequent years, particularly among the Soviet elite. The proceeds of globalization, which had been carefully managed by the Soviet state, were exploited as private gain by well-connected individuals who moved capital abroad and established residence in foreign cities. Meanwhile, non-elite migrants found themselves free to leave at the Cold War's end, but with fewer places to go.

The stateless position in which many migrants found themselves after the Cold War had always lurked in the shadow of defection, which offered few guarantees and protected the privileges of the superpowers. Statelessness was arguably produced by an abundance of state power rather than an absence of it. It could take the form of enforced exclusion from the protections of citizenship, the sanctioning of individuals found to be in violation of international treaties, and the relegation of certain people to the margins of political communities.[62] Yuri Nosenko, who defected from the KGB in 1964 but was suspected of being a Soviet plant, was held in excruciating limbo for years in a CIA safe house in Maryland; Pranas and Algirdas Brazinskas, though not physically confined, lived under assumed names as virtual outcasts until the father's life was violently taken by the son; Svetlana Allilueva, after returning to the Soviet Union, was kept at arm's length by the party leadership after her initial press conference and finally chose to come back to the United States a second time.[63] While defection created a small opening for migrants to exploit Cold War divisions, gain fame, and insert themselves into the competition between the superpowers, it was a dangerous game that left many lives in the balance. By illegally crossing out of the Soviet state, defectors severed connections with family and friends and destabilized their identities. As their life stories became narratives that served Cold War needs, some were forced to lose their pasts and change their names.

The cost of defection could be seen even among the first group of Soviet citizens to flee in the early Cold War. Igor Gouzenko, whose defection uncovered a massive Soviet spying effort in North America, appeared in public only while wearing a hood to conceal his identity and was buried in 1982 in an unmarked grave. Oksana Kasenkina went from jumping from a consulate to being sequestered in a Miami hotel. Even Victor Kravchenko, following his victory in the "Trial of the Century," felt uncomfortable with the role assigned to him and was disenchanted with Eisenhower-era politics in the United States. Much to the dismay of his patrons in the American intelligence community, he forged ties with leftists in South America, pursued a string of unsuccessful business ventures in Peru and Chile, and ended up committing suicide in his Manhattan apartment in 1966.[64]

It is possible that some defectors preserved a sense of personal integrity by constructing a new identity whose very legibility in Cold War terms concealed and protected their core experiences, which remained private. Outward compliance, selective silence, and evasion were perhaps the most effective means of avoiding state scrutiny for those in a position of vulnerability.[65] Though such a strategy is difficult to discern in governmental records, it is suggested in Anna Seghers's *Transit*, a novel of exile set against the backdrop of the Second World War. The novel's narrator, having assumed the identity of another man, sits for an immigration interview with a US consular official that recalls the interrogations Soviet defectors faced in the Cold War. He recounts: "She [the official] carefully typed out my answers, all the facts of my past, my goal in life. The web of questions was so dense, so cleverly thought out, so unavoidable, that no detail of my life could have escaped the consul, if only it had been *my* life."[66] Seghers, who fled Nazi Germany and later crossed Cold War borders to settle in socialist East Berlin, was aware of the small but crucial space that existed between emigres' identity and their official identification in state documents.[67]

Defection had helped define the contours of the Western-backed refugee regime, and state efforts to govern the movement of defectors during the Cold War anticipated broader restrictions on refugee mobility. To be sure, the Refugee Convention originally reached in 1951 was eventually strengthened in the name of universal human rights, theoretically encompassing the ongoing flow of refuge-seekers across the world. Yet, for most of the Cold War, the number of people fleeing remained comparatively small, hemmed in by the exit restrictions maintained by socialist states. It was all too convenient to adopt an expansive stance on refugee rights while their demographic impact was limited. It was when larger numbers arrived that the international refugee regime faltered: in 1956 with the Hungarian Uprising, and even more so in the 1970s, with the massive outflow of "boat people" from Vietnam, a wave that only subsided when the Southeast Asian country agreed to limit exit and instead promote "orderly departures."[68]

Below the surface of Cold War competition, both superpowers shared a mutual wariness of spontaneous movement and uncontrolled migration. And both sides viewed decolonization as a potential challenge to the bipolar world order they had established. The new states that emerged from colonialism, such as Vietnam, were not only battlefields in a global ideological struggle but also sites of rising outmigration, with post-colonial populations clamoring for increased mobility or simply taking flight without authorization. In many cases, the United States and the Soviet Union, their respective allies, and even post-colonial elites in Africa, Asia, and Latin America colluded to keep migrants in place. As legal scholar E. Tendayi Achiume has observed, promoting the formal independence of post-colonial countries was far easier than recognizing their interdependence, which would have meant allowing for free migration between former colonies and their metropoles.[69] The United Nations played a central role in restraining post-colonial mobility, since it accorded representation to a "club" of territorially defined states and provided a forum to govern interstate migration. Even as they competed for individual migrants, the superpowers worked together to tame global migration.

The regulation of mobility followed in the wake of defectors. When the United States and the Soviet Union sought to claim Soviets displaced by World War II, both states honed their methods for tracking, sorting, and channeling migrants. Out of the chaos of the postwar period and amid the growth of the socialist bloc, a new vocabulary was used to categorize spontaneous migrants as defectors and escapees. The 1950s saw the corralling of unrestrained movement into an international asylum system backed by the United States. It also witnessed the launch of a creative repatriation campaign extended by the Soviet Union in response. Faced with the promotion of defection by the United States and its allies, socialist states tightened their borders and built new barriers to prevent exit, from the Berlin Wall to the system of restricted zones and surveillance networks that reached eastward into the Soviet heartland. As other migrants followed the journey made by Kravchenko, Gouzenko, and Kasenkina by fleeing Soviet diplomatic missions—or finding refuge in a foreign embassy—a framework was created to close off embassies and consulates while limiting the scope of diplomatic asylum. At sea, the United States and the Soviet Union promoted the freedom of navigation but maximized control of their own ships and sailors. In the skies, those who sought to cross the Iron Curtain by hijacking an airplane found themselves grounded by an international accord that criminalized irregular movement in the air. The Cold War era was not defined by superpower competition alone. It was also shaped by the ongoing contest between states and migrants, in which superpower collusion tipped the balance and helped states gain the upper hand.

THE WORLD THE COLD WAR MADE

If the plight of Soviet migrants at the end of the Cold War seemed a faint echo of the situation facing displaced persons after the Second World War, then the rising tide of refugees that crested in the mid-2010s was a clamorous reverberation of the past. Seventy years after the end of World War II, six decades after the global wave of decolonization, and nearly thirty years after the demise of defection as a pathway for non-elite migration, desperate migrants clustered in makeshift camps across Europe. In Rome, not far from the beach town of Ladispoli where Soviet emigres once gathered, refuge-seekers from around the world could be found eking out an existence in the city's margins. They squatted in an abandoned office building facing the Piazza di Indipendenza and slept in pitched tents in a parking lot near the Tiburtina railway station. They sought shelter in Palazzo Selam, a ramshackle former university building originally constructed as a "palace of peace," and occupied a former penicillin factory on the outskirts of the Italian capital.[70] Some had fled fighting in Syria, Iraq, Afghanistan, Ethiopia, and Eritrea; others had run from economic hardship and political instability in Tunisia, Nigeria, and Pakistan. Many found that they did not meet the formal criteria of a "refugee." Unlike Soviet migrants after the Second World War, most were as unwanted by the countries they had left as they were undesired by the countries where they sought refuge.[71]

Far more refuge-seekers were held along Europe's periphery or in post-colonial countries far from its borders, including Pakistan, Kenya, Sudan, and Uganda.[72] A 2016 deal the European Union brokered with Turkey granted Turkish citizens visa-travel to Europe and provided billions of euros in aid money in exchange for Turkey's agreement to take back migrants fleeing to nearby Greece.[73] Some likened the edge of the Schengen zone, within which Europeans—and now Turks—could travel freely, to a new "iron curtain" that closed Europe off to unwanted migrants, many from countries that once been colonized by Europe's empires.[74]

The situation was described as a "refugee crisis," but it was more than simply a passing episode, and the conditions that gave rise to it were not new. While the fall of the Berlin Wall spawned dreams of a borderless world, the model of globalization forged in the Cold War included barriers to guide and limit the movement of people. Capital and transnational elites flowed free, but many ordinary migrants remained trapped in precarious positions. For all the talk among scholars about the demise of the nation-state and the rise of deterritorialized polities, governments retained the right to exclude, and their ability to enforce borders was arguably greater than ever, assisted by drone surveillance, biometric screening, and metadata collection from social media.[75] The Soviet Union broke apart, but the agreements that the United States and the USSR had brokered at the UN remained in effect, and they were built upon further: Western countries continued their retreat from granting asylum at embassies; the UN Conventions on the Law of the Sea became the accepted rules governing the world's waters; and airport security checks proliferated in number and scope. Although state-imposed exit restrictions were a rarity after 1991, and the term "defection" was seldom used except to describe people fleeing socialist holdout North Korea, the Cold War's impact on global mobility was lasting.

The refugee system forged in the Cold War was designed to assert US interests over global migration flows, filtering migrants based on desirability, channeling most to neighboring Europe or distant Latin America and Australia, and bringing a relatively small number to the United States, with a preference for those with specialized knowledge who were readily employable. It was assumed that most migrants who hoped to reach the capitalist superpower would instead be resettled in third countries. Through embassies and intelligence networks embedded in allied countries across the globe, the United States encouraged socialist migrants to flee but then rerouted them as it saw fit. The practice was just the latest manifestation of the United States running its immigration policy by "remote control," selecting migrants long before they reached American shores.[76] The remote screening of migrants by the United States and the "offshoring" of migration enforcement to third countries would endure after the Cold War's end.[77]

While many scholars of globalization have either overlooked or downplayed the USSR's role, the socialist superpower helped craft the rules that governed global mobility and did so for its own reasons. The Soviet Union, too, sought to pursue the "remote control" of migrants, but in most cases this control was exerted over those who sought to leave the boundaries of citizenship. Wherever they went, Soviet citizens were thought to carry the state's border with them, keeping them tethered to Soviet embassies, Soviet ships, and Soviet airplanes. While other "buffer zones"—such as the refugee screening facilities located in Mexico near the US border or the refugee camps in Turkey built at the frontier of the European Union—have been designed to keep migrants out, the Soviet KGB and the border troops it supervised sought to turn the socialist camp into an even more expansive buffer where wayward Soviets could be retrieved before they reached the capitalist West. When it could, the Soviet Union sought to extend this zone of migration control into capitalist states such as Finland, which was obligated to return Soviet escapees. The socialist superpower engaged a globalizing world and increased the flow of its citizens abroad even as it sought to control the terms of their movement. For the most part, Soviet restrictions on exit were compatible with the advance of global capitalism and were deftly worked into a string of international agreements.

Some Soviet border management practices even anticipated those that would be adopted by the post–Cold War world, especially after the attacks of September 11, 2001. Decades before the post-9/11 sorting of migrants by risk rather than citizenship alone, the Soviet Union surveilled populations on a massive scale for ideological reliability and employed "prophylactic" methods of border control to identify those likely to flee. Soviet borders, like those of the post-9/11 world, stretched deep into Soviet territory and reached outward to monitor citizens abroad.[78] While the Cold-War-era KGB and CIA could only dream of possessing the data made publicly available on social media in the twenty-first century, both sides screened migrants for speech and behavior in their competition for defectors.

In the decades after the Cold War, the United States and Russia continued to reach far beyond their borders to monitor, restrain, and direct migrants. In the global "War on Terror," policymakers in Washington used extraordinary rendition to seize and transfer opponents from one country to another and to carry out harsh interrogations, which recalled those directed against defectors suspected of being covert agents. Across the globe, the United States oversaw a sprawling network of liminal spaces that built on its Cold War–era capabilities and even borrowed from its erstwhile opponent. One of the secret "black sites" utilized by the US government for rendition and detention was located in Poland on the grounds of what had once been a socialist-era intelligence training facility. Taking advantage of ambiguities in international law, US officials moved people to extraterritorial spaces, such as Cuba's Guantanamo Bay, and allegedly placed them on board floating prison ships in international waters.[79]

While the United States' capacity to move migrants across the globe surpassed that of post-Soviet Russia, President Vladimir Putin ostentatiously brandished Russia's power over people living in nearby countries as well as those far beyond them. Looking back to the Soviet period with nostalgia, he cast Russia's projection of influence abroad to punish opponents, claim Russian speakers, and resettle populations as evidence of the country's enduring "great power" status.[80] In 2006, Aleksander Litvinenko, who fled to the West after serving in the KGB and its successor agency, the FSB, died in a London hospital, poisoned with the radioactive isotope polonium-210. An inquiry launched by the British government pointed to the hand of Russian intelligence, but in Moscow, there was little effort to conceal the state's contempt for Litvinenko. Aleksandr Gusak, Litvinenko's former supervisor in the FSB, declared that Litvinenko had "defected abroad" and "deserved to be executed" according to Soviet-era practice.[81] At a televised awards show in 2016, Putin remarked that "Russia's border does not end anywhere." Although the Russian president passed the comment off as a half-joke, it later proliferated on billboards in Russian-occupied Ukraine.[82] The full-scale invasion that Russia launched in 2022 displaced millions of Ukrainian citizens. Some were routed through Russian-operated "filtration camps" and forcibly deported to Russia, grimly evoking Soviet policies after the Second World War.[83]

The limits on movement put in place during the Cold War continue to be felt around the world. They may expand further as the planet warms and global inequalities deepen. The refugee system, designed to meet the needs of the Cold War, is ill-suited to shelter migrants fleeing the "slow violence" of climate change, deforestation, toxic drift, and other human-made disasters whose effects unfold gradually but destructively.[84] As such migrants seek to escape global changes rather than the oppressive policies of a single state, many will try to move in a direction already difficult to traverse, from the Global South to the Global North. In the face of mass migration that could exceed the levels recorded during the Second World War, it is possible to imagine the return of emigration controls, tolerated or even encouraged by wealthier countries fearful of an influx of migrants. Criticism of "mass emigration countries" has already been raised by influential voices in the United States and Europe.[85] Migrants lacking the resources to navigate a globalized world risk being left in perpetual limbo, either behind borders or in camps far from their intended destinations. While defectors could hope to cross the Cold War world by betting on a dramatic escape, many people seeking to move in the Cold War's wake find themselves held in place, waiting.

NOTES

INTRODUCTION

1. The Oreshkov case is detailed in GARF, f. 8131, op. 31, d. 85592.
2. NACP, RG 59, AAD, Telegram from Secretary of State to American Embassy Moscow, August 22, 1974.
3. NACP, RG 59, AAD, Telegram from American Embassy Moscow to Secretary of State, April 3, 1976.
4. Gerard Daniel Cohen, *In War's Wake: European Refugees in the Postwar Order* (New York: Oxford University Press, 2012); Susan L. Carruthers, *Cold War Captives: Imprisonment, Escape, and Brainwashing* (Berkeley: University of California Press, 2009); Tara Zahra, *The Great Departure: Mass Migration from Eastern Europe and the Making of the Free World* (New York: W. W. Norton, 2017).
5. Manfred Steger, *Globalization: A Very Short Introduction* (Oxford: Oxford University Press, 2013).
6. In Oscar Sanchez-Sibony's crucial study of the Soviet Union's engagement with globalization, it is the United States that sets the terms for global trade. Sanchez-Sibony, *Red Globalization: The Political Economy of the Soviet Cold War from Stalin to Khrushchev* (Cambridge: Cambridge University Press, 2017). For an even more forceful claim of America's exceptional role, see Daniel Bessner and Fredrik Logevall, "Recentering the United States in the Historiography of American Foreign Relations," *Texas National Security Review* 3, no. 2 (2020): 38–55.
7. See Paul Kramer, "Geopolitics of Mobility: Immigration Policy and American Global Power in the Long Twentieth Century," *American Historical Review* 123, no. 2 (2018): 393–438 on the global ambitions of US immigration policy; on the concept of a "mobility regime," see Ronen Shamir, "Without Borders? Notes on Globalization as a Mobility Regime," *Sociological Theory* 23, no. 2 (2005): 197–217; on the Soviet mobility regime's history, see Lewis Siegelbaum and Leslie Page Moch, *Broad Is My Native Land: Repertoires and Regimes of Migration in Russia's Twentieth Century* (Ithaca, NY: Cornell University Press, 2015).
8. On the United States and the Soviet Union as heirs to European imperialism, see Odd Arne Westad, *The Global Cold War: Third World Interventions and the Making of Our Times* (Cambridge: Cambridge University Press, 2005).
9. On the relative porousness of Cold War borders, at least for goods, ideas, and authorized travelers, see György Péteri, "Nylon Curtain—Transnational and Transsystemic Tendencies in the Cultural Life of State-Socialist Russia and East-Central Europe," *Slavonica* 10, no. 2 (2004): 113–24; Michael David-Fox,

"The Implications of Transnationalism," *Kritika: Explorations in Russian and Eurasian History* 12, no. 4 (2011): 895–904; and Anne E. Gorsuch and Diane P. Koenker, eds. *The Socialist Sixties: Crossing Borders in the Second World* (Bloomington: University of Indiana Press, 2013).

10. This argument builds on Edith Sheffer's microhistorical analysis of the division of Germany in *Burned Bridge: How East and West Germans Made the Iron Curtain* (New York: Oxford University Press, 2011).

11. Peter Schneider, *The Wall Jumper: A Berlin Story*, trans. Leigh Hafrey (Chicago: University of Chicago Press, 1998), 59.

12. On tensions between the Global North and South, see Matthew Connelly, "Taking Off the Cold War Lens: Visions of North-South Conflict during the Algerian War for Independence," *American Historical Review* 105, no. 3 (2000): 739–69.

13. In *Red Globalization,* Sanchez-Sibony makes a persuasive case that the Soviet Union was a keen participant in international trade. On the establishment of international rules and institutions to safeguard capital from decolonization, see Quinn Slobodian, *Globalists: The End of Empire and the Birth of Neoliberalism* (Cambridge, MA: Harvard University Press, 2018).

14. For a parallel effort to preserve the "unevenness" of empire in the global financial system, see Vanessa Ogle, "Archipelago Capitalism: Tax Havens, Offshore Money, and the State, 1950s–1970s," *American Historical Review* 122, no. 5 (2017): 1431–58.

15. Michel Foucault, *Security, Territory, Population: Lectures at the College de France, 1977–1978*, ed. M. Senellart, trans. G. Burchell (New York: Picador, 2007). See Benjamin D. Hopkins, *Ruling the Savage Periphery: Frontier Governance and the Making of the Modern State* (Cambridge, MA: Harvard University Press, 2020) for how "frontier governmentality" contained and confined certain populations to the periphery of European empires.

16. Based on Google Books Ngram analysis of term's use from 1900 to 2000.

17. On the US immigration system, see Aristide Zolberg, *A Nation by Design: Immigration Policy in the Fashioning of America* (Cambridge, MA: Harvard University Press, 2006); on how Cold War refugees sometimes crossed long-standing boundaries, see Carl J. Bon Tempo, *Americans at the Gate: The United States and Refugees during the Cold War* (Princeton, NJ: Princeton University Press, 2008).

18. On the evolution of "political opinion" as a basis for seeking refuge, see Peter Gatrell, *The Making of the Modern Refugee* (Oxford: Oxford University Press, 2013).

19. Akademiia Nauk SSSR, *Slovar' sovremennogo russkogo iazyka*, vol. 7 (Moscow: Izdatel'stvo AN SSSR, 1958), 754.

20. The Soviet term for treason, *izmena Rodine*, literally translates as "betrayal of the Motherland." *Rodina* can also be rendered as "homeland," but it is a gendered term and sometimes elaborated as *Rodina-mat'* (Rodina-Mother).

21. NACP, RG 59, Policy Planning Staff, microfiche 1171, card 62, Policy Relating to Defection and Defectors from Soviet Power, June 28, 1949.

22. FRUS, Intelligence Community, 1950–1955, Doc. 252, National Security Council Intelligence Directive No. 13, January 19, 1950.

23. On "psychological exploitation," see Monica Kim, *Interrogation Rooms of the Korean War: The Untold History* (Princeton, NJ: Princeton University Press, 2020).

24. NACP, RG 59, Policy Planning Staff, microfiche 1171, card 23, Utilization of Refugees from the Soviet Union in U.S. National Interest, February 5, 1948.
25. The directive remained secret long after the Cold War's end. In 2011, the US National Archives declassified a tranche of files originally belonging to Rose Conway, President Truman's personal secretary. Among them was a collection of NSC directives intended for the president; tucked away in the fourth volume of this compilation was a complete copy of NSC 86/1. TPL, President's Secretary Files, Box 171, NSC 86/1, United States Policy on Soviet and Satellite Defectors, April 19, 1951.
26. For a comparative view of state efforts to channel movement, see Valeska Huber, *Channelling Mobilities: Migration and Globalisation in the Suez Canal Region and Beyond, 1869–1914* (Cambridge: Cambridge University Press, 2013).
27. "Ingenious Escapees Choose All Avenues to Freedom Lest We Forget." *USEP News*, 1958, EPL, Robert K. Gray, Box 2.
28. Helena Merriman, "The Story of Tunnel 29," *BBC News*, accessed October 25, 2022, https://www.bbc.co.uk/news/extra/Od4dL9Lip2/tunnel_29.
29. Vladislav Krasnov, *Soviet Defectors: The KGB Wanted List* (Stanford, CA: Hoover Institution Press, 1986). For a study of the National Alliance of Russian Solidarists and other emigre groups, see Benjamin Tromly, *Cold War Exiles and the CIA: Plotting to Free Russia* (Oxford: Oxford University Press, 2019).
30. I refer here to the notes of former KGB archivist Vasili Mitrokhin. Christopher Andrew worked with Mitrokhin to publish a series of books, including *The Mitrokhin Archive: The KGB in Europe and the West* (London: Allen Lane, 1999) and *The Mitrokhin Archive II: The KGB and the World* (London: Allen Lane, 2005).
31. Among important recent works are Kevin P. Riehle, *Soviet Defectors: Revelations of Renegade Intelligence Officers, 1924–1954* (Edinburgh: Edinburgh University Press, 2020); Mark Edele, *Stalin's Defectors: How Red Army Soldiers Became Hitler's Collaborators, 1941–1945* (Oxford: Oxford University Press, 2019); Tromly, *Cold War Exiles and the CIA*.
32. See, for example, Boris Volodarsky, *Stalin's Agent: The Life and Death of Alexander Orlov* (Oxford: Oxford University Press, 2019); Serhii Plokhy, *The Man with the Poison Gun* (London: One World, 2017).
33. Gabriel Popescu, *Bordering and Ordering the Twenty-First Century: Understanding Borders* (Lanham, MD: Rowman and Littlefield, 2012); Matthew Longo, *The Politics of Borders: Sovereignty, Security, and the Citizen after 9/11* (Cambridge: Cambridge University Press, 2018.
34. Étienne Balibar, *Politics and the Other Scene*, trans. Christine Jones, James Swenson, and Chris Turner (London: Verso, 2012), 75–86.
35. Thomas Nail, *Theory of the Border* (New York: Oxford University Press, 2018).
36. Giorgio Agamben, *State of Exception*, trans. Kevin Attell (Chicago: University of Chicago Press, 2005).
37. On the militarization of borders, see Reece Jones, *Violent Borders: Refugees and the Right to Move* (London: Verso, 2017).
38. Pierre Bourdieu, *Language and Symbolic Power*, trans. and ed. John B. Thompson (Cambridge: Polity, 2011), 117–25.
39. For a long-term history of the territorialization of state power, see Charles S. Maier, *Once within Borders: Territories of Power, Wealth, and Belonging since 1500* (Cambridge, MA: Harvard University Press, 2016); on the extension of law, see Lauren Benton, *A Search for Sovereignty: Law and Geography in European Empires, 1400–1900* (Cambridge: Cambridge University Press, 2010).

40. Plato, *Laws*, trans. Benjamin Jowett, accessed October 25, 2022, http://class ics.mit.edu/Plato/laws.12.xii.html; discussed in Alan Dowty, *Closed Borders: The Contemporary Assault on Freedom of Movement* (New Haven, CT: Yale University Press, 1989), 8–9.

41. Nancy L. Green, "The Politics of Exit: Reversing the Immigration Paradigm," *Journal of Modern History* 77, no. 2 (2005): 263–89.

42. Shelly Chan, *Diaspora's Homeland: Modern China in the Age of Global Migration* (Durham, NC: Duke University Press, 2018).

43. Nancy L. Green and François Weil, eds., *Citizenship and Those Who Leave: The Politics of Emigration and Expatriation* (Urbana: University of Illinois Press, 2007).

44. A point emphasized by Zahra in *The Great Departure*.

45. Dowty, *Closed Borders*, 186.

46. John Torpey, *The Invention of the Passport: Surveillance, Citizenship, and the State* (Cambridge: Cambridge University Press, 2000).

47. Torpey, *Invention of the Passport*, 163.

48. Eric Lohr, *Russian Citizenship: From Empire to Soviet Union* (Cambridge, MA: Harvard University Press, 2012).

49. On the experiences of the Bolsheviks in emigration, see Faith Hillis, *Utopia's Discontents: Russian Émigrés and the Quest for Freedom, 1830s–1930s* (New York: Oxford University Press, 2021).

50. Gatrell, *Making of the Modern Refugee*, 21–84.

51. Iurii Fel'shtinskii, *K istorii nashei zakrytosti* (Moscow: Terra, 1991), 69–122.

52. RGASPI, f. 17, op. 3, d. 766, l. 15. On early Soviet "nonreturners," see Vladimir Genis, *Nevernye slugi rezhima: pervye sovetskie nevozvrashchentsy (1920–1933)*, 2 vols. (Moscow: Informkniga, 2009–2010).

53. Nathalie Moine, "Passeportisation, statistique des migrations et contrôle de l'identité sociale," *Cahiers du monde russe* 38, 4 (1997): 587–99; David R. Shearer, *Policing Stalin's Socialism: Repression and Social Order in the Soviet Union, 1924–1953* (New Haven, CT: Yale University Press, 2009).

54. On the border with Turkey, see Mathjis Pelkmans, *Defending the Border: Identity, Religion, and Modernity in the Republic of Georgia* (Ithaca, NY: Cornell University Press, 2006); on China, see Alsu Tagirova, "Transgressing the Boundaries: The Migration of Uighurs into Soviet Central Asia after World War II," *Asian Perspective* 42, no. 4 (2018): 575–96.

55. In *Broad Is My Native Land*, Siegelbaum and Moch discuss Eurasia's "itinerants"; Sheila Fitzpatrick examines the wanderings of a "marginal" Soviet citizen in "The Tramp's Tale: Travels within the Soviet Union and across its Borders, 1925–1950," *Past & Present* 241, no. 1 (2018): 259–90.

56. For an institutional history, see Andrea M. Chandler, *Institutions of Isolation: Border Controls in the Soviet Union and Its Successor States, 1917–1993* (Montreal-Kingston: McGill-Queen's University Press, 1998).

57. See Sabine Dullin's thorough study of border enforcement before World War II, *La frontière épaisse: aux origins des politiques soviétiques, 1920–1940* (Paris: EHESS, 2014).

58. RGANI, f. 3, op. 22, d. 70, ll. 92–101. Established in 1954, the KGB inherited responsibility for the intelligence and secret police functions that had once been the purview of Ezhov's NKVD.

59. RGANI, f. 3, op. 22, d. 70, ll. 102–20.

60. GARF, f. 7523, op. 10, d. 71; GARF, f. 7523, op. 59, d. 5, ll. 6–8.

61. RGANI, f. 89, op. 73, d. 11.

62. A. Kolpakidi and D. Prokhorov, *KGB prikazanno likvidirovat': Spetsoperatsii sovetskikh spetssluzhb 1918–1941* (Moscow: Iauza, 2004).

63. RGVA, f. 4, op. 12, d. 98, ll. 617–22. For background, see Edele, *Stalin's Defectors*, 41.

64. For a comparative perspective, see Anna Mazurkiewicz, ed., *East Central European Migrations during the Cold War: A Handbook* (Berlin: De Gruyter Oldenbourg, 2019).

65. Linda K. Kerber, "The Stateless as the Citizen's Other: A View from the United States," *American Historical Review* 112, no. 1 (2007): 1–34; Mae M. Ngai, *Impossible Subjects: Illegal Aliens and the Making of Modern America* (Princeton, NJ: Princeton University Press, 2014).

66. Dowty in *Closed Borders* and Zahra in *Great Departure* both point to the long-term legacies of Russian serfdom. Both serfdom and slavery were perpetuated by criminalizing the flight of those enserfed and enslaved.

67. Laura Madokoro, *Elusive Refuge: Chinese Migrants in the Cold War* (Cambridge, MA: Harvard University Press, 2016).

68. Kelly Lytle Hernández, *Migra! A History of the U.S. Border Patrol* (Berkeley: University of California Press, 2010); Ana Raquel Minian, "Offshoring Migration Control: Guatemalan Transmigrants and the Construction of Mexico as a Buffer Zone," *American Historical Review* 125, no. 1 (2020): 89–111; Zolberg describes "remote control" of immigration by the United States in *A Nation by Design*.

69. Charles S. Maier outlines the supposed dichotomy in "The Cold War as an Era of Imperial Rivalry," in Silvio Pons and Federico Romero, eds., *Reinterpreting the End of the Cold War: Issues, Interpretations, Periodization* (London: Frank Cass, 2005). In *Empires in World History: Power and the Politics of Difference* (Princeton, NJ: Princeton University Press, 2010), Jane Burbank and Frederick Cooper treat Russia and the Soviet Union as Eurasian land empires but also discuss how Russian and Soviet rulers borrowed techniques from other imperial states. Daniel Immerwahr foregrounds the role of territory in America's "pointillist" empire in *How to Hide an Empire: A History of the Greater United States* (New York: Farrar, Straus and Giroux, 2019).

70. On the rooting of migrants in Soviet territory, see Erik R. Scott, *Familiar Strangers: The Georgian Diaspora and the Evolution of Soviet Empire* (New York: Oxford University Press, 2016).

71. In *Power and Protest: Global Revolution and the Rise of Détente* (Cambridge, MA: Harvard University Press, 2003), Jeremi Suri makes the case for tacit collusion across the Iron Curtain but argues that it was primarily a response to internal dissent.

72. In this sense, it resembled forms of collusion more typically described by economists examining cartels than by jurists scrutinizing cases of overt conspiracy. See Robert C. Marshall and Leslie M. Marx, *The Economics of Collusion: Cartels and Bidding Rings* (Cambridge, MA: MIT Press, 2014).

73. George Orwell, "You and the Atomic Bomb," *Tribune*, October 19, 1945.

74. By emphasizing the mutual constitution of Cold War borders by the superpowers, this book departs from the framework of bipolarity described by John Lewis Gaddis in *The Long Peace* (New York: Oxford University Press, 1987), which rests on the notion of the "mutual independence" of the United States and the Soviet Union. See Gaddis, *Long Peace*, 225.

75. Recent scholarship on the Cold War has highlighted the role of actors besides the United States and the Soviet Union. For an ambitious study that emphasizes regional dynamics, see Lorenz M. Lüthi, *Cold Wars: Asia, the Middle East, Europe* (Cambridge: Cambridge University Press, 2020).

76. On international law's history in the Soviet Union and elsewhere, see Lauri Mälksoo, *Russian Approaches to International Law* (Oxford: Oxford University Press, 2017); Anthea Roberts, *Is International Law International?* (Oxford: Oxford University Press, 2019). On the postwar Soviet effort to shape international law, see Francine Hirsch, *Soviet Judgment at Nuremberg: A New History of the International Military Tribunal after World War II* (New York: Oxford University Press, 2020).

77. For a comparative look at how Cold War migrants navigated the interstate order, see Meredith Oyen, *The Diplomacy of Migration: Transnational Lives and the Making of US-Chinese Relations in the Cold War* (Ithaca, NY: Cornell University Press, 2016).

78. On international relief workers, see Sharif Gemie, Laure Humbert, and Fiona Reid, *Outcast Europe: Refugees and Relief Workers in an Era of Total War, 1936–1948* (London: Continuum, 2011).

CHAPTER 1

1. Based on descriptions in Nina Berberova, *Poslednye i pervye; Delo Kravchenko* (Moscow: Idz-vo im. Sabashnikovykh, 2000), 143–45; Victor Kravchenko, *I Chose Justice* (New York: Scribner, 1950), 48–50; Victor Kravchenko et al., *Kravchenko versus Moscow* (London: Wingate, 1950), 11; Gary Kern, *The Kravchenko Case: One Man's War against Stalin* (New York: Enigma, 2012), 391–93.

2. Victor Kravchenko et al., *Le procès Kravchenko contre les Lettres francaises: Compte rendu des audiences d'après la sténographie suivi d'un index des noms cites* (Paris: Jeune Parque, 1949), vol. 2, 278–92.

3. Kravchenko et al., *Le procès Kravchenko*, vol. 1, 10.

4. For background see Irwin M. Wall, *The United States and the Making of Postwar France, 1945–1954* (Cambridge: Cambridge University Press, 2002).

5. For a description of the camp, see Nikolai Tolstoy, *The Secret Betrayal* (New York: Scribner, 1978), 376–77; on the French political context, see Catherine Gousseff, *Le Paris des étrangers depuis 1945* (Paris: Éditions de la Sorbonne, 1995), 189–204; on the Soviet response, see GARF, f. 9526, op. 6, d. 352, ll. 10–20.

6. Translation provided in Kravchenko, *I Chose Justice*, 32.

7. Kravchenko, *I Chose Justice*, 65.

8. Cited in Kravchenko, *I Chose Justice*, 65–66.

9. Kravchenko et al., *Le procès Kravchenko*, vol. 2, 282–92.

10. According to Soviet messages decrypted by the US Venona project, NACP, RG 263, Venona Messages, 1939–1951, Box 3.

11. Kern, *Kravchenko Case*, 418.

12. Konstantin Simonov, "Iuda Kravchenko i ego khoziaeva," *Pravda*, February 1, 1949, 3–4.

13. NACP, RG 65, Office of the Director, Official and Confidential Subject Files, 1924–1972, Box 19, FBI Memorandum on Kravchenko, February 9, 1966.

14. On use of term "deserter," see Kern, *The Kravchenko Case*, 308; a headline in the *Christian Science Monitor*, April 6, 1944, 13, read "Kravchenko Resignation Serves Nazi Propaganda."

15. Benjamin Tromly, *Cold War Exiles and the CIA: Plotting to Free Russia* (Oxford: Oxford University Press, 2019), 100.
16. Kern claims Kravchenko proposed the idea of a trial in *Kravchenko Case*, 333–34; on the role of the US government, see Wall, *United States and the Making of Postwar France*, 152.
17. Kern, *Kravchenko Case*, 342–47, 378–88.
18. NACP, Bureau of Public Affairs, Subject Files of Policy Plans and Guidance Staff, Box 70, Memoranda on Kravchenko's lecture tour, 1951; NACP, RG 59, Records Relating to the IRO and DPC, Resettlement File, 1941–1952, Box 6, Department of State Telegrams, January 1951.
19. For a sampling of this important field of scholarship, see Seth Bernstein, "Ambiguous Homecoming: Retribution, Exploitation and Social Tensions during Repatriation to the USSR, 1944–1946," *Past & Present* 242, no. 1 (2019): 193–226; Gerard Daniel Cohen, *In War's Wake: European Refugees in the Postwar Order* (New York: Oxford University Press, 2012); Melissa Feinberg, *Curtain of Lies: The Battle over Truth in Stalinist Eastern Europe* (New York: Oxford University Press, 2017); Atina Grossmann, *Jews, Germans, and Allies: Close Encounters in Occupied Germany* (Princeton, NJ: Princeton University Press, 2007); Anna Holian, *Between National Socialism and Soviet Communism: Displaced Persons in Postwar Germany* (Ann Arbor: University of Michigan Press, 2011); Andrew Janco, "Soviet 'Displaced Persons' in Europe," PhD diss., University of Chicago, 2012; Mark Wyman, *DPs: Europe's Displaced Persons, 1945–1951* (Ithaca, NY: Cornell University Press, 1998).
20. Mark Edele's *Stalin's Defectors: How Red Army Soldiers Became Hitler's Collaborators* (Oxford: Oxford University Press, 2019) focuses on wartime flight; Vladislav Krasnov's *Soviet Defectors: The KGB Wanted List* (Stanford, CA: Hoover Institution Press, 1986), considers defection as a phenomenon dating back to the establishment of Soviet rule; Kevin P. Riehle's *Soviet Defectors: Revelations of Renegade Intelligence Officers, 1924–1954* (Edinburgh: Edinburgh University Press, 2020) similarly treats defection as a constant from the 1920s onward.
21. An abbreviation of its official name: the Administration of the Plenipotentiary of the Soviet of People's Commissars for the Affairs of Repatriation. I use the term "Soviet-claimed" since some migrants would not have identified as citizens, especially those fleeing from annexed territories.
22. GARF, f. 9526, op. 1, d. 220, l. 229.
23. On the sizable number of Russian-speaking DPs who went to Australia and their subsequent lives there, see Sheila Fitzpatrick, *White Russians, Red Peril: A Cold War History of Migration to Australia* (London: Routledge, 2021).
24. Mark Edele, "The Second World War as a History of Displacement: The Soviet Case," *History Australia* 12, no. 2 (2015): 17–40.
25. Precise numbers are difficult to pin down, but these commonly cited figures are from Eugene Kulischer, *Europe on the Move: War and Population Changes, 1917–1947* (New York: Columbia University Press, 1948), 305. An even greater number of Germans from East Central Europe were expelled in the war's aftermath, though they fled from different countries and their migration would continue until 1950.
26. For a case study, see Liudmila Novikova, "Criminalized Liaisons: Soviet Women and Allied Sailors in Wartime Arkhangel'sk," *Journal of Contemporary History* 55, no. 4 (2020), 745–763.
27. AVP RF, f. 192, op. 11, p. 74, d. 1.

28. Victor Kravchenko, *I Chose Freedom: The Personal and Political Life of a Soviet Official* (New York: C. Scribner's Sons, 1946), 2–4.

29. "Soviet Official Here Resigns; Assails 'Double-Faced' Policies," *New York Times*, April 4, 1944; Kravchenko, *I Chose Freedom*, 4; AVP RF, f. 192, op. 11, p. 74, d. 2, l. 43.

30. "Soviet Official Here Resigns," *New York Times*, April 4, 1944.

31. AVP RF, f. 192, op. 11, p. 74, d. 1, l. 10.

32. Kevin P. Riehle, "Early Cold War Evolution of British and US Defector Policy and Practice," *Cold War History* 19, no. 3 (2019): 343–61; for background, see Elizabeth Kimball Maclean, *Joseph E. Davies: Envoy to the Soviets* (Westport, CT: Praeger, 1992).

33. NACP, RG 65, Office of the Director, Official and Confidential Subject Files, 1924–1972, Box 19, FBI Memorandum on Kravchenko, February 9, 1966.

34. Tolstoy, *The Secret Betrayal*; for a more balanced view, see Jason Kendall Moore, "Between Expediency and Principle: US Repatriation Policy toward Russian Nationals, 1944–1949," *Diplomatic History* 24, no. 3 (2000): 381–404.

35. FRUS, Diplomatic Papers, 1945, Europe, Vol. V, Doc. 631, Memorandum to the Secretary of State, April 19, 1945.

36. Mark Elliott, "The United States and the Forced Repatriation of Soviet Citizens, 1944–47," *Political Science Quarterly* 88, no. 2 (1973): 253–75; Janco, "Soviet 'Displaced Persons' in Europe."

37. On the significance of demographics, see Tara Zahra, *The Great Departure: Mass Migration from Eastern Europe and the Making of the Free World* (New York: W. W. Norton, 2017).

38. For background, see Aristide Zolberg, *A Nation by Design: Immigration Policy in the Fashioning of America* (Cambridge, MA: Harvard University Press, 2006), 243–92.

39. US Holocaust Museum, "How Many Refugees Came to the United States from 1933–1945?" accessed October 25, 2022, https://exhibitions.ushmm.org/americans-and-the-holocaust/how-many-refugees-came-to-the-united-states-from-1933-1945.

40. GARF, f. 9526, op. 6, d. 380.

41. Bernstein, "Ambiguous Homecoming," 207.

42. AVP RF, f. 192, op. 11, p. 74, d. 1, ll. 73–76.

43. NACP, RG 43, Country Files, Box 201, "Repatriation of Enemy and Ex-Enemy Nationals," October 14, 1946.

44. Figures from Zemskov, *Vozvrashchenie sovetskikh peremeshchennykh lits*, and Louise Holborn, *The International Refugee Organization: Its History and Work, 1946–1952* (London: Oxford University Press, 1956).

45. Liisa Helena Malkki, "Refugees and Exile: From 'Refugee Studies' to the National Order of Things," *Annual Review of Anthropology* 24 (1995): 495–523.

46. Jayne Persian, "Displaced Persons and the Politics of International Categorisation(s)," *Australian Journal of Politics and History* 58, no. 4 (2012): 481–96; on the possibilities of statelessness, which narrowed in the postwar period, see Mira L. Siegelberg, *Statelessness: A Modern History* (Cambridge, MA: Harvard University Press, 2020).

47. Anna Holian, "The Ambivalent Exception: American Occupation Policy in Postwar Germany and the Formation of Jewish Refugee Spaces," *Journal of Refugee Studies* 25, no. 3 (2012): 428–51.

48. For background, see R. M. Douglas, *Orderly and Humane: The Expulsion of the Germans after the Second World War* (New Haven, CT: Yale University Press, 2013).

49. Elliott, "The United States and Forced Repatriation," 256.

50. GARF, f. 9526, op. 6, d. 43-, ll. 186–89.

51. Holian, "The Ambivalent Exception," 456.

52. GARF, f. 9526, op. 1, d. 743, l. 180.

53. GARF, f. 9526, op. 6, d. 431, ll. 111–13.

54. GARF, f. 9526, op. 6, d. 431, l. 20.

55. Holian, "The Ambivalent Exception," 456.

56. For two critical studies of the evolving political context navigated by migrants, see Holian, *Between National Socialism and Soviet Communism*; and Feinberg, *Curtain of Lies*.

57. On interactions between DPs and international organizations, see Ruth Balint, *Destination Elsewhere: Displaced Persons and Their Quest to Leave Postwar Europe* (Ithaca, NY: Cornell University Press, 2021).

58. Moore, "Between Expediency and Principle," 395–96.

59. TFA, Escapees/Karlsfeld Files, "Betrayal of the Cossacks at Lienz." The role of British and American soldiers received renewed attention in the 1970s with the publication of Nicholas Bethell's *The Last Secret: Forcible Repatriation to Russia, 1944–7* (London: Deutsch, 1974) and Julius Epstein's *Operation Keelhaul: The Story of Forced Repatriation from 1944 to the Present* (Old Greenwich, CT: Devin-Adair, 1974).

60. On the relationship between emigres and policymakers, see Tromly, *Cold War Exiles and the CIA*.

61. Pauli Heikkilä, "Baltic States: Estonia, Latvia and Lithuania," in *East Central European Migrations*, ed. Anna Mazurkiewicz, 45–67 (Berlin: De Gruyter Oldenbourg, 2019).

62. Persian, "Displaced Persons and the Politics of International Categorisation(s)," 489–90.

63. Translated in Atle Grahl-Madsen, *Territorial Asylum* (Stockholm: Almqvist & Wiksell, 1980), 32.

64. Elliott, "The United States and Forced Repatriation," 269–70

65. George Ginsburgs, "The Soviet Union and the Problem of Refugees and Displaced Persons, 1917–1956," *American Journal of International Law* 51, no. 2 (1957): 325–61. Russian speakers from Manchuria were the first to be offered Soviet citizenship, with decrees in November 1945 and January 1946. See Laurie Manchester, "Repatriation to a Totalitarian Homeland: The Ambiguous Alterity of Russian Repatriates from China to the U.S.S.R.," *Diaspora: A Journal of Transnational Studies* 16, no. 3 (2007): 353–88.

66. Jo Laycock, "Belongings: People and Possessions in the Armenian Repatriations, 1945–1949," *Kritika: Explorations in Russian and Eurasian History* 18, no. 3 (2017): 511–37.

67. Sheila Fitzpatrick, "The Motherland Calls: 'Soft' Repatriation of Soviet Citizens from Europe, 1945–1953," *Journal of Modern History* 90, no. 2 (2018): 323–50.

68. Holian, "The Ambivalent Exception," 462.

69. M. Lesnov, *Tvoi dolg pered rodinoi* (Voennoe izdatel'stvo Narodnogo Kommissariata Oborony, 1945).

70. GARF, f. 9526, op. 6, d. 262, l. 109.

71. GARF, f. 9526, op. 6, d. 262, ll. 188–205.

72. GARF, f. 9526, op. 6, d. 606, ll. 1–40.
73. TFA, Karlsfeld Files, Tatiana Schaufuss letter to Paul McCormack, October 2, 1945.
74. TFA, Karlsfeld Files, translation of article from *Novoe Russkoe Slovo*, February 19, 1947.
75. GARF, f. 10055, op. 3, d. 657, l. 20; GARF, f. 9526, op. 6, d. 254.
76. Anatol Shmelev, *Tracking a Diaspora: Emigres from Russia and Eastern Europe in the Repositories* (Hoboken, NJ: Taylor and Francis, 2012), 163.
77. GARF, f. 9526, op. 6, d. 262, l. 287.
78. NACP, RG 59, Records Relating to the IRO and the DPC, IRO Subject File, 1946–1952, Box 13, IRO Manual for Eligibility Officers.
79. Tolstoy Foundation, *Who Are the DPs?* (New York: Tolstoy Foundation, 1953).
80. Louis Fischer and Boris Yakovlev, eds., *Thirteen Who Fled* (New York: Harper, 1949); Tromly discusses the background of Fischer's interview subjects in *Cold War Exiles*, 1–2.
81. David S. Foglesong, *The American Mission and the "Evil Empire"* (New York: Cambridge University Press, 2007).
82. Alexandra Tolstoy, "The Russian DPs" *Russian Review* 9, no. 1 (1950): 57.
83. Kevin R. Johnson, "The Intersection of Race and Class in U.S. Immigration Law and Enforcement," *Law and Contemporary Problems* 72, no. 4 (2009): 1–35.
84. NACP, RG 59, Records Relating to the International Refugee Organization, IRO Subject File, 1946-1952, Box 13, IRO Manual for Eligibility Officers.
85. Lieselotte Luyckx, "Soviet DPs for the Belgian Mining Industry: The Daily Struggle against Yalta of a Forgotten Minority," PhD thesis, European University Institute, 2012.
86. Fitzpatrick, "The Motherland Calls."
87. NACP, RG 59, Displaced Persons, 1945–1949, Box 4105, Correspondence from the Ukrainian Congress Committee of America, December 17, 1945.
88. NACP, RG 59, Displaced Persons, 1945–1949, Box 4104, Draft report from Johns Hopkins University, 1945.
89. NYPL, David J. Dallin Papers, Box 1, Interviews, 1948–1955.
90. On the project's scope, see David Brandenberger, "A Guide to Working with the Harvard Project on the Soviet Social System Online," accessed October 25, 2022, https://library.harvard.edu/sites/default/files/static/collections/hpsss/HPSSSguide2020.pdf; on American Sovietology, see David C. Engerman, *Know Your Enemy: The Rise and Fall of America's Soviet Experts* (New York: Oxford University Press, 2011).
91. GARF, f. 9526, op. 6, d. 1024, l. 280.
92. TFA, Schleissheim Files, Report on DP Camp Feldmoching-Schleissheim, 1949.
93. UN, UNRRA Germany Photographs, accessed October 25, 2022, https://www.flickr.com/photos/70217867@N07/albums/72157629547616745.
94. On the former, see Michel Foucault, *Security, Territory, Population: Lectures at the College de France, 1977–1978*, ed. M. Senellart, trans. G. Burchell (New York: Picador, 2007); on the latter, see Giorgio Agamben, *State of Exception*, trans. Kevin Attell (Chicago: Chicago University Press, 2005).
95. Moore, "Between Expediency and Principle," 401.
96. GARF, f. 9526, op. 6, d. 430, l. 114.
97. See, for example, letters in GARF, f. 9526, op. 1, d. 663.

98. NACP, RG 59, Records Relating to the IRO and the DPC, Resettlement File, 1941–1952, Box 1, Letter from US Political Adviser for Germany to Secretary of State, December 22, 1947.

99. GARF f. 8131, op. 31, d. 83803, ll. 10–21.

100. Susan L. Carruthers, *Cold War Captives: Imprisonment, Escape, and Brainwashing* (Berkeley: University of California Press, 2009), 9–10, 182–83.

101. "Universal Declaration of Human Rights," Office of the High Commissioner for Human Rights, accessed October 25, 2022, https://www.ohchr.org/EN/UDHR/Documents/UDHR_Translations/eng.pdf.

102. For a sample of the debate over the origins of postwar human rights, see Samuel Moyn, *The Last Utopia: Human Rights in History* (Cambridge, MA: Belknap, 2012) and the rebuttal by Johannes Morsink, *The Universal Declaration of Human Rights and the Holocaust* (Washington, DC: Georgetown University Press, 2019).

103. Ginsburgs, "The Soviet Union and the Problem of Refugees and Displaced Persons," 351.

104. Andrew Janco has traced the notion of refugees being "unwilling" to return to the Soviet invasion of Poland and the Baltic states in 1939–40. See "'Unwilling': The One-Word Revolution in Refugee Status, 1940–51," *Contemporary European History* 23, no. 3 (2014): 429–46.

105. "Convention and Protocol Relating to the Status of Refugees," United Nations High Commissioner for Refugees, accessed October 25, 2022, https://www.unhcr.org/en-us/3b66c2aa10.

106. AVP RF, f. 54, op. 40, p. 718, d. 8, ll. 76–77.

107. TPL, George L. Warren Files, Box 1, *The New International Yearbook*, 1948.

108. Based on analysis of cases in GARF, f. 9526, op. 6, d. 433.

109. GARF, f. 9526, op. 1, d. 410, ll. 72–85.

110. The term was invoked during the NKVD's mass operations against national minorities and foreign-born residents of the USSR in the 1930s, which targeted them as potential spies. See, for example, the Politburo's decree of March 9, 1936, which set the stage for these operations, RGASPI, f. 17, op. 3, d. 9575.

111. TPL, President's Secretary Files, Box 171, NSC 86/1, United States Policy on Soviet and Satellite Defectors, April 19, 1951.

112. Annie Jacobsen, *Operation Paperclip: The Secret Intelligence Program that Brought Nazi Scientists to America* (New York: Back Bay, 2015).

113. FRUS, Diplomatic Papers, 1945, Europe, Volume V, Doc. 884, Aide-Mémoire from Department of State to Soviet Embassy, April 12, 1945.

114. NACP, RG 65, Office of the Director, Official and Confidential Subject Files, 1924–1972, Box 19, FBI Memorandum on Kravchenko, February 9, 1966.

115. Amy Knight, *How the Cold War Began: The Igor Gouzenko Affair and the Hunt for Soviet Spies* (New York: Basic, 2007).

116. Kevin P. Riehle, "Early Cold War Evolution of British and US Defector Policy and Practice."

117. "The Gloomy Diary of a Russian Deserter," *Life*, September 12, 1949, 57–60.

118. The Barsov case and its aftermath is discussed in Carruthers, *Cold War Captives*, 59. The defector's name is more correctly rendered as Borzov, but he was almost universally referred to as Barsov in the Western press.

119. Engerman, *Know Your Enemy*; on the recruitment of skilled workers as a strategy to undermine socialist economies, see Emmanuel Comte, "Waging the Cold War: The Origins and Launch of Western Cooperation to Absorb Migrants from Eastern Europe," *Cold War History* 20, no. 4 (2020): 461–81.

120. NACP, RG 59, Records of the Policy and Planning Staff, 1947–1954, M1171, Card 62.
121. NACP, RG 59, Political Refugees, Soviet Union, 1945–1949, Box 6641, Policy on Defectors, September 21, 1949.
122. NACP, RG 59, Political Refugees, Soviet Union, 1945–1949, Box 6641, Soviet Defector Interrogation Report (SPONGE #1), November 25, 1949.
123. NACP, RG 59, Political Refugees, Soviet Union, 1945–1949, Box 6641, Confidential Memorandum, August 19, 1949.
124. Gregory Mitrovich, *Undermining the Kremlin: America's Strategy to Subvert the Soviet Bloc, 1947–1956* (Ithaca, NY: Cornell University Press, 2009), 78.
125. FRUS, National Security Council Intelligence Directive No. 13.
126. FRUS, The Intelligence Community, 1950–1955, Doc. 253, National Security Council Intelligence Directive No. 14, March 3, 1950.
127. FRUS, The Intelligence Community, 1950–1955, Doc. 18, Director of Central Intelligence Directive 14/1, July 17, 1950.
128. FRUS, National Security Council Intelligence Directive No. 13.
129. Riehle, "Early Cold War Evolution of British and US Defector Policy."
130. The program's origins are detailed in the declassified 2003 CIA working paper by Kevin Conley Ruffner, "Eagle and Swastika: CIA and Nazi War Criminals and Collaborators," from CIA, CREST 519697e8993294098d50c2a4, Chapter 13, 1.
131. TPL, President's Secretary Files, Box 171, NSC 86/1.
132. TPL, President's Secretary Files, Box 171, NSC 86/1.
133. DDO, Text of NSC action toward US policy regarding the resettling of Soviet bloc defectors, undated, tinyurl.galegroup.com/tinyurl/4Xm7HX.
134. The details of Phase B remain classified, though the Psychological Strategy Board's document, "A National Psychological Program with Respect to Escapees from the Soviet Orbit," dated December 5, 1952, outlines Phase B's general contours. TPL, Psychological Strategy Board Files, Box 4.
135. NACP, Psychological Operations Plan for Soviet Orbit Escapees Phase A, December 20, 1951, accessed October 25, 2022, https://www.archives.gov/files/declassification/iscap/pdf/2012-089-doc1.pdf.
136. Discussed in Carruthers, *Cold War Captives*, 70–73.
137. TPL, Psychological Strategy Board Files, Box 4, Phase B overview.
138. Benjamin Tromly, "The Making of a Myth: The National Labor Alliance, Russian Emigres, and Cold War Intelligence Activities," *Journal of Cold War Studies* 18, no. 1 (2016): 80–111.
139. TPL, Psychological Strategy Board Files, Box 4, Phase B overview.
140. Carruthers, *Cold War Captives*, 4–5.
141. CIA, Letter to PSB from Eisenhower, March 6, 1953, CREST CIA-RDP RDP80R01731R000700450020-8.
142. Ned O'Gorman, "'The One Word the Kremlin Fears': C. D. Jackson, Cold War 'Liberation,' and American Political-Economic Adventurism," *Rhetoric and Public Affairs* 12, no. 3 (2009): 389–427.
143. DDO, Psychological Value of Escapees from the Soviet Orbit, March 26, 1953.
144. On the role of dancers in the Cold War, see David Caute, *The Dancer Defects: The Struggle for Cultural Supremacy in the Cold War* (Oxford: Oxford University Press, 2003).
145. Carruthers, *Cold War Captives*, 83.
146. WCD, Office of Policy Coordination, History of American Committee for Liberation, August 21, 1951, accessed October 25, 2022, https://digitalarchive.

wilsoncenter.org/document/114354. On the organization's history, see Tromly, *Cold War Exiles*, 95–120.

147. NACP, RG 59, Political Refugees, Soviet Union, 1950–1954, Box 3810, Despatch from American Consul General to Department of State, May 18, 1954.

148. NACP, RG 466, Peripheral Reporting Unit, 1953–55, Box 2, Questionnaire for Interviewing Recent Refugees, February 1, 1954.

149. NACP, RG 59, Political Refugees, Eastern Europe, 1950–1954, Box 3787, Coordination of Escapee Program with VOA, March 17, 1953.

150. "3 Francs for Kravchenko," *New York Times*, February 8, 1950, 5.

151. Cited in Kern, *Kravchenko Case*, 496.

152. DDO, Psychological Value of Escapees from the Soviet Orbit, March 26, 1953.

153. AVP RF, f. 129, op. 44, p. 325, d. 58.

154. EPL, White House Office, National Security Council Staff: Papers, Disaster File Series, Box 41, NSC Report on Admission of Certain European Temporary Visitors Excludable Under Existing Law, March 26, 1955.

155. TPL, Psychological Strategy Board Files, Box 28, Freedom Train Correspondence, January 18, 1952.

CHAPTER 2

1. Alexandra Richie, *Faust's Metropolis: A History of Berlin* (London: HarperCollins, 2008), 715–18; on the inner German border's evolution, see Astrid M. Eckert, *West Germany and the Iron Curtain: Environment, Economy, and Culture in the Borderlands* (New York: Oxford University Press, 2019).

2. NACP, RG 59, Political Refugees, Soviet Union, 1953–1959, Box 3503, "Soviet Confrontation with Soviet Defector Pronin," June 19, 1959.

3. On "brainwashing," see Monica Kim, *Interrogation Rooms of the Korean War: The Untold History* (Princeton, NJ: Princeton University Press, 2020), esp. 303–48; Susan L. Carruthers, *Cold War Captives: Imprisonment, Escape, and Brainwashing* (Berkeley: University of California Press, 2009), 174–216.

4. DDO, Psychological Value of Escapees from the Soviet Orbit, March 26, 1953.

5. United Nations High Commissioner for Refugees (UNHCR), "States Parties to the 1951 Convention relating to the Status of Refugees and the 1967 Protocol," accessed October 25, 2022, https://www.unhcr.org/protect/PROTECTION/ 3b73b0d63.pdf.

6. On mid-century psychiatry, see Anne Harrington, *Mind Fixers: Psychiatry's Troubled Search for the Biology of Mental Illness* (New York: W. W. Norton, 2019); on "psychological citizenship," see Andrea Friedman, *Citizenship in Cold War America: The National Security State and the Possibilities of Dissent* (Amherst: University of Massachusetts Press, 2014), 16–47.

7. For background, see Patrick Major, *Behind the Berlin Wall: East Germany and the Frontiers of Power* (Oxford: Oxford University Press, 2010); Paul Steege, *Black Market, Cold War: Everyday Life in Berlin, 1946–1949* (Cambridge: Cambridge University Press, 2009); Rolf Steininger, *Austria, Germany, and the Cold War: From the Anschluss to the State Treaty, 1938-1955* (New York: Berghahn, 2012).

8. On the concept of borderlands, see Paul Readman, Cynthia Radding, and Chad Bryant, eds., *Borderlands in World History, 1700–1914* (Basingstoke: Palgrave Macmillan, 2014).

9. While Kim describes the interrogation rooms of the Korean War as the "testing ground" for psychological techniques, such tactics had been trained on Soviet

migrants in Europe before the outbreak of conflict in Korea; after the cessation of fighting in Korea, they continued to be deployed in Austria and Germany. Kim, *Interrogation Rooms of the Korean War*, 81.

10. On America's "empire of bases," see Chalmers Johnson, *The Sorrows of Empire: Militarism, Secrecy, and the End of the Republic* (London: Verso, 2006); Daniel Immerwahr, *How to Hide an Empire: A History of the Greater United States* (New York: Farrar, Straus and Giroux, 2019).

11. On the more coercive forms of Soviet control, see Norman Naimark, *The Russians in Germany: A History of the Soviet Zone of Occupation* (Cambridge, MA: Belknap, 2001). Recent scholarship has emphasized subtler forms of coercion in encouraging repatriation. See Simo Mikkonen, "Not by Force Alone: Soviet Return Migration in the 1950s," in *Coming Home? Conflict and Return Migration in the Aftermath of Europe's Twentieth Century Civil Wars*, ed. Sharif Gemie, Scott Soo, and Norry LaPorte, vol. 1 (Newcastle upon Tyne: Cambridge Scholars, 2013), 183–200; and Sheila Fitzpatrick, "The Motherland Calls: 'Soft' Repatriation of Soviet Citizens from Europe, 1945–1953," *Journal of Modern History* 90, no. 2 (2018): 323-50.

12. The committee's name in Russian was *Komitet za vozvrashchenie na Rodinu*. While I translate *Rodina* as "Motherland" in other cases, I use the more common translation of the committee's name, which renders it as "Homeland."

13. Ted Shackley, with Richard A. Finney, *Spymaster: My Life in the CIA* (Washington, DC: Potomac Books, 2005), 81.

14. On the logic of compartmentation as revealed in the construction of the CIA's main headquarters in Langley, see Andrew Friedman, *Covert Capital: Landscapes of Denial and the Making of U.S. Empire in the Suburbs of Northern Virginia* (Berkeley: University of California Press, 2016).

15. Shackley, *Spymaster*, 80.

16. *The Kremlin's Espionage and Terror Organizations: Testimony of Petr S. Deriabin, Former Officer of the USSR's Committee of State Security (KGB)* (Washington, DC: US Government Printing Office, 1959).

17. On the KGB's structure, see A. I. Kokurin, N. V. Petrov, and P. G. Pikhoia, *Lubianka: VChK-OGPU-KVD-NKGB-MGB, MVD, KGB 1917–1960* (Moscow: MFD, 1997); on the monitoring of emigres, including Ukrainians, see Serhii Plokhy, *The Man with the Poison Gun* (London: One World, 2017), 201–2.

18. *The Kremlin's Espionage and Terror Organizations*, 9–10.

19. On panopticism, see Michel Foucault, *Discipline and Punish: The Birth of the Prison*, trans. Alan Sheridan (London: Penguin, 2020).

20. Truman's statement is cited and contextualized in Harrington, *Mind Fixers*, 86–87. The notion of writers as "engineers of human souls" was coined by Soviet author Yuri Olesha and later used by Stalin.

21. Martin Miller, *Freud and the Bolsheviks: Psychoanalysis in Imperial Russia and the Soviet Union* (New Haven, CT: Yale University Press, 1998).

22. NACP, RG 84, US Mission to the United Nations, Central Subject Files, 1946–1963, Box 69, Interpretive Comment on First Ten Sponge Reports, May 1950.

23. NACP, RG 59, US Department of State, Political Refugees, Soviet Union, 1950–1954, Box 3799, Education and the Teacher in the Soviet Union, April 29, 1950.

24. NACP, RG 59, US Department of State, Political Refugees, Soviet Union, 1950–1954, Box 3799, Office Memorandum, March 3, 1950.

25. For an overview, see Margaret Mead, "The Swaddling Hypothesis: Its Reception," *American Anthropologist* 56, no. 3 (1954): 12–27.

26. NACP, RG 59, US Department of State, Political Refugees, Soviet Union, 1950–1954, Box 3799, Paper on Russian Character by Soviet Source (Sponge No. 3), March 21, 1950.

27. NACP, RG 59, US Department of State, Political Refugees, Soviet Union, 1950–1954, Box 3799, Nekotorye cherty russkogo kharaktera.

28. NACP, RG 59, Box 3799, Paper on Russian Character by Soviet Source (Sponge No. 3).

29. On Stalinist self-presentation, see Sheila Fitzpatrick, *Tear off the Masks! Identity and Imposture in Twentieth-Century Russia* (Princeton, NJ: Princeton University Press, 2005).

30. On Soviet self-fashioning, see Jochen Hellbeck, *Revolution on My Mind: Writing a Diary under Stalin* (Cambridge, MA: Harvard University Press, 2006); on self-improvement in the United States, see Timothy Aubry and Trysh Travis, eds., *Rethinking Therapeutic Culture* (Chicago: University of Chicago Press, 2015).

31. NACP, RG 84, Box 69, Interpretive Comment on First Ten Sponge Reports, May 1950.

32. "Convention and Protocol Relating to the Status of Refugees," UNHCR, accessed October 25, 2022, https://www.unhcr.org/3b66c2aa10.

33. NACP, RG 84, US Mission to the United Nations, Central Subject Files, 1946–1963, Box 69, Background of Attached Sponge Report, April 1, 1952.

34. EPL, Gerald D. Morgan Records, Box 36, Shanley letter to Patrick J. Hillings, April 29, 1954.

35. Fitzpatrick, *Tear off the Masks!* On the importance of confessions, see Igal Halfin, *Stalinist Confessions: Messianism and Terror at the Leningrad Communist University* (Pittsburgh: University of Pittsburgh Press, 2009).

36. DNSA, "Kubark Counterintelligence Interrogation," July 1963.

37. Shackley, *Spymaster*, 81.

38. Stanley B. Farndon, "The Interrogation of Defectors," *Studies in Intelligence* 4 (Summer 1960): 9–30.

39. DNSA, "Kubark Counterintelligence Interrogation."

40. Farndon, "The Interrogation of Defectors," 27–28.

41. John Debevoise, "Soviet Defector Motivation," *Studies in Intelligence* 2, no. 4 (1958): 33–42.

42. Delmege Trimble, "Defector Disposal (US)," *Studies in Intelligence* 2, no. 4 (1958): 43–54.

43. Martin L. Brabourne, "More on the Recruitment of Soviets," *Studies in Intelligence* 9 (1965): 39–60.

44. Farndon, "The Interrogation of Defectors," 14.

45. Trimble, "Defector Disposal," 52. On the ambivalent position of Russians and other Slavs in America's racial hierarchy, see David S. Foglesong, *The American Mission and the "Evil Empire"* (New York: Cambridge University Press, 2007).

46. John Ankerbrand, "What to Do with Defectors," *Studies in Intelligence* 5 (Fall 1961): 33–43.

47. Trimble, "Defector Disposal," 43.

48. US Congress, House Committee on Un-American Activities, Testimony of Nikolai Khokhlov, Thought Control in Soviet Art and Literature and the Liberation of Russia, April 17, 1956.

49. HIA, Personal Papers of Nikolai E. Khokhlov, Box 3.

50. See, for example, from the KGB's own journal, V. A. Mal'tsev and V. Ia. Matvievskii, "K voprosu tipologii lichnosti i prestupnogo povedeniia izmennika Rodiny," *Trudy vysshei shkoly KGB* 11 (1976): 194–206.

51. Brabourne, "More on the Recruitment of Soviets," 58–59.

52. NACP, Research Aid: Cryptonyms and Terms in Declassified CIA Files, accessed October 25, 2022, https://www.archives.gov/files/iwg/declassified-records/rg-263-cia-records/second-release-lexicon.pdf.

53. The CIA subsidy is mentioned in CIA, Project Harvard Renewal, July 11, 1963, CREST 5197c265993294098d50e2c7; the organization's private nature was emphasized in Frank R. Barnett, "America's Strategic Weakness-Redefection," *Russian Review* 15, no. 1 (1956): 29–36.

54. NACP, RG 59, US Department of State, Political Refugees, Eastern Europe, 1950–1954, Box 3787, Telegram from Dulles to HICOG Frankfurt, April 3, 1953.

55. TFA, Karlsfeld, Speech by Tatiana Schaufuss, September 4, 1953.

56. NACP, RG 59, Box 3787, Telegram from Dulles to HICOG Frankfurt, April 3, 1953.

57. TFA, Karlsfeld, Report on Karlsfeld Escapee Center, April 4, 1955.

58. NACP, RG 59, US Department of State, Political Refugees, Soviet Union, 1955–1959, Box 3494, MOA on Assistance for Tolstoy Foundation, July 25, 1955.

59. TFA, Karlsfeld, Breakdown of the Total Candidatures for Karlsfeld, October 12, 1953.

60. Keith Allen, *Interrogation Nation: Refugees and Spies in Cold War Germany* (London: Rowman & Littlefield, 2017), 60–61.

61. NACP, RG 59, US Department of State, Political Refugees, Eastern Europe, 1950–1954, Box 3788, Despatch on Camp Valka, June 4, 1953.

62. GARF, f. 10015, op. 1, d. 1170, l. 35.

63. TFA, Karlsfeld, Notes on Karlsfeld Escapee Center, January 20, 1954; TFA, Karlsfeld, Report on Karlsfeld Escapee Center, April 4, 1955.

64. David L. Hoffmann, *Stalinist Values: The Cultural Norms of Soviet Modernity, 1917–1941* (Ithaca, NY: Cornell University Press, 2003).

65. Peabody would go on to complete his doctorate in psychology at Harvard in 1960 and later became chair of Swarthmore's psychology department. Walter F. Naedele, "Dean Peabody, 85, Professor of Psychology," *Philadelphia Inquirer*, October 10, 2013, accessed October 25, 2022, https://www.inquirer.com/philly/obituaries/20131010_Dean_Peabody__85__professor_of_psychology.html.

66. TFA, Karlsfeld, Report on Karlsfeld Escapee Center, January 30–March 25, 1954.

67. TFA, Karlsfeld, Report on Karlsfeld Escapee Center, April 26–May 25, 1954.

68. TFA, Karlsfeld, Report on Karlsfeld Escapee Center, January 30–March 25, 1954.

69. TFA, Karlsfeld, Letter from Tatiana Schaufuss to Elmer M. Falk, April 6, 1954.

70. Cited and discussed in Benjamin Tromly, "Ambivalent Heroes: Russian Defectors and American Power in the Early Cold War," *Intelligence and National Security* 33, no. 5 (2018): 642–58.

71. Allen, *Interrogation Nation*, 131.

72. TFA, Karlsfeld, Report on Karlsfeld Escapee Center, April 4, 1955; GARF. f. 10015, op. 1, d. 1170, l. 39.

73. GARF, f. 10015, op. 1, d. 1170, l. 35.

74. NCAP, RG 59, General Records, Subject Files, Committees Escapee & Refugee Subcommittee, Box 28, Background on Valentin Sokolov, June 23, 1954.

75. TFA, Karlsfeld, Annual Report of Karlsfeld Center, 1958.

76. NACP, RG 59, US Department of State, Political Refugees, Eastern Europe, 1950–1954, Report on "Black Marketing" by East European Refugees," July 24, 1952.

77. NACP, RG 59, Political Refugees, Soviet Union, 1955–1959, Box 3493, Article in *Posev* on the Arrest of V. M. Denisov by West German Authorities, May 13, 1955.

78. NACP, RG 59, US Department of State, Political Refugees, Soviet Union, 1950–1954, Box 3804, Forthcoming Congress of Soviet Post-War Defectors, September 22, 1952.

79. Benjamin Tromly, in *Cold War Exiles and the CIA* (Oxford: Oxford University Press, 2019), 232–34, claims that Denisov was a "Soviet agent," but it remains unknown when and why he became one.

80. NACP, RG 59, Political Refugees, Soviet Union, 1950–1954, Box 3808, Memorandum of Conversation with Vasili M. Denisov, July 12, 1953.

81. GARF, f. 10015, op. 1, d. 1221, ll. 1–12.

82. NACP, RG 59, Political Refugees, Soviet Union, 1955–1959, Box 3493, Press Conference of Re-defector Vladimir Vasilaky, April 18, 1955.

83. A secret report written for the KGB's school in 1968 referred to the Committee's "use" by Soviet intelligence since its founding in 1955 and noted the KGB's "help" in organizing Vasilaky's press conference. A. A. Fabrichnikov and I. A. Ovchinnikov, *Ispol'zovanie vozmozhnostei sovetskogo komiteta po kul'turnym sviaziam s sootechestvennikami za rubezhom v razvedyvatel'noi rabote* (Moscow: Nauchno-izdatel'skii otdel KGB, 1968), 12–13.

84. NACP, RG 59, Political Refugees, Soviet Union, 1955–1959, Box 3493, Soviet-Satellite Anti-Emigration Campaign, April 13, 1955.

85. Josef L. Junz, "The State Treaty with Austria," *American Journal of International Law*, 49, no. 4 (1955): 535–42; FRUS, 1955–1957, Austrian State Treaty, Summit and Foreign Ministers Meetings, 1955, Volume V, Doc. 44, Telegram from the Department of State to the Delegation at the Vienna Ambassadorial Conference, May 3, 1955.

86. Analyses voiced in the 1950s and 1960s and summarized in Robert L. Ferring, "The Austria State Treaty of 1955 and the Cold War," *Western Political Quarterly*, 21, no. 4 (1968): 651–67.

87. On Serov's role, see Mikkonen, "Not by Force Alone," 188; on Bulganin, see EPL, White House Central Files, Confidential File Series, Box 63, Report of Donovan Emergency Commission, Exhibit 8, March 20, 1956.

88. "Ukaz ot 17 sentiabria 1955 goda ob amnistii sovetskikh grazhdan, sotrudnichavshikh s okkupantami v period Velikoi Otechestvennoi voiny 1941–1945 gg.," *Vedomosti Verkhovnogo Soveta SSSR*, 17 (1955): 345.

89. EPL, White House Central Files, Confidential File Series, Box 63, Report of Donovan Emergency Commission, Exhibit 2.

90. EPL, White House Central Files, Confidential File Series, Box 63, Report of Donovan Emergency Commission, 10.

91. Various issues of *Za vozvrashchenie na Rodinu*, 1955–1960.

92. EPL, White House Central Files, Confidential File Series, Box 63, Report of Donovan Emergency Commission, 5.

93. NACP, RG 59, Political Refugees, Soviet Union, 1955–1959, Box 3502, Redefection of Soviet emigres Ivan Vasilyevich Ovchinnikov and Viktor Semyonovich Ilyinsky, November 21, 1958. Ovchinnikov's case is discussed in Tromly, *Cold War Exiles and the CIA*, 249–51. He later published a memoir, *Na pereput'iakh Rossii* (Moscow: Panorama, 1995).

94. Mal'tsev and Matvievskii, "K voprosu tipologii lichnosti i prestupnogo povedeniia izmennika Rodiny."

95. K. G. Fetisenko, "Nekotorye voprosy poniatiia izmeny Rodine v forme perekhoda na storonu vraga," *Trudy vysshei shkoly KGB* 13 (1977): 91–98; N. F. Murashov, Iu. F. Karasev, V. G. Mishchenko, "K voprosu o vozbuzhdenii ugolovnykh del ob izmene Rodine v forme begstva za granitsu i otkaza vozvratit'sia iz-za granitsy v SSSR," *Trudy vysshei shkoly KGB* 13 (1977): 99–106.

96. Rehabilitation was extended even to those who had died. See Samuel Arthur Casper, "The Bolshevik Afterlife: Posthumous Rehabilitation in the Post-Stalin Soviet Union, 1953–1970," PhD diss., University of Pennsylvania, 2018.

97. Steven A. Barnes, *Death and Redemption: The Gulag and the Shaping of Soviet Society* (Princeton, NJ: Princeton University Press, 2017).

98. HDA SBU, f. 1, op. 11 (1959), d. 7, t. 7, l. 191.

99. HDA SBU, f. 1, op. 11 (1959), d. 7, t. 7, ll. 148–66.

100. HDA SBU, f. 1, op. 11 (1959), d. 7.

101. AVP RF, f. 129, op. 45, p. 109, d. 71.

102. HIA, Eesti NSV Riikliku Julgeoleku Komitee Selected Records, ERAF.137SM.1.19, ll. 54–57.

103. NACP, RG 59, Political Refugees, Soviet Union, 1955-1959, Box 3502, Leaflet for Returnees, 1958.

104. Igal Halfin, *Terror in My Soul: Communist Autobiographies on Trial* (Cambridge, MA: Harvard University Press, 2003); Hellbeck, *Revolution on My Mind.*

105. EPL, White House Central Files, Confidential File Series, Box 63, Report of Donovan Emergency Commission, Exhibit 6.

106. NACP, RG 59, Political Refugees, Eastern Europe, Box 3479, Report on Redefection to Soviet and Satellite Countries, April 25, 1958.

107. See, for example, *Shpionskii tsentr pod vyveskoi "Amerikanskogo komiteta"* (Berlin: Izdatel'stvo Komiteta za vozvrashchenie na Rodinu, 1960).

108. FRUS, Eastern Europe, 1955–1957, Vol. XXV, Doc. 58, Memorandum of Discussion at the 285th Meeting of the National Security Council, Washington, May 17, 1956.

109. Barnett, "America's Strategic Weakness—Redefection," 30.

110. CIA, Defector Kidnappings, August 10, 1955, CREST CIA-RDP59-00882R000100040053-6.

111. DDO, Operations Coordinating Board, Detailed Development of Major Actions Concerning Escapees Under NSC 86/1 and Other Related Policies, November 2, 1955.

112. EPL, White House Office, NSC Series, Briefing Notes, Box 6, Operations Coordinating Board Progress Report on Defectors, Escapees, and Refugees from Communist Areas, December 9, 1957.

113. DDO, Psychological Operations Plan for Soviet Orbit Escapees Phase A, December 20, 1951.

114. UNHCR, "State parties, including reservations and declarations, to the 1951 Refugee Convention," accessed October 25, 2022, https://www.unhcr.org/5d9ed32b4.

115. EPL, White House Central Files, Confidential File Series, Box 63, Report of Donovan Emergency Commission, 1.

116. EPL, White House Office, NSC Staff, Papers, 1948–1961, Disaster File, Box 52, National Security Council Progress Report on United States Policy on Soviet and Satellite Defectors, April 18, 1956.

117. DNSA, US Policy on Defectors, Escapees and Refugees from Communist Areas, March 8, 1957.
118. EPL, White House Office, NSC Staff, Papers, 1948–1961, Disaster File, Box 52, National Security Council Progress Report on United States Policy on Soviet and Satellite Defectors, April 18, 1956.
119. UNHCR, "States parties, including reservations and declarations, to the 1967 Protocol Relating to the Status of Refugees," accessed October 25, 2022, https://www.unhcr.org/en-us/protection/convention/5d9ed66a4/states-parties-including-reservations-declarations-1967-protocol-relating.html.
120. EPL, White House Central Files, Confidential File Series, Box 63, Report of Donovan Emergency Commission, 4.
121. EPL, White House Central Files, Confidential File Series, Box 63, Report of Donovan Emergency Commission, 7; for background, see Carl J. Bon Tempo, *Americans at the Gate: The United States and Refugees during the Cold War* (Princeton, NJ: Princeton University Press, 2008).
122. DDO, Draft Report to the NSC, December 14, 1954.
123. EPL, White House Central Files, Confidential File Series, Box 63, Report of Donovan Emergency Commission, 7.
124. EPL, White House Central Files, Confidential File Series, Box 63, Report of Donovan Emergency Commission, 6.
125. TFA, Karlsfeld, Analysis of the Report of the Donovan Emergency Commission," May 23, 1956.
126. EPL, White House Office, NSC Staff, Papers, 1948–1961, Disaster File, Box 52, Progress Report to National Security Council on United States Policy on Soviet and Satellite Defectors, April 18, 1956.
127. Gordon Rottman and Chris Taylor, *The Berlin Wall and the Intra-German Border, 1961–89* (Oxford: Osprey, 2008).
128. S. Sidorov, "U chasovykh granits novoi Germanii," *Pogranichnik*, 12 (1966): 57–61.
129. KPL, Presidential Papers, White House Central Subject Files, Box 71, Memorandum for the President, March 30, 1962.
130. DDO, Psychological Value of Escapees from the Soviet Orbit, March 26, 1953; US Immigration and Naturalization Service Refugee Law and Policy Timeline, 1891–2003, accessed October 25, 2022, https://www.uscis.gov/history-and-genealogy/our-history/refugee-timeline.
131. EPL, White House Office, NSC Staff, Papers, 1948–1961, Disaster File, Box 52, Operations Coordination Board Report, September 14, 1960.
132. And finally, in 1975, it was transformed from a "committee" to an even more neutral "society." See opis' to GARF, f. 9651.
133. Pronin's fate was described in "Sentenced for 'Betraying the Motherland,'" *A Chronicle of Current Events* 4, no. 4 (1968), translated and available online, accessed October 25, 2022, https://chronicle-of-current-events.com/2013/09/22/4-4-concerning-certain-political-prisoners-sentenced-for-betraying-the-motherland/.
134. Craig R. Whitney, *Spy Trade: Germany's Devil's Advocate and the Darkest Secrets of the Cold War* (New York: Times, 1993); author interview with Jeffrey Smith, former General Counsel of the CIA, March 23, 2017.
135. NACP RG 84, US Mission to the United Nations, Central Subject Files, 1946-1963, Box 69, Background of Sponge Report, April 1, 1952.
136. EPL, US NSC Presidential Records, Intelligence Files, Box 2, MIG Defector," November 12, 1953.

137. On the defector program in Vietnam, see FRUS, 1964–1968, Vol. VI, Vietnam, January–August 1968, Doc. 296, CIA Programs to Induce Desertions and Defections in South Vietnam, undated; on Khokhlov's work there, see Vladislav Krasnov, *Soviet Defectors: The KGB Wanted List* (Stanford, CA; Hoover Institution Press, 1986), 30.

138. EPL, Papers as President, NSC Series, Box 13, "US Policy on Defectors, Escapees, and Refugees from Communist Areas," September 20, 1960.

CHAPTER 3

1. Vladislav Krasnov, *Soviet Defectors: The KGB Wanted List* (Stanford, CA; Hoover Institution Press, 1986), 109–11. For a fuller discussion of the Black Sea region's significance, see Erik R. Scott, "The Black Sea Coast as a Landscape of Cold War Intelligence," *Kritika: Explorations in Russian and Eurasian History* 23, no. 3 (2022): 581–604.

2. SShSSA, f. 6, d. 28496-63, t. 5, ll. 133.

3. SShSSA, f. 6, d. 28496-63, t. 5, ll. 184–85. George Feifer would go on to write several books based on his encounters with Soviet citizens, including *Russia Close-Up* (London: Cape, 1973).

4. SShSSA, f. 6, d. 28496-63, t. 1, l. 150.

5. Cooperation on returning Soviet defectors was part of the "Agreement of Friendship Cooperation, and Mutual Assistance" between the Soviet Union and Finland signed in 1948, accessed October 25, 2022, http://heninen.net/sopi mus/1948_e.htm.

6. On foreign influences in the western borderlands, see Amir Weiner, "Foreign Media, the Soviet Western Frontier, and the Hungarian and Czechoslovak Crises," in *Cold War Broadcasting: Impact on the Soviet Union and Eastern Europe*, ed. A. Ross Johnson and R. Eugene Parta, 299–318 (Budapest: Central European University Press, 2010).

7. Andrea M. Chandler, *Institutions of Isolation: Border Controls in the Soviet Union and Its Successor States, 1917–1993* (Montreal and Kingston: McGill-Queen's University Press, 1998); Sabine Dullin, *La frontière épaisse: aux origins des politiques soviétiques. 1920–1940* (Paris: EHESS, 2014); Terry Martin, "The Origins of Soviet Ethnic Cleansing," *Journal of Modern History* 70, 4 (1998): 813–61; Nathalie Moine, "Passeportisation, statistique des migrations et contrôle de l'identité sociale," *Cahiers du monde russe* 38, 4 (1997): 587–99; David R. Shearer, *Policing Stalin's Socialism: Repression and Social Order in the Soviet Union, 1924–1953* (New Haven, CT: Yale University Press, 2009).

8. For an exceptional study that moves beyond the Stalinist period, see Sabine Dullin, "Des frontieres s'ouvrent et se ferment: la mise en place d'un espace socialiste derriere le rideau de fer, 1953-1970," *Relations Internationales* 147 (2011): 35–48.

9. P. I. Zyrianov, ed., *Uchebnik pogranichnika* (Moscow: Voennoe izdatel'stvo Ministerstvo oborony SSSR, 1967), 35–36.

10. Zyrianov, ed. *Uchebnik pogranichnika*, 52.

11. Mathjis Pelkmans, *Defending the Border: Identity, Religion, and Modernity in the Republic of Georgia* (Ithaca, NY: Cornell University Press, 2006), 22.

12. Oscar Sanchez-Sibony, *Red Globalization: The Political Economy of the Soviet Cold War from Stalin to Khrushchev* (Cambridge: Cambridge University Press, 2017),182.

13. Johanna Conterio, "'Our Black Sea Coast': The Sovietization of the Black Sea Littoral under Khrushchev and the Problem of Overdevelopment," *Kritika: Explorations in Russian and Eurasian History* 19, 2 (2018): 327–61; Diane P. Koenker, "The Taste of Others: Soviet Adventures in Cosmopolitan Cuisines," *Kritika: Explorations in Russian and Eurasian History* 19, no. 2 (2018): 243–72.

14. HDA SBU, f. 24, op. 7 (1969), d. 1.

15. World War II thus supplanted the Civil War, which had earlier been emphasized. The latter's importance is discussed in Dullin, *La frontière épaisse*.

16. See map of American-led alliances in *Pogranichnik* 22 (1962): 9; Sergei Goliakov, "Radiodiversanty," *Pogranichnik* 6 (1976): 90–92; V. Cherniavskii, "Shpionskaia monopoliia," *Pogranichnik* 8 (1984): 88–91.

17. RGVA, f. 40926, op. 1, d. 453.

18. Dullin, "Des frontieres s'ouvrent et se ferment," 41.

19. RGVA, f. 40926, op. 1, d. 538.

20. HIA, Lietuvos SSR Valstybės Saugumo Komitetas, f. K-1, op. 10, d. 64.

21. See, for example, HDA SBU, f. 24, op. 9 (1965), d. 3.

22. SShSSA, f. 6, d. 4713–58.

23. HDA SBU, f. 13, d. 310.

24. In some ways, this tendency built on interwar trends. See Rogers Brubaker, *Nationalism Reframed: Nationhood and the National Question in the New Europe* (Cambridge: Cambridge University Press, 1996).

25. Many of these ethnic Hungarians had become Soviet citizens upon the Soviet annexation of the Transcarpathian region in 1945. HDA SBU f. 1, op. 92 (1954), d. 21.

26. For an overview, see Anna Mazurkiewicz, ed., *East Central European Migrations during the Cold War: A Handbook* (Berlin: De Gruyter Oldenbourg, 2019).

27. Gerhard Saelter, *Grenzpolizisten: Konformitaet, Verweigerung und Repression in der Grenzpolizei und den Grenztruppen der DDR 1952 bis 1965* (Berlin: Christoph Links, 2009).

28. Gordon Rottman and Chris Taylor, *The Berlin Wall and the Intra-German Border, 1961–89* (Oxford: Osprey, 2008), 44.

29. Rottman and Taylor, *The Berlin Wall and the Intra-German Border,* 4–23.

30. "Memorial to the Division of Germany in Marienborn," accessed October 25, 2022, https://gedenkstaette-marienborn.sachsen-anhalt.de/fileadmin/Bibliot hek/STGS/Marienborn/Bilder_neue_Homepage/bls_englisch_neu_2008.pdf.

31. GARF, f. 9474, op. 41, d. 3217.

32. HDA SBU, f. 24, op. 9 (1965), d. 1, l. 3.

33. A. Skrypnik, "V gostiakh u boevykh druzei," *Pogranichnik* 3 (1964): 52–54.

34. HDA SBU, f. 24, op. 2 (1968), d. 3, ll. 2–7, 129.

35. HDA SBU, f. 24, op. 2 (1968), d. 3, ll. 206–207.

36. On the state's struggle with contraband trade before the Cold War, see Andrei Shlyakhter, "Smuggler States: Poland, Latvia, Estonia, and Contraband Trade across the Soviet Frontier, 1919–1924," PhD diss., University of Chicago, 2020.

37. HDA SBU, f. 1, op. 4 (1961), d. 6, ll. 17–22.

38. Raymond L. Garthoff, "When and Why Romania Distanced Itself from the Warsaw Pact," *Cold War International History Project Bulletin* 5 (Spring 1995): 111.

39. HDA SBU, f. 24, op. 1 (1970), d. 1; HDA SBU, f. 24, op. 1 (1973), d. 1; HDA SBU, f. 24, op. 2 (1972), d. 4; HDA SBU, f. 24, op. 15 (1988), d. 1.

40. RGANI, f. 3, op. 22, d. 70, ll. 186–188.

41. Pelkmans, *Defending the Border*, 33–35.

42. Martin, "The Origins of Soviet Ethnic Cleansing."

43. RGANI, f. 5, op. 47, d. 305, ll. 144, 170–76.

44. HDA SBU, f. 24, op. 2 (1968), d. 3.

45. On treasonous behavior, see HDA SBU, f. 1, op. 17 (1965), d. 12, ll. 1–2.

46. M. Lykov, "Kak i pochemu proizoshlo beznakazannoe narushenie granitsy," *Sbornik statei zhurnala* Pogranichnik 2 (1958).

47. HDA SBU, f. 24, op. 9 (1965), d. 1, l. 9; HDA SBU, f. 1, op. 17 (1965), d. 12, ll. 1–2.

48. HDA SBU, f. 24, op. 2 (1968), d. 3, ll. 329-33; HDA SBU, f. 24, op. 2 (1968), d. 3, l. 363.

49. William E. Butler, *The Soviet Union and the Law of the Sea* (Baltimore: Johns Hopkins University Press, 1971), 72.

50. HDA SBU, f. 24, op. 9 (1965), d. 1, l. 7.

51. HDA SBU, f. 24, op. 15 (1988), d. 1, l. 164.

52. Peter King, "The Extraordinary Life of Interpreter Pyotr Patrushev," *Sydney Morning Herald*, April 29, 2016, accessed October 25, 2022, https://www.smh.com.au/national/the-extraordinary-life-of-interpreter-pyotr-patrushev-20160 429-goi425.html. Additional cases are discussed in Scott, "The Black Sea Coast as a Landscape of Cold War Intelligence."

53. "Komsomol'skie kordony deistvuiut," *Pogranichnik* 19 (1962): 49–50.

54. RGANI, f. 5, op. 47, d. 305, ll. 144, 170–76.

55. RGANI, f. 5, op. 60, d. 250, ll. 11–13.

56. On the Baltic Sea, see Tomasz Blusiewicz, "Kaliningrad, Pribaltika, Leningrad: Trade and the Cold War in Soviet Port Cities, 1956–1991," accessed October 25, 2022, https://scholar.harvard.edu/tomaszblusiewicz/publicati ons/kaliningrad-pribaltika-leningrad-trade-and-cold-war-soviet-port-cities; on Odesa, see HDA SBU, f. 24, op. 4 (1965), d. 1.

57. HDA SBU, f. 24, op. 3 (1967), d. 1.

58. HDA SBU, f. 24, op. 4 (1972), d. 1.

59. SShSSA, f. 6, d. 22125–61.

60. SShSSA, f. 6, d. 297–56; SShSSA, f. 6, d. 903–57.

61. Based upon a reading of cases in RGANI, f. 5, op. 66, d. 1034.

62. For the text of the criminal code initially instituted in 1927 and updated in 1950, see https://prorivists.org/doc_criminal_code-1950/. For the 1960 criminal code, see https://dokipedia.ru/document/5160972. Both accessed October 25, 2022.

63. SShSSA, f. 6, d. 28496-63, t. 6, ll. 7–8.

64. SShSSA, f. 6, d. 28496-63, t. 6, ll. 11–17.

65. GARF, f. 9474, op. 16, d. 842.

66. GARF, f. 8131, op. 31, d. 82148, l. 10.

67. GARF, f. 8131, op. 31, d. 82148, l. 10.

68. SShSSA, f. 6, d. 25703-62.

69. HDA SBU, f. 24, op. 2 (1968), d. 3, l. 374.

70. V. A. Mal'tsev and V. Ia. Matvievskii, "K voprosu tipologii lichnosti i prestupnogo povedeniia izmennika Rodiny," *Trudy vysshei shkoly KGB* 11 (1976): 194–206.

71. On "prophylaxis," see Edward Cohn, "Coercion, Reeducation, and the Prophylactic Chat: *Profilaktika* and the KGB's Struggle with Political Unrest in Lithuania, 1953–64," *Russian Review* 76, no. 2 (2017): 272–93; and Cohn, "A Soviet Theory of Broken Windows: Prophylactic Policing and the KGB's Struggle with Political Unrest in the Baltic Republics," *Kritika: Explorations in Russian and Eurasian History* 19, no. 4 (2018): 769–92.

72. HDA SBU, f. 24, op. 2 (1968), d. 3, l. 163.

73. HDA SBU, f. 24, op. 2 (1972), d. 4, l. 87.
74. HDA SBU, f. 24, op. 2 (1968), d. 3, l. 163.
75. SShSSA, f. 6, d. 28496-63, t. 1.
76. Tarik Cyril Amar, "Between James Bond and Iosif Stalin: *Seventeen Moments of Spring*, a Soviet Cultural Event of the Cold War and Post-Thaw," *Kritika: Explorations in Russian and Soviet History* 21, no. 3 (2020): 627–28; Christine E. Evans, *Between Truth and Time: A History of Soviet Central Television* (New Haven, CT: Yale University Press, 2016), 152–73.
77. *Oshibka rezidenta*, film directed by Veniamin Dorman, 1968.
78. Stalin-era representations of Soviet border troops are discussed in Dullin, *La frontière épaisse*.
79. RGALI, f. 2458, op. 6, d. 326.
80. HDA SBU, f. 27, op. 10 (1974), d. 3, ll. 10–12.
81. NACP, RG 466, Peripheral Reporting Unit, Records of Interrogations of Defectors, 1953–1955, Box 2, Soviet Defector Interrogation Report (SPONGE 55, DS-617), February 28, 1955.
82. See, for example, RGANI, f. 5, op. 66, d. 1034.
83. HDA SBU, f. 27, op. 23 (1982), d. 2, l. 31.
84. HDA SBU, f. 27, op. 23 (1982), d. 2.
85. HDA SBU, f. 24, op. 4 (1965), d. 1, l. 246.
86. "Okhrana granitsy—iskusstvo," *Pogranichnik* 16 (1966). Soviet authorities had long criticized "formalist" tendencies in art and music.
87. HDA SBU, f. 24, op. 7 (1969), d. 1, ll. 33–37.
88. SBU, f. 27, op. 10 (1974), d. 3, l. 35.
89. Based on the family names of the border troops' officers in the region discussed in KGB files and profiled in *Pogranichnik*.
90. Timofei Strokach served in this capacity from 1956 to 1957, and Il'ia Kalinichenko served from 1989 to 1991.
91. On Ukrainian nationalism's growing political potency in the late Soviet period, see Serhii Plokhy, *The Last Empire: The Final Days of the Soviet Union* (New York: Basic Books, 2014).
92. HDA SBU, f. 27, op. 109 (1990), d. 7.
93. HDA SBU, f. 27, op. 109 (1990), d. 7, ll. 54–55.
94. See, for example, HDA SBU, f. 27, op. 113 (1991), d. 4, one of the final bundle of reports compiled by the Special Department.
95. Based on a reading of *Pogranichnik* from 1986–1991. The cover featuring a woman border guard is from issue 3 (1986); the image with the cat is from issue 7 (1991).
96. V. Roshchupkin, "Kakoi 'detonator' oni podkladyvaiut," *Pogranichnik* 11 (1988): 114–20; I. Kalinichenko, "Kontsepsiia okhrany granitsy: vzgliad v budushchee," *Pogranichnik* 1 (1991): 8–12; V. Tkachenko, "Vozdukh, kotorym dyshim," *Pogranichnik* 11 (1990): 2–4.
97. Thomas de Waal, *Black Garden: Armenia and Azerbaijan through Peace and War* (New York: New York University Press, 2013); Dmitrii Okunev, "'Razozhgli kostry': pochemu azerbaidzhantsy prorvali granitsu SSSR," *Gazeta.ru*, December 31, 2019, accessed October 25, 2022, https://www.gazeta.ru/science/2019/12/31_a_12892628.shtml.
98. Christine Evans and Lars Lundgren, "Geographies of Liveness: Time, Space, and Satellite Networks as Infrastructures of Live Television in the *Our World* Broadcast," *International Journal of Communication* 10 (2016): 5362–77.

99. On the internalization of the border among everyday Soviet citizens, see Pelkmanns, *Defending the Border*, and Zbigniew Wojnowski, *The Near Abroad: Socialist Eastern Europe and Soviet Patriotism in Ukraine, 1956–1985* (Toronto: University of Toronto Press, 2017).

100. Matthew A. Light, "What Does It Mean to Control Migration? Soviet Mobility Policies in Comparative Perspective," *Law and Social Inquiry* 37, no. 2 (2012): 395–429.

CHAPTER 4

1. FRUS, 1948, Eastern Europe, the Soviet Union, Vol. IV, Doc. 678, Embassy of the Soviet Union to the Department of State, August 14, 1948.

2. Oksana Kasenkina, *Leap to Freedom* (Philadelphia: Lippincott, 1949), 264.

3. TFA, VIP, Kasenkina Files, Statement of Alexandra L. Tolstoy, August 9, 1949.

4. Kasenkina, *Leap to Freedom*, 230.

5. On Kasenkina's coverage in the American press, see Susan L. Carruthers, *Cold War Captives: Imprisonment, Escape, and Brainwashing* (Berkeley: University of California Press, 2009), 49–50. The "Swedish Kasenkina" was nineteen-year-old Lydia Makarova, who was featured in a large photograph on the front page of the *New York Daily News* on August 19, 1948.

6. Carruthers, *Cold War Captives*, 32, 248 (note 39).

7. Lomakin's recognition was "revoked by an Act of the President" on August 23, 1948. FRUS, 1948, Eastern Europe, the Soviet Union, Vol. IV, Doc. 683, Secretary of State to the Ambassador of the Soviet Union, August 27, 1948.

8. D. B. Levin, *Diplomaticheskii immunitet* (Moscow, 1949), 238–41.

9. Steven Press, "Sovereignty at Guantánamo: New Evidence and a Comparative Historical Interpretation," *Journal of Modern History* 85, no. 3 (2013): 592–631.

10. D. I. Bogatikov, *Ugolovnaia otvetstvennost' sovetskikh grazhdan, lits bez grazhdanstva i inostrantsev za prestupleniia, sovershennye na territorii SSSR i za granitsei* (Moscow: Vysshaia shkola KGB, 1965), accessed in HDA SBU, f. 13, d. 882.

11. RGANI, f. 89, op. 31, d. 7, ll. 9–22.

12. On Mindszenty, see Peter Kenez, "The Hungarian Communist Party and the Catholic Church, 1945–1948," *Journal of Modern History* 75, no. 4 (2003): 864–89.

13. On Kasenkina's leap as a media event, see Carruthers, *Cold War Captives*, 23–58.

14. On post-colonial efforts to transcend the nation-state, see Christopher J. Lee, ed., *Making a World after Empire: The Bandung Moment and Its Political Afterlives* (Athens: Ohio University Press, 2010); Adom Getachew, *Worldmaking after Empire: The Rise and Fall of Self-Determination* (Princeton, NJ: Princeton University Press, 2020).

15. Final Communiqué of the Asian-African Conference of Bandung, April 24, 1955, accessed October 25, 2022, https://www.cvce.eu/en/obj/final_communique_of_the_asian_african_conference_of_bandung_24_april_1955-en-676237bd-72f7-471f-949a-88b6ae513585.html.

16. On the importance of the Security Council, see David L. Bosco, *Five to Rule Them All: The UN Security Council and the Making of the Modern World* (New York: Oxford University Press, 2009).

17. John D. Kelly and Martha Kaplan, "Legal Fictions after Empire," in *The State of Sovereignty: Territories, Laws, Populations*, ed. Douglas Howland, 169–95 (Bloomington: Indiana University Press, 2009); Mark Mazower, *No Enchanted*

Palace: The End of Empire and the Ideological Origins of the United Nations (Princeton, NJ: Princeton University Press, 2009).

18. Frederick Cooper, "Alternatives to Empire: France and Africa after World War II," in *The State of Sovereignty: Territories, Laws, Populations*, ed. Douglas Howland, 94–123 (Bloomington: Indiana University Press, 2009.

19. London Declaration, April 26, 1949, accessed October 25, 2022, https://thec ommonwealth.org/sites/default/files/inline/London-Declaration.pdf.

20. TNA, Colonial Immigrants, August 22, 1955, accessed October 25, 2022, http:// filestore.nationalarchives.gov.uk/pdfs/small/cab-129-77-cp-55-102-2.pdf.

21. Martti Koskenniemi, *The Gentle Civilizer of Nations: The Rise and Fall of International Law, 1870–1960* (Cambridge: Cambridge University Press, 2001).

22. See Francine Hirsch, *Soviet Judgment at Nuremberg: A New History of the International Military Tribunal after World War II* (New York: Oxford University Press, 2020).

23. Hans J. Morgenthau, *Politics among Nations: The Struggle for Power and Peace* (New York: Alfred A. Knopf, 1948), 211.

24. Koskenniemi, *Gentle Civilizer of Nations*, 197. In a similar vein, Mark Mazower refers to international law after 1945 as a "shadow of its former self." Mazower, *Governing the World: The History of an Idea, 1815 to the Present* (New York: Penguin Books, 2013), 93.

25. On the space treaty, see Stephen Buono, "Merely a 'Scrap of Paper'? The Outer Space Treaty in Historical Perspective," *Diplomacy & Statecraft* 31, no. 2 (2020): 350–72.

26. Eileen Denza, *Diplomatic Law: Commentary on the Vienna Convention on Diplomatic Relations*, 4th ed. (Oxford: Oxford University Press, 2016), 1.

27. In the words of Dutch jurist Hugo Grotius, embassies were to be "treated as *quasi extra territorium*" (as if outside the country). Linda S. Frey and Marsha L. Frey, *The History of Diplomatic Immunity* (Columbus: Ohio State University Press, 1999), 186–87.

28. Charles S. Maier, *Once within Borders: Territories of Power, Wealth, and Belonging since 1500* (Cambridge, MA: Harvard University Press, 2019), 72–81; Frey and Frey, *History of Diplomatic Immunity*, 343–73.

29. Pär Kristoffer Cassel, *Grounds of Judgment: Extraterritoriality and Imperial Power in Nineteenth-Century China and Japan* (New York: Oxford University Press, 2012).

30. Frey and Frey, *History of Diplomatic Immunity*, 364.

31. Carroll Neale Ronning, *Diplomatic Asylum: Legal Norms and Political Reality in Latin American Relations* (The Hague: Nijhoff, 1965); Maarten Den Heijer, "Diplomatic Asylum and the Assange Case," *Leiden Journal of International Law* 26, no. 2 (2013): 399–425, esp. 403.

32. Frey and Frey, *History of Diplomatic Immunity*, 439–44.

33. "Question of Diplomatic Asylum: Report of the Secretary General," September 2, 1975, accessed October 25, 2022, https://www.unhcr.org/en-us/protection/his torical/3ae68bee0/question-diplomatic-asylum-report-secretary-general.html.

34. René Värk, "Diplomatic Asylum: Theory, Practice and the Case of Julian Assange," *Sisekaitseakadeemia Toimetised* 11 (2012): 240–57, esp. 245.

35. For an example, in 1973 a Greek Communist Party member sought refuge in the Soviet Embassy in Japan, while his homeland was ruled by a right-wing military junta. RGANI, f. 5, op. 66, d. 1034, l. 176.

36. On athletes, see Robert Edelman and Christopher Young, eds., *The Whole World Was Watching: Sport in the Cold War* (Stanford, CA: Stanford University Press, 2020); on musicians, see Kiril Tomoff, *Virtuosi Abroad: Soviet Music and Imperial Competition during the Early Cold War, 1945–1958* (Ithaca, NY: Cornell University Press, 2015); on dancers, see Anne Searcy, *Ballet in the Cold War: A Soviet-American Exchange* (New York: Oxford University Press, 2020); on tourists, see Anne E. Gorsuch, *All This Is Your World: Soviet Tourism at Home and Abroad after Stalin* (Oxford: Oxford University Press, 2013), and I. B. Orlov and A. D. Popov, *Russo turisto: sovetskii vyezdnoi turizm, 1955–1991* (Moscow: Izdatel'skii dom Vysshei shkoly ekonomiki, 2016).

37. D. I. Bogatikov, *Ugolovnaia otvetstvennost' sovetskikh grazhdan, lits bez grazhdanstva i inostrantsev za prestupleniia*, accessed in HDA SBU, f. 13, d. 882, l. 25.

38. For background and two contrasting views of the purges' origins, see Robert Conquest, *The Great Terror: A Reassessment* (New York: Oxford University Press, 2008), and J. Arch Getty and Oleg V. Naumov, *The Road to Terror: Stalin and the Self-Destruction of the Bolsheviks, 1932–1939* (New Haven, CT: Yale University Press, 2002).

39. RGANI, f. 3, op. 22, d. 70, ll. 93–101.

40. RGANI, f. 3, op. 22, d. 70, ll. 121–132.

41. RGANI, f. 3, op. 22, d. 70, ll. 192–196.

42. Kevin C. Ruffner, "Trying to Warm Up the Cold War: A Futile Fling with Sexspionage in Austria," *Studies in Intelligence* (1999), 43–57, esp. 44. For background on REDCAP, see Kevin P. Riehle, "Early Cold War Evolution of British and US Defector Policy and Practice," *Cold War History* 19, no. 3 (2019): 343–61.

43. Martin L. Brabourne, "More on the Recruitment of Soviets," *Studies in Intelligence* 9 (1965): 43–45.

44. Quotations from 1979 version, RGANI, f. 89, op. 31, d. 7.

45. Vladimir Vysotskii, "Instruktsiia pered poezdkoi za rubezh," 1973, accessed October 25, 2022, https://rupoem.ru/vysotskiy/ya-vchera-zakonchil-kovku.aspx.

46. HIA, Lietuvos SSR Valstybės Saugumo Komitetas, f. k-1, op. 14, d. 185, l. 33.

47. Kai S. Bruns, "'A Hazardous Task': Britain and the 1961 Vienna Convention on Diplomatic Relations," *International History Review* 39, no. 2 (2017): 196–215, esp. 200.

48. KGBD, Lietuvos SSR Valstybės Saugumo Komitetas, f. k-1, op. 3, d. 754, ll. 144–51.

49. Aleksandr Kaznacheev, *Inside a Soviet Embassy: Experiences of a Russian Diplomat in Burma* (Philadelphia: Lippincott, 1962), 18, 59–63.

50. Victor Kravchenko, *I Chose Freedom: The Personal and Political Life of a Soviet Official* (New York: C. Scribner's Sons, 1946), 457–58.

51. Kasenkina, *Leap to Freedom*, 157.

52. Kravchenko, *I Chose Freedom*, 461, 464.

53. Kasenkina, *Leap to Freedom*, esp. 154.

54. Kaznacheev, *Inside a Soviet Embassy*, 52–53.

55. Kaznacheev, *Inside a Soviet Embassy*, 223.

56. One of the most famous cases was that of T. E. Lawrence. For a biographical study, see John E. Mack, *A Prince of Our Disorder: The Life of T. E. Lawrence* (Cambridge, MA: Harvard University Press, 1998).

57. GARF, f. 8131, op. 31, d. 88075.

58. RGANI, f. 6, op. 4, d. 2237, ll. 1–10.
59. The time span of the program is listed in NACP, Research Aid: Cryptonyms and Terms in Declassified CIA Files.
60. WCD, Mitrokhin Archive, KGB Practices, Folder 70, The Chekist Anthology, accessed October 25, 2022, https://digitalarchive.wilsoncenter.org/document/110319.
61. Ruffner, "Trying to Warm Up the Cold War."
62. FRUS, 1955–1957, Africa, Vol. XVIII, Doc. 186, Memorandum from the Assistant Secretary of State for Near Eastern, South Asian, and African Affairs, January 5, 1956; FRUS, 1955–1957, Africa, Vol. XVIII, Doc. 199, Note from the Ambassador in Morocco, October 6, 1956.
63. James R. Blaker, *United States Overseas Basing: The Anatomy of a Dilemma* (New York: Praeger, 1990); Chalmers Johnson, *The Sorrows of Empire: Militarism, Secrecy, and the End of the Republic* (London: Verso, 2006); Maria Höhn and Seungsook Moon, eds., *Over There: Living with the U.S. Military Empire* (Durham, NC: Duke University Press, 2010).
64. C. T. Sandars, *America's Overseas Garrisons: The Leasehold Empire* (New York: Oxford University Press, 2000).
65. Gretchen Heefner, "'A Slice of Their Sovereignty': Negotiating the U.S. Empire of Bases, Wheelus Field, Libya, 1950–1954," *Diplomatic History* 14, no. 1 (2017): 50–77.
66. Heefner, "'A Slice of Their Sovereignty,'" 71–75.
67. FRUS, 1977–1980, Southeast Asia and the Pacific, Vol. XXII, Doc. 292. Telegram from the Embassy in Malaysia, February 9, 1977.
68. FRUS, 1969–1976, Vol. XVIII, China, 1973–1976, Doc. 60, Memorandum of Conversation, November 13–14, 1973.
69. Brabourne, "More on the Recruitment of Soviets," 50.
70. Andrew Friedman, *Covert Capital: Landscapes of Denial and the Making of U.S. Empire in the Suburbs of Northern Virginia* (Berkeley: University of California Press, 2016), 83.
71. FRUS, 1949, Eastern Europe, Soviet Union, Vol. 5, Doc. 335, The Chargé in the Soviet Union to the Secretary of State, March 4, 1949; Yuri Rastvorov, "Red Fraud and Intrigue in Far East," *Life*, December 6, 1954, 174–92; Walter Bedell Smith, *My Three Years in Moscow* (Philadelphia: Lippincott, 1950), 186–87.
72. Discussed in George Ginsburgs, "Soviet Citizenship Legislation and Statelessness as a Consequence of the Conflict of Nationality Laws," *International and Comparative Law Quarterly* 15, no. 1 (1966): 1–54.
73. NACP, RG 59, Political Refugees, Soviet Union, 1955–1959, Box 3502, Telegram from Dulles to American Embassy Moscow, July 7, 1958.
74. NACP, RG 59, Political Refugees, Soviet Union 1955–1959, Box 3502, Telegram from Dulles to Berlin, July 7, 1958.
75. NACP, RG 59, Political Refugees, Soviet Union, 1955–1959, Box 3502, Telegram from Gulfer to Secretary of State, July 23, 1958.
76. Based on reading of files in NACP, RG 59, Political Refugees, Soviet Union, 1955–1959; NACP, RG 59, Political Refugees, Soviet Union, 1960–1963; NACP, RG 59, Bureau of Security and Consular Affairs, 1953–1960.
77. The 1958 instructions are summarized and the 1959 instructions included as an attachment in NACP, RG 59, POL 30, USSR 1970–73, Box 2761, Summary Procedures for the Handling of Requests for Political Asylum by Foreign Nationals, December 2, 1970.

78. Summary Procedures for the Handling of Requests for Political Asylum by Foreign Nationals, December 2, 1970.

79. NACP, RG 59, Political Refugees, Soviet Union, 1955–1959, Box 3503, Request of Soviet Citizen for Asylum, September 15, 1959.

80. GARF, f. 8131, op. 32, d. 92062.

81. NACP, RG 59, US Department of State, Political Refugees, Soviet Union, 1960–63, Box 1856, Request for Political Asylum by Soviet Citizen," November 23, 1959.

82. NACP, RG 59, POL 30, USSR 1964–66, Box 2893, Soviet Citizen Requests Political Asylum, January 17, 1964.

83. NACP, RG 59, US Department of State, Political Refugees, Soviet Union, 1955–1959, Box 3503, Telegram from Rangoon to Secretary of State, June 30, 1959; EPL, NSC Presidential Records, Intelligence Files, 1953–1961, Box 1, Memorandum of June 2, 1960.

84. GARF, f. 8131, op. 31, d. 88075.

85. Focusing on Algeria, historian Matthew Connelly has emphasized the growing importance of the North-South divide. Connelly, *A Diplomatic Revolution: Algeria's Fight for Independence and the Origins of the Post-Cold War Era* (New York: Oxford University Press, 2002).

86. UN, Documents, A/C6/SR313, 53–55, October 29, 1952; UN, Documents, A/C6/SR316, October 31, 1952.

87. Richard Langhorne, "The Regulation of Diplomatic Practice: The Beginnings of the Vienna Convention on Diplomatic Relations, 1961," *Review of International Studies* 18, no. 1 (1992): 13.

88. UN, Documents, A/C6/SR316, October 31, 1952.

89. NACP, RG 59, Class 3 Files, 1950-1954, Box 1301, Yugoslav Candidate for Membership in the International Law Commission of the United Nations, June 2, 1953.

90. EPL, White House Office, National Security Council Staff, Papers, Disaster File Series, Box 52, US Policy on Defectors, Escapees and Refugees from Communist Areas," March 8, 1957.

91. Ilya V. Gaiduk, *Divided Together: The United States and the Soviet Union in the United Nations* (Washington, DC: Woodrow Wilson Center Press, 2012), 155–57.

92. Gaiduk, *Divided Together*, 205.

93. Mazower, *Governing the World*, 249.

94. Mazower, *Governing the World*, 259.

95. Gaiduk, linking events in the Middle East and East Central Europe, goes so far as to suggest the "virtual collusion of both superpowers on their attitudes toward the dual crisis" in Egypt and Hungary. *Divided Together*, 219.

96. TNA, FO 371/103647.

97. TNA, DO 211/30.

98. TNA, CAB 129/81.

99. TNA, CAB/128/32.

100. On the coup, see Stephen Schlesinger and Stephen Kinzer, *Bitter Fruit: The Story of the American Coup in Guatemala* (Cambridge, MA: Harvard University Press, 2005); for the text of the agreement, see the Organization of American States, Convention on Diplomatic Asylum, accessed October 25, 2022, https://www.oas.org/juridico/english/sigs/a-46.html.

101. Gaiduk, *Divided Together*, 263

102. Evan Luard, *The History of the United Nations: The Age of Decolonization, 1955–1965* (New York: St. Martin's, 1989), 181; Mazower, *Governing the World*, 263.

103. GARF, 9540, op. 1, d. 106, l. 18.

104. Frey and Frey, *History of Diplomatic Immunity*, 465.

105. UN, Documents, A/CN.4/110, 1957.

106. On tacit collusion from an organizational perspective, see Jean Tirole, *The Theory of Industrial Organization* (Cambridge, MA: MIT Press, 1988). Such a perspective differs from the legal definition of collusion, which typically rests on an explicit, though conspiratorial, agreement.

107. Lawrence Preuss, "Consular Immunities: The Kasenkina Case," *American Journal of International Law* 41, 1 (1949): 37–56.

108. See the text obtained and translated by the CIA, Ivan A. Serov, "Work with Walk-Ins," *Studies in Intelligence* 8, no. 1 (1964), 47.

109. For a discussion of the operation of these networks after World War II, see Hirsch, *Soviet Judgment at Nuremberg*.

110. Levin, *Diplomaticheskii immunitet*, 379–81.

111. TNA, FO 371/100889.

112. FRUS, 1952–1954, American Republics, Vol. IV, Doc. 67, Secretary of State to Diplomatic Offices in the American Republics, January 15, 1954.

113. TNA, DO 161/137.

114. NACP, RG 59, Class 3 Files, 1960–1963, Box 730, Telegram from American Embassy in Vienna to American Embassy in Budapest, March 13, 1961.

115. There were thirty-four original signatories to the VCDR, plus another twenty-six countries that signed before it was registered in 1964. Today, 192 countries are party to the VCDR. See the UN Treaties Collection, accessed October 25, 2022, https://treaties.un.org/pages/ViewDetails.aspx?src=TREATY&mtdsg_no=III-3&chapter=3&clang=_en.

116. TNA, DO 161/138; British attitudes are discussed further in Bruns, "'A Hazardous Task.'"

117. United Nations, Vienna Convention on Consular Relations, 1963, accessed October 25, 2022, https://legal.un.org/ilc/texts/instruments/english/conventions/9_2_1963.pdf.

118. Some post-colonial states also marginalized minority populations in the same period. See "The Spirit of Bandung," in *Bandung, Global History, and International Law: Critical Pasts and Pending Futures*, ed. Luis Eslava, Michael Fakhri, and Vasuki Nesiah, 3–32, esp. 26 (Cambridge: Cambridge University Press, 2017).

119. Den Heijer, "Diplomatic Immunity and the Assange Case," 408.

120. This development is in line with Giorgio Agamben's argument that sovereignty rests in the "power to proclaim the exception." Giorgio Agamben, *State of Exception*, trans. Kevin Attell (Chicago: University of Chicago Press, 2005).

121. Randall Hansen, "The Kenyan Asians, British Politics, and the Commonwealth Immigrants Act, 1968," *Historical Journal* 42, no. 3 (1999): 809–34

122. TNA, DO 211/30.

123. Erik R. Bickstrom, *Pathways and Consequences of Legal Irregularity: Senegalese Migrants in France, Italy, and Spain* (Cham: Springer Nature, 2019), 29–74.

124. Rosemary Sullivan, *Stalin's Daughter: The Extraordinary and Tumultuous Life of Svetlana Alliluyeva* (New York: HarperCollins, 2015), 277.

125. DDO, Comments of George Kennan on Svetlana, March 27, 1967.

126. WCD, Radio Free Europe and Radio Liberty, CIA Guidelines on Svetlana (Stalin) Defection, March 13, 1967.

127. Sullivan, *Stalin's Daughter*, 298–30.
128. TNA, FCO 95/14.
129. DDO, Summary of Indian Government Official's Swiss Meeting with Soviet Defector Svetlana Alliluyeva, March 21, 1967.
130. RGASPI, f. 558, op. 11, d. 1562; RGASPI, f. 558, op. 11, d. 1565.
131. DDO, Summary of Indian Government Official's Swiss Meeting with Soviet Defector Svetlana Alliluyeva.
132. NACP, RG 59, Central Foreign Policy Files, 1967–1969, Box 2684, Request for Political Asylum, May 30, 1967.
133. NACP, RG 59, POL 30, 1970–73, Summary of Present Procedures, December 2, 1970.
134. FRUS, 1964–1968, Volume XIV, Soviet Union, Office of the Historian Press Release, February 21, 2001.
135. Värk, "Diplomatic Asylum: Theory, Practice and the Case of Julian Assange," 250.
136. "Mrs. Oksana Kasenkina Dies; Fled from Russians Here in '48," *New York Times*, July 27, 1960, 29.
137. Biographical details drawn from Kasenkina, *Leap to Freedom*.
138. NACP, RG 59, Political Refugees, Soviet Union 1955–1959, Box 3502, Memorandum of Conversation on Oksana Kasenkina, March 12, 1959.
139. On these more revolutionary strands, see Getachew, *Worldmaking after Empire*. While Getachew locates the decline of radical "worldmaking" in the 1970s and notes the power of American hegemony, a focus on the history of diplomatic representation suggests an earlier decline and accords an important role to the Soviet Union.
140. On détente, see Jeremi Suri, *Power and Protest: Global Revolution and the Rise of Détente* (Cambridge, MA: Harvard University Press, 2003).
141. Manu Bhagavan, "A New Hope: India, the United Nations, and the Making of the Universal Declaration of Human Rights," *Modern Asia Studies* 44, no. 2 (2010): 311–47.
142. Luard, *History of the United Nations: The Age of Decolonization*, 7.
143. Paul Behrens, "The Law of Diplomatic Asylum: A Contextual Approach," *Michigan Journal of International Law* 35, no. 2 (2014): 319–67, esp. 323.
144. Frey and Frey, *History of Diplomatic Immunity*, 510.
145. Frey and Frey, *History of Diplomatic Immunity*, 512–14; Bernhard Blumenau, *The United Nations and Terrorism: Germany, Multilateralism, and Antiterrorism Efforts in the 1970s* (Basingstoke: Palgrave Macmillan, 2014).
146. For historical context, see Samuel Moyn, *The Last Utopia: Human Rights in History* (Cambridge, MA: Belknap, 2012).
147. DDO, Recommended USG Posture on the Emigration of the Embassy Pentecostals.
148. Oleg Sofianik, "'Povedat' svobodnomu miru'—pobeg bez pobega," *Tainy istorii*, April 5, 2020, accessed October 25, 2022, https://secrethistory.su/2043-kak-sovetskie-grazhdane-pytalis-sbezhat-iz-sssr-cherez-posolstva-drugih-gosudarstv.html?fbclid=IwAR3Np6pq3BTa5jtC5wUsy5XvfZvT5Yb1bOnebjxpwsRvv6IPB8DBmliRVZs.
149. See Arkady Shevchenko's autobiography, *Breaking with Moscow* (New York: Knopf, 1985).
150. Den Heijer, "Diplomatic Asylum and the Assange Case," 404–5.
151. Susanne Riveles, "Diplomatic Asylum as a Human Right: The Case of the Durban Six," *Human Rights Quarterly* 11, no. 1 (1989): 139–59.

CHAPTER 5

1. V. Kalinin, *Net liubvi sil'nee* (Odesa: Odesskoe knizhnoe izdatel'stvo, 1961), 10. The song Kalinin refers to is "U chernogo moria."
2. Kalinin, *Net liubvi sil'nee*, 11.
3. HDA SBU, f. 6, d. 75112, t. 1, ll. 155–59.
4. For background, see Bill Hayton, *The South China Sea: The Struggle for Power in Asia* (New Haven, CT: Yale University Press, 2014); Marwyn S. Samuels, *Contest for the South China Sea* (London: Routledge, 2014).
5. NACP, RG 59, Class 9 Files, 1950–1954, Box 6002, Letter from the Secretary of the US Navy to the Secretary of State, September 20, 1954.
6. V. Kalinin and D. Kuznetsov, *Tanker 'Tuapse': dokumental'naia povest'* (Moscow: Molodaia gvardiia, 1956), 6.
7. Kalinin and Kuznetsov, *Tanker 'Tuapse,'* 6.
8. NACP, RG 59, Class 9 Files, 1950–54, Box 6002, Note transcribed in US Department of State Telegram, June 24, 1954.
9. NACP RG 59, Class 9 Files, 1950–54, Box 6002, Report transcribed in US Department of State Telegram, June 26, 1954.
10. Jeremy Black, *The British Seaborne Empire* (New Haven, CT: Yale University Press, 2004).
11. Truman's proclamation may have been preceded by underseas petroleum claims by smaller Latin American states, but it far exceeded them in its geographical scope. Gregory T. Cushman, *Guano and the Opening of the Pacific World* (New York: Cambridge University Press, 2013), 294–95.
12. CIA, Soviet Shipping Expansion since 1972, September 2, 1974, CREST 0000484023.
13. NACP, RG 59, Class 9 Files, 1950–54, Box 6002, Protest note of the Soviet Embassy, August 22, 1950.
14. Michel Foucault, "Of Other Spaces," *Diacritics* 16, no. 1 (1986): 22–27.
15. Vladislav Krasnov, *Soviet Defectors: The KGB Wanted List* (Stanford, CA: Hoover Institution Press, 1986), 203–4.
16. Denver Brunsman, "Men of War: British Sailors and the Impressment Paradox," *Journal of Early Modern History* 14 (2010): 9–44.
17. Donald W. Mitchell, *A History of Russian and Soviet Sea Power* (New York: Macmillan, 1974).
18. NACP, RG 59, Class 9 Files, 1950–54, Box 6002, Notes on Requested Return of Two U.S. Merchant Ships Transferred to USSR, September 5, 1950.
19. NACP, RG 59, Class 9 Files, 1950–54, Box 6002, Department of State Secret Despatch, March 15, 1950.
20. NACP, RG 59, Class 9 Files, 1950–54, Box 6002, Construction by Burmeister & Wain of Second Tanker for the USSR, July 3, 1953.
21. DNSA, CIA Briefing to NSC, July 14, 1954.
22. On the sea as a space of opportunity and risk for imperial rule, see Glen O'Hara, "'The Sea Is Swinging into View': Modern British Maritime History in a Globalised World," *English Historical Review* 124, no. 510 (2009): 1109–34; Niklas Frykman, *The Bloody Flag: Mutiny in the Age of Atlantic Revolution* (Berkeley: University of California Press, 2020).
23. On class and race in the British maritime empire, see Marcus Rediker, *Between the Devil and the Deep Blue Sea: Merchant Seamen, Pirates and the Anglo-American Maritime World, 1700–1750* (Cambridge: Cambridge University Press, 1987);

W. Jeffrey Bolster, *Black Jacks: African American Seamen in the Age of Sail* (Cambridge, MA: Harvard University Press, 1998).

24. HDA SBU, f. 24, op. 2 (1968), d. 2, l. 194.
25. For instances of Soviet sailors being prosecuted for smuggling, see SShSSA, f. 6, d. 29150-72 (1971–1972); SShSSA, f. 6, d. 29156072 (1972); SShSSA, f. 6, d. 29150-72 (1972); SShSSA, f. 6, d. 29195-75 (1974).
26. For an example of an "elder" waiting hours to inform the ship's administration of a missing sailor in New York for fear of punishment, see AVP RF, f. 129, op. 44, p. 325, d. 58.
27. The case was followed by the Commonwealth Office, whose archives contain records of the trial. See TNA, FCO 168/911.
28. "Defection of a Russian Seaman," House Committee on Un-American Activities, September 19, 1963; Richard Zowie, "Short Swim to Freedom: An Account of the Defection of Vladislav Tarasov," *DLIFLC & POM Globe*, September 1997, 22–23.
29. GARF, f. 8131, op. 31, d. 98943.
30. HIA, Lietuvos SSR Valstybės Saugumo Komitetas, f. K-1, op. 14, d. 659.
31. Akram Akzamovich Gindulin, "Datskaia 'sensatsiia' i istina: Triuk NTSovtsev sorvalsia," *Za vozvrashchenie na Rodinu* March 1957, 1.
32. GARF, f. 8131, op. 31, d. 81144.
33. On Soviet relations with the PRC and the ROC, see Alexander Lukin, *The Bear Watches the Dragon: Russia's Perceptions of China and the Evolution of Russian-Chinese Relations since the Eighteenth Century* (New York: Routledge, 2003).
34. DNSA, Central Intelligence Agency report, June 25, 1954.
35. Steve Tsang, "Chiang Kai-shek and the Kuomintang's Policy to Reconquer the Chinese Mainland, 1949–1958," in *In the Shadow of China: Political Developments in Taiwan since 1949*, ed. Steve Tsang, 48–72 (London: Hurst, 1993).
36. UN, Digital Library, Additional Measures to Be Employed to Meet the Aggression in Korea, May 18, 1951, accessed October 25, 2022, https://digitallibr ary.un.org/record/863534?ln=en.
37. Xin-zhu J. Chen, "China and the US Trade Embargo, 1950–1972," *American Journal of Chinese Studies* 13, no. 2 (2006): 169–86.
38. DNSA, National Security Council Briefing, July 13, 1954.
39. Robert Accinelli, *Crisis and Commitment: United States Policy toward Taiwan, 1950–1955* (Chapel Hill: University of North Carolina Press, 1996), 185–210.
40. On "White Terror," see Steven E. Phillips, *Between Assimilation and Independence: The Taiwanese Encounter Nationalist China, 1945–1950* (Stanford, CA: Stanford University Press, 2003), 99–100.
41. CIA, NSC Briefing, July 14, 1954, CREST CIA-RDP80R01443R000200360010-1.
42. NACP, RG 59, A1 5412, US State Department Memorandum, Bureau of East Asian and Pacific Affairs, June 13, 1966,
43. "Convention and Protocol Relating to the Status of Refugees," UNHCR, accessed October 25, 2022, https://www.unhcr.org/3b66c2aa10.
44. EPL, White House Office, National Security Council Staff Papers, OCB Report, January 21, 1959.
45. NACP, RG 59, US Department of State, Records of the Bureau of Security and Consular Affairs, 1953–60, Box 43, Memorandum of Conversation between Commissioner Swing and Scott McLeod, October 21, 1954.
46. FRUS, 1952–1954, China and Japan, Vol. XIV, Doc. 229, Secretary of State to the Embassy in the Republic of China, July 9, 1954; on the kerosene, see DNSA, Current Intelligence Bulletin, June 24, 1954.

47. DNSA, Disruption of Soviet Shipping in Far East, July 13, 1954.
48. FRUS, 1952–1954, China and Japan, Volume XIV, Part 1, Doc. 256, Chargé in the Republic of China (Cochran) to the Department of State, August 16, 1954; DNSA, Letter from Henry Cabot Lodge, Jr. to John Foster Dulles, October 6, 1954.
49. UN General Assembly, *Official Records* 9 (December 13, 1954), 251–53.
50. Lauren Benton, *A Search for Sovereignty: Law and Geography in European Empires, 1400–1900* (Cambridge: Cambridge University Press, 2010; Michael Kempe, "Even in the Remotest Corners of the World: Globalized Piracy and International Law, 1500–1900," *Journal of Global History* 5, no. 3 (2010): 353–72; Julia Leikin, "The Prostitution of the Russian Flag": Privateers in Russian Admiralty Courts, 1787–98," *Law and History Review* 35, no. 4 (November 2017), 1049–81.
51. AVP RF, f. 7, op. 31, p. 4, d. 56, ll. 7–8.
52. AVP RF, f. 47, op. 2, p. 81, d. 26, ll. 24–26.
53. Alina Cherviatsova and Oleksandr Yarmysh, "Soviet International Law: Between Slogans and Practice," *Journal of the History of International Law* 19, no. 2 (2017): 296–327.
54. UN General Assembly, *Official Records* 9 (December 13, 1954), 251–52.
55. UN General Assembly, *Official Records* 9 (December 13, 1954), 252–57.
56. NACP, RG 59, Class 9 Files, 1950–54, US State Department Telegram, December 14, 1954.
57. CIA, Interception of Soviet Tanker in Luzon Strait, June 25, 1954, CREST CIA-RDP91T01172R000300010022-5.
58. *US Participation in the UN: Report by the President to the Congress for the Year 1954* (Washington, DC: Department of State, 1955), 51–54.
59. FRUS, 1955–1957, China, Vol. II, Doc. 276, Memorandum of Conversation, San Francisco, June 23, 1955.
60. FRUS, 1952–1954, China and Japan, Vol. XIV, Part 1, Doc. 329, Secretary of State to the Embassy in the Republic of China, October 8, 1954.
61. UN General Assembly, *Official Records* 9 (December 13, 1954), 252.
62. AVP RF, f. 6, op. 13a, p. 44, d. 310, l. 1.
63. AVP RF, f. 6, op. 14, p. 7, d. 81, l. 57–62.
64. AVP RF, f. 6, op. 14, p. 7, d. 81, ll. 63, 71.
65. DDO, Operations Coordinating Board, Progress Report on NSC 5503, July 11, 1955.
66. AVP RF, f. 6, op. 14, p. 7, d. 81, ll. 79–80.
67. "The Episode of the Russian Seamen." Report of the Subcommittee to Investigate the Administration of the Internal Security Act to the Committee on the Judiciary, May 24, 1956 (Washington, DC: United States Government Printing Office, 1956).
68. AVP RF, f. 6, op. 14, p. 7, d. 81, ll. 79–80.
69. "The Episode of the Russian Seamen," 15.
70. "The Episode of the Russian Seamen," 7.
71. NACP, RG 59, Bureau of European Affairs, Office of Soviet Union Affairs, Special Collection Subject Files, 1950–1982, Box 18, Tuapse Crewmen Tell of US Escape, April 13, 1956.
72. NACP, RG 59, US Department of State, Political Refugees, Soviet Union, 1955–1959, Box 3500, Telegram from Department of State in Hong Kong to Secretary of State, August 26, 1957; NACP, RG 59, US Department of State, Political Refugees, Soviet Union, 1955–1959, Box 3496, Despatch from American Embassy in Taipei to Department of State, March 15, 1956.

73. NACP, RG 59, A1 5412, US State Department Memorandum, Bureau of East Asian and Pacific Affairs, June 13, 1966.

74. Clyde Sanger, *Ordering the Oceans: The Making of the Law of the Sea* (Toronto: University of Toronto Press, 1987), 13–15; Hunter Miller, "The Hague Codification Conference," *American Journal of International Law* 24, no. 4 (1930): 674–93.

75. UN, Documents, A/CN.4/13, April 12, 1949.

76. UN, Documents, A/CN.4/32, July 15, 1950, 5–6, 60, 112.

77. UN, Documents, A/CN.4/L.53, May 6, 1955.

78. UN, Documents, A/CN.4/L.53, May 2–July 8, 1955.

79. NACP, RG 59, Class 3 Files, 1955–1959, Box 1637, Telegram from Geneva to Secretary of State, March 14, 1958.

80. NACP, RG 59, Class 3 Files, 1955–1959, Box 1634, Department of State Instruction on Preparation for the 1958 Law of the Sea Conference, January 31, 1957; NACP, RG 59, Class 3 Files, 1955–1959, Box 1634, Memorandum on Law of the Sea Conference, September 19, 1957.

81. NACP, RG 59, Class 3 Files, 1955–1959, Box 1634, Department of State Instruction on Draft Resolution, October 31, 1956.

82. DDO, Eisenhower and British Prime Minister Macmillan Discuss Three-Mile Territorial Sea, March 14, 1958.

83. TNA, FO 371/133745.

84. Convention on the Territorial Sea and the Contiguous Zone, 1958, Article 24, accessed October 25, 2022, https://www.gc.noaa.gov/documents/8_1_1958_terr itorial_sea.pdf.

85. Convention on the Territorial Sea and the Contiguous Zone, 1958, Article 5.

86. UN Treaty Collection, Convention on the Territorial Sea and the Contiguous Zone, accessed October 25, 2022, https://treaties.un.org/Pages/ViewDetails. aspx?src=IND&mtdsg_no=XXI-1&chapter=21&clang=_en.

87. Convention on the Territorial Sea and the Contiguous Zone, 1958, Article 19.

88. William Butler, *The Soviet Union and the Law of the Sea* (Baltimore: Johns Hopkins University Press), 182.

89. UN Treaty Collection, Convention on the High Seas, accessed October 25, 2022, https://treaties.un.org/pages/ViewDetails.aspx?src=TREATY&mtdsg_no=XXI-2&chapter=21.

90. TNA, FO 371/133745.

91. UN, Digital Library, Question of Diplomatic Asylum, 1975.

92. Renaud Morieux discusses the ambiguities of "liquid borders" in *The Channel: England, France and the Construction of a Maritime Border in the Eighteenth Century* (Cambridge: Cambridge University Press, 2016).

93. The role of the secret police as "co-authors" in such productions is discussed by Cristina Vatulescu in *Police Aesthetics: Literature, Film, and the Secret Police in Soviet Times* (Stanford, CA: Stanford University Press, 2010).

94. AVP RF, f. 6, op. 14, p. 7, d. 81, l. 52.

95. RGANI, f. 89, op. 67, d. 8.

96. RGALI, f. 2932, op. 3, d. 263.

97. On US POWs in Korea, see Susan L. Carruthers, *Cold War Captives: Imprisonment, Escape, and Brainwashing* (Berkeley: University of California Press, 2009), and Monica Kim, *Interrogation Rooms of the Korean War: The Untold History* (Princeton, NJ: Princeton University Press, 2020).

98. RGALI, f. 2932, op. 1, d. 473.

99. RGALI, f. 2932, op. 1, d. 474.

100. The book's production notes reveal that it was ghostwritten by Anatoly Agranovskii, a Soviet journalist who would later serve as the unacknowledged author of Leonid Brezhnev's memoirs. RGALI, f. 1580, op. 2, d. 40. The Robinsonade genre was popular among Soviet readers.

101. Kalinin and Kuznetsov, *Tanker 'Tuapse,'* 6–9.

102. Kalinin and Kuznetsov, *Tanker 'Tuapse,'* 26.

103. Kalinin and Kuznetsov, *Tanker 'Tuapse,'* 32.

104. Kalinin and Kuznetsov, *Tanker 'Tuapse,'* 82.

105. Kalinin and Kuznetsov, *Tanker 'Tuapse,'* 96–98.

106. Kalinin and Kuznetsov, *Tanker 'Tuapse,'* 28.

107. Kalinin and Kuznetsov, *Tanker 'Tuapse,'* 55–56, 66.

108. Kalinin and Kuznetsov, *Tanker 'Tuapse,'* 56.

109. Kalinin and Kuznetsov, *Tanker 'Tuapse,'* 96–97.

110. Kalinin and Kuznetsov, *Tanker 'Tuapse,'* 116.

111. Kalinin and Kuznetsov, *Tanker 'Tuapse,'* 128.

112. *Ch. P.—Chrezvychainoe proisshestvie,* directed by Viktor Ivchenko, 1958.

113. "Kogda liud'mi dvizhet liubov' k Otchizne, ikh ne voz'mesh' ni nasiliem, ni podkupom, *Za vozvrashchenie na Rodinu,* May 18, 1956, 2.

114. "Eshche chetvero spaseny," *Za vozvrashchenie na Rodinu,* July 11, 1958, 2.

115. GARF, f. 8131, op. 31, d. 96483.

116. GARF, f. 8131, op. 31, d. 85513.

117. GARF, f. 8131, op. 31, d. 96483.

118. HDA SBU, f. 6, d. 75112, t. 1.

119. HDA SBU, f. 6, d. 75112, t. 2, l. 72–74.

120. HDA SBU, f. 6, d. 75112, t. 1, ll. 155–56.

121. HDA SBU, f. 6, d. 75112, t. 1, ll. 155–56.

122. HDA SBU, f. 6, d. 75112, t. 1, ll. 125–35.

123. HDA SBU, f 6, d. 75112, t. 1, ll. 136–53.

124. HDA SBU, f. 6, d. 75112, t. 1, ll. 156–58.

125. HDA SBU, f. 6, d. 75112, t. 1, ll. 136–53.

126. Summary of testimonies in HDA SBU, f. 6, d. 75112, t. 1.

127. HDA SBU, f. 6, d. 75112, t. 1, ll. 262–67.

128. HDA SBU, f. 6, d. 75112, t. 2, ll. 47–50.

129. HDA SBU, f. 6, d. 75112, t. 2, ll. 65.

130. Kalinin, *Net liubvi sil'nee,* 4–6.

131. HDA SBU, f. 6, d. 75112, t. 2, ll. 237–38.

132. NACP, RG 59, Bureau of East Asian and Pacific Affairs, Office of the Country Director, Subject Files, 1951–1978, Box 11, Conversation between Ambassador McConaughy and Ambassador Kohler, January 24, 1967.

133. Reece Jones, *Violent Borders: Refugees and the Right to Move* (London: Verso, 2017), 116.

134. L. A. Ivanashchenko, "Svoboda otkrytogo moria i problemy voennogo moreplavaniia," in *Aktual'nye problemy soveremennogo mezhdunarodnogo morskogo prava* (Moscow: Nauka, 1972), 92–93.

135. NACP, RG 59, Records Relating to Maritime Affairs and Port Security, 1949–1975, Box 1, US State Department Memorandum on Incidents at Sea, November 23, 1970.

136. CIA, "Soviet Shipping Expansion since 1972," September 2, 1974, CREST 0000484023.

137. CIA, "The Emerging Role of the Soviet Merchant Fleet in World Shipping," March 5, 1977, CREST 0000681969.

138. Robin R. Churchill and Alan Vaughan Lowe, *The Law of the Sea* (Manchester: Manchester University Press, 2008).

139. UN Treaty Collection, UN Convention on the Law of the Sea, 1982, accessed October 25, 2022, https://treaties.un.org/pages/ViewDetailsIII.aspx?src=TRE ATY&mtdsg_no=XXI-6&chapter=21&Temp=mtdsg3&clang=_en.

140. Roncevert Ganan Almond, "US Ratification of the Law of the Sea Convention," *The Diplomat*, May 24, 2017, accessed October 25, 2022, https://thediplomat. com/2017/05/u-s-ratification-of-the-law-of-the-sea-convention/.

141. UN, Documents, United Nations Convention on the Law of the Sea, 1982.

142. NACP, RG 59, POL 30 USSR, 1970–74, Box 2761, US State Department Memorandum for the President on Kudirka's Attempted Defection, December 2, 1970.

143. These changes were announced in the face of US congressional hearings. See *Attempted Defection by Lithuanian Seaman Simas Kudirka: Hearings, Ninety-First Congress Second Session* (Washington, DC: Government Printing Office, 1971).

144. Medvid's case was raised in later hearings on the treatment of Soviet defectors. See *Federal Government's Handling of Soviet and Communist Bloc Defectors: Hearings, One Hundredth Congress, First Session* (Washington, DC: Government Printing Office, 1988).

145. Joel Brinkley, "Was Soviet Seaman Switched for a Non-Defector," *New York Times*, March 2, 1986.

146. NACP, AAD, US State Department Telegram on Kurilov by Secretary of State, December 30, 1974.

147. Kurilov's story is detailed in his memoir, Slava Kurilov, *Alone in the Ocean* (Jerusalem: Paloma, 2016).

148. See his memoir, Sergei Kourdakov, *The Persecutor* (New York: Ballantine, 1974); see also the 2004 documentary, *Forgive Me, Sergei*, which investigates the account of his defection.

149. David Meadows, "Lillian Gasinskaya: The Russian in the Red Bikini Who Captivated Sydney," *Daily Telegraph*, January 13, 2016, accessed October 25, 2022, https://www.dailytelegraph.com.au/news/lillian-gasinskayoy-the-russian-in-the-red-bikini-who-captivated-sydney/news-story/9c993fd5179c2bedf57e4 bd4cfdeb1ce.

150. DDO, Memorandum of Telephone Call Regarding Two Soviet Seamen Requesting Asylum, November 18, 1971.

151. NACP, RG 59, POL 30 USSR, 1970–73, Box 2761, Memorandum of Conversation with Talyshevs, March 8, 1972.

152. Cases detailed in NACP, RG 59, POL 30 USSR, 1964–1966, Box 2893.

153. W. Courtland Robinson, *Terms of Refuge: The Indochinese Exodus and the International Response* (London: Zed Books, 1998); Jana K. Lipman, *In Camps: Vietnamese Refugees, Asylum Seekers, and Repatriates* (Berkeley: University of California Press, 2020).

154. TNA, FCO 58/1773.

155. The program, *Vremia*, aired August 18, 1988. Available at the Open Society Archives, file:///Users/erikscott/Zotero/storage/RKC8U8EC/osaba9abda4-aa41-41c4-bf5e-558f15b2f7bf.html. The subsequent fate of the sailors is discussed in "Tragicheskaia istoriia tankera 'Tuapse' i ego ekipazha," *Korabel'nyi portal*, July 17, 2010, accessed October 25, 2022, http://korabley.net/news/tragicheskaja_ istorija_tankera_tuapse_i_ego_ehkipazha/2010-07-17-603.

CHAPTER 6

1. This account relies on the investigative records of the Georgian KGB. SShSSA, f. 6, d. 7020.
2. On the relationship between civil aviation and state power in the American context, see Jenifer Van Vleck, *Empire of the Air: Aviation and the American Ascendancy* (Cambridge, MA: Harvard University Press, 2013).
3. Van Vleck, *Empire of the Air*, 228, 262.
4. Van Vleck, *Empire of the Air*, 228.
5. KPL, National Security Files, Box 182, Policy Statement on Bilateral Civil Air Transport Relations between the United States and the Sino-Soviet Bloc, January 28, 1963.
6. "United States and Soviet Union Sign Civil Air Transport Agreement," *International Legal Materials*, 6, no. 1 (1967): 82–91.
7. On the expansion of immigration controls at Heathrow Airport, see James Vernon, "Heathrow and the Making of Neoliberal Britain," *Past & Present* 261, no. 1 (2021): 213–47.
8. On the feminized role of flight attendants, see Kathleen M. Barry, *Femininity in Flight: A History of Flight Attendants* (Durham, NC: Duke University Press, 2007).
9. On hijacking to Cuba, see Teishan A. Latner, "Take Me to Havana! Airline Hijacking, U.S.-Cuba Relations, and Political Protest in Late Sixties' America," *Diplomatic History* 39, no. 1 (2015): 16–44.
10. On globalization in this period, see Thomas Borstelmann, *The 1970s: A New Global History from Civil Rights to Economic Inequality* (Princeton, NJ: Princeton University Press, 2013); Niall Ferguson et al., eds., *The Shock of the Global: The 1970s in Perspective* (Cambridge, MA: Harvard University Press, 2011). For a popular history of hijacking, see Brendan I. Koerner, *The Skies Belong to Us: Love and Terror in the Golden Age of Hijacking* (New York: Broadway, 2013); for a study emphasizing film, see Annette Vowinckel, *Flugzeugentführungen: eine Kulturgeschichte* (Göttingen: Wallstein, 2011).
11. On terrorism, see Jussi M. Hanhimäki and Bernhard Blumenau, eds., *An International History of Terrorism: Western and Non-Western Experiences* (London: Routledge, 2013); Bruce Hoffman, *Inside Terrorism* (New York: Columbia University Press, 2017).
12. The phrase is from Mark Mazower, *No Enchanted Palace: The End of Empire and the Ideological Origins of the United Nations* (Princeton, NJ: Princeton University Press, 2009), 23. Mira Siegelberg, looking at the interwar period in *Statelessness: A Modern History* (Cambridge, MA: Harvard University Press, 2020), recovers the possibilities of non-state belonging without neglecting its perils. The ninth chapter of Hannah Arendt's *The Origins of Totalitarianism* (New York: Schocken, 1951), deals with the issue in the interwar and immediate postwar periods.
13. Albert White (Algirdas Brazinskas) correspondence with author, October 28, 2016.
14. White (Brazinskas) correspondence with author, October 2, 2016.
15. White (Brazinskas) correspondence with author, October 28, 2016.
16. For a historical overview, see David Gero, *Flights of Terror: Aerial Hijack and Sabotage since 1930* (Somerset: Haynes, 2009); on the representation of Cold War hijackings, see Annette Vowinckel, "Flying Away: Civil Aviation and the Dream of Freedom in East and West," in *Divided Dreamworlds? The Cultural Cold War in East and West*, ed. Peter Romijn, Giles Scott-Smith, and Joes Segal, 181–200 (Amsterdam: Amsterdam University Press, 2012).

17. Kevin Riehle argues that this incident paved the way for the general criminalization of flight as treason in *Soviet Defectors: Revelations of Renegade Intelligence Officers, 1924–1954* (Edinburgh: Edinburgh University Press, 2020), 37.

18. EPL, Robert K. Gray Records, 1954–1960, Box 2, "Three Czechs Force Plane into Austria," *USEP News*, June 1958, no. 24.

19. CIA, Summary of International Repercussions of Gary Powers Incident, July 1, 1960, CREST 0000022337.

20. Diane Solway, *Nureyev: His Life* (New York: William Morrow, 1998), 158.

21. Jeffrey Smith, interview with author, Washington, DC, March 23, 2017.

22. NACP, RG 59, Records of Warren Christopher, Box 1, Comments by Jeffrey Smith in US Department of State Note, September 5, 1979.

23. Robert T. Holden, "The Contagiousness of Aircraft Hijacking," *American Journal of Sociology*, XCI (1986).

24. Latner, "Take Me to Havana!," 16.

25. KPL, National Security Files, Box 297, Memorandum on Hijacking, August 1961.

26. Technologies discussed by Matthew Connelly in "Future Shock: The End of the World as They Knew It," in *The Shock of the Global*, ed. Niall Ferguson et al., 337–50 (Cambridge, MA: Harvard University Press, 2011).

27. David G. Hubbard, *The Skyjacker: His Flights of Fantasy* (New York: Macmillan, 1971); James A. Arey, *The Sky Pirates* (New York: C. Scribner's Sons, 1972).

28. On the history of piracy, see Michael Kempe, "Even in the Remotest Corners of the World: Globalized Piracy and International Law, 1500–1900," *Journal of Global History* 5, no. 3 (2010): 353–72; Marcus Rediker, *Villains of All Nations: Atlantic Pirates in the Golden Age* (Boston: Beacon Press, 2004); and Kris E. Lane, *Pillaging the Empire: Global Piracy on the High Seas, 1500–1750* (New York: Routledge, 2016).

29. UN Treaty Collection, Convention on the High Seas, accessed October 25, 2022, https://treaties.un.org/pages/ViewDetails.aspx?src=TREATY&mtdsg_no=XXI-2&chapter=21; UN Treaty Collection, Convention on the Territorial Sea and the Contiguous Zone, accessed October 25, 2022, https://treaties.un.org/Pages/ViewDetails.aspx?src=IND&mtdsg_no=XXI-1&chapter=21&clang=_en.

30. "Hijack No Stunt by Allen Funt," *Ocala Star-Banner*, February 4, 1969, 1.

31. Vowinckel, "Flying Away," 193.

32. Recounted in Joseph K. Valiunas, *Serving Lithuania* (Southampton, NY: Valiunas, 1988), 133.

33. DDO, Transcript of Conversation between Richard Nixon and Henry Kissinger, October 15, 1970; on détente, see Jeremi Suri, *Power and Protest: Global Revolution and the Rise of Détente* (Cambridge, MA: Harvard University Press, 2003).

34. Richard Nixon, "Statement Announcing a Program to Deal with Airplane Hijacking," September 11, 1970, accessed October 25, 2022, https://www.presidency.ucsb.edu/documents/statement-announcing-program-deal-with-airplane-hijacking.

35. Van Vleck, *Empire of the Air*.

36. Hans Heymann Jr., "The Soviet Role in International Civil Aviation," *Journal of Air Law and Commerce* 25, no. 3 (1958): 265–80. On Aeroflot's growth and global ties, see Steven Harris, "The World's Largest Corporation: How Aeroflot Learned to Stop Worrying and Become a Corporation," *Laboratorium: Russian Review of Social Research* 13, no. 1 (2021): 20–56; and Steven Harris, "Dawn of the Soviet Jet Age: Aeroflot Passengers and Aviation Culture under Khrushchev," *Kritika: Explorations in Russian and Eurasian History* 21, no. 3 (2020): 591–626.

37. On Soviet ties with the PLO and the PFLP, see transcribed KGB reports in Christopher Andrew and Vasili Mitrokhin, *The Sword and the Shield: The Mitrokhin Archive and the Secret History of the KGB* (New York: Basic Books, 2001), 380–83.

38. Viktor Maevskii, "Farisei," *Pravda*, September 17, 1970, 4.

39. Nancy Douglas Joyner, *Aerial Hijacking as an International Crime* (Dobbs Ferry, NY: Oceana, 1974), 177.

40. Quoted in Hoffman, *Inside Terrorism*, 66. On the PLO's relationship to the state system, see Paul Thomas Chamberlin, *The Global Offensive: The United States, the Palestine Liberation Organization, and the Making of the Post-Cold War Order* (New York: Oxford University Press, 2012).

41. For a participant's account, see Eduard Kuznetsov, *Mordovskii marafon* (Moscow: Eksmo, 2008).

42. Documents suggest that the KGB knew about the hijacking plot in April 1970 if not sooner; other Soviet records show the state's concerns with international coverage of the would-be hijackers' arrest and trial. See Boris Morozov, *Documents on Soviet Jewish Emigration* (London: Routledge, 2015), 85–85, 90–93, 150; on international reaction, especially in Israel, see Jonathan Dekel-Chen, "Israeli Reactions in a Soviet Moment: Reflections on the 1970 Leningrad Affair," *Kennan Cable* 58 (September 2020): 1-9.

43. Evtim Kostadinov, ed., *Mezhdunarodniiat terorizm v dosietata na DS: dokumentalen sbornik* (Sofia: KRDOPBGDSPSBNA, 2010), 20–21.

44. AVP RF, f. 192, op. 60, p. 371, d. 1. 39.

45. Edward McWhinney, *Aerial Piracy and International Terrorism: The Illegal Diversion of Aircraft and International Law* (Dordrecht: Nijhoff, 1987), 32–33.

46. McWhinney, *Aerial Piracy and International Terrorism*, 43.

47. NACP, RG 59, Political Refugees, Eastern Europe, 1955–1959, Box 3473, Letter from Anthony J. Rudis to President Dwight D. Eisenhower, June 16, 1956.

48. NACP, RG 59, POL 30 USSR, 1970–1973, Telegram from US Embassy in Ankara to US State Department, October 19, 1970.

49. NACP, RG 59, POL 30 USSR, 1970–1973, Telegram from US Embassy in Ankara to US State Department, October 22, 1970.

50. DNSA, Telegram from US State Department to Geneva, Rome, Ankara, Istanbul, January 18, 1971.

51. Van Vleck, *Empire of the Air*, 230–31.

52. White (Brazinskas) correspondence with author, October 28, 2016.

53. GARF, f. 8131, op. 36, d. 4362, ll. 235–47.

54. "2 U.S. Generals in Ankara after Detention," *New York Times*, November 11, 1970, 1.

55. GARF, f. 8131, op. 36, d. 4366, l. 100; GARF, f. 8131, op. 36, d. 4362, l. 192.

56. Valiunas, *Serving Lithuania*, 145.

57. For background, see Bülent Gökay, *Soviet Eastern Policy and Turkey, 1920–1991: Soviet Foreign Policy, Turkey and Communism* (London: Routledge, 2012).

58. Valiunas, *Serving Lithuania*, 146.

59. GARF, f. 8131, op. 36, d. 4366, t. 5, l. 98.

60. GARF, f. 8131, op. 36, d. 4366, l. 94.

61. GARF, f. 8131, op. 36, d. 4364.

62. SShSSA, f. 6, d. 7020.

63. GARF, f. 8131, op. 36, d. 4362, ll. 290–92.

64. GARF, f. 8131, op. 36, d. 4366, ll. 154–55.

65. GARF, f. 8131, op. 36, d. 4366, ll. 160–68.

66. GARF, f. 8131, op. 36, d. 4366, ll. 150–87.

67. GARF, f. 8131, op. 36, d. 4366, ll. 102–4

68. GARF, f. 8131, op. 36, d. 4363, l. 13.

69. Valiunas, *Serving Lithuania*, 146.

70. GARF, f. 8131, op. 36, d. 4366, l. 110.

71. The trial is documented in A. Rozhanskii, ed., *Antievreiskie protsessy v Sovetskom Soiuze (1969–1971)* (Jerusalem: Evreiskii universitet, 1979).

72. "Mrs. Meier Warns on Soviet Trials," *New York Times*, November 17, 1970, 7.

73. Gal Beckerman, "Hijacking Their Way Out of Tyranny," *New York Times*, June 18, 2010, A29.

74. The trials are detailed in Morozov, *Documents on Soviet Jewish Emigration*, and in NACP, RG 59, Bureau of European Affairs, Records Relating to Soviet Jewry, 1964–1973, Box 1, Memorandum on Leningrad Trial, May 21, 1971.

75. GARF, f. 7928, op. 3, d. 2626, ll. 1–3.

76. Foreign Broadcast Information Service Daily Report, USSR International Affairs, October 23, 1970, A6, citing *TASS*, October 22, 1970.

77. AVP RF, f. 129, op. 56, p. 421, d. 25, ll. 3–5.

78. RGANI, f. 89, op. 76, d. 2.

79. GARF, f. 5446, op. 104, d. 1375, ll. 1–3.

80. RGALI, f. 2944, op. 4, d. 2288. The film, *Abiturentka*, was released in 1974.

81. G. Bocharov, *Smert' stiuardessy* (Moscow: Pravda, 1980). On Kurchenko's place in the longer history of Soviet martyrdom, see Yuliya Minkova, *Making Martyrs: The Language of Sacrifice in Russian Culture from Stalin to Putin* (Rochester, NY: University of Rochester Press, 2018).

82. GARF, f. 8131, op. 36, d. 4367, l. 130.

83. Ahmet Emin Yaman, "Dünya Savaşında Türkiye' de Askeri Mülteciler ve Gözaltı Kampları (1941–1942)," accessed October 25, 2022, https://dergipark.org.tr/tr/pub/tariharastirmalari/issue/47812/603958.

84. For a comparative look at the growing influence of the Cuban diaspora in Miami in the 1970s and 1980s and its relationship to US foreign policy, see Hideaki Kami, *Diplomacy Meets Migration: US Relations with Cuba during the Cold War* (New York: Cambridge University Press, 2018).

85. Algirdas Brazinskas-Baltas, *Už mylimą Baltiją: eilėraščiai* (New York: Amerikos Lietuvių Tautinės sąjungos Richmond Hill skyrius, 1973), 4–5.

86. '"Freedom Flight' Plea in Soviet Plane Case," *Times*, August 24, 1972, 5.

87. SShSSA, f. 6, d. 7020; GARF, f. 8131, op. 36, d. 4362–66.

88. Valiunas, *Serving Lithuania*, 147.

89. White (Brazinskas) correspondence with author, November 9, 2016.

90. NACP, RG 59, AAD, US State Department Telegram to US Embassy in Ankara, May 24, 1974; NACP, RG 59, AAD, US Embassy in Ankara Telegram to Department of State, May 29, 1974.

91. NACP, RG 59, AAD, US Embassy in Ankara Telegram to Department of State, June 12, 1974.

92. Andrew and Mitrokhin, *Sword and Shield*, 382.

93. NACP, RG 59, AAD, US Department of State Telegram to US Embassy in Ankara, July 8, 1974.

94. Kasım Cindemir, "Cinayetten yargılanan korsan, babasını öldürdü," *Hürriyet*, February 11, 2002, accessed October 25, 2022, https://www.hurriyet.com.tr/gundem/cinayetten-yargilanan-korsan-babasini-oldurdu-53799.

95. Sami Shubber, "Aircraft Hijacking under the Hague Convention 1970: A New Regime?" *International and Comparative Law Quarterly* 22, no. 4 (1973): 687–726; Linda S. Frey and Marsha L. Frey, *The History of Diplomatic Immunity* (Columbus: Ohio State University Press, 1999), 512.

96. Michael McGuire, "A Saga of Two Lithuanian 'Refugees,'" *Chicago Tribune*, September 29, 1976, 1–4.

97. NACP, RG 59, AAD, US Embassy in Ankara Telegram to Department of State, July 3, 1976.

98. NACP, RG 59, AAD, US Embassy in Ankara Telegram to Department of State, July 8, 1976; NACP, RG 59, AAD, US Embassy in Rome Telegram to US Embassy in Ankara, July 10, 1976.

99. NACP, RG 59, AAD, US Embassy in Rome Telegram to Department of State, July 9, 1976.

100. NACP, RG 59, AAD, US Consulate in Istanbul Telegram to US Embassy in Ankara, July 10, 1976; NACP, RG 59, AAD, US Embassy in Rome Telegram to Department of State, July 11, 1976.

101. NACP, RG 59, AAD, US Embassy in Rome Telegram to Secretary of State, July 27, 1976.

102. NACP, RG 59, AAD, US Department of State Telegram to US Embassy in Caracas, July 30, 1976; NACP, RG 59, AAD, US Department of State Telegram to US Embassy in Rome, July 30, 1976.

103. McGuire, "A Saga of Two Lithuanian 'Refugees,'" 4.

104. NACP, RG 59, AAD, Philip C. Habib Telegram to Kazys Robelis, August 2, 1976; NACP, RG 59, AAD, Arthur Adair Hartman Telegram to Philip C. Habib, August 30, 1976.

105. White (Brazinskas) correspondence to author, November 9, 2016.

106. NACP, RG 59, AAD, US Embassy in Ankara Telegram to Department of State, May 29, 1974.

107. McGuire, "A Saga of Two Lithuanian 'Refugees,'" 4.

108. On the domestic politics of the issue, see Carl Bon Tempo, *Americans at the Gate: The United States and Refugees during the Cold War* (Princeton, NJ: Princeton University Press, 2008).

109. Algis Ruksenas, *Day of Shame: The Truth about the Murderous Happenings aboard the Cutter Vigilant during the Russian-American Confrontation off Martha's Vineyard* (New York: McKay, 1973); Kudirka's story was given further attention in the 1978 CBS television movie, *The Defection of Simas Kudirka*.

110. Hoffman, *Inside Terrorism*, 65–66.

111. Hoffman, *Inside Terrorism*, 77.

112. Hoffman, *Inside Terrorism*, 68; on the 1983 hijacking in Georgia and its aftermath, see Erik R. Scott, *Familiar Strangers: The Georgian Diaspora and the Evolution of Soviet Empire* (New York: Oxford University Press, 2016), 195–97.

113. Bernhard Blumenau, "The United Nations and West Germany's Efforts against International Terrorism in the 1970s," in *An International History of Terrorism*, ed. Jussi M. Hanhimäki and Bernhard Blumenau, 66–87 (London: Routledge, 2013).

114. NACP, RG 59, AAD, US Department of State Telegram to US Embassy in Caracas, October 4, 1977; NACP, RG 59, AAD, US Embassy in Caracas Telegram to US Secretary of State, October 26, 1977.

115. RGANI, f. 5, op. 66, d. 1034, ll. 27–37.

116. "U. N. Assails Iran's Return of Flier to Soviet Union," *New York Times*, November 2, 1976.

117. The case is discussed in Stern's *Judgment in Berlin* (New York: Universe, 1984); it was later dramatized in a 1988 film by the same name.

118. See Michael Cotey Morgan, *The Final Act: The Helsinki Accords and the Transformation of the Cold War* (Princeton, NJ: Princeton University Press, 2020).

119. NACP, RG 59, AAD, US Department of State Telegram to US Embassy in Caracas, October 4, 1977.

120. According to White's (Brazinskas') testimony at his trial. See LexisNexis Academic, "2006 Appeal Albert Victor White," December 7, 2006, accessed October 25, 2022, http://www.lexisnexis.com/Academic.

121. Bernhard Blumenau, *The United Nations and Terrorism: Germany, Multilateralism, and Antiterrorism Efforts in the 1970s* (Basingstoke: Palgrave Macmillan, 2014), 169.

122. The initial announcement alleged that the US government harbored "extremist" and "anti-Soviet" organizations that threatened the safety of Soviet athletes. See "Zaiavlenie natsional'nogo olimpiiskogo komiteta SSSR," *Pravda*, May 9, 1984, 6. Subsequent press coverage brought up the Brazinskases to support this allegation: discussed in Rokas Tracevskis, "Bloody End to Story of Legendary Hijackers," *Baltic Times*, March 21, 2002, accessed October 25, 2022, https://www.baltictimes.com/news/articles/6162/.

123. On the Gilev and Pozdeev case, see HDA SBU, f. 5, d. 67322.

124. On airline deregulation, see Borstelmann, *The 1970s*, 149–51.

125. The most famous case was that of Iranian refugee Mehran Karimi Nasseri, whose eighteen-year sojourn at Charles de Gaulle Airport in Paris inspired two films and an opera.

126. Carolin Liebisch-Gümüş, "Airborne Asylum: Migration by Airplane in (West) Germany, 1945–1980s," *Bulletin of the German Historical Institute* 68 (Spring 2021): 39–60.

127. B. Martin Tsamenyi, "The 'Boat People': Are They Refugees?" *Human Rights Quarterly* 5, no. 3 (1983): 348–73; Jana K. Lipman's *In Camps* (Berkeley: University of California Press, 2020) rightly notes the importance of Vietnamese activism in refugee camps and in the diaspora, though individual Vietnamese refugees were never accorded the media attention enjoyed by the Brazinskases.

128. White (Brazinskas) correspondence with author, October 28, 2016.

129. Based on a summary of his testimony in "2006 Appeal Albert Victor White."

130. Eric Malnic, "Hijackers' Saga: Dad Slain, Son Arrested," *Los Angeles Times*, February 9, 2002, accessed October 25, 2022, https://www.latimes.com/archi ves/la-xpm-2002-feb-09-me-charge9-story.html.

131. Andrei Sidorchik, "Vydache ne podlezhat," *Argumenty i fakty*, October 15, 2015, accessed October 25, 2022, https://aif.ru/society/history/vydache_ne_ podlezhat_pervye_sovetskie_aviaugonshchiki_nashli_ubezhishche_v_ssha.

CONCLUSION

1. This account is based on the recollections of emigres gathered by HIAS in Russian and English and available at HIAS, My Story, accessed October 25, 2022, https://www.hias.org/mystory. It also draws on footage from the 2014 documentary film, *Stateless*.

2. Victor Rosenberg, "Refugee Status for Soviet Jewish Immigrants to the United States," *Touro Law Review* 19, no. 2 (2015): 419–50, esp. 427–28.

3. George H. W. Bush, Speech at Freedom Rally for Soviet Jews, December 6, 1987, *CSPAN*, accessed October 25, 2022, https://www.c-span.org/video/?537-1/freedom-rally-soviet-jews.

4. George H. W. Bush, News Conference in Helena, Montana, September 18, 1989, American Presidency Project, accessed October 25, 2022, https://www.presidency.ucsb.edu/documents/the-presidents-news-conference-helena-montana.

5. Barry R. Chiswick, "Soviet Jews in the United States: Language and Labour Market Adjustments Revisited," in *Russian Jews on Three Continents: Migration and Resettlement*, ed. Noah Lewin-Epstein, Yaacov Ro'i, and Paul Ritterband, 234 (London: Cummings Center, 1997), 234; Mark Tolts, "Postsovetskaia evreiskaia diaspora: noveishie otsenki," *Demoskop* 497–498 (2012): 1–2.

6. Cheryl Shanks, *Immigration and the Politics of American Sovereignty, 1890–1990* (Ann Arbor: University of Michigan Press, 2001), esp. 144–86.

7. William D. Montalbano, "Italian Resort Finds Itself Swamped by Flood of Soviet Emigres," *Los Angeles Times*, February 19, 1989, accessed October 25, 2022, https://www.latimes.com/archives/la-xpm-1989-02-19-mn-420-story.html.

8. Geliia Pevzner, "'Tuda, gde kormili': Geliia Pevzner o kolbasnoi emigratsii," *Rossiia segodnia*, July 15, 2014, accessed October 25, 2022, https://inosmi.ru/world/20140715/221672178.html.

9. On Soviet dreams of "the West," see Eleonory Gilburd, *To See Paris and Die: The Soviet Lives of Western Culture* (Cambridge, MA: Harvard University Press, 2018).

10. María Cristina García, *The Refugee Challenge in Post–Cold War America* (New York: Oxford University Press, 2020).

11. Based on data from UNHCR's Refugee Data Finder, accessed October 25, 2022, https://www.unhcr.org/refugee-statistics/download/?url=7iOQ.

12. John Tellaray and Michael Sulick, "A Defection Case that Marked the Times," *Studies in Intelligence* 56, no. 4 (2012): 1–4.

13. Discussed in Keith Gave, *The Russian Five: A Story of Espionage, Defection, Bribery, and Courage* (Cork: BookBaby, 2018).

14. NYPL, Mikhail Baryshnikov Archive, Box 5, Draft Publicity File, 1975.

15. NACP, RG 59, Bureau of European Affairs, Defector and Confrontation File, 1964–1970, Box 1, Correspondence between Department of Defense and Department of State, January 31, 1968.

16. NACP, RG 59, AAD, Message from US Secretary of State to US Embassy in Moscow, October 5, 1973.

17. Tim Weiner, *Legacy of Ashes: The History of the CIA* (London: Penguin, 2011), 375–81.

18. "Afghan Soviet 'Defector Pipeline' Resolution," House Concurrent Resolution 169, Congressional Record Daily Edition 133, 127 (July 30, 1987): E3167.

19. TFA, Escapees/Karlsfeld, Soviet POWS and Defectors in Afghanistan, selected files.

20. Rosemary Sullivan, *Stalin's Daughter: The Extraordinary and Tumultuous Life of Svetlana Alliluyeva* (New York: HarperCollins, 2015) 525.

21. DNSA, Vitaly Sergeyevich Yurchenko Biography, November 8, 1985.

22. Gene Kramer, "Pipeline to West Urged for Red Army Afghanistan Defectors," *Associated Press*, March 23, 1988, accessed October 25, 2022, https://apnews.com/article/18ff4803ea37e68449b6df875efd217f; Vincent J. Schodolski, "Soviet Who Fled to US Recants Story," *Chicago Tribune*, July 28, 1988, accessed October 25, 2022, https://www.chicagotribune.com/news/ct-xpm-1988-07-28-8801180306-story.html.

23. *Federal Government's Handling of Soviet and Communist Bloc Defectors: Hearings, One Hundredth Congress, First Session* (Washington, DC: Government Printing Office, 1988), 2–3.

24. *Federal Government's Handling of Soviet and Communist Bloc Defectors*, 14.

25. *Federal Government's Handling of Soviet and Communist Bloc Defectors*, 22.

26. "Public Law 110: Central Intelligence Agency Act of 1949," Homeland Security Digital Library, accessed October 25, 2022, https://www.hsdl.org/?abstract&did=472434.

27. Burton Gerber, interview with author, March 23, 2017.

28. Definition from NSC 86/1.

29. *Federal Government's Handling of Soviet and Communist Bloc Defectors*, 73.

30. Alexey Antoshin, "USSR," in *East Central European Migrations during the Cold War: A Handbook* (Berlin: De Gruyter Oldenbourg, 2019), ed. Anna Mazurkiewicz, 326–67.

31. NACP RG 59, RG 59 Bureau of European Affairs, Office of Soviet Union Affairs, Bilateral Political Relations, Records Relating to Soviet Jewry, 1964–1973, Box 1, Memorandum on Soviet Jews from Assistant Secretary of State for European Affairs to Secretary of State, July 23, 1964.

32. RGANI, f. 89, op. 18, d. 45, ll. 2–3. In *Documents on Soviet Jewish Emigration* (London: Routledge, 2015), Boris Morozov concurs that the quote concerns the potential use of emigrants for espionage. See Morozov, 16.

33. The story was published abroad by an NTS-affiliated journal. Valerii Tarsis, "Skazanie o sinei mukhe," *Grani* 52 (1962): 5–85.

34. Valerii Tarsis, *Palata No. 7* (Frankfurt: Posev, 1966).

35. RGANI, f. 89, op. 25, d. 22, l. 3.

36. RGANI, f. 89, op. 25, d. 22, l. 5.

37. RGANI, f. 89, op. 25, d. 21; RGANI, f. 89, op. 25, d. 37. On their lives in emigration, see Liudmila Shtern, *Brodksy: A Personal Memoir* (Fort Worth, TX: Baskerville, 2004); Aleksandr Solzhenitsyn, *Between Two Millstones*, trans. Clare Kitson and Melanie Moore, Books 1–2 (Notre Dame: University of Notre Dame Press, 2018–2020).

38. See GARF, f. 7523, op. 10, 59, 65, 68, 71, 88, and 93 for a range of cases on the revocation of Soviet citizenship.

39. On the stripping of Allilueva's citizenship, see RGASPI, f. 558, op. 11, d. 1565.

40. See discussion among agents of Soviet intelligence recorded in WCD, Vassiliev Notebooks, Yellow Notebook #2.

41. Serhii Plokhy, *The Man with the Poison Gun* (London: One World, 2017), 320.

42. Christopher M. Andrew and Vasili Mitrokhin, *The Mitrokhin Archive: The KGB in Europe and the West* (London: Allen Lane, 1999), 480–82.

43. Christopher Andrew, *The Secret World: A History of Intelligence* (London: Penguin, 2019), 699.

44. RGANI, f. 89, op. 37, d. 32, ll. 3–4.

45. RGANI, f. 89, op. 37, d. 32, ll. 5–6.

46. Andrew and Mitrokhin, *The Mitrokhin Archive: The KGB in Europe and the West*, 477–78.

47. Brigitte Le Normand, "Yugoslavia," in *East Central European Migrations during the Cold War*, ed. Mazurkiewicz, 381.

48. Sławomir Łukasiewicz, "Poland," in *East Central European Migrations during the Cold War*, ed. Mazurkiewicz, 205–7.

49. Beatrice Scutaru, "Romania," in *East Central European Migrations during the Cold War*, ed. Mazurkiewicz, 258.

50. Radu Ioanid, *Ransom of the Jews: The Story of the Extraordinary Secret Bargain between Romania and Israel* (Lanham: Rowman & Littlefield, 2021).

51. Beatrice Hicks, "Germany," in *East Central European Migrations during the Cold War*, ed. Mazurkiewicz, 150.

52. For the perspectives of the migrants themselves, see José Manuel García, *Voices from Mariel: Oral Histories of the 1980 Cuban Boatlift* (Gainesville: University Press of Florida, 2018).

53. Alexandra Richie, *Faust's Metropolis: A History of Berlin* (London: HarperCollins, 2008), 715–18.

54. A common Soviet slogan.

55. On the punishment of Armenian repatriates who illegally fled abroad, see RGANI, f. 5, op. 66, d. 1034, l. 811.

56. N. F. Chistiakov and M. E. Karyshev, eds., *Neotvratimoe vozmedie* (Moscow: Voenizdat, 1984).

57. "Kamera smotrit v mir: Byvshie," September 19, 1986, Open Society Archives, accessed October 25, 2022, https://catalog.osaarchivum.org/catalog/osa:9a98b 1b2-a895-4445-afc9-d2323b684d85#https://www.ku.edu.

58. RGANI, f. 89, op. 37, d. 36.

59. RGANI f. 89, op. 11, d. 37.

60. RGANI, f. 89, op. 13, d. 6.

61. RGANI, f. 89, op. 19, d. 40, l. 1; Michael Cotey Morgan, *The Final Act: The Helsinki Accords and the Transformation of the Cold War* (Princeton, NJ: Princeton University Press, 2020).

62. Linda K. Kerber, "The Stateless as the Citizen's Other: A View from the United States," *American Historical Review* 112, no. 1 (2007): 1–34.

63. On the Politburo's views of Allilueva, see RGANI, f. 89, op. 36, d. 18.

64. Gary Kern, *The Kravchenko Case: One Man's War against Stalin* (New York: Enigma, 2012), 518–33.

65. James C. Scott, *Weapons of the Weak: Everyday Forms of Peasant Resistance* (New Haven, CT: Yale University Press, 1985).

66. Anna Seghers, *Transit*, trans. Margot Bettauer Dembo (New York: New York Review of Books, 2013), 181–82.

67. On Seghers, see Marike Janzen, *Writing to Change the World: Anna Seghers, Authorship, and International Solidarity in the Twentieth Century* (Rochester, NY: Camden House, 2018).

68. Judith Kumin, "Orderly Departure from Vietnam: Cold War Anomaly or Humanitarian Innovation?" *Refugee Survey Quarterly* 27, no. 1 (2008): 104–17.

69. E. Tendayi Achiume, "Migration as Decolonization," *Stanford Law Review* 71 (2019): 1509–74; E. Tendayi Achiume, "The Postcolonial Case for Rethinking Borders," *Dissent*, Summer 2019, accessed October 25, 2022, https://www.diss entmagazine.org/article/the-postcolonial-case-for-rethinking-borders.

70. Mattha Busby and Carlotta Dotto, "'I Love Rome, but Rome Doesn't Love Us': The City's New Migrant Crisis," *Guardian*, February 19, 2018, accessed October 25, 2022, https://www.theguardian.com/cities/2018/feb/19/rome-italy-migrant-crisis-squatting-emergency-shelters-asylum-seekers; Caitlin L. Chandler, "Rome: Where Migrants Face Eviction as Fascists Find a Home," *New York Review*, January 28, 2019, accessed October 25, 2022, https://www.nybooks.com/daily/2019/01/28/rome-where-migrants-face-eviction-while-fasci sts-find-a-home/.

71. "Migration to Europe in Charts," *BBC News*, September 11, 2018, accessed October 25, 2022, https://www.bbc.com/news/world-europe-44660699.

72. Amnesty International, "The World's Refugees in Numbers," accessed October 25, 2022, https://www.amnesty.org/en/what-we-do/refugees-asylum-seekers-and-migrants/global-refugee-crisis-statistics-and-facts/.

73. Berkay Mandıracı, "Sharing the Burden: Revisiting the EU-Turkey Migration Deal," International Crisis Group, March 13, 2020, accessed October 25, 2022, https://www.crisisgroup.org/europe-central-asia/western-europemediterran ean/turkey/sharing-burden-revisiting-eu-turkey-migration-deal.

74. Parallels are discussed in Libora Oates-Indruchova and Wolfgang Mueller, "From the Iron Curtain to the Schengen Area: Memory Cultures of Bordering Communist and Postcommunist Europe," *East European Politics & Societies* 31, no. 2 (2017): 227–33.

75. Wendy Brown, *Walled States, Waning Sovereignty* (New York: Zone, 2010); Matthew Longo, *The Politics of Borders: Sovereignty, Security, and the Citizen after 9/11* (Cambridge: Cambridge University Press, 2018).

76. The notion of "remote control" is from Aristide Zolberg, *A Nation by Design: Immigration Policy in the Fashioning of America* (Cambridge, MA: Harvard University Press, 2006).

77. Ana Raquel Minian, "Offshoring Migration Control: Construction of Mexico as a Buffer Zone," *American Historical Review* 125, no. 1 (2020): 89–111.

78. On post-9/11 security measures, see Longo, *The Politics of Borders*; on the "thick" Soviet border, see Sabine Dullin, *La frontière épaisse: aux origines des politiques soviétiques, 1920-1940* (Paris: EHESS, 2014).

79. Trevor Paglen, *Blank Spots on the Map: The Dark Geography of the Pentagon's Secret World* (New York: New American Library, 2010).

80. On continuity and change in Russia's foreign policy, see Mark Kramer, "The Soviet Legacy in Russian Foreign Policy," *Political Science Quarterly* 134, no. 4 (2019–20): 585–609.

81. Sir Robert Owen, chair, *The Litvinenko Inquiry: Report into the Death of Alexander Litvinenko* (London: Her Majesty's Stationery Office, 2016), 66-67.

82. "Russia's Border Doesn't End Anywhere, Vladimir Putin Says," *BBC News*, November 26, 2016, accessed October 25, 2022, https://www.bbc.com/news/world-europe-38093468; "'Granitsy Rossii nigde ne zakanchivaietsia,'" *Dialog. UA*, September 22, 2017, accessed October 25, 2022, https://www.dialog.ua/news/131624_1506100574.

83. Claire Parker, "New Findings Expose Machinery of Russia's 'Filtration' of Ukrainians," *Washington Post*, September 1, 2022, accessed October 25, 2022, https://www.washingtonpost.com/world/2022/09/01/russia-ukraine-filtration-forced-transfer/.

84. Rob Nixon, *Slow Violence and the Environmentalism of the Poor* (Cambridge, MA: Harvard University Press, 2011).

85. Ira Mehlman, "It's Time to Treat Mass Emigration Countries as Rogue States," *The Hill*, October 31, 2018, accessed October 25, 2022, https://thehill.com/opin ion/immigration/413907-its-time-to-treat-mass-emigration-countries-as-rogue-states.

SOURCES AND SELECT BIBLIOGRAPHY

A NOTE ON SOURCES

Defectors crossed and gave meaning to political and cultural borders in the Cold War. To understand the significance of their journeys, I followed the traces they left in multiple state archives in several countries. Because the central KGB archives in Moscow remain closed, I utilized the substantial swath of documents in Russia that are declassified along with the records of former Soviet republics where KGB files have been made accessible to researchers. I found a wealth of materials in Ukraine and Georgia, and I was able to use the extensive Estonian, Latvian, and Lithuanian KGB documents available at the Hoover Institution Archives. These countries formed the western flank of the Soviet Union, and their local KGB branches were tasked with enforcement along the sections of the border most frequently crossed by defectors in the Cold War. I also relied on the records of the two states most invested in encouraging and tracking defectors' global journeys: the United States and the United Kingdom. My work was bolstered by several online archival collections that are international in scope, including those of the Wilson Center and the United Nations.

Emigre collections, some still privately maintained, gave me another opportunity to listen to the voices of Cold War migrants and those who spoke on their behalf. I found diaries, notes, and letters written by defectors evoking experiences that later reappeared in reworked form in media coverage, published memoirs, and films. In cases where I was able to locate surviving defectors as well as those who encountered them, personal correspondence and interviews helped me to appreciate the difficult decisions these migrants faced.

This book was also an effort to cross historiographical and disciplinary boundaries. I am indebted to the work my fellow historians are doing to reconsider the Soviet Union's engagement with the world and its role in the Cold War. I benefited from the broader scholarship devoted to the history of migration, the history of empires, legal history, and diplomatic history. Works written by anthropologists, literary scholars, political theorists, and sociologists helped shape the way I think about borders and mobility.

The archival collections I consulted are listed below, followed by a select bibliography of secondary sources that informed my approach. Additional secondary sources, published document collections, and the Cold War–era films, memoirs, and periodicals utilized for this project are provided in the notes.

ARCHIVAL SOURCES

Georgia
SShSSA—sakartvelos shinagan sakmeta saministro arkivi
Archive of the Ministry of Internal Affairs of Georgia, Tbilisi
Fond 6 Criminal Cases of the Georgian KGB
Russian Federation
AVP RF—Arkhiv vneshnei politiki Rossiiskoi Federatsii
Foreign Policy Archive of the Russian Federation, Moscow
Fond 6 Secretariat of Viacheslav Molotov
Fond 7 Secretariat of Andrei Vyshinsky
Fond 47 Section for United Nations and International Organizations
Fond 54 Treaty and Legal Directorate
Fond 129 Referentura (Desk) for the United States
Fond 192 Embassy of the USSR in the United States
Fond 197 Embassy of the USSR in France
GARF—Gosudarstvennyi arkhiv Rossiiskoi Federatsii
State Archive of the Russian Federation, Moscow
Fond 8131 Procuracy of the USSR
Fond 9474 Supreme Court of the USSR
Fond 9526 Administration for Repatriation
Fond 9651 Committee for the Return to the Homeland
Fond 10015 Collection of Nikolai Troitskii
Fond 10078 Collection of Aleksandr Gorkin
RGALI—Rossiiskii gosudarstvennyi arkhiv literatury i iskusstva
Russian State Archive for Literature and the Arts, Moscow
Fond 2458 Directorship of Art Exhibitions and Panoramas
Fond 2932 Central House of the Arts of the USSR
Fond 2944 State Committee for Cinematography (Goskino)
RGANI—Rossiiskii gosudarstvennyi arkhiv noveishei istorii
Russian State Archive of Contemporary History, Moscow
Fond 3 Politburo of the Central Committee of the Communist Party of the Soviet
    Union (CPSU)
Fond 5 Apparat of the Central Committee of the CPSU
Fond 6 Party Control Commission of the Central Committee of the CPSU
Fond 89 Collection of Declassified Documents
RGASPI—Rossiiskii gosudarstvennyi arkhiv sotsial'no-politicheskoi istorii
Russian State Archive of Socio-Political History, Moscow
Fond 17 Central Committee of the CPSU
Fond 558 Collection of Joseph Stalin
RGVA—Rossiiskii gosudarstvennyi voennyi arkhiv
Russian State Military Archive, Moscow
Fond 444-P Section for Repatriation and Retrieval of Citizens of the Soviet Control
    Commission in Germany
Fond 40926 Political Directorate of the Border Troops of the USSR
Ukraine
HDA SBU—Haluzevii derzhavnii arkhiv Sluzhby bezpeky Ukraïny
Sectoral State Archive of the Security Services of Ukraine, Kyiv
Fond 1 Second Chief Directorate of the Ukrainian KGB
Fond 5 Criminal Cases of the Ukrainian KGB against Unrehabilitated Persons

Fond 6 Criminal Cases of the Ukrainian KGB against Rehabilitated Persons
Fond 13 Collection of Publications of the KGB of the USSR
Fond 16 Secretariat of the Ukrainian KGB
Fond 24 Intelligence Departments of the KGB of the USSR for the Western Border District
Fond 27 Special Department of the KGB of the USSR for the Western Border District
United Kingdom
TNA—The National Archives of the UK, Kew
Cabinet Office (CAB)
Dominions Office (DO)
Foreign and Commonwealth Office (FCO)
Foreign Office (FO)
United States
EPL—Eisenhower Presidential Library Archives, Abilene, KS
Dwight D. Eisenhower Papers as President (Ann Whitman File)
Dwight D. Eisenhower Records as President (White House Central File)
Gerald D. Morgan Records
US National Security Council Presidential Records
White House Office
HIA—Hoover Institution Archives, Stanford, CA
Eesti NSV Riikliku Julgeoleku Komitee (Estonian KGB) Selected Records
Latvijas PSR Valsts Drosibas Komiteja (Latvian KGB) Selected Records
Lietuvos SSR Valstybės Saugumo Komitetas (Lithuanian KGB) Selected Records
Nikolai E. Khokhlov Papers
KPL—Kennedy Presidential Library Archives, Boston, MA
National Security Files
Presidential Papers
NACP—US National Archives, College Park, MD
Access to Archival Databases (AAD)
RG 43 International Conferences, Commissions, and Expositions
RG 59 Department of State
    RG 65 Federal Bureau of Investigation
RG 84 Foreign Service Posts of the Department of State
RG 263 Central Intelligence Agency
RG 466 High Commissioner for Germany
NYPL—New York Public Library, New York, NY
David J. Dallin Papers
Mikhail Baryshnikov Archive
TFA—Tolstoy Foundation Archives, Valley Cottage, NY
Escapees/Karlsfeld Files
VIP Files
TPL—Truman Presidential Library Archives, Independence, MO
Harry S. Truman Papers, Psychological Strategy Board Files
Online Archival Collections
CIA—Central Intelligence Agency Freedom of Information Act Electronic Reading Room
DDO—Declassified Documents Online
DNSA—Digital National Security Archive
FRUS—Foreign Relations of the United States
HPSSS—Harvard Project on the Soviet Social System Online

KGBD—KGB Documents Online
UN—United Nations Documents and Digital Library
WCD—Wilson Center Digital Archive

SELECT BIBLIOGRAPHY

Achiume, E. Tendayi. "Migration as Decolonization." *Stanford Law Review* 71 (2019): 1509–74.

Agamben, Giorgio. *State of Exception*. Translated by Kevin Attell. Chicago: University of Chicago Press, 2005.

Allen, Keith. *Interrogation Nation: Refugees and Spies in Cold War Germany*. London: Rowman & Littlefield, 2017.

Andrew, Christopher M. and Vasili Mitrokhin. *The Mitrokhin Archive: The KGB in Europe and the West*. London: Allen Lane, 1999.

Andrew, Christopher M. and Vasili Mitrokhin. *The Mitrokhin Archive II: The KGB and the World*. London: Allen Lane, 2005.

Baiburin, Al'bert. *Sovetskii pasport: Istoriia, struktura, praktiki*. St. Petersburg: Izdatel'stvo Evropeiskogo universiteta, 2019.

Balibar, Étienne. *Politics and the Other Scene*. Translated by Christine Jones, James Swenson, and Chris Turner. London: Verso, 2012.

Balint, Ruth. *Destination Elsewhere: Displaced Persons and Their Quest to Leave Postwar Europe*. Ithaca, NY: Cornell University Press, 2021.

Benton, Lauren. *A Search for Sovereignty: Law and Geography in European Empires, 1400–1900*. Cambridge: Cambridge University Press, 2010.

Bernstein, Seth. "Ambiguous Homecoming: Retribution, Exploitation and Social Tensions during Repatriation to the USSR, 1944–1946." *Past & Present* 242, no. 1 (2019): 193–226.

Bon Tempo, Carl J. *Americans at the Gate: The United States and Refugees during the Cold War*. Princeton, NJ: Princeton University Press, 2008.

Bosco, David L. *Five to Rule Them All: The UN Security Council and the Making of the Modern World*. New York: Oxford University Press, 2009.

Brown, Wendy. *Walled States, Waning Sovereignty*. New York: Zone, 2010.

Bruns, Kai S. "'A Hazardous Task': Britain and the 1961 Vienna Convention on Diplomatic Relations." *International History Review* 39, no. 2 (2017): 196–215.

Burbank, Jane and Frederick Cooper. *Empires in World History: Power and the Politics of Difference*. Princeton, NJ: Princeton University Press, 2010.

Butler, William E. *The Soviet Union and the Law of the Sea*. Baltimore: Johns Hopkins University Press, 1971.

Carruthers, Susan L. *Cold War Captives: Imprisonment, Escape, and Brainwashing*. Berkeley: University of California Press, 2009.

Caute, David. *The Dancer Defects: The Struggle for Cultural Supremacy in the Cold War*. Oxford: Oxford University Press, 2003.

Chan, Shelly. *Diaspora's Homeland: Modern China in the Age of Global Migration*. Durham, NC: Duke University Press, 2018.

Chandler, Andrea M. *Institutions of Isolation: Border Controls in the Soviet Union and Its Successor States, 1917–1993*. Montreal and Kingston: McGill-Queen's University Press, 1998.

Cherviatsova, Alina and Oleksandr Yarmysh. "Soviet International Law: Between Slogans and Practice." *Journal of the History of International Law* 19, no. 2 (2017): 296–327.

Cohen, Gerard Daniel. *In War's Wake: European Refugees in the Postwar Order*. New York: Oxford University Press, 2012.

Cohn, Edward. "Coercion, Reeducation, and the Prophylactic Chat: *Profilaktika* and the KGB's Struggle with Political Unrest in Lithuania, 1953–64." *Russian Review* 76, no. 2 (2017): 272–93.

Comte, Emmanuel. "Waging the Cold War: The Origins and Launch of Western Cooperation to Absorb Migrants from Eastern Europe," *Cold War History* 20, no. 4 (2020): 461–81.

Connelly, Matthew. *A Diplomatic Revolution: Algeria's Fight for Independence and the Origins of the Post–Cold War Era*. New York: Oxford University Press, 2002.

David-Fox, Michael. "The Implications of Transnationalism." *Kritika: Explorations in Russian and Eurasian History* 12, no. 4 (Fall 2011): 895–904.

Denza, Eileen. *Diplomatic Law: Commentary on the Vienna Convention on Diplomatic Relations*. 4th ed.. Oxford: Oxford University Press, 2016.

Dowty, Alan. *Closed Borders: The Contemporary Assault on Freedom of Movement*. New Haven, CT: Yale University Press, 1989.

Dullin, Sabine. *La frontière épaisse: aux origins des politiques soviétiques, 1920–1940*. Paris: EHESS, 2014.

Eckert, Astrid M. *West Germany and the Iron Curtain: Environment, Economy, and Culture in the Borderlands*. New York: Oxford University Press, 2019.

Edele, Mark. *Stalin's Defectors: How Red Army Soldiers Became Hitler's Collaborators, 1941–1945*. Oxford: Oxford University Press, 2019.

Engerman, David C. *Know Your Enemy: The Rise and Fall of America's Soviet Experts*. New York: Oxford University Press, 2011.

Fainberg, Dina. *Cold War Correspondents: Soviet and American Reporters on the Ideological Frontlines*. Baltimore: Johns Hopkins University Press, 2021.

Feinberg, Melissa. *Curtain of Lies: The Battle over Truth in Stalinist Eastern Europe*. New York: Oxford University Press, 2017.

Fel'shtinskii, Iurii. *K istorii nashei zakrytosti*. Moscow: Terra, 1991.

Fitzpatrick, Sheila. *White Russians, Red Peril: A Cold War History of Migration to Australia*. London: Routledge, 2021.

Foglesong, David S. *The American Mission and the "Evil Empire."* New York: Cambridge University Press, 2007.

Frey, Linda S. and Marsha L. Frey. *The History of Diplomatic Immunity*. Columbus: Ohio State University Press, 1999.

Foucault, Michel. *Security, Territory, Population: Lectures at the College de France, 1977–1978*. Edited by M. Senellart. Translated by G. Burchell. New York: Picador, 2007.

Friedman, Andrea. *Citizenship in Cold War America: The National Security State and the Possibilities of Dissent*. Amherst: University of Massachusetts Press, 2014.

Friedman, Andrew. *Covert Capital: Landscapes of Denial and the Making of U.S. Empire in the Suburbs of Northern Virginia*. Berkeley: University of California Press, 2016.

Gaddis, John Lewis. *The Long Peace*. New York: Oxford University Press, 1987.

Gaiduk, Ilya V. *Divided Together: The United States and the Soviet Union in the United Nations*. Washington, DC: Woodrow Wilson Center Press, 2012.

García, María Cristina. *The Refugee Challenge in Post–Cold War America*. New York: Oxford University Press, 2020.

Gatrell, Peter. *The Making of the Modern Refugee*. Oxford: Oxford University Press, 2013.

Gatrell, Peter. *The Unsettling of Europe: How Migration Reshaped a Continent.* New York: Basic Books, 2019.

Genis, Vladimir. *Nevernye slugi rezhima: pervye sovetskie nevozvrashchentsy (1920–1933).* 2 vols. Moscow: Informkniga, 2009–2010.

Getachew, Adom. *Worldmaking after Empire: The Rise and Fall of Self-Determination.* Princeton, NJ: Princeton University Press, 2020.

Gilburd, Eleonory. *To See Paris and Die: The Soviet Lives of Western Culture.* Cambridge, MA: Harvard University Press, 2018.

Green, Nancy L. "The Politics of Exit: Reversing the Immigration Paradigm." *Journal of Modern History* 77, no. 2 (2005): 263–89.

Gorsuch, Anne. E. *All This Is Your World: Soviet Tourism at Home and Abroad after Stalin.* Oxford: Oxford University Press, 2013.

Gorsuch, Anne E. and Diane P. Koenker, eds. *The Socialist Sixties: Crossing Borders in the Second World.* Bloomington: University of Indiana Press, 2013.

Grossmann, Atina. *Jews, Germans, and Allies: Close Encounters in Occupied Germany.* Princeton, NJ: Princeton University Press, 2007.

Harris, Steven. "Dawn of the Soviet Jet Age: Aeroflot Passengers and Aviation Culture under Khrushchev." *Kritika: Explorations in Russian and Eurasian History* 21, no. 3 (2020): 591–626.

Hernández, Kelly Lytle. *Migra! A History of the U.S. Border Patrol.* Berkeley: University of California Press, 2010.

Hillis, Faith. *Utopia's Discontents: Russian Émigrés and the Quest for Freedom, 1830s–1930s.* New York: Oxford University Press, 2021.

Hirsch, Francine. *Soviet Judgment at Nuremberg: A New History of the International Military Tribunal after World War II.* New York: Oxford University Press, 2020.

Holian, Anna. *Between National Socialism and Soviet Communism: Displaced Persons in Postwar Germany.* Ann Arbor: University of Michigan Press, 2011.

Hopkins, Benjamin D. *Ruling the Savage Periphery: Frontier Governance and the Making of the Modern State.* Cambridge, MA: Harvard University Press, 2020.

Howland, Douglas, ed. *The State of Sovereignty: Territories, Laws, Populations.* Bloomington: Indiana University Press, 2009.

Huber, Valeska. *Channelling Mobilities: Migration and Globalisation in the Suez Canal Region and Beyond, 1869–1914.* Cambridge: Cambridge University Press, 2013.

Immerwahr, Daniel. *How to Hide an Empire: A History of the Greater United States.* New York: Farrar, Straus and Giroux, 2019.

Janco, Andrew. "Soviet 'Displaced Persons' in Europe." PhD diss., University of Chicago, 2012.

Janco, Andrew. "'Unwilling': The One-Word Revolution in Refugee Status, 1940–51." *Contemporary European History* 23, no. 3 (2014): 429–46.

Jones, Reece. *Violent Borders: Refugees and the Right to Move.* London: Verso, 2017.

Kami, Hideaki. *Diplomacy Meets Migration: US Relations with Cuba during the Cold War.* New York: Cambridge University Press, 2018.

Kerber, Linda K. "The Stateless as the Citizen's Other: A View from the United States." *American Historical Review* 112, no. 1 (2007): 1–34.

Kern, Gary. *The Kravchenko Case: One Man's War against Stalin.* New York: Enigma, 2012.

Kim, Monica. *Interrogation Rooms of the Korean War: The Untold History.* Princeton, NJ: Princeton University Press, 2020.

Knight, Amy. *How the Cold War Began: The Igor Gouzenko Affair and the Hunt for Soviet Spies.* New York: Basic, 2007.

Koskenniemi, Martti. *The Gentle Civilizer of Nations: The Rise and Fall of International Law, 1870–1960*. Cambridge: Cambridge University Press, 2001.

Kramer, Mark. "The Soviet Legacy in Russian Foreign Policy." *Political Science Quarterly* 134, no. 4 (2019–20): 585–609.

Kramer, Paul. "Geopolitics of Mobility: Immigration Policy and American Global Power in the Long Twentieth Century." *American Historical Review* 123, no. 2 (2018): 393–438.

Krasnov, Vladislav. *Soviet Defectors: The KGB Wanted List*. Stanford, CA: Hoover Institution Press, 1986.

Latner, Teishan A. "Take Me to Havana! Airline Hijacking, U.S.-Cuba Relations, and Political Protest in Late Sixties' America." *Diplomatic History* 39, no. 1 (2015): 16–44.

Laycock, Jo. "Belongings: People and Possessions in the Armenian Repatriations, 1945–1949." *Kritika: Explorations in Russian and Eurasian History* 18, no. 3 (2017): 511–37.

Light, Matthew A. "What Does It Mean to Control Migration? Soviet Mobility Policies in Comparative Perspective." *Law and Social Inquiry* 37, no. 2 (2012): 395–429.

Lipman, Jana K. *In Camps: Vietnamese Refugees, Asylum Seekers, and Repatriates*. Berkeley: University of California Press, 2020.

Lohr, Eric. *Russian Citizenship: From Empire to Soviet Union*. Cambridge, MA: Harvard University Press, 2012.

Longo, Matthew. *The Politics of Borders: Sovereignty, Security, and the Citizen after 9/11*. Cambridge: Cambridge University Press, 2018.

Lüthi, Lorenz M. *Cold Wars: Asia, the Middle East, Europe*. Cambridge: Cambridge University Press, 2020.

Madokoro, Laura. *Elusive Refuge: Chinese Migrants in the Cold War*. Cambridge, MA: Harvard University Press, 2016.

Maier, Charles S. *Once within Borders: Territories of Power, Wealth, and Belonging since 1500*. Cambridge, MA: Harvard University Press, 2016.

Major, Patrick. *Behind the Berlin Wall: East Germany and the Frontiers of Power*. Oxford: Oxford University Press, 2010.

Mälksoo, Lauri. *Russian Approaches to International Law*. Oxford: Oxford University Press, 2017.

Manchester, Laurie. "Repatriation to a Totalitarian Homeland: The Ambiguous Alterity of Russian Repatriates from China to the U.S.S.R." *Diaspora: A Journal of Transnational Studies* 16, no. 3 (2007): 353–88.

Mark, James, Artemy M. Kalinovsky, and Steffi Marung, eds. *Alternative Globalizations: Eastern Europe and the Postcolonial World*. Bloomington: Indiana University Press, 2020.

Mazower, Mark. *No Enchanted Palace: The End of Empire and the Ideological Origins of the United Nations*. Princeton, NJ: Princeton University Press, 2009.

Mazurkiewicz, Anna, ed. *East Central European Migrations during the Cold War: A Handbook*. Berlin: De Gruyter Oldenbourg, 2019.

Mëhilli, Elidor. *From Stalin to Mao: Albania and the Socialist World*. Ithaca, NY: Cornell University Press, 2018.

Minian, Ana Raquel. "Offshoring Migration Control: Guatemalan Transmigrants and the Construction of Mexico as a Buffer Zone." *American Historical Review* 125, no. 1 (2020): 89–111.

Mitrovich, Gregory. *Undermining the Kremlin: America's Strategy to Subvert the Soviet Bloc, 1947–1956*. Ithaca, NY: Cornell University Press, 2009.

Morgan, Michael Cotey. *Final Act: The Helsinki Accords and the Transformation of the Cold War*. Princeton, NJ: Princeton University Press, 2020.

Moyn, Samuel. *The Last Utopia: Human Rights in History*. Cambridge, MA: Belknap, 2012.

Nail, Thomas. *Theory of the Border*. New York: Oxford University Press, 2018.

Ngai, Mae M. *Impossible Subjects: Illegal Aliens and the Making of Modern America*. Princeton, NJ: Princeton University Press, 2014.

Ogle, Vanessa. "Archipelago Capitalism: Tax Havens, Offshore Money, and the State, 1950s–1970s." *American Historical Review* 122, no. 5 (2017): 1431–58.

Orlov, I. B. and A. D. Popov. *Russo turisto: sovetskii vyezdnoi turizm, 1955–1991*. Moscow: Izdatel'skii dom Vysshei shkoly ekonomiki, 2016.

Oyen, Meredith. *The Diplomacy of Migration: Transnational Lives and the Making of US-Chinese Relations in the Cold War*. Ithaca, NY: Cornell University Press, 2016.

Pelkmans, Mathjis. *Defending the Border: Identity, Religion, and Modernity in the Republic of Georgia*. Ithaca, NY: Cornell University Press, 2006.

Persian, Jayne. "Displaced Persons and the Politics of International Categorisation(s)." *Australian Journal of Politics and History* 58, no. 4 (2012): 481–96.

Péteri, György. "Nylon Curtain—Transnational and Transsystemic Tendencies in the Cultural Life of State-Socialist Russia and East-Central Europe." *Slavonica* 10, no. 2 (2004): 113–24.

Plokhy, Serhii. *The Man with the Poison Gun*. London: One World, 2017.

Pomeranz, William. *Law and the Russian State: Russia's Legal Evolution from Peter the Great to Vladimir Putin*. London: Bloomsbury, 2019.

Popescu, Gabriel. *Bordering and Ordering the Twenty-First Century: Understanding Borders*. Lanham, MD: Rowman and Littlefield, 2012.

Polian, Pavel. *Zhertvy dvukh diktatur: ostarbaitery i voennoplennye v Tret'em Reikhe i ikh repatriatsiia*. Moscow: TSIRZ, 1996.

Press, Steven. "Sovereignty at Guantánamo: New Evidence and a Comparative Historical Interpretation." *Journal of Modern History* 85, no. 3 (2013): 592–631.

Riehle, Kevin P. *Soviet Defectors: Revelations of Renegade Intelligence Officers, 1924–1954*. Edinburgh: Edinburgh University Press, 2020.

Roberts, Anthea. *Is International Law International?* Oxford: Oxford University Press, 2019.

Sassen, Saskia. *Territory, Authority, Rights: From Medieval to Global Assemblages*. Princeton, NJ: Princeton University Press, 2006.

Sanchez-Sibony, Oscar. *Red Globalization: The Political Economy of the Soviet Cold War from Stalin to Khrushchev*. Cambridge: Cambridge University Press, 2017.

Scott, James C. *Seeing Like a State: How Certain Schemes to Improve the Human Condition Have Failed*. New Haven, CT: Yale University Press, 1998.

Shamir, Ronen. "Without Borders? Notes on Globalization as a Mobility Regime." *Sociological Theory* 23, no. 2 (2005): 197–217.

Shanks, Cheryl. *Immigration and the Politics of American Sovereignty, 1890–1990*. Ann Arbor: University of Michigan Press, 2001.

Sheffer, Edith. *Burned Bridge: How East and West Germans Made the Iron Curtain*. New York: Oxford University Press, 2011.

Shlyakhter, Andrei. "Smuggler States: Poland, Latvia, Estonia, and Contraband Trade across the Soviet Frontier, 1919–1924." PhD diss., University of Chicago, 2020.

Siegelbaum, Lewis and Leslie Page Moch. *Broad Is My Native Land: Repertoires and Regimes of Migration in Russia's Twentieth Century*. Ithaca, NY: Cornell University Press, 2015.

Siegelberg, Mira L. *Statelessness: A Modern History*. Cambridge, MA: Harvard University Press, 2020.

Slobodian, Quinn. *Globalists: The End of Empire and the Birth of Neoliberalism*. Cambridge, MA: Harvard University Press, 2018.

Sullivan, Rosemary. *Stalin's Daughter: The Extraordinary and Tumultuous Life of Svetlana Alliluyeva*. New York: HarperCollins, 2015.

Suri, Jeremi. *Power and Protest: Global Revolution and the Rise of Détente*. Cambridge, MA: Harvard University Press, 2003.

Torpey, John. *The Invention of the Passport: Surveillance, Citizenship, and the State*. Cambridge: Cambridge University Press, 2000.

Tromly, Benjamin. *Cold War Exiles and the CIA: Plotting to Free Russia*. Oxford: Oxford University Press, 2019.

Van Vleck, Jenifer. *Empire of the Air: Aviation and the American Ascendancy*. Cambridge, MA: Harvard University Press, 2013.

Vatulescu, Cristina. *Police Aesthetics: Literature, Film, and the Secret Police in Soviet Times*. Stanford, CA: Stanford University Press, 2010.

Vowinckel, Annette. *Flugzeugentführungen: eine Kulturgeschichte*. Göttingen: Wallstein, 2011.

Weiner, Tim. *Legacy of Ashes: The History of the CIA*. London: Penguin, 2011.

Weiss, Linda. *The Myth of the Powerless State: Governing the Economy in a Global Era*. Cambridge: Polity, 1998.

Westad, Odd Arne. *The Global Cold War: Third World Interventions and the Making of Our Times*. Cambridge: Cambridge University Press, 2005.

Wojnowski, Zbigniew. *The Near Abroad: Socialist Eastern Europe and Soviet Patriotism in Ukraine, 1956–1985*. Toronto: University of Toronto Press, 2017.

Wyman, Mark. *DPs: Europe's Displaced Persons, 1945–1951*. Ithaca, NY: Cornell University Press, 1998.

Zahra, Tara. *The Great Departure: Mass Migration from Eastern Europe and the Making of the Free World*. New York: W. W. Norton, 2017.

Zolberg, Aristide. *A Nation by Design: Immigration Policy in the Fashioning of America*. Cambridge, MA: Harvard University Press, 2006.

INDEX

For the benefit of digital users, indexed terms that span two pages (e.g., 52–53) may, on occasion, appear on only one of those pages.

Tables, figures, and boxes are indicated by an italic *t*, *f*, and *b* following the page number.

debriefing questionnaires, 52–53
defection generally
　border making impacts of, 3–8, 6*f*,
　　243n.6, 244n.13
　by border troops, 115–16
　defector psychological profile, 63–69
demise of, 222, 224–25
　desertion relationship to, 27–31
　encouragement of by
　　superpowers, 18–19
　foreign ships in, 92, 104–5
　hearing testimony, 228
　mobility regimes, 58–60, 59*f*, 128–29
　perceptions of, 10–11
　personal costs of, 235–37
　portrayal of, 46, 54, 67, 69, 162–
　　63, 177–87
　prevention/prosecution of, 107–14
　as psychological phenomenon, 69
　as rite of institution, 13
　source access, 11–12
　Soviet government notification
　　policy, 225
　Soviet migrants final wave, 222–23
　statistics, 105–6, 223–24
　terminology, 8–11, 26–27, 244n.20,
　　245n.25
Defector Program (US), 43–49, 53–55,
　58, 63, 89, 222, 225–28
Defector Reception Center (Germany),
　56, 61, 67
Demirel, Süleyman, 205
Denisov, V. M., 74–75
Denmark, 162
Deriabin, Petr, 61–62
détente, 153, 189, 209
desertor político, 9
desirability of defectors, 166, 169–70,
　171–73, 227
Dien Bien Phu battle, 168
diplomatic asylum. *see* extraterritoriality
Diplomatic Immunity (Levin), 146–47
displaced persons (DPs)
　anti-Soviet attitudes among, 35–37
　Baltic refugees, 31–32, 33–34, 35–
　　36, 229
　camps, 23, 26, 27*f*
　citizenship for, 219
　Cold War contestation of, 34–40
　collaboration screening, 39

eligibility criteria, 37
emigre groups assisting, 35–39
family networks in repatriation of,
　40–41, 78–79, 170–71
forced repatriation, 33–34, 36–37, 38,
　40–41, 54, 77–78, 88, 96–98, 237
German, 31–32
individual agency among, 39–40
Jewish, 31–32, 229
Mönchehof camp, 36–37
motivations, 33, 46
nationality as criterion, 31–32
persecution criterion, 32–34, 41–42
political history documentation
　requirement, 85–86
productive labor capability
　criterion, 38
recruitment of for political gain, 35–
　36, 39, 44–47, 74
refoulement, 42
resettlement centers, 70–75
sorting by nationality, 228–29
sorting/classification of, 31–34
storytelling as weapon, 49–53
as strategic source of knowledge, 38–
　39, 44–47, 139–41
typology of displacement criterion, 32
Ukrainians, 31–32
work as rehabilitation of, 35, 36–37,
　38, 71–72
Donovan, William, 79
Donovan Report, 82, 84, 85–86
double agents, 74–75
Draugas (The Friend), 211
druzhina/druzhiny, 95, 103
Dubrovsky, Vasyl, 75
Dulles, John Foster, 70–71, 166–67, 168

economic liberalism, 13–14
Ecuador, 174–75
Eden, Anthony, 144–45
Egypt, 144
Eisenhower, Dwight, 50–51, 83, 85–86,
　163–64, 166–67, 175
embassies/consulates, 126, 131–42, 152–
　55, 177
Emergency, 181–82, 183–84
employment for defectors, 73, 84–
　85, 166
Eremenko, Venedikt, 183–84, 185

Macmillan, Harold, 175
Makarova, Natalia, 231
Malik, Iakov, 143, 167–68, 174
Marchenko, Olga, 23, 24, 25,
    34–35, 51
Mariel Boatlift, 155, 232
maritime law. *see also* extraterritoriality
    citizen regulation by state, 176
    decolonization context, 168, 174
    defection to foreign ships in,
        92, 104–5
    defector legal status, 165–66, 187–91,
        278n.144
    extradition, 162
    fishing rights, 176–77
    freedom of navigation, 176, 188
    jurisdiction/global shipping, 156–59,
        174, 273n.11
    loyalty/treason at sea Soviet
        narrative, 177–87
    piracy, 159, 167, 168, 173–74, 176
    sovereignty/citizenship, 163–73, 174–
        75, 177
    Soviet power rise, 160–63
    state-registered vessels, 174, 175–
        76, 188
    territorial waters limits, 174–76, 188
    UN Conference/Law of the Sea, 173–
        77, 187, 188
    US continental shelf claims, 157–58,
        173–74, 176–77
Markovskii, Leonid, 140–41
Marshall Plan, 40, 43
McCarran, Pat, 85–86
McCarthy, Joseph, 54
McCormack, Paul, 36
Medvid, Mirsolav, 189–90, 278n.144
Meir, Golda, 208
Meskhetian Turks, 102–3
Mikhailov, Maksim, 179–80
Mikhailov, Nikolai, 76–77
Mindszenty, Jozsef, 127, 142, 147–48
Mitrokhin, Vasili, 231, 245n.30
Mkheidze, Revaz, 4–5, 91–92, 93–94,
    104–5, 107–8, 109–10
Moldova, 29–30, 100, 101–2
Morgenthau, Hans, 128–29
Morocco, 147
Moscow Trials/Great Purge, 167. *see also*
    Great Terror

motivations
    defectors as interpreters of, 33
    discernment of, 2, 43, 63–64, 65–66
    of displaced persons, 33, 46
    economic, 88–89
    ideological, 7–8, 46, 67, 88–89, 108–9
    Kravchenko, 7–8, 25, 46
    as legal criterion, 108–13
    Oreshkov, 2
    personal issues as, 67–68, 107, 109–
        10, 162–63, 206–7
    portrayal of, 46, 54, 67, 69, 162–63,
        177–87, 206–7, 208
    psychopathologies, 67–69, 110–11,
        124, 139, 141, 185–86
    rebirth/metamorphosis, 68
    Sokolov, 73–74
    statistics on, 111
    Tuapse crew, 165, 169–71, 178–79
musicians, 131–32, 234
Myanmar. *see* Burma

Nasseri, Mehran Karimi, 284n.125
National Committee/Free Europe, 51–52
National Alliance of Russian Solidarists
    (NTS), 36–37, 185
NATO, 137–38
Nazi Germany, 14, 23–25, 26–28, 29–30,
    33–34, 36–38, 44, 60–61, 128–29
nevozvrashchenets, 8
New York Times, 29
New Zealand, 147
Nichols, Michael, 186
Nigeria, 144–45
Nikolaev, Vladimir, 29
Nixon, Richard, 200, 202–4
NKVD, 15–16, 132
Nosenko, Yuri, 235
Notting Hill riots, 144–45
NSC 86/1, 10, 44, 49, 245n.25
Nunn, Sam, 226–27
Nuremberg trials, 128–29
Nureyev, Rudolf, 197, 231

Odesa, Ukraine, 106, 113
Operation Paperclip, 44
Operation REDCAP, 48, 132–33, 136
Orekhov, Yuri, 4–5, 91–94, 104–5, 107–
    8, 109–10
Oreshkov, Viktor, 1–3, 7–8